# Mastering Identity and Access Management with Microsoft Azure

Start empowering users and protecting corporate data, while managing Identities and Access with Microsoft Azure in different environments

Jochen Nickel

BIRMINGHAM - MUMBAI

# Mastering Identity and Access Management with Microsoft Azure

Copyright © 2016 Packt Publishing

First published: September 2016

Production reference: 1260916

Published by Packt Publishing Ltd.
Livery Place
35 Livery Street
Birmingham
B3 2PB, UK.
ISBN 978-1-78588-944-8

www.packtpub.com

# Credits

**Author**
Jochen Nickel

**Reviewer**
Ronny de Jong

**Commissioning Editor**
Kartikey Pandey

**Acquisition Editor**
Rahul Nair

**Content Development Editor**
Trusha Shriyan

**Technical Editor**
Sachit Bedi

**Copy Editors**
Safis Editing

**Project Coordinator**
 Kinjal Bari

**Proofreader**
Safis Editing

**Indexer**
Pratik Shirodkar

**Graphics**
Kirk D'Penha

**Production Coordinator**
Shantanu N. Zagade

# About the Author

**Jochen Nickel** is a Cloud, Identity and Access Management Solution Architect with a focus and technical deep knowledge of Identity and Access Management. He is currently working for inovit GmbH in Switzerland and spends the majority of each work day planning, designing, and implementing Identity and Access Management solutions, single parts such as Microsoft Azure Active Directory Premium and Microsoft Azure Rights Management Services, or complete Enterprise Mobility Suite solutions. He has also been part of many projects, proofs of concepts, reviews, reference architectures, and workshops in this field of technology. Furthermore, he is a Microsoft V-TSP Security, Identity and Access Management, Microsoft Switzerland, and uses his experience for directly managed business accounts in Switzerland. He has also been an established speaker at many technology conferences. As an active writer and reviewer, Jochen authored Learning Microsoft Windows Server 2012 Dynamic Access Control and reviewed Windows Server 2012 Unified Remote Access Planning and Deployment by Erez Ben-Ari and Bala Natarajan, as well as Windows Server 2012 R2 Administrator Cookbook by Jordan Krause, a Microsoft MVP. He is also reviewing Microsoft Identity Manager 2016 Handbook for Packt Publishing. Committed to continuous learning, he holds Microsoft certifications such as MCSD Azure Solutions Architect, MCITP, MCSE/A Office 365/Private Cloud, MCTS, and many other security titles such as Certified Information Systems Auditor (CISA). He enjoys spending as much time as possible with his family to recharge, in order to handle such interesting technologies.

# About the Reviewer

As senior consultant and Microsoft MVP Ronny is working for inovativ, a Dutch Microsoft gold partner specialized in Microsoft datacenter, workplace, productivity and security solutions.

Ronny's primary focus is on Enterprise Mobility + Security, Identity and Access management and Data- and Threat protection. As proud community domain lead he is responsible for a great team of highly skilled consultant's caring for product innovation and adoption.

In his role as Microsoft Valuable Professional (MVP) for Enterprise Mobility he's working closely with various Microsoft product groups to provide customer feedback, product improvements and most important his contributions to the community by sharing knowledge and experience. As Microsoft Partner Technical Solution Professional (P-TSP) for Enterprise Mobility + Security and Windows 10 he is working closely with Microsoft SSP/TSP counterparts on customer engagements for corporate accounts and enterprise segments.

His presence at various community events as well as international conferences like Experts live Europe, TechDays and various user group meetings are dedicated by meeting people and again sharing knowledge. Furthermore, Ronny is active via various social media channels, his blogs and is member of the System Center User Group NL.

# www.PacktPub.com

For support files and downloads related to your book, please visit www.PacktPub.com.

Did you know that Packt offers eBook versions of every book published, with PDF and ePub files available? You can upgrade to the eBook version at www.PacktPub.com and as a print book customer, you are entitled to a discount on the eBook copy. Get in touch with us at service@packtpub.com for more details.

At www.PacktPub.com, you can also read a collection of free technical articles, sign up for a range of free newsletters and receive exclusive discounts and offers on Packt books and eBooks.

https://www.packtpub.com/mapt

Get the most in-demand software skills with Mapt. Mapt gives you full access to all Packt books and video courses, as well as industry-leading tools to help you plan your personal development and advance your career.

## Why subscribe?

- Fully searchable across every book published by Packt
- Copy and paste, print, and bookmark content
- On demand and accessible via a web browser

# Table of Contents

# Preface

Mastering Identity and Access Management with Microsoft Azure is a practical, hands-on guide, packed with project experience and tailored to roles/scenarios and architecture and hands-on guide. *Business decision makers, architects, and system engineers* are the audience of this book. The book builds a very helpful reference for the three main Identity and Access Management cloud scenarios to help the reader survive in future projects. The reader will also be able to transition between the different scenarios and adapt the information gathered from this book directly to a design, architecture, or implementation. With this great resource, the reader gets an information package that also covers future functionalities of Windows 10 and Windows Server 2016.

## What this book covers

Chapter 1, *Getting Started with a Cloud-Only Scenario,* explains the main features and licensing information, including some basic cost calculations for such an approach. The challenging aspects with security and legal requirements will round off this chapter.

Chapter 2 , *Planning and Designing Cloud Identities,* teaches everything you need in order to understand and design identities for a cloud-only architecture. Starting with understanding the user and group life cycles, you will learn how to design roles and administrative units for Role-Based Access Control.

Chapter 3 , *Planning and Designing Authentication and Application Access,* teaches you how to design Azure AD as an identity provider and how to provide flexible and secure access to SaaS applications. Furthermore, you will learn about the rich authentication reporting functionality.

Chapter 4 , *Building and Configuring a Suitable Azure AD,* explains how to configure a suitable Azure AD tenant based on the appropriate architecture. You will also learn how to configure and manage users, groups, roles, and administrative units to provide user- and group-based application and self-service access, including the audit functionality.

Chapter 5, *Shifting to a Hybrid Scenario,* explores all the necessary information for a transition process into a hybrid Identity and Access Management architecture with a single or multi-forest on-premise Active Directory environment. You will be able to describe the necessary architecture changes and relevant tasks to provide a successful solution shift.

Chapter 6, *Extending to a Basic Hybrid Environment,* guides you through all the business-relevant information to plan and make the right decisions for a hybrid approach. You will learn to adopt the correct features, licensing models, and security strategy for the typical legal requirements.

Chapter 7, *Designing the Hybrid Identity Management Architecture,* teaches you how to take advantage of managing common identities with Microsoft Identity Manager 2016 and to build cloud identities with the Azure AD Connect utility. You will also explore all the various functions for Identities by building a solid hybrid Identity Management solution.

Chapter 8, *Planning the Authorization and Information Protection Options,* explores the various functions for authorization and information protection for building a solid hybrid Access Management solution. Furthermore, you will get in touch with risk-based access control and the future functionality of Windows Server 2016.

Chapter 9, *Building Cloud from Common Identities,* teaches you how to configure and manage the Identity Synchronization and Federation environment. You will also be able to include on-premise applications and Multi-Factor Authentication.

Chapter 10, *Implementing Access Control Mechanisms,* teaches you how to configure access-control mechanisms in the hybrid environment. You will configure Multi-Factor Authentication, Conditional Access, and Information Protection scenarios to apply the required security functionality.

Chapter 11, *Managing Transition Scenarios with Special Scenarios,* guides you through the transition process and principles for moving to a cloud-only or multi-forest approach. Additionally, you will learn how to identify the right strategy to decide the correct direction of a coming project. Furthermore, an effective change-management process will be discussed in this chapter.

Chapter 12, *Advanced Considerations for Complex Scenarios,* discusses complex and hybrid Identity and Access Management scenarios and teaches you all the necessary features and licensing models to go ahead. You will learn to understand the special business requirements and security and legal requirements in a complex hybrid infrastructure.

Chapter 13, *Delivering Multi-Forest Hybrid Architectures*, teaches you the capabilities of directory synchronization and single-sign on over different Active Directory forests. You will also learn about Identity Management over company borders, such as in Business-to-Customer (B2C) and Business-to-Business (B2B) scenarios. Furthermore, you will learn how to enhance the management of identities, authentication, and authorization.

Chapter 14, *Installing and Configuring the Enhanced Identity Infrastructure*, teaches you how configure and manage a Multi-Forest Synchronization and Single-Sign-On high available identity and access management environment based on AAD Connect and ADFS in order to provide the required infrastructure for several use cases in a hybrid identity and access-management solution. You will also work with capabilities across company borders and publish the most common on-premise services.

Chapter 15, *Installing and Configuring Information Protection Features*, shows you how to configure information protection features with Azure RMS to secure access to sensitive data in order to provide an extended access-management solution. You will configure and publish custom Rights Policy templates, use RMS logging, and get a first view of the new Azure Information Protection capabilities.

Chapter 16, *Choosing the Right Transition, Method, and Future Trends*, is the final destination of our journey, where we will discuss additional information that will help you manage several cloud scenarios and support new initiatives. We will jump into some upcoming features and innovations of Microsoft.

# What you need for this book

To use the book efficiently, you should have some understanding of security solutions, Active Directory, access privileges/rights, and authentication methods. Programming knowledge is not required but will be helpful for using PowerShell or working with APIs to customize your solutions.

# Who this book is for

This book is for business decision makers, IT consultants, and system and security engineers who wish to plan, design, and implement Identity and Access Management solutions with Microsoft Azure.

# Conventions

In this book, you will find a number of text styles that distinguish between different kinds of information. Here are some examples of these styles and an explanation of their meaning.

Code words in text, database table names, folder names, filenames, file extensions, pathnames, dummy URLs, user input, and Twitter handles are shown as follows: "Mount the downloaded `WebStorm-10*.dmg` disk image file as another disk in your system."

A block of code is set as follows:

```
"use strict";
//---- Start custom code ----
function loadJquery(callback) {
  var jqueryScript = document.createElement('script');
jqueryScript.setAttribute('src',
'https://code.jquery.com/jquery-1.11.2.min.js');
document.getElementsByTagName('head')[0].appendChild(jqueryScript);
```

Any command-line input or output is written as follows:

```
New-Item C:\inetpub\basicroot -type Directory
Import-Module Webadministration
```

**New terms** and **important words** are shown in bold. Words that you see on the screen, for example, in menus or dialog boxes, appear in the text like this: "The shortcuts in this book are based on the `Mac OS X 10.5+` scheme."

Warnings or important notes appear in a box like this.

Tips and tricks appear like this.

# Reader feedback

Feedback from our readers is always welcome. Let us know what you think about this book-what you liked or disliked. Reader feedback is important for us as it helps us develop titles that you will really get the most out of. To send us general feedback, simply e-mail `feedback@packtpub.com`, and mention the book's title in the subject of your message. If there is a topic that you have expertise in and you are interested in either writing or contributing to a book, see our author guide at `www.packtpub.com/authors`.

# Customer support

Now that you are the proud owner of a Packt book, we have a number of things to help you to get the most from your purchase.

# Downloading the example code

You can download the example code files for this book from your account at `http://www.packtpub.com`. If you purchased this book elsewhere, you can visit `http://www.packtpub.com/support` and register to have the files e-mailed directly to you.

You can download the code files by following these steps:

1. Log in or register to our website using your e-mail address and password.
2. Hover the mouse pointer on the **SUPPORT** tab at the top.
3. Click on **Code Downloads & Errata**.
4. Enter the name of the book in the **Search** box.
5. Select the book for which you're looking to download the code files.
6. Choose from the drop-down menu where you purchased this book from.
7. Click on **Code Download**.

Once the file is downloaded, please make sure that you unzip or extract the folder using the latest version of:

- WinRAR / 7-Zip for Windows
- Zipeg / iZip / UnRarX for Mac
- 7-Zip / PeaZip for Linux

The code bundle for the book is also hosted on GitHub at `https://github.com/PacktPubl ishing/Mastering-Identity-and-Access-Management-with-Microsoft-Azure`. We also have other code bundles from our rich catalog of books and videos available at `https://gi thub.com/PacktPublishing/`. Check them out!

# Downloading the color images of this book

We also provide you with a PDF file that has color images of the screenshots/diagrams used in this book. The color images will help you better understand the changes in the output. You can download this file from `https://www.packtpub.com/sites/default/files/down loads/MasteringIdentityandAccessManagementwithMicrosoftAzure_ColorImages.pdf`.

# Errata

Although we have taken every care to ensure the accuracy of our content, mistakes do happen. If you find a mistake in one of our books-maybe a mistake in the text or the code-we would be grateful if you could report this to us. By doing so, you can save other readers from frustration and help us improve subsequent versions of this book. If you find any errata, please report them by visiting `http://www.packtpub.com/submit-errata`, selecting your book, clicking on the **Errata Submission Form** link, and entering the details of your errata. Once your errata are verified, your submission will be accepted and the errata will be uploaded to our website or added to any list of existing errata under the Errata section of that title.

To view the previously submitted errata, go to `https://www.packtpub.com/books/conten t/support` and enter the name of the book in the search field. The required information will appear under the **Errata** section.

# Piracy

Piracy of copyrighted material on the Internet is an ongoing problem across all media. At Packt, we take the protection of our copyright and licenses very seriously. If you come across any illegal copies of our works in any form on the Internet, please provide us with the location address or website name immediately so that we can pursue a remedy.

Please contact us at `copyright@packtpub.com` with a link to the suspected pirated material.

We appreciate your help in protecting our authors and our ability to bring you valuable content.

# Questions

If you have a problem with any aspect of this book, you can contact us at questions@packtpub.com, and we will do our best to address the problem.

# 1
# Getting Started with a Cloud-Only Scenario

Before jumping into the architecture and deployment of the Microsoft Azure IAM capabilities, we will first start with a business view to identify the important business needs and challenges of a cloud-only environment and scenario. Throughout this chapter, we will also discuss the main features of and licensing information for such an approach. Finally, we will round up with the challenges surrounding security and legal requirements.

The topics we will cover in this chapter are as follows:

- Identifying business needs and challenges
- An overview of feature and licensing decisions
- Defining the benefits and costs
- Principles of security and legal requirements

## Identifying business needs and challenges

Oh! Don't worry, we don't intend to bore you with a lesson of typical IAM stories – we're sure you've come across a lot of information in this area. However, you do need to have an independent view of the actual business needs and challenges in the cloud area, so that you can get the most out of your own situation.

# Common Identity and Access Management needs

**Identity and Access Management (IAM)** is the discipline that plays an important role in the actual cloud era of your organization. It's also of value to small and medium-sized companies, so that they can enable the right individuals to access the right resources from any location and device, at the right time and for the right reasons, to empower and enable the desired business outcomes. IAM addresses the mission-critical need of ensuring appropriate and secure access to resources inside and across company borders, such as cloud or partner applications.

The old security strategy of only securing your environment with an intelligent firewall concept and access control lists will take on a more and more subordinated role. There is a recommended requirement of reviewing and overworking this strategy in order to meet higher compliance and operational and business requirements. To adopt a mature security and risk management practice, it's very important that your IAM strategy is business-aligned and that the required business skills and stakeholders are committed to this topic. Without clearly defined business processes you can't implement a successful IAM functionality in the planned timeframe. Companies that follow this strategy can become more agile in supporting new business initiatives and reduce their costs in IAM.

The following three groups show the typical indicators for missing IAM capabilities on the premises and for cloud services:

- Your employees/partners:
    - Same password usage across multiple applications without periodic changes (also in social media accounts)
    - Multiple identities and logins
    - Passwords are written down in Sticky Notes, Excel, etc.
    - Application and data access allowed after termination
    - Forgotten usernames and passwords
    - Poor usability of application access inside and outside the company (multiple logins, VPN connection required, incompatible devices, etc.)

- Your IT department:
    - High workload on Password Reset Support
    - Missing automated identity lifecycles with integrity (data duplication and data quality problems)

- No insights in application usage and security
- Missing reporting tools for compliance management

- Complex integration of central access to **Software as a Service (SaaS)**, Partner and On-Premise applications (missing central access/authentication/authorization platform)
- No policy enforcement in cloud services usage
- Collection of access rights (missing processes)

- Your developers:
    - Limited knowledge of all the different security standards, protocols, and APIs
    - Constantly changing requirements and rapid developments
    - Complex changes of the Identity Provider

# Implications of Shadow IT

On top of that, often the IT department will hear the following question: *When can we expect the new application for our business unit?* Sorry, but the answer will always take too long. Why should I wait? All I need is a valid credit card that allows me to buy my required business application, but suddenly another popular phenomenon pops up: *The shadow IT!* Most of the time, this introduces another problem – uncontrolled information leakage. The following figure shows the flow of typical information – *and that which you don't know can hurt!*

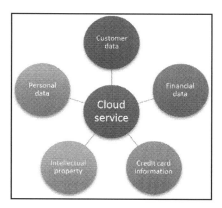

The previous figure should not give you the impression that cloud services are inherently dangerous, rather that before using them you should first be aware that, and in which manner, they are being used. Simply migrating or ordering a new service in the cloud won't solve common IAM needs. This figure should help you to imagine that, if not planned, the introduction of a new or migrated service brings with it a new identity and credential set for the users, and therefore multiple credentials and logins to remember! You should also be sure which information can be stored and processed in a regulatory area other than your own organization. The following table shows the responsibilities involved when using the different cloud service models. In particular, you should identify that you are responsible for data classification, IAM, and end point security in every model:

| Cloud Service Modell | IaaS | | PaaS | | SaaS | |
| --- | --- | --- | --- | --- | --- | --- |
| Responsibility | Customer | Provider | Customer | Provider | Customer | Provider |
| Data Classification | X | | X | | X | |
| End Point Security | X | | X | | X | |
| Identity and Access Management | X | | X | X | X | X |
| Application Security | X | | X | X | | X |
| Network Controls | X | | X | X | | X |
| Host Security | | X | | X | | X |
| Physical Security | | X | | X | | X |

# The mobile workforce and cloud-first strategy

Many organizations are facing the challenge of meeting the expectations of a mobile workforce, all with their own device preferences, a mix of private and professional commitments, and the request to use social media as an additional means of business communication.

Let's dive into a short, practical, but extreme example. The *AzureID* company employs approximately 80 employees. They work with a SaaS landscape of eight services to drive all their business processes. On premises, they use **Network-Attached Storage(NAS)** to store some corporate data and provide network printers to all of the employees. Some of the printers are directly attached to the C-level of the company. The main issues today are that the employees need to remember all their usernames and passwords of all the business applications, and if they want to share some information with partners they cannot give them partial access to the necessary information in a secure and flexible way. Another point is if they want to access corporate data from their mobile device, it's always a burden to provide every single login for the applications necessary to fulfil their job. The small IT department with one **Full-time Employee** (FTE) is overloaded with having to create and manage every identity in each different service. In addition, users forget their passwords periodically, and most of the time outside normal business hours. The following figure shows the actual infrastructure:

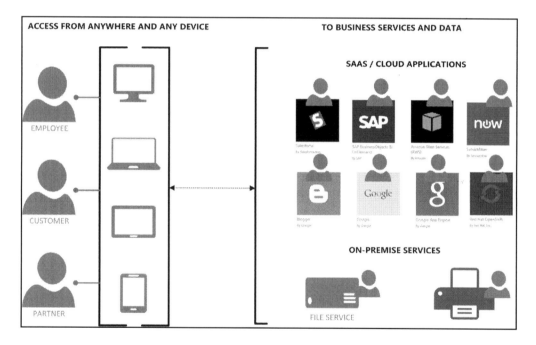

Let's analyze this extreme example to reveal some typical problems, so that you can match some ideas to your IT infrastructure:

- Provisioning, managing, and de-provisioning identities can be a time-consuming task

- There are no single identity and credentials
- There is no collaboration support for partner and consumer communication
- There is no Self-Service Password Reset functionality
- Sensitive information leaves the corporation over email
- There are no usage or security reports about the accessed applications/services
- There is no central way to enable **Multi-Factor Authentication (MFA)** for sensitive applications
- There is no secure strategy for accessing social media
- There is no usable, secure, and central remote access portal

 Remember, shifting applications and services to the cloud just introduces more implications/challenges, not solutions. First of all, you need your IAM functionality accurately in place. You also need to always handle on-premises resources with minimal printer management.

# An overview of feature and licensing decisions

With the cloud-first strategy of Microsoft, the Azure platform and their number of services grow constantly, and we have seen a lot of costumers lost in a paradise of wonderful services and functionality. This brings us to the point of how to figure out the relevant services for IAM for you and how to give them the space for explanation. Obviously, there are more services available that stripe this field with a small subset of functionality, but due to the limited page count of this book and our need for rapid development, we will focus on the most important ones, and will reference any other interesting content. The primary service for IAM is the Azure Active Directory service, which has also been the core directory service for Office 365 since 2011. Every other SaaS offering of Microsoft is also based on this core service, including Microsoft Intune, Dynamics, and Visual Studio Online. So, if you are already an Office 365 customer you will have your own instance of Azure Active Directory in place. For sustained access management and the protection of your information assets, the Azure Rights Management services are in place. There is also an option for Office 365 customers to use the included Azure Rights Management services. You can find further information about this by visiting the following link: http://bit.ly/1 KrXUxz.

Let's get started with the feature sets that can provide a solution, as shown in the following screenshot:

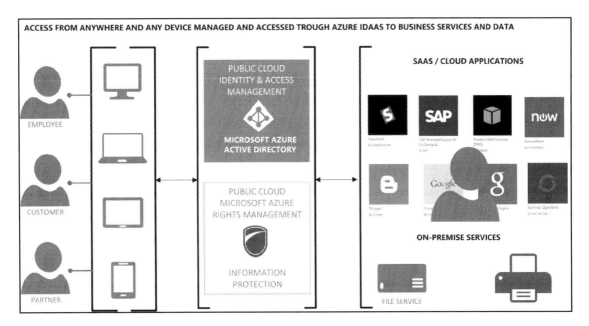

Including Azure Active Directory and **Rights Management** helps you to provide a secure solution with a central access portal for all of your applications with just one identity and login for your employees, partners, and customers that you want to share your information with. With a few clicks you can also add MFA to your sensitive applications and administrative accounts. Furthermore, you can directly add a **Self-Service Password Reset** functionality that your users can use to reset their password for themselves. As the administrator, you will receive predefined security and usage reports to control your complete application ecosystem. To protect your sensible content, you will receive digital rights management capabilities with the Azure Rights Management services to give you granular access rights on every device your information is used.

Doesn't it sound great? Let's take a deeper look into the functionality and usage of the different Microsoft Azure IAM services.

# Azure Active Directory

Azure Active Directory is a fully managed multi-tenant service that provides IAM capabilities as a service. This service is not just an instance of the Windows Server Domain Controller you already know from your actual Active Directory infrastructure. Azure AD is not a replacement for the Windows Server Active Directory either. If you already use a local Active Directory infrastructure, you can extend it to the cloud by integrating Azure AD to authenticate your users in the same way as on-premise and cloud services.

Staying in the business view, we want to discuss some of the main features of Azure Active Directory. Firstly, we want to start with the Access panel that gives the user a central place to access all his applications from any device and any location with SSO.

 The combination of the Azure Active Directory Access panel and the Windows Server 2012 R2/2016 Web Application Proxy / ADFS capabilities provide an efficient way to securely publish web applications and services to your employees, partners, and customers. It will be a good replacement for your retired Forefront TMG/UAG infrastructure.

Over this portal, your users can do the following:

- User and group management
- Access their business relevant applications (On-premise, partner, and SaaS) with single-sign-on or single logon
- Delegation of access control to the data, process, or project owner
- Self-service profile editing for correcting or adding information
- Self-service password change and reset

- Manage registered devices

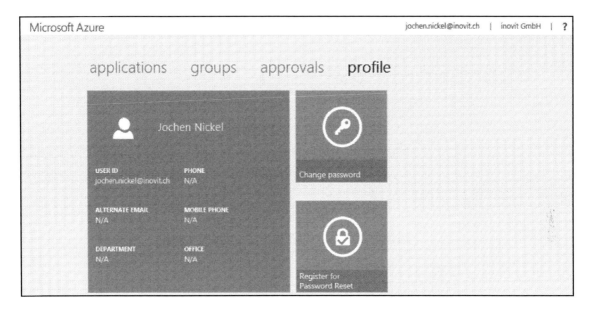

With the Self-Service Password Reset functionality, a user gets a straight forward way to reset his password and to prove his identity, for example through a phone call, email, or by answering security questions.

The different portals can be customized with your own **Corporate Identity** branding. To try the different portals, just use the following links: `https:/ /myapps.microsoft.com` and `https://passwordreset.microsoftonline .com`.

To complete our short introduction to the main features of the Azure Active Directory, we will take a look at the reporting capabilities. With this feature you get predefined reports with the following information provided. With viewing and acting on these reports, you are able to control your whole application ecosystem published over the Azure AD access panel.

- Anomaly reports
- Integrated application reports
- Error reports
- User-specific reports
- Activity logs

| REPORT | DESCRIPTION |
|---|---|
| ◢ ANOMALOUS ACTIVITY | |
| Sign ins from unknown sources | May indicate an attempt to sign in without being traced. |
| Sign ins after multiple failures | May indicate a successful brute force attack. |
| Sign ins from multiple geographies | May indicate that multiple users are signing in with the same account. |
| Sign ins from IP addresses with suspicious activity | May indicate a successful sign in after a sustained intrusion attempt. |
| Sign ins from possibly infected devices | May indicate an attempt to sign in from possibly infected devices. |
| Irregular sign in activity | May indicate events anomalous to users' sign in patterns. |
| Users with anomalous sign in activity | Indicates users whose accounts may have been compromised. |
| ◢ ACTIVITY LOGS | |
| Audit report | Audited events in your directory |
| Password reset activity | Provides a detailed view of password resets that occur in your organization. |
| Password reset registration activity | Provides a detailed view of password reset registrations that occur in your organization. |
| Groups activity | Provides an activity log to all group related activity in your directory |
| ◢ INTEGRATED APPLICATIONS | |
| Application usage | Provides a usage summary for all SaaS applications integrated with your directory. |
| Account provisioning activity | Provides a history of attempts to provision accounts to external applications. |
| Account provisioning errors | Indicates an impact to users' access to external applications. |

From our discussions with customers we recognize that, a lot of the time, the differences between the different Azure Active Directory editions are unclear. For that reason, we will include and explain the feature tables provided by Microsoft. We will start with the common features and then go through the premium features of Azure Active Directory.

# Common features

First of all, we want to discuss the Access panel portal so we can clear up some open questions. With the Azure AD Free and Basic editions, you can provide a maximum of 10 applications to every user. However, this doesn't mean that you are limited to 10 applications in total. Next, the portal link: right now it cannot be changed to your own company-owned domain, such as `https://myapps.inovit.ch`. The only way you can do so is by providing an alias in your DNS configuration; the accessed link is `https://myapps.microsoft.com`. Company branding will lead us on to the next discussion point, where we are often asked how much corporate identity branding is possible. The following link provides you with all the necessary information for branding your solution: `http://bit.ly/1Jjf2nw`. Rounding up this short Q&A on the different feature sets is Application Proxy usage, one of the important differentiators between the Azure AD Free and Basic editions. The short answer is that with Azure AD Free, you cannot publish on-premises applications and services over the Azure AD Access Panel portal.

| Features | AAD Free | AAD Basic | AAD Premium |
|---|---|---|---|
| Directory as a Service (objects) | 500k | unlimited | unlimited |
| User/Group management (UI or PowerShell) | X | X | X |
| Access Panel portal for SSO (per user) | 10 apps | 10 apps | unlimited |
| User-based application access management/provisioning | X | X | X |
| Self-service password change (cloud users) | X | X | X |
| Directory synchronization tool | X | X | X |
| Standard security reports | X | X | X |
| High availability SLA (99.9%) | | X | X |
| Group-based application access management and provisioning | | X | X |
| Company branding | | X | X |
| Self-service password reset for cloud users | | X | X |

| | | |
|---|---|---|
| Application Proxy | X | X |
| Self-service group management for cloud users | X | X |

# Premium features

The Azure Active Directory Premium edition provides you with the entire IAM capabilities, including the usage licenses of the on-premises used Microsoft Identity Manager. From a technical perspective, you need to use the Azure AD Connect utility to connect your on-premises Active Directory with the cloud and the Microsoft Identity Manager to manage your on-premises identities and prepare them for your cloud integration. To acquire Azure AD Premium, you can also use the **Enterprise Mobility Suite** (**EMS**) license bundle, which contains Azure AD Premium, Azure Rights Management, Microsoft Intune, and **Advanced Threat Analytics** (**ATA**) licensing. You can find more information about EMS by visiting `http://bit.ly/1cJLPcM` and `http://bit.ly/29rupF4`.

| Features | Azure AD Premium |
|---|---|
| Self-service password reset with on-premises write-back | X |
| Microsoft Identity Manager server licenses | X |
| Advanced anomaly security reports | X |
| Advanced usage reporting | X |
| Multi-Factor Authentication (cloud users) | X |
| Multi-Factor Authentication (On-premises users) | X |

Azure AD Premium reference:

`http://bit.ly/1gyDRoN`

 MFA for cloud users is also included in Office 365. The main difference is that you cannot use it for on-premises users and services such as VPN or web servers.

# Azure Active Directory Business to Business

One of the newest features based on Azure Active Directory is the new **Business to Business (B2B)** capability. The new product solves the problem of collaboration between business partners. It allows users to share business applications between partners without going through inter-company federation relationships and internally-managed partner identities. With Azure AD B2B, you can create cross-company relationships by inviting and authorizing users from partner companies to access your resources. With this process, each company federates once with Azure AD and each user is then represented by a single Azure AD account. This option also provides a higher security level, because if a user leaves the partner organization, access is automatically disallowed. Inside Azure AD, the user will be handled as though a guest, and they will not be able to traverse other users in the directory. Real permissions will be provided over the correct associated group membership.

# Azure Active Directory Business to Consumer

Azure Active Directory **Business to Consumer (B2C)** is another brand new feature based on Azure Active Directory. This functionality supports signing in to your application using social networks like Facebook, Google, or LinkedIn and creating developed accounts with usernames and passwords specifically for your company-owned application. Self-service password management and profile management are also provided with this scenario. Additionally, MFA introduces a higher grade of security to the solution. Principally, this feature allows small, medium and large companies to hold their customers in a separated Azure Active Directory with all the capabilities, and more, in a similar way to the corporate-managed Azure Active Directory. With different verification options, you are also able to provide the necessary identity assurance required for more sensible transactions. Azure B2C takes care about all the IAM tasks for own development application.

# Azure Active Directory Privileged Identity Management

Azure AD Privileged Identity Management provides you with the functionality to manage, control, and monitor your privileged identities. With this option, you can build up an **Role-based Access Control (RBAC)** solution over your Azure AD and other Microsoft online services, such as Office 365 or Microsoft Intune. The following activities can be carried out with this functionality:

- You can discover the actual configured Azure AD Administrators
- You can provide *just in time* administrative access

- You can get reports about administrator access history and assignment changes
- You can receive alerts about access to a privileged role

The following built-in roles can be managed with the current version:

- Global Administrator
- Billing Administrator
- Service Administrator
- User Administrator
- Password Administrator

# Azure MFA

Protecting sensible information or application access with additional authentication is an important task not just in the on-premises world. In particular, it needs to be extended to every sensible cloud service used. There are a lot of variations for providing this level of security and additional authentication, such as certificates, smart cards, or biometric options. For example, smart cards depend on special hardware used to read the smart card and cannot be used in every scenario without limiting the access to a special device or hardware or. The following table gives you an overview of different attacks and how they can be mitigated with a well designed and implemented security solution.

| Attacker | Security solution |
| --- | --- |
| Password brute force | Strong password policies |
| Shoulder surfing<br>Key or screen logging | One-time password solution |
| Phishing or pharming | Server authentication (HTTPS) |
| Man-in-the-Middle<br>Whaling (Social engineering) | Two-factor authentication<br>Certificate or one-time password solution |
| Certificate authority corruption<br>Cross Channel Attacks (CSRF) | Transaction signature and verification<br>Non repudiation |
| Man-in-the-Browser<br>Key loggers | Secure PIN entry<br>Secure messaging<br>Browser (read only)<br>Push button (token)<br>Three-factor authentication |

The Azure MFA functionality has been included in the Azure Active Directory Premium capabilities to address exactly the attacks described in the previous table. With a one-time password solution, you can build a very capable security solution to access information or applications from devices that cannot use smart cards as the additional authentication method. Otherwise, for small or medium business organizations a smart card deployment, including the appropriate management solution, will be too cost-intensive and the Azure MFA solution can be a good alternative for reaching the expected higher security level.

In discussions with our customers, we recognized that many don't realize that Azure MFA is already included in different Office 365 plans. They would be able to protect their Office 365 with multi-factor out-of-the-box but they don't know it! This brings us to Microsoft and the following table, which compares the functionality between Office 365 and Azure MFA.

| Feature | O365 | Azure |
| --- | --- | --- |
| Administrators can enable/enforce MFA to end-users | X | X |
| Use mobile app (online and OTP) as second authentication factor | X | X |
| Use phone call as second authentication factor | X | X |
| Use SMS as second authentication factor | X | X |
| App passwords for non-browser clients (for example, Outlook, Lync) | X | X |
| Default Microsoft greetings during authentication phone calls | X | X |
| Remember Me | X | X |
| IP Whitelist | | X |
| Custom greetings during authentication phone calls | | X |
| Fraud alert | | X |
| Event confirmation | | X |
| Security reports | | X |
| Block/unblock users | | X |
| One-time bypass | | X |
| Customizable caller ID for authentication phone calls | | X |
| MFA Server – MFA for on-premises applications | | X |
| MFA SDK – MFA for custom apps | | X |

With the Office 365 capabilities of MFA, the administrators are able to use basic functionality to protect their sensible information. In particular, if integrating on-premises users and services, the Azure MFA solution is needed.

 Azure MFA and the on-premises installation of the MFA server cannot be used to protect your Windows Server DirectAccess implementation. Furthermore, you will find the customizable caller ID limited to special regions.

# Azure Rights Management

More and more organizations are in the position of providing a continuous and integrated information protection solution to protect sensible assets and information. On the one hand is the department, which carries out its business activities, generates the data, and then processes. Furthermore, it uses the data inside and outside the functional areas, passes it, and runs a lively exchange of information.

On the other hand, revision is required by legal requirements that prescribe measures to ensure that information is dealt with and dangers such as industrial espionage and data loss are avoided. So, this is a big concern when safeguarding sensitive information.

While staff appreciate the many methods of communication and data exchange, this development starts stressing the IT security officers and makes managers worried. The fear is that critical corporate data stays in an uncontrolled manner and leaves the company or moves to competitors. The routes are varied, but data is often lost in inadvertent delivery via email. In addition, sensitive data can leave the company on a USB stick and smartphone, or IT media can be lost or stolen. In addition, new risks are added, such as employees posting information on social media platforms. IT must ensure the protection of data in all phases, and traditional IT security solutions are not always sufficient. The following figure illustrates this situation and leads us to the Azure Rights Management services.

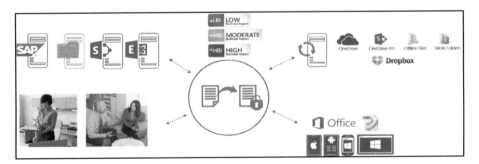

Like its other additional features, the base functional is included in different Office 365 plans. The main difference between the two is that only the Azure RMS edition can be integrated in an on-premises file server environment in order to be able to use the File Classification Infrastructure feature of the Windows Server file server role.

The Azure RMS capability allows you to protect your sensitive information based on classification information with a granular access control system. The following table, provided by Microsoft, shows the differences between the Office 365 and Azure RMS functionality. Azure RMS is included with E3, E4, A3, and A4 plans.

| Feature | RMS O365 | RMS Azure |
|---|---|---|
| Users can create and consume protected content by using Windows clients and Office applications | X | X |
| Users can create and consume protected content by using mobile devices | X | X |
| Integrates with Exchange Online, SharePoint Online, and OneDrive for Business | X | X |
| Integrates with Exchange Server 2013/Exchange Server 2010 and SharePoint Server 2013/SharePoint Server 2010 on-premises via the RMS connector | X | X |
| Administrators can create departmental templates | X | X |
| Organizations can create and manage their own RMS tenant key in a hardware security module (the Bring Your Own Key solution) | X | X |
| Supports non-Office file formats: Text and image files are natively protected; other files are generically protected | X | X |
| RMS SDK for all platforms: Windows, Windows Phone, iOS, Mac OSX, and Android | X | X |
| Integrates with Windows file servers for automatic protection with FCI via the RMS connector | | X |
| Users can track usage of their documents | | X |
| Users can revoke access to their documents | | X |

In particular, the tracking feature helps users to find where their documents are distributed and allows them to revoke access to a single protected document.

# Microsoft Azure security services in combination

Now that we have discussed the relevant Microsoft Azure IAM capabilities, you can see that Microsoft provides more than just single features or subsets of functionality. Furthermore, it brings a whole solution to the market, which provides functionality for every facet of IAM. Microsoft Azure also combines clear service management with IAM, making it a rich solution for your organization. You can work with that toolset in a native cloud-first scenario, hybrid, and a complex hybrid scenario and can extend your solution to every possible use case or environment. The following figure illustrates all the different topics that are covered with Microsoft Azure security solutions:

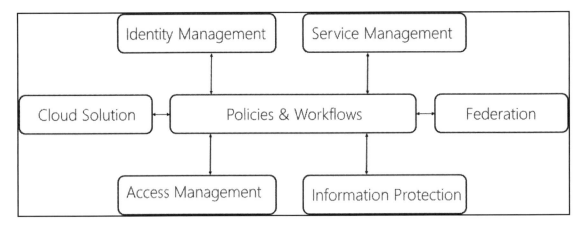

# Defining the benefits and costs

The Microsoft Azure IAM capabilities help you to empower your users with a flexible and rich solution that enables better business outcomes in a more productive way. You help your organization to improve the regulatory compliance overall and reduce the information security risk. Additionally, it can be possible to reduce IT operating and development costs by providing higher operating efficiency and transparency. Last but not least, it will lead to improved user satisfaction and better support from the business for further investments.

The following toolset gives you very good instruments for calculating the costs of your special environment.

- Azure Active Directory Pricing Calculator: http://bit.ly/1fspdhz
- Enterprise Mobility Suite Pricing: http://bit.ly/1V42RSk
- Microsoft Azure Pricing Calculator: http://bit.ly/1JojUfA

# Principles of security and legal requirements

The classification of data, such as business information or personal data, is not only necessary for an on-premises infrastructure. It is the basis for the assurance of business-related information and is represented by compliance with official regulations. These requirements are of greater significance when using cloud services or solutions outside your own company and regulation borders. They are clearly needed for a controlled shift of data in an area in which responsibilities on contracts must be regulated. Safety limits do not stop at the private cloud, and are responsible for the technical and organizational implementation and control of security settings.

The subsequent objectives are as follows:

- Construction, extension, or adaptation of the data classification to the Cloud Integration
- Data classification as a basis for encryption or isolated security silos
- Data classification as a basis for authentication and authorization

Microsoft itself has strict controls that restrict access to Azure to Microsoft employees. Microsoft also enables customers to control access to their Azure environments, data, and applications, as well as allowing them to penetrate and audit services with special auditors and regulations on request.

A statement from Microsoft: Customers will only use cloud providers in which they have great trust. They must trust that the privacy of their information will be protected, and that their data will be used in a way that is consistent with their expectations. We build privacy protections into Azure through Privacy by Design.

You can get all the necessary information about security, compliance, and privacy by visiting the following link `http://bit.ly/1uJTLAT`.

# Summary

Now that you are fully clued up with information about typical needs and challenges and feature and licensing information, you should be able to apply the right technology and licensing model to your cloud-only scenario. You should also be aware of the benefits and cost calculators that will help you calculate a basic price model for your required services. Furthermore, you can also decide which security and legal requirements are relevant for your cloud-only environments.

In the next chapter, we will design a sustainable cloud-only IAM environment. We will discuss the user and group life cycle and the roles and administrative units with the relevant identity reporting capabilities. We look forward to seeing you work on your design in the next chapter.

# 2
# Planning and Designing Cloud Identities

Having read through the first chapter, you will have realized that Microsoft Azure provides a whole bunch of functionality for Identity and Access Management. Now, after hearing the relevant business information, we will dive into the architecture of Azure Active Directory to understand the relevant concepts and design dependencies for cloud-only identities. Furthermore, we will see that small or innovative companies often follow the cloud-only strategy. This is perfectly normal, as most companies have an existing local IT infrastructure. Often you will find a domain controller and file/print services on-premises, but Azure Active Directory also provides users with important Identity Management as a Service and identity repository features for a more flexible and value added IT ecosystem. After reading this chapter, you will also be able to design and construct roles and administrative units for **Role Based Access Control** (**RBAC**) in your current or planned Microsoft Azure environment. We will go through these topics, starting with these cloud-only capabilities and then on to basic and complex hybrid designs in the following chapters. In this chapter, we will focus on the following main topics:

- Understanding the user and group life cycle
- Designing roles and administrative units
- Managing identity reporting capabilities

# Understanding the user and group life cycle

One of the basic concepts to understand is the user and group life cycle, so it's very important to understand the different repositories and capabilities where objects are stored and managed. In this section, we will provide you with the necessary information for designing your solution.

# Microsoft Azure Identity repositories and capabilities

IAM is a very broad field in technology. Internet threats are becoming more intelligent and effective, so IAM solutions must constantly evolve to keep up. In particular, these solutions must address the four most important fields in order to be successful. The four main topics are the administration, authentication, authorization, and auditing of identities. With Microsoft Azure, you get several options for leveraging identity and access management solutions.

Azure Active Directory is the central and main identity repository for the whole Microsoft Azure landscape. The existence of an Azure AD directory is a requirement for an Azure subscription, and you can find out more information on that by visiting: `http://bit.ly/2a rPa54`.

Each Azure tenant has at least one directory associated with it. Azure tenants can have multiple directories and these directories are all separate and unique. For example, if two Azure AD directories exist in the same tenant, they have their own set of administrators and there is no data shared between them. The administrator of one directory in the tenant does not have access to another directory in the same tenant, unless you explicitly grant access to it.

- **Mandatory:** There is always one directory in a tenant (`.onmicrosoft.com`)
- **Recommended:** There should be an Azure AD directory for testing purposes
- **Optional:** Developers may have their own Azure AD directory for development reasons

Azure Active Directory is used for logging into and accessing the Azure portal, Office 365, Dynamics, Intune, and other Microsoft cloud services. It also offers a variety of specific manifestations for addressing the most important use cases in actual environments. The following figure shows the main subsets of Azure Active Directory and further identity services that can be designed and implemented:

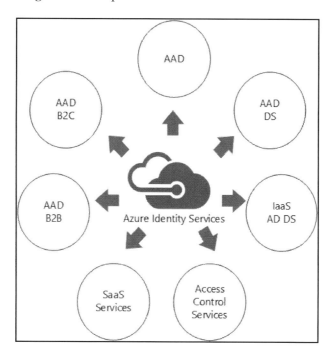

All the shown services allow you to work in a cloud-only and hybrid Identity and Access Management approach, so it's important that you can map the specific service to the requirements and use cases to provide a suitable solution for your company.

- **Azure Active Directory**: Azure AD is a single, multi-tenant directory and cloud-scale identity service. Azure AD has features that rely on cloud services, such as Azure **Multi-Factor Authentication(MFA)**. You can use the cloud **Identity Management as a Service (IdMaaS)** feature, such as Self Service Password Reset, to enable new identity management features that traditionally take weeks of months to deploy on-premises.

- **Azure Active Directory Domain Services**: They allow you to move workloads to the cloud with Kerberos, **NT LAN Manager** (**NTLM**) as authentication protocols. You are also able to connect by **Lightweight Directory Access Protocol** (**LDAP**) to the directory service. Basic group policies are also available in this scenario. This service is an extension of your current Azure Active Directory and you can take advantage of the functionality.
- **Active Directory Domain Services on IaaS**: This is a Domain Controller hosted on a virtual machine in Microsoft Azure IaaS and allows you to provide an Active Directory that you are familiar with from on-premises infrastructures.

- **Azure Active Directory Access Control Services**: This does not own any identities; it federates identities. It is a federation provider and allows you to adopt social media logins.
- **Identities in SaaS identity repositories**: These services rely on their own user repositories and can be integrated in a federation scenario.
- **Azure Active Directory B2B**: This is an extension of your Azure Active Directory that allows you to provide your application ecosystem to partners and other external parties with focus on the authorization process. The authentication process will be simplified both for organizations with Azure Active Directory and without.
- **Azure Active Directory B2C**: This has an own directory in your tenant that allows you to provide customer facing applications with the entire capabilities of Azure Active Directory, including the integration of social media identity providers. It allows developers to focus on the application and not on the identity and access management functionalities.

# Azure Active Directory conceptual architecture

Essentially, Azure Active Directory is a scalable directory infrastructure that provides functionality for data access, replication and synchronization, device registration, and **Security Token Services(STS)**. Azure AD follows the **Windows Server AD(WSAD)** data model with special modifications for the cloud usage scenario. The core data model contains the following main information:

- Directory contexts, one or multiple per tenant plus a system
- Each object has an object class or type (`ObjectType`)

- An object contains a set of properties
- An object may contain a set of navigation properties
- Object (link) instances

 Objects do not have distinguished names and are not arranged into a distinguished multi-level hierarchy. Also, the directory doesn't support object class inheritance.

The following figure shows the Azure AD core directory, the administration, and authentication endpoints, including the capabilities for integrating On-premises Active Directory Federation Services for a better understanding of the whole architecture:

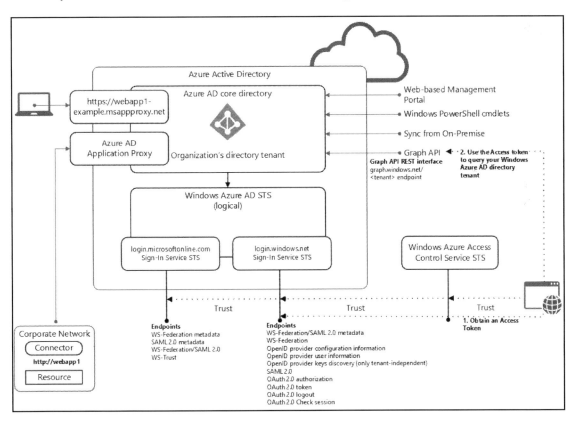

# Usage scenarios of Azure Active Directory Premium

With the premium version of Azure Active Directory, you get a rich set of capabilities that allow users and administrators to manage identities in the cloud. Beginning the design process, we separate the key areas into two sections: basic and advanced modules. You will mainly start to design a solid user and group life cycle, followed by advanced topics such as administrative units and role-based access management. Finally, you will move to the reporting features to provide a variety of activity, security, and audit reports. The following figure gives you a graphical overview of the next sections:

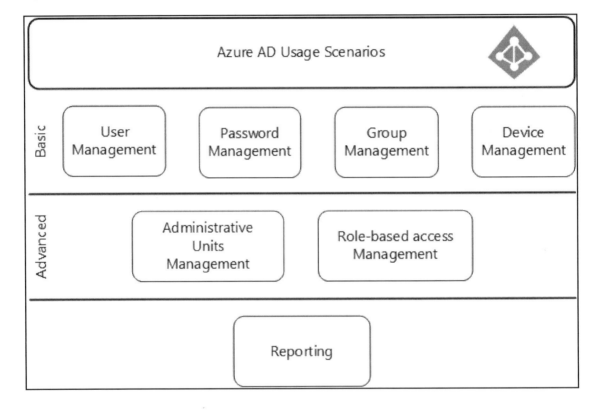

Generally, you can use different methods to manage the various scenarios. In no particular order, here are some common methods:

- **UX management**: This manually uses the Azure Management Portal. This portal is very intuitive and easy to understand. In special companies without on-premises directories or a small number of employees, this approach is used to manage their identities. It's also very handy for tests, small proof of concepts, and application development. The following figure gives you an idea about how to manage users with the Management Portal:

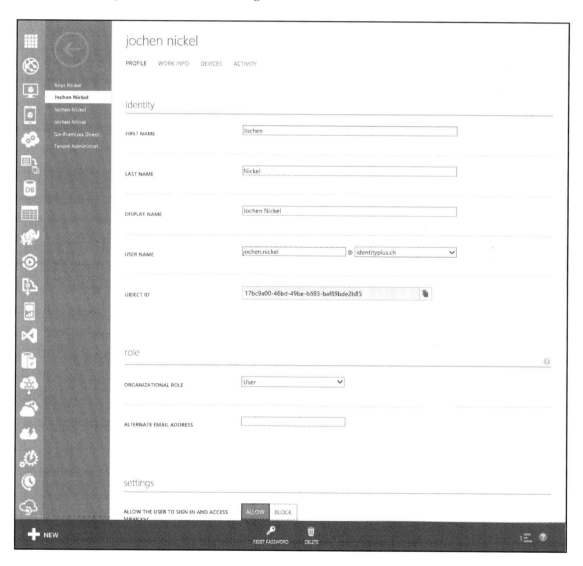

- **PowerShell management**: This is a scripted way of using PowerShell and the Azure Active Directory `cmdlets`. This method provides you with a simple way to automate tasks such as user licensing or bulk modification operations.
- **Graph API management**: This programatically uses the Azure AD Graph API. This is an extremely powerful option that essentially gives you full control of how identities are managed in Azure Active Directory. To be able to design a powerful management solution and to get a better understanding of this option, we will provide a short introduction to this field of technology.

Basically, we start with the question: *What is a graph?* The simplest answer to this question is to say that it's a RESTful interface for Azure AD. This interface allows you to perform tenant-specific queries and programmatically access directory objects like users, groups, and roles. You can also access relationships like members, `memberOf`, and `directReports`. The requests use the HTTP standard methods `get`, `post`, and `delete` to create, read, update, and delete objects in the Azure Active Directory. The Graph API also provides the following functionality:

- The responses support JSON, XML, and standard HTTP status codes
- Compatibility with OData V3
- Uses OAuth 2.0 for authentication and role based assignment

The following shows a simplified interaction flow between the application and the graph API to understand the architecture of this interface:

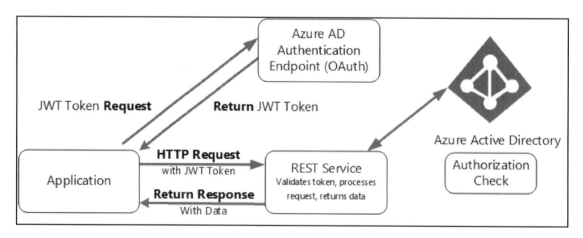

For completeness, we need a short answer to the question: *What is REST?* REST stands for Representational State Transfer and is an architecture style and not a protocol. It gives a description of how HTTP should be used for accessing data and follows these characteristics:

- RESTful Web Services expose resources through a URI
- Clients use HTTP Verbs
- Single resource, with multiple representations
- Stateless

After studying the theory, it's time to show you an example of how to create a new user in Azure Active Directory. You can also use the online Graph Explorer to get a deeper understanding of this material. There is the option to use the provided demo company or your own tenant at: `https://graphexplorer.cloudapp.net/`.

| **Example: Create new user** |
|---|
| Method: POST<br>`https://graph.windows.net/identityplus.ch/users?api-version=2013-04-05` |
| HEADERS<br>Content-Type: application/json<br>Authorization: Bearer<br>eyJ0eXArOiJLV1QiLCJhbGciOiJSAzI1NiIsEng1dCI6Ik8HVEZSZEstZnl0aEV1T.... |
| BODY<br>`{`<br>`"accountEnabled":true,`<br>`"userPrincipalName":"NewUser@identityplus.ch",`<br>`"displayName":"New User",`<br>`"passwordProfile":{ "password":"NewStartWithGr@phAP1",`<br>`"forceChangePasswordNextLogin":true},`<br>`"mailNickname":"NewUser"`<br>`}` |
| RESPONSE:<br>`201 Created` |

The previous example fulfills the following requirements:

- Password meets the tenant's accepted password complexity
- Uses the minimum set of properties to create a user
- Usage location is not set by the example above

You can use this functionality in the different reading scenarios, such as:

- Simply reading from Azure Active Directory
- Receiving *Deltas* from changes
- Using it for authorization decisions, like getting users group and role memberships
- Designing workflows that look up relationships (Manager/Direct Report)
- Checking subscribed services such as Exchange, SharePoint, Skype, or Dynamics CRM
- For designing people or group pickers with list, search user, or groups functions

Also for typical writing scenarios, such as:

- Updating users, groups, and roles
- Adding users to groups or roles
- Setting the user password
- Provisioning and de-provisioning of users

After discussing the different management methods and scenarios for designing an administrative solution, we will move on to the first basic module: *User Management*.

# Important user principles

The main focus of an Identity and Access management solution is to reflect an end-to-end life cycle. The identity lifecycle with the main principles of hiring, transition, and termination is also valid for a cloud identity scenario and can be represented with the necessary work items, as follows:

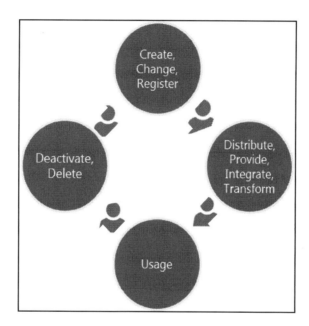

# Employee life cycle (word smart)

The relationship starts when a new employee joins the organization and his identity and corresponding information must be provided. Initially, an identification of the employee as a user will be created and an assignment of standard access rights to applications will be implemented.

The following partial processes run in a typical end-to-end process:

- Provisioning
    - Creation of the person and identifier(s)
    - Definition of group and role memberships
    - Definition of the required system and application access

- Authentication and Authorization
    - Validation of the person's identity
    - Determination of the right-to-access
    - Audit and security reporting
    - Management of system authorizations

- Self-Service
    - Registration for Password Reset and maintenance of other verification options
    - Password Reset and Changes, Account Unlock
    - Maintenance of personal information

- De-provisioning
    - Revoking of permissions/authorizations based on current role(s)
    - Deactivation of the user account
    - Deletion of the user account
    - Security controls

After a brief refresher of the standard processes and work items, we will now dive into the specialties of Azure Active Directory, starting with the different account types you can create. In Azure Active Directory, you can use three main types:

- Azure Active Directory Accounts
- Microsoft Accounts
- Organizational Accounts

The following figure shows the manual process of creating a new user account in Azure Active Directory over the Azure Web Management Portal:

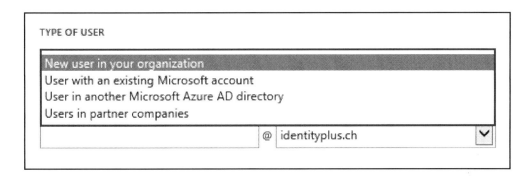

- **Azure Active Directory Accounts:** In Azure Active Directory, you can create users and groups in your directory. This service works independently because it's able to perform the authentication of a user without any on-premises infrastructure integration. With the integration of on-premises directory services, users and groups can directly access resources within Azure. Every user is then represented in the Azure Active Directory.

- **Microsoft Accounts**: These are normally used for private usage scenarios and without any organizational control.

### Recommendation

Provide access to resources whenever possible with Organization Accounts in Azure subscriptions. Do not allow the use of existing personal Microsoft accounts. Depending on the individual permissions, these accounts may be tied to the company Azure Subscriptions, have access to storage accounts, and billing information. Also, aliases are used in the naming of the account, like `alias4711@outlook.com`.

A valid design principle for Microsoft Accounts is to map them to a person and use a format like `FirstName.LastName@outlook.com`. A format like `FirstName.LastName.Suffix@outlook.com` can also be used to identify different environments, such as DEV for the development account.

| Jochen Nickel | jochen.nickel@identityplus.ch | Microsoft Azure Active Directory |
|---|---|---|
| Jochen Nickel | jochen.nickel@azureid.ch | Local Active Directory |
| Jochen Nickel | jochen.nickel@outlook.com | Microsoft account |
| Jochen Nickel | jochen.nickel@identityplus.onmicrosoft.com | Microsoft Azure Active Directory |

- **Organizational Accounts**: The recommended way to manage Azure subscriptions is to use Organizational Accounts. The form of an organizational account can be the organization's email address, such as `FirstName.LastName@organizationalname.com`. This happens if a company configures a custom domain and uses a cloud only, directory synchronization, or federation scenario. The main reason for using Organizational Accounts is that the organization has more control over the user account. Furthermore, many of the Azure Service offerings depend heavily on Organizational Accounts.

| Jochen Nickel | jochen.nickel@identityplus.ch | Microsoft Azure Active Directory |
|---|---|---|
| Jochen Nickel | jochen.nickel@azureid.ch | Local Active Directory |
| Jochen Nickel | jochen.nickel@outlook.com | Microsoft account |
| Jochen Nickel | jochen.nickel@identityplus.onmicrosoft.com | Microsoft Azure Active Directory |

If we create a user account in Azure Active Directory, we are already using another very important design principle. The **User Principal Name (UPN)** is used as the user's sign-in name. The following figure shows the re-usage of this convention for a user account in a pure cloud identity scenario.

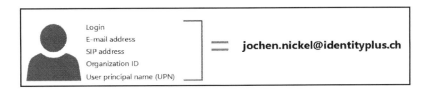

As an architect or engineer of such a solution, you should be aware of the following statements about the user principal name:

- **Alternate Login ID**: This is a way to achieve UPN alignment without having to modify the UPN attribute of user accounts (AAD Connect – Synchronization Scenario)
- **UPN requirements**:
    - Can only contains letters, numbers, periods, dashes, and underscores
    - Must be known by users
    - The domain suffix must be under the domain chosen for Single sign-on
    - UPN alignment
    - The domain selected to federate must be registered as a public domain
    - A required change of UPNs in on-premises Active Directory domains

- **Limitations**:
    - No usage in an Exchange Hybrid Online Deployment.
    - Current Azure AD Connect deployments with synchronized objects; need to change the UPN of every user account.
    - Kerberos-based SSO no longer works for applications that rely on the Sign-in Assistant for example, S4B or OD4B
    - Azure AD Application Proxy and Kerberos Constrained Delegation requires a UPN match between Azure AD and the on-premise Active Directory

- If you start thinking about the integration of your on-premises infrastructure, you should also think about what implications a change of the UPN has on the rest of your infrastructure. Just to give you an idea of this, think about the certificates and applications that depend on this attribute. We will discuss and give you further information on this topic in the hybrid scenarios later on in the book. Next, we will discuss the different ways to manage your users in Azure Active Directory.

Whenever possible, try to have the e-mail address aligned with the UPN for a better user experience and the usage of the most compatible scenario.

# Defining the correct user management

The user management in Azure Active Directory can be arranged in three different ways. We have already discussed this issue more generally in the section on usage scenarios in this chapter. Now we will focus on managing user accounts. The first, and easiest, way to administer user accounts is to use the Azure Web Management Portal, as you can see in the following figure:

With the portal you are able to create, change, and delete user accounts and their attributes. In the local Active Directories you are able to disable user accounts. Azure Active Directory allows you to `Allow` or `Block` the user to sign in and access services. This helps you to manage temporary staff or the deactivation of a user account before you delete it:

The portal also allows you to monitor the used devices and applications directly on the user's properties, as you can see in the following example:

| | | | | |
|---|---|---|---|---|
| 11/25/2015 11:42:57 PM | Microsoft Device Registration Cli... | 84.75.23.101 | Zuerich, Zuerich, CH | Windows |
| 11/25/2015 11:42:40 PM | Universal Store Native Client | 84.75.23.101 | Zuerich, Zuerich, CH | Windows |
| 11/25/2015 11:42:37 PM | Accounts Control UI | 84.75.23.101 | Zuerich, Zuerich, CH | Windows |
| 11/25/2015 11:40:22 PM | Unknown First-Party App | 84.75.23.101 | Zuerich, Zuerich, CH | Windows |
| 11/25/2015 11:40:05 PM | Device Registration Service | 84.75.23.101 | Zuerich, Zuerich, CH | Windows |

Another important aspect is to set the user's manager. You can do that just by copying the user's object ID of the manager to the managed user.

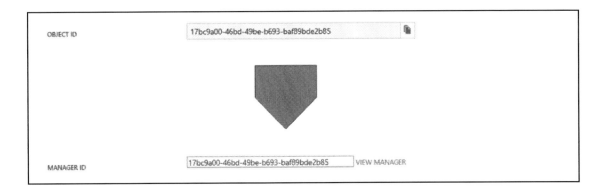

Your user management solution can also use PowerShell with the Azure Active Directory module. This option should be used for bulk or detailed operations or for scenarios with a higher number of employees. The `cmdlets` help you to perform many tasks, such as managing users, passwords, and user principle names. After installing the Azure Active Directory module (`http://bit.ly/1OdZTIS`), you can use the PowerShell to administer your Azure AD. See the following figure, which shows you some example `cmdlets` that you can use to design your solution scripts:

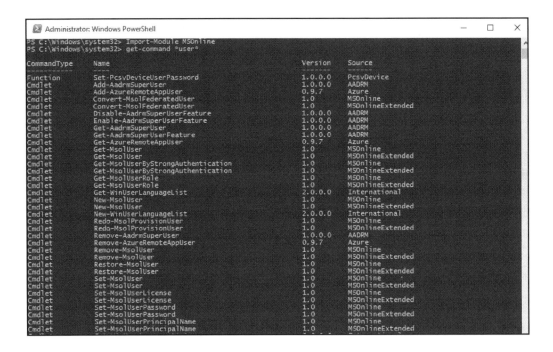

The following link provides you with all the necessary user management references:

PowerShell reference: `http://bit.ly/1TerDQj`.

A typical task you can't do over the management portal is restoring a deleted user account from the Azure AD Recycle Bin. For that, you can use the following `cmdlet` to view the deleted user accounts and provide a valuable restore capability:

- **View deleted users**: `Get-MsolUser -ReturnDeletedUsers`
- **Restore deleted users**: `Restore -MsolUser -UserPrincipalName <string>`
- **Retention time**: 30 days

Another way is to use the Office 365 management portal, `https://portal.office.com`, with the following option:

The third option is to use the Graph API. For most companies, there should be a real need, or a special integration scenario, to develop their own Graph API application for managing their user accounts and groups. The implementation for creating a new user could be like the following example in C#:

```
// Example for Graph API
// Create a new user object in Azure Active Directory.
var newUser = new User()
{
    // Set Required settings
    DisplayName = "John Smith",
    UserPrincipalName = "john.smith@identityplus.ch",
    PasswordProfile = new PasswordProfile()
    {
        Password = "ImS@Strong!",
        ForceChangePasswordNextLogin = false
    },
    MailNickname = "John.Smith",
    AccountEnabled = true,
    // Set some optional settings
    GivenName = "John",
    Surname = "Smith",
    JobTitle = "Senior Sales Agent",
    Department = "Sales",
    City = "Zuerich",
    State = "ZH",
    Mobile = "0041-123-4567",
};
// Add the user to the Azure Active directory
adClient.Users.AddUserAsync(newUser).Wait();
```

For designing and implementing an application by calling the Azure AD Graph API, you could use the following references:

Operations on users and Graph API: `http://bit.ly/1PYMdE1`

Sample console application: `http://bit.ly/1YUnGn1`

Sample web application: `http://bit.ly/1PQM9bw`

 Be aware that the Graph API and the PowerShell methods don't offer all the management capabilities.

The last section has demonstrated the different ways of administering your cloud-only identity scenario. We recommend that you design an administrative solution with the management portal and the PowerShell as a starting point. Because you will often need to integrate on-premises infrastructures, the Microsoft synchronization toolset allows you to automate many tasks. The authority will be on the known Active Directory management console or a local identity management system, such as Microsoft Identity Manager 2016.

# Addressing successful user scenarios

In addition to the previously discussed management solutions, there are some other important options for technically implementing an end-to-end user life cycle. In this section, we want to focus on two special scenarios: *Workday HCM* and the future functionality of *Azure AD Connect synchronization* capabilities. The *Workday* example provides insight into a Microsoft partner solution with the goal that user data is mastered by HR and provisioned by Azure Active Directory. In future releases, the Azure AD Connect utility is able to connect to directories other than Active Directory. If this feature set is enabled, you can connect directly to your on-premises HR system and provide a similar way of provisioning user accounts to Azure Active Directory. You need to do that with your on-premises Identity Management system, such as **Microsoft Identity Manager(MIM)** 2016.

The following figure gives you a graphical summary of the solutions:

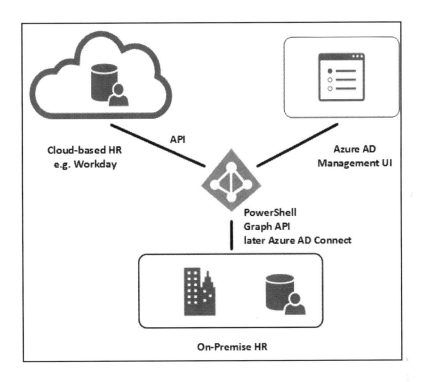

For example, if you use Workday **Human Capital Management(HCM)** (`http://bit.ly/1j 3M4jI`) as your cloud HR system, you are able to use the inbound provision of user accounts in your Azure Active Directory and build with the outbound provisioning, for example, using Salesforce, ServiceNow, and Citrix GoTo Meeting in a completely automated way to get user data out of your HR system and into your cloud applications.

The following figure shows the capabilities of integrating Workday in your Azure Identity and Access management solution:

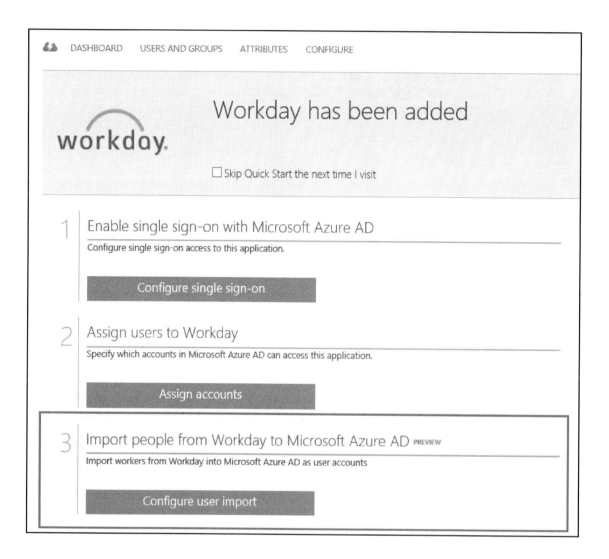

The following reference link `http://bit.ly/1TTTQfy` gives you all the necessary details to design and implement the solution with Workday HCM.

As discussed, you can enable user provisioning to other SaaS applications, such as Salesforce, to complete the solution. In this scenario, Azure Active Directory can be used to manage user access, to synchronize user accounts, and to provide SSO to Salesforce. In this case, you configure the outbound provisioning process to the application, like the following example with the Salesforce sandbox system:

To design and implement this solution, you need to decide the correct attribute mappings to use the outbound provisioning process. Microsoft provides the standard attribute mappings shown below to integrate with Salesforce. Furthermore, you can use the reference link `http://bit.ly/1fQer6q` to get the required tutorials and then design criteria to implement such a solution:

## attribute mappings

| TARGET ATTRIBUTE (SALESFORCE SAND... | TARGET OBJECT | SOURCE ATTRIBUTE (AZURE AD) | SOURCE OBJECT | REQUIR... |
|---|---|---|---|---|
| IsActive | User | Not([IsSoftDeleted]) | User | Yes |
| Alias | User | Mid([userPrincipalName], 1, 8) | User | Yes |
| Email | User | mail | User | Yes |
| EmailEncodingKey | User | "ISO-8859-1" (default) | - | Yes |
| LanguageLocaleKey | User | "en_US" (default) | - | Yes |
| FirstName | User | givenName | User | Yes |
| LastName | User | surname | User | Yes |
| LocaleSidKey | User | Replace([preferredLanguage], "-",..."_"...) | User | Yes |
| ProfileName | User | SingleAppRoleAssignment([appRoleAssignments]) | User | Yes |
| TimeZoneSidKey | User | "America/Los_Angeles" (default) | - | Yes |
| Username | User | userPrincipalName | User | Yes |
| UserPermissionsCallCenterAutoLogin | User | "False" (default) | - | Yes |
| UserPermissionsMarketingUser | User | "False" (default) | - | Yes |
| UserPermissionsOfflineUser | User | "False" (default) | - | Yes |

These two examples give you an idea of a complete end-to-end scenario and you can try this scenario and find all the information to feel confident during design and implementation. To capture all these scenarios in this book would take us far beyond the possible number of pages.

For the **Azure AD Connect** tool, Microsoft plans two major innovations. The first is the capability to connect additional directories like databases, LDAP directories, and more. This option will give you the chance to adopt local LDAP directories and, for example, HR systems. The other innovation is to allow a *User write back*, which allows you to provision user accounts to your local Active Directory and use Azure AD as **Identity Management as a Service (IdMaaS)**. Special, smaller organizations can use the Management Portal as their primary management tool and profit from services like Self-Service Password Reset, MFA, and SSO. Equipped with all this information, we will move on to the next section: *Password management*.

# Designing an added value with password management

Oops, I forgot my password. I'm sure you've been in that situation before. Azure Active Directory Premium provides the functionality of a Self-Service Password Reset (SSPR). With this service, users can reset their forgotten passwords in Azure AD without the help or assistance of the help desk.

Password management in Azure Active Directory Premium provides the following capabilities:

- **Self-Service password change**: This allows the changing of expired or non-expired passwords.
- **Self-Service password reset**: This allows the resetting of forgotten passwords.
- **Administrator-initiated password reset**: This allows users to reset passwords of end users or other administrators within the Azure Management Portal.
- **Password write-back**: New passwords can optionally be written back to the on-premises Active Directory. In order to support password write-back, the following services and connections must be in place:
    - AAD Sync or AAD Connect must be used for synchronizing user accounts to Azure AD

Microsoft Identity Manager 2016 with the AAD Connector is not supported with password synchronization. Azure AD Connect also provides an auto-update mechanism without the need of re-installation. This is very helpful because there is currently a monthly release of the tool at the moment.

- Password hash synchronization must be enabled so that a hash of the on-premises password hashes is synchronized into the Azure AD tenant for each user

The password write-back design will be discussed in the section on hybrid identity scenarios later on in Chapter 7, *Designing Hybrid Identity Management Architecture*, of this book.

With the following 10 point list, you will be able to design a password management solution based on Azure Active Directory with all the relevant information.

- **Password Reset:** Enabled/Disabled
- **Restrict Access to password Reset:** All Users/Limited Users

SSPR can be enabled for all users or only for a subset of users in the directory. To enable SSPR for a subset of users, the users can be added to an Azure AD security group, which is referenced in the SSPR configuration. There are two options for adding users into this group:

- Create the group in the cloud and manage members through Azure AD. This process would work well for organizations with a smaller amount of people where administrators can effectively manage users through the Azure Management Portal.

- Create the group in the on-premises AD, manage its membership in the on-premises AD, and synchronize it into Azure AD via AAD Connect. This is the preferred process for large and medium-sized organizations that already have a process for managing group memberships on-premises.

- **Authentication Methods:** Azure AD SSPR supports the following forms of authentication for forgotten passwords:
    - Phone call with a one-time code
    - Text message with a one-time code
    - Email with a one-time code to an alternate email address
    - Security Questions
- **Number of Authentication methods required:** 1 or 2
- **Number of questions required to register:** 3 to 5
- **Number of questions required to reset:** 3 to 5
- **Security Questions**: Limit of 20 questions
- **Require users to register when signing in to the Access Panel. During registration they are asked to enter their contact information:** Yes/No
- **Number of days before users must confirm their contact data**: Range from 0 to 730 days
- **Customize the contact for your administrator link**: Disabled/Enabled

The following figure shows you the relevant settings in the Azure Management Portal:

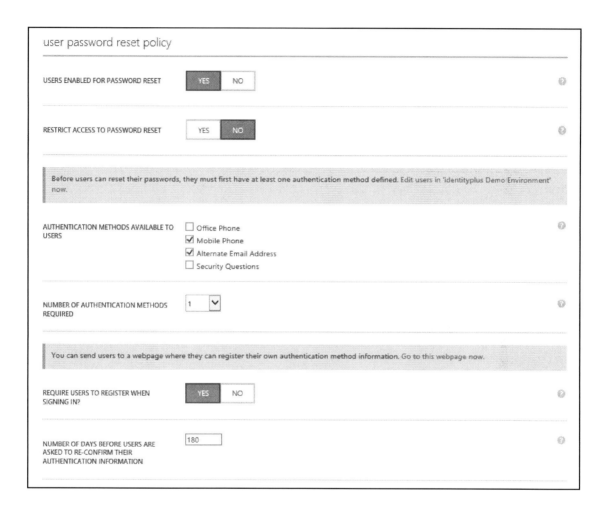

The authentication methods are one of the most important design criteria, because if a user initiates the password reset process, he needs to be verified by an alternate authentication method in order to successfully reset his forgotten password. As discussed previously, Azure AD SSPR supports different methods, and we need to discuss them in more detail. The following figure shows the user's registration process:

**Design Tip 1:** The user can be required and prompted to register his verification methods before being allowed to access any application. There is also a direct link you can provide to the users, which is as follows:
`https://account.activedirectory.windowsazure.com/PasswordReset/Register.aspx?tenantIdentifier=e98b729a-add6-4565-b21-454`

If you enforce registration, the user will be prompted with the following message:

Your administrator has required you to verify your contact info. You can use this to reset your password if you ever lose access to your account.

verify now

- **Phone-Based Authentication**: To use the phone-based method, the user must register his mobile phone or office phone number. This can be done with the registration process mentioned previously or pre-populated through the administrator over the web interface, PowerShell, or the AAD Connect tool.

**Design Tip 2**
Please be aware that not every employee provides his private mobile number or is in possession of a mobile phone.

- **E-mail-Based Authentication**: If you want to use the email option, the Alternate Email Address attribute of the user account needs to be populated with a valid external email address. Similar to the phone number, this can be done with options such as phone-based authentication.

**Design Tip 3**
Please be aware that not every employee provides his private email address.

- **Question-Based Authentication**: To use this option, a user needs to answer a pre-defined pool of security questions. Azure AD will require that some number of questions must be answered during enrollment and either all or a subset of those questions need to be answered during a password reset event.

**Design Tip 4**

This option is the last choice in terms of the usability and comfort of the password reset process. It's also important to ensure that questions don't inappropriately ask users for sensitive PII information, and that the questions are secure with the answers hard to guess.

# Reset your password

**verification step 1** > verification step 2 > choose a new password

Please choose the first contact method we should use for verification:

○ Email my alternate email

○ Text my mobile phone

○ Call my mobile phone

○ Call my office phone

◉ Answer my security questions

What is your favorite food?

[                                    ]

What was the name of your first pet?

[                                    ]

What was the make and model of your first car?

[                                    ]

[ Next ]

It is recommended to create an end-user communication plan to provide users with details on how to register for SSPR, reset their password, and what to expect. From a practical perspective, a small video about the process is very helpful.

After successful registration, a user will be able to reset or change his password in many different ways:

- Over the `https://myapps.microsoft.com` portal
- Over the `https://portal.office.com` portal
- Over the `https://manage.windowsazure.com` portal

The following figure shows the example over the Azure Web Management Portal:

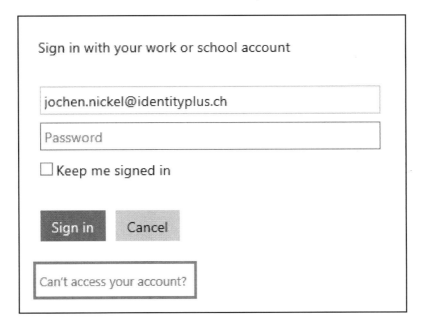

If you want to reset your password, you can use the **Can't access your account?** link that will request your User ID and where you answer a captcha, as you can see in the following figure:

 The user can use also the direct link `https://passwordreset.microsofto nline.com` to reset the password.

The following standard values for passwords are set in Azure AD:

- **Password restrictions**: 8 characters minimum and 16 characters maximum
- **Password expiry duration**: 90 days
- **Password expiry notification**: 14 days

- **Account Lockout**: After 10 unsuccessful logon attempts
- **On-premises account**: Will be respected

To see whether a single user's password is set to never expire, run the following `cmdlet` by using the UPN (for example, `jochen.nickel@identityplus.ch`) or the user ID of the user you want to check:

```
Get-MSOLUser -UserPrincipalName user@example.com | Select
PasswordNeverExpires
```

To verify your newly-designed and implemented password management solution, you should provide a small test plan with the following test cases:

| TC-01 | **Verify that a user can successful sign in to the access panel** `https://myapps.microsoft.com` **and register for a password reset using the contact methods.** |
|---|---|
| TC-02 | Verify that users can reset their password by visiting `https://myapps.microsoft.com` and clicking on **Can't access your account?**. The user needs to provide the UPN and contact details to complete the verification process and set up a new password. Users should be able to log in with the new password. |

# Describing the required group principles

The Azure Active Directory **Self-Service Group Management** (**SSGM**) functionality enables users to manage their own groups and group memberships. The following scenarios are supported:

- A user can create their own groups, which can be used to authorize people to access applications that are integrated with Azure AD
- A user can manage the memberships of groups that were created in Azure AD
- A user can request to join groups that were created in Azure AD

Azure Directory differs between two types of group management scenarios: delegated and SSGM.

Self-Service Group Management requires an Azure Active Directory Premium license. The user performing group management must have a license assigned. We highly recommend that you study Office 365 and visit the following link:
`https://support.office.com/en-us/article/Learn-about-Office-365-groups-b565caa1-5c40-40ef-9915-60fdb2d97fa2`.

The group management switches in Azure Active Directory are shown in the following figure:

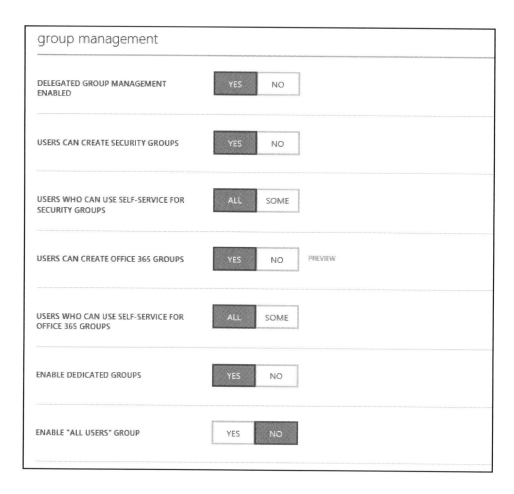

The Delegated Group Management feature provides the following capabilities:

- Administrators can assign applications to groups
- Enables group owners to maintain group memberships
- Azure Groups must be managed within Azure
- Synced on-premises groups cannot be delegated in Azure
- Azure-created groups do not synchronize back to on-premises

Group write-back is in preview: `https://azure.microsoft.com/en-us/d ocumentation/articles/active-directory-aadconnect-feature-prev iew/#group-writeback`.

The Self-Service Group Management feature provides the following capabilities:

- Azure AD Premium empowers users to request membership to security groups and permits group owners to approve or deny access
- Currently supported on Azure AD are groups created from within the myapps portal (`myapps.microsoft.com`)

The group membership policy is controlled via one of three methods:

- Open access
- Only owners can add members
- Group owner approval

SSGM can be enabled for all users or a subset of users in a specific Azure AD security group. There are two options for adding users into this group:

- Create the group in the cloud and manage members through Azure AD

**Design Tip**

This works well for organizations with a smaller amount of people, where administrators can effectively manage the users through the Azure Management Portal.

- Create the group in the on-premises AD, manage its membership in the on-premises AD, and synchronize it into Azure AD using AAD Connect (which will be discussed in the hybrid identity scenarios section later on in this book)

**Design Tip 2**

This is the preferred process for large and medium-sized organizations that already have a process for managing group memberships on-premises.

# Group management in action

When enabling a user for Self-Service Group Management, the user will be able to create groups and submit requests to join groups. After activating SSGM, a variety of options are available:

- **Allow users to create their own groups**: This is not always the preferred option for organizations. Organizations are able to turn off the feature.
- **Restrict who can use SSGM**: This option limits which users are enabled for SSGM.

The following figure shows the option to create your own groups in the access panel on `htt ps://myapps.microsoft.com`. The user is allowed to set owners and members, and as the owner he needs to approve the joining requests.

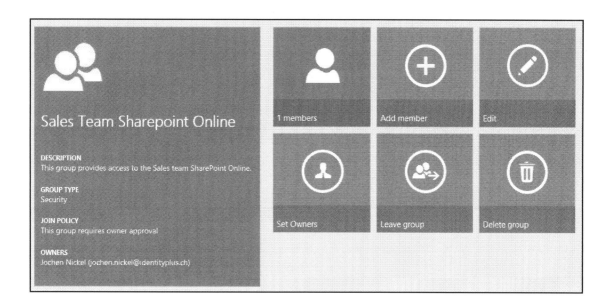

 Groups that are created in the Azure Management Portal have SSGM disabled by default. Groups cannot be enabled for SSGM unless they have an identified owner.

Often, groups have no valid owners because the previous owner may have left the organization or the group may have been created without an owner and no one is sure what organization the group should be managed by. For analysis, you can use PowerShell to find all groups without a valid owner.

Dedicated groups are special groups that are created and managed by Azure AD automatically. One example is the dedicated group for `All Users`, which contains every user account in Azure AD.

 You can choose to enable or disable dedicated groups. In order to use Dedicated Groups, SSGM must be enabled in Azure AD.

Dynamic groups allow an administrator to specify some criteria, by which all users who meet the criteria are automatically members of the group.

 These criteria take the form of a user attribute query based on attributes that are present in the directory.

The following example shows the mechanism of dynamic groups:

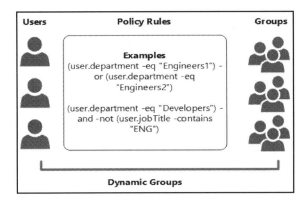

 Limitations and Extensions: The number of dynamic groups at the time of writing is limited to 10 dynamic groups in the Azure AD tenant. All attributes that you want to use for group membership evaluation must be present on the user objects in Azure AD. You are also able to extend your Azure AD with custom attributes. With these additional attributes, you can also populate group memberships; see the following example: `http:/ /bit.ly/2afrAan`.

You should be aware of the following characteristics when designing a successful solution:

- Converting a standard group in a dynamic group will result in losing the previous membership.
- When creating a custom (advanced) membership evaluation policy, there is a limit of 255 characters. Therefore, complex evaluations that involve multiple attributes and `and`/`or` conditions should be limited.

The following figure shows the configuration of dynamic group memberships. You can use the following reference `http://bit.ly/29WohSS` to construct advanced rules for dynamic group memberships:

To manage groups, you can use the following group management references:

- **PowerShell:** `https://msdn.microsoft.com/en-us/library/azure/dn919663.aspx`
- **Graph API:** `https://msdn.microsoft.com/Library/Azure/Ad/Graph/api/groups-operations`

# Defining the required device principles

With Azure Active Directory, you're able to connect personal or corporate devices to the directory service. After joining the device, it becomes a known device and the user is able to use single sign-on with his corporate resources and applications.

This functionality works very well for the following usage scenarios:

- **Scenario 1:** When most user apps and resources are in the cloud, for example, if a company uses Office 365 as their collaboration platform and Workday as their HR system, employees can connect Windows 10 devices to Azure AD independently during the first-run experience or from System Settings. They can also sign in to Windows 10 using their Azure AD credentials. The applications are accessed with single sign-on – including the Azure AD Access Panel `https://myapps.microsoft.com`.

- **Scenario 2:** Seasonal workers, students, and externals don't need a fully equipped and domain-joined corporate PC or notebook. They can choose their own device and can profit from single sign-on application access. The Azure AD joined device can also be used as a second factor.

The following figure shows the capabilities in a solution overview, including the necessary settings in the Azure Management Portal:

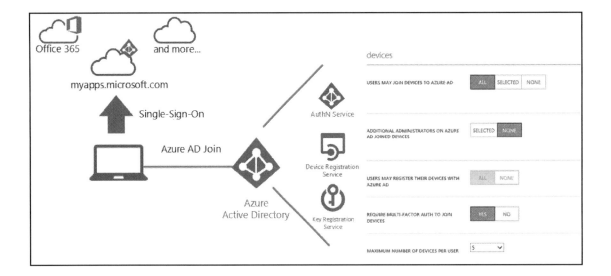

# Online device management

With the Azure AD join scenario, the user is able to join the device in a self-service manner. With Windows 10, for example, the user can directly log on to Azure AD and his/her user account is managed with the device in a known state.

This user process is shown in the following figure:

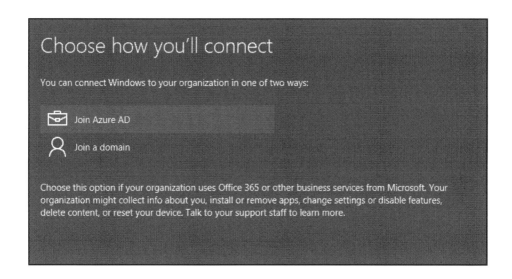

 Administrators are also able to configure an automatic device registration process:
https://azure.microsoft.com/en-us/documentation/articles/active-directory-conditional-access-automatic-device-registration-windows7/

This feature will be discussed in more depth in the section on hybrid identity scenarios later on in this book.

# Designing roles and administrative units

In this section, we will discuss the designing of roles and administrative units that we can use to provide Role-based Access Control and the delegation of rights to several types of administrative persons.

## Roles and RBAC

RBAC is well implemented in the Microsoft Azure platform and has a security model to perform access control of resources by users on a more granular level. Users can access and execute actions on the resources within their scope of work.

There is an actual limit of 200 co-administrators per subscription. RBAC is only available in the new Azure Portal `https://portal.azure.com`, in addition to the usage of the Azure Resource Manager APIs.

RBAC allows more users to manage their Azure services, and at the same time limits access to only specific resources, rather than the entire subscription.

Practical Notes:

- **Administrators and co-administrators**: They will see all resources in all portals and through APIs
- **Users defined in RBAC**: They will not have access to Service Management portals or APIs
- **Users not assigned to either**: They will only see the empty ARM portal, and will not be able to access the Service Management Portal
- **The subscription**: This is no longer the management boundary for permissions in Azure
- **Role permissions**: There are 22 built-in Azure RBAC roles for controlling access to Azure resources

The following figure shows a schematic overview of the Azure RBAC capabilities:

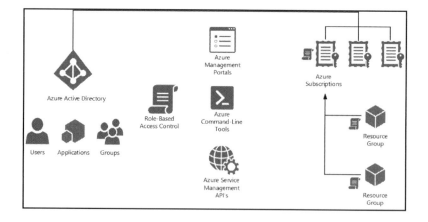

The following articles can be used for more information about the whole RBAC solution and help you gain confidence in your ability to provide a solution design for your customers.

- http://blogs.technet.com/b/ad/archive/214/12/18/azure-active-directory-now-with-group-claims-and-application-roles.aspx
- https://azure.microsoft.com/en-us/documentation/articles/role-based-access-control-configure/

# Designing administrative units

With the Azure AD Premium features, you get the capabilities of administrative units. Administrative units help you to delegate administrative access in large enterprises. For example, you can allow a set of people to manage a subset of users in your company or delegate administrative tasks to special regions or business units. From a design perspective, you are able to model and delegate administrative access in the cloud. If you are familiar with role-based access control, you can think about administrative units as a custom resource scope that can be defined to represent the administrative boundaries. The following figure gives you an idea of the possible design scenarios:

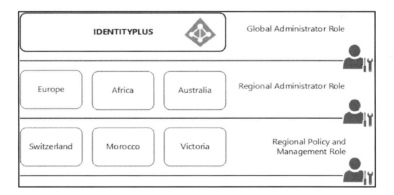

The following limitations are available in the current state of implementation:

- Administrative units are only available in PowerShell
- Administrative unit-scoped user account administrators cannot create or delete users

- Groups are not supported as members of administrative units, and administrative unit-scoped user account administrators cannot create or delete groups
- Currently, only user objects are supported as members of administrative units

# Managing identity reporting capabilities

Azure Active Directory contains a series of reports that can be used to gain insight into various activities around the user. These reports are broken down into three categories:

- **Anomalous Activity:** This reports potentially suspicious activity that could be an indicator of a security incident
- **Activity Logs:** This provides reports on various activities that are taking place within the directory, such as password management or self-service identity activities
- **Integrated Applications**: This provides statistics regarding which applications are being used

The following figure represents the Azure AD reporting architecture and informs us of the different interfaces and capabilities:

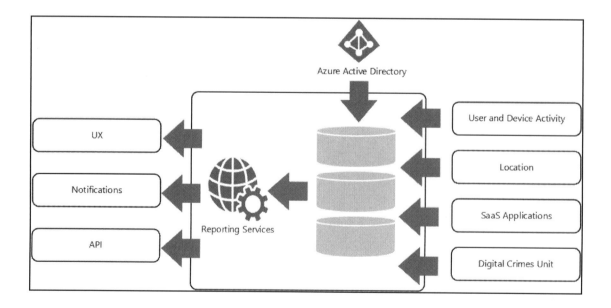

# Azure Active Directory Audit Report events

With Azure AD Audit Reports, you can identify the following possible causes:

- User is sharing their password
- User is using a remote desktop to launch a web browser for sign in
- User is using a VPN or going through a proxy in another region
- A hacker has signed in to the account of a user from a different country

- User has forgotten their password
- User is the victim of a successful password guessing brute force attack

The following figure shows an example report on the dashboard:

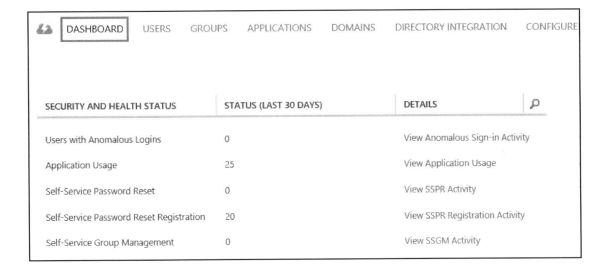

In particular, the marked causes in the following figure are interesting to note when identifying attacks to user accounts in Azure Active Directory:

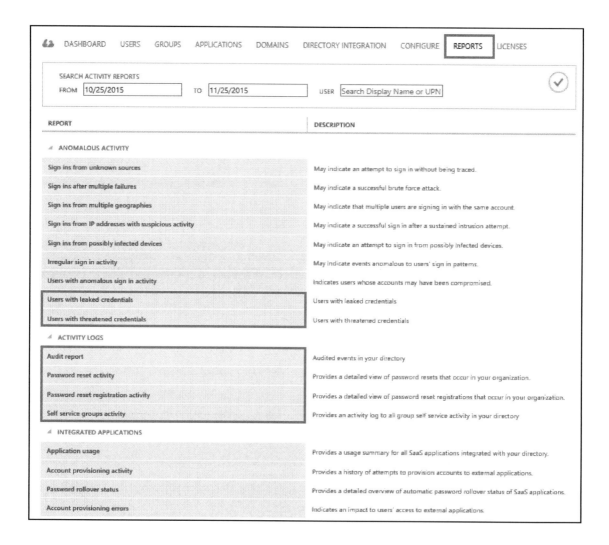

There is also the capability to download the reports as a CSV file for further analysis or presentation.

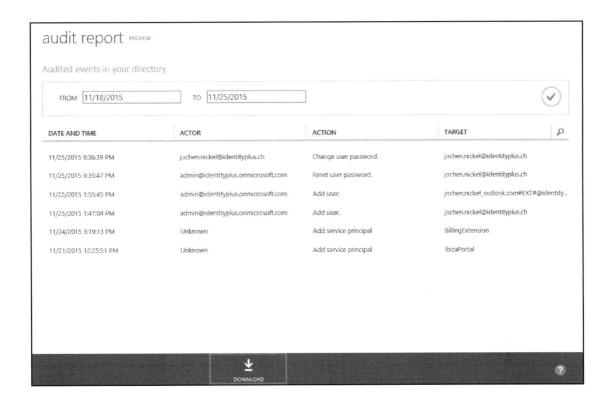

Additionally, you can use the different notifications shown in the following figure to actively get informed about sensitive interactions, such as password changes in administrative accounts:

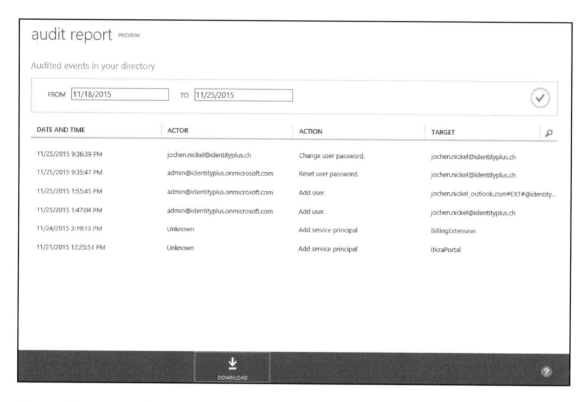

To provide more in-depth reports, you can develop your own application against the Azure AD Reporting API.

 With the following references, you can design and use the Azure AD Reporting API:
Sample Application in C#: http://bit.ly/1OspFKq
Getting Started Guide: http://bit.ly/11KGFCh

# Summary

After reading this chapter, you should be able to describe the Azure Active Directory architecture and to design a complete user and group life cycle. You should also be able to describe the different roles, administrative units, and the identity reporting capabilities. This chapter has captured the principles, features, and functionality that are integral to the designing and architecture of cloud identities.

In the next chapter, we will plan and design the authentication and application access. You will learn how to use Azure AD as an Identity Provider. Furthermore, we will dive into user and group-based access management, including the associated reporting capabilities. We hope to see you in the next chapter as you learn how to design the authentication and authorization capabilities of Microsoft Azure.

# 3
# Planning and Designing Authentication and Application Access

Now that we have finished going through the relevant architecture and the principal identity management capabilities of Azure Active Directory, it's time to move on to authentication and authorization. This chapter will discuss the essential topics for using Azure AD as an identity provider and for providing flexible and secure access to SaaS applications. Furthermore, we will get to know the rich authentication reporting functionality. This chapter deals with the following topics:

- Using Azure AD as an identity provider
- User and group-based application access management
- Managing authentication reporting capabilities

# Using Azure AD as an identity provider

In the new cloud era, the externalization and consumerization of IT is playing a main role. Users need to access all their data and resources from many different places and devices without thinking about where the application is actually installed. SaaS applications are very useful for meeting this demand. Here enters another issue, however, because purchasing and using SaaS applications is easier than ever and various departments are bypassing their IT departments. Shadow IT is born – application usage without central management. This trend called **Shadow IT** will be seen more often as more companies try to adopt cloud-based SaaS apps.

Typical questions we hear in our projects are as follows:

- How can I arrange collaboration without managing foreign users? (management)
- How do I monitor the usage of these applications? (management)
- How do I enforce the correct set of permissions to these applications? (access control)
- How do I ensure that only legitimate users have access to these applications? (security)

Shadow IT also introduces challenges surrounding user experience because in an unmanaged SaaS application landscape, the user needs to remember and manage multiple usernames and passwords in order to access his applications. Just imagine a user accessing six different SaaS applications and trying to manage six different credential sets. You know what will happen – the passwords will be very easy to guess, written on post-its, or managed in Microsoft Excel sheets. Furthermore, the user will be forced to enter his credentials several times and the user experience is highly compromised.

This brings us to another point: modern authentication, such as federation with other identity providers. Federated Identity Management requires that the organization have a common set of policies, practices, and protocols in place to manage the identity and trust of IT users and devices across organizations. Federation also often requires that users are provisioned in SaaS platforms.

Microsoft Azure Active Directory will help organizations and IT administrators to bridge the gap and address these challenges mentioned previously. The following figure summarizes the graphically:

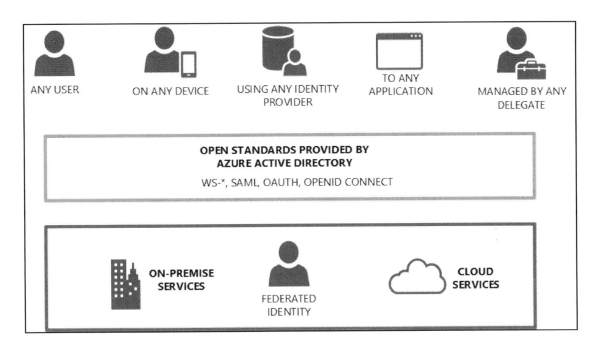

# Azure Active Directory Authentication endpoints

Today, the common authentication mechanisms like Kerberos or NTLM (Identity 1.0) no longer apply to the needs of inter-organizational or cloud usage. Identity federation protocols are increasingly taking on the role to meet these requirements. Azure Active Directory provides the most important open standards in this technology field. The following figure shows the different authentication endpoints that can be used with Microsoft Azure:

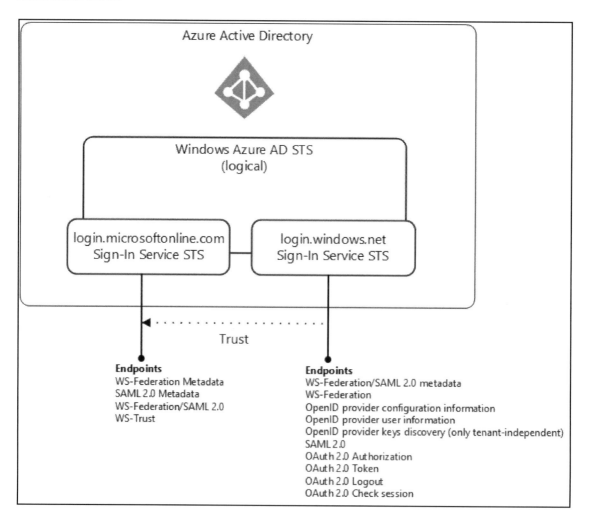

Azure Active Directory supports these most widely used authentication and authorization protocols (Identity 2.0) using a **Security Token Service** (**STS**). This STS is implemented by a combination of two security token services.

- The `login.microsoftonline.com` sign-in service handles the user authentication with an optional second-form of authentication
- The `login.windows.net`, used for modern business applications handles the policy and claims generation steps for modern application

**Design Note 1**

The complete references are available on `http://bit.ly/1k62QkV`. In this chapter, we capture the most important facts about this protocol standard.

# Common features for application access in Azure AD

Microsoft provides two methods for providing SSO with the Azure Active Directory implementation:

- Federation-based SSO
- Password-based SSO

The following two sections will provide a short overview of these methods.

## Federation-based SSO

The configuration of federation-based SSO enables the users in your organization to be automatically signed in to a third-party SaaS application. For example, when you have already been logged into Azure AD by the Access Control Panel `https://myapps.microsoft.com` and you want to access resources that are controlled by a third-party SaaS application, federation eliminates the need for a user to be re-authenticated. Federated SSO is available for end user browsers that support JavaScript and CSS.

**Design Note 2**
Applications with support of SSO and full user management:
`http://bit.ly/1OVYvgZ`
Complete list of all SaaS applications in the actual catalog:
`http://bit.ly/1Pcxu9h`

# Password-based SSO

The configuration of password-based SSO enables the users in your organization to be automatically signed in to a third-party SaaS application by Azure Active Directory using the user account information from the third-party SaaS application. When you enable this feature, Azure AD collects and securely stores the user account information and the related password.

Password-based SSO relies on a browser extension to securely retrieve the application and user specific information from Azure AD.

Password-based SSO provides two different models in the case of identity provisioning:

- Password-based SSO without identity provisioning
- Password-based SSO with identity provisioning

Most third-party SaaS applications that are supported by Azure AD support this feature.

The following end user browsers can be used:

- IE 11, remember IE 8 and IE9 are EOL, IE10 on Windows 7 EOL or later.
- Chrome on Windows 7 or later or Mac OS X or later
- Edge isn't supported

## Password-based SSO without identity provisioning

This option allows the administrator to pre-stage applications for the user. You need to choose the option **Users authenticate with their existing application account** in the Azure Management Portal.

 All users in the directory will see all applications that have been configured in this mode.

The user will be prompted to install the Password SSO plugin for Internet Explorer or Chrome the first time he clicks the application. The browser requires a restart after installing this plugin. The user needs to return to the Access Panel and click on the application tile again and will then be prompted for a username and password for the application. Once the username and password are entered, these credentials will be securely stored in Windows Azure Active Directory and linked to their account.

The next time a user clicks on the application tile, they will be automatically signed into the application without needing to enter the credentials again.

## Password-based SSO with identity provisioning

This option allows the administrator to add applications and pre-configure a central credential set for the applications. You need to choose the option **Users authenticate with their existing application account** in the Azure Management Portal.

The user will also be prompted to install the Password SSO plugin for Internet Explorer or Chrome the first time he clicks the application. The browser requires a restart after installing this plugin. When the user returns to the Access Panel and clicks on the application tile again, he will then be automatically signed in to the application.

The next section gives you an overview of all the relevant protocols supported by Azure Active Directory.

# Common token standards in a federated world

When a digital identity is transferred across a network, it's only a collection of bytes. It's common to refer to a set of bytes containing identity information as a security token or just a token. In a claims-based world, a token contains one or more claims, each of which carries some piece of information about the user it identifies.

Today, the tokens come in different flavors, like the following token formats:

- **SAML** – Security Assertion Markup Language
    - XML-based
    - Very descriptive metadata
- **JWT** – JSON Web Token
    - More easily human readable
    - Smaller token size
- **SWT** – Simple Web Token
    - Form-encoded attribute/value pairs
    - Not very common
- **Kerberos**

 For the following protocol specifications we recommend a good basic knowledge of claims-based authentication. You can download the Microsoft Claims-based authentication handbook to prepare yourself. Use the following download link `http://bit.ly/1MkAOsk` to get the book.

# Security Assertion Markup Language (SAML) 2.0

SAML is the foundation for much of the current identity federation activity and SAML 2.0 is preceded by SAML 1.0 and 1.1. SAML 1.1 was released in 2003 and had just two scenarios (also known as profiles), and both were IdP-initiated. Shibboleth 1.3 and Liberty Alliance–WS-FF 1.2 extended SAML 1.1, and SAML 2.0 was released by OASIS in 2005.

The following table shows the SAML core principles:

| Assertions | Protocols | Bindings |
|---|---|---|
| **Package of identity information** | Request / Response Based | Associates a message (protocol) with transport (communication mechanism) |
| **Synonym Token** | Defines the messaging requirements | Examples:<br>HTTP Redirect<br>HTTP POST<br>SOAP |
| **XML-based** | Examples:<br>Authentication Request<br>Single Logout<br>Artifact Resolution | |

# Key facts about SAML

SAML precisely defines messages for exchanging queries and assertions (claims). The SAML standard defines a transport-neutral protocol that can be used with various bindings, SOAP being one of them. The SAML standard defines identity information in the form of assertions. Large parts of the standard go into defining the assertions and attribute profiles. Logout information will always be sent to as many receivers as possible. There is no notion of session timeout.

SAML 2.0 uses profiles, which describe how assertions, protocols, and bindings combine to form a federation scenario. For example, a Web SSO Profile will be used like the following:

- AuthN Request Protocol
- HTTP Redirect Binding at IdP
- HTTP POST Binding at SP

There are many different SSO profiles available that are defined in the specification:

- Web Browser SSO Profile
- **Enhanced Client or Proxy (ECP)** Profile
- Identity provider Discovery Profile
- Single Logout Profile
- Name Identifier Management Profile
- Artifact Resolution Profile
- Assertion Query/Request Profile
- Name Identifier Mapping Profile

There are also SAML attribute profiles, such as the following, available to use:

- Basic Attribute Profile
- X.500/LDAP Attribute Profile
- UUID Attribute Profile
- DCE PAC Attribute Profile
- XACML Attribute Profile

To give an example, we use the typical SAML WebSSO profile in the following figure:

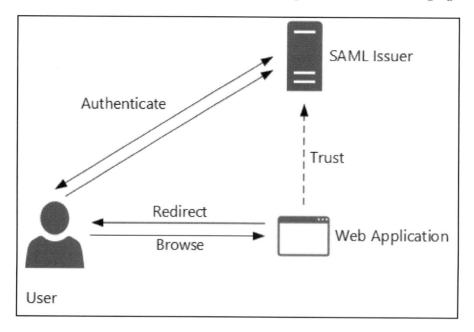

1. Trust is established between the web application and the SAML issuer.
2. The user browses to the web application.
3. The web application detects that the user is not authenticated and redirects him to the SAML Issuer.
4. The user automatically browses to the SAML Issuer.
5. The user authenticates to the SAML Issuer.
6. The SAML Issuer builds the token and passes it back to the user.
7. The user POSTs the token to the web application.

 In summary, we can say that SAML 2.0 was released in 2005 by OASIS and is commonly used in Web Sign-in scenarios, particularly for web applications with an XML token format.

# WS-Federation

WS-Federation was developed by an industry consortium and was released in December 2006 with Microsoft being a key contributor. WS-Federation is also part of a larger framework, WS-Security, and builds on the work of WS-Trust from February 2005, defining the following two key principals:

- The protocol for requesting/receiving security tokens
- How trust should be brokered between parties (using an STS)

It also defines two profiles:

- Active Requestor Profile
- Passive Requestor Profile

WS-* Federation Suite:

- WS-Trust
- WS-Federation
- WS-Policy

# Key facts about WS-Federation

The token format in WS-Federation is agnostic, and unlike SAML, the token can be anything. WS-Federation does not define any specific messages but suggests using a web service for this purpose.

The WS-Federation specification defines its services using SOAP and then builds facilities for tunneling SOAP through the browser. There is no definition of what the security token looks like; the token is opaque, with one possible security token being a SAML assertion as defined in the SAML standard. Thereby, WS-Federation can leverage part of SAML, which is well in line with the composability concept normally used in WS-* specifications. An application has to register to receive logout information. There is no notion of session timeout.

There are also some relationships regarding SAML-P with the WS-Federation and the passive requestor profile:

- Similar to SAML WebSSO Profile
- Incompatible:
    - Different request and response messages
    - No IdP-initiated use case
    - No Assertion Query Profile

The following figure gives us an example of the WS-Federation Passive Requestor Profile:

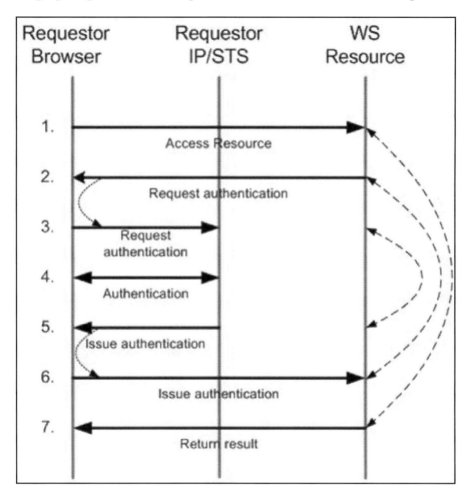

Source: Microsoft

 In summary, we can say that this standard was established in 2006 and is commonly used for Web Sign-In scenarios, and in particular .NET web applications. The token format is agnostic like SAML, JWT, etc.

# OAuth 2.0

In simple words, authentication is the act of proving who you are, whereas authorization is the act of determining what you can do. OAuth 2.0 is about delegated authorization and not about authentication. It is not a protocol, it's an authorization framework defined in the *RFC 6749, The OAuth 2.0 Authorization Framework*. This can be confusing because there are many cases in which you use OAuth 2.0 to log in to a client Web Application.

The authentication process must end by figuring out and validating the identity of the end user, but OAuth doesn't do that. OAuth provides time-based tokens, which can be used to access a resource on behalf of the end user without providing any identity information about the end user.

OAuth 2.0 is the de facto standard for API security and is a major breakthrough in identity delegation.

## The principal facts about OAuth 2.0

The following are the principal facts about OAuth 2.0:

- It is an Internet Protocol/specification for creating and managing application identity
- It is a cross-platform mechanism
- It has delegated authorization to APIs
- Its main purpose is to get the client an Access Token
- It is not an authentication protocol
- It is preceded by OAuth 1.0 and OAuth **Web Resource Authorization Profiles (WRAP)**
- It is an Internet standard used by Facebook, Google, and Twitter
- Microsoft, for example, uses OAuth with Azure Active Directory and SharePoint 2013

The OAuth framework differs between two client (application) types when accessing a service on behalf of a user. The two types of application can be described as follows:

- **Public**: Runs locally on a device. Not trusted to hold a secret.
- **Private**: Runs behind firewalls. Can be trusted with secrets.

The following figure gives an example of the roles in the OAuth framework:

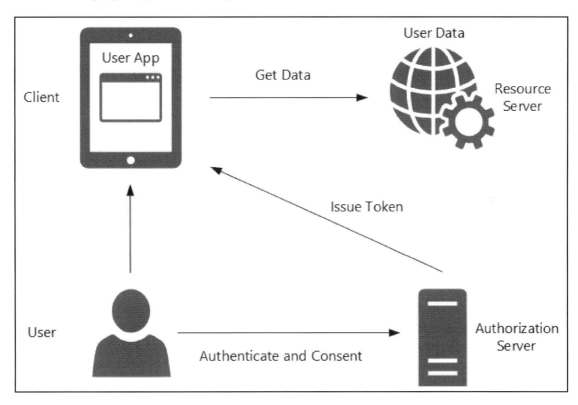

It is also important to understand the flows in OAuth 2.0 that define the process for obtaining an Access Token.

# Main flow facts

There are four flows defined in the specification:

1. Authorization Code flow.

    - One-time code issued to client
    - Client redeems code for access token

2.  Client Credentials flow.

    - Authenticates the client, not the user
    - Client receives an access token for itself

3.  Resource Owner Password flow.

    - Client collects username/password from user
    - Exchange username/password for access token

4.  Implicit flow.

    - Client is untrusted (public)
    - No refresh token issued

**Practical Note**
The main practically used flows in the real world are the Authorization Code and Client Credentials flows.

# Authorization code flow (very common)

The main concept of this flow is that the client gets an authorization code first and uses the code to redeem the access token. It's recommended for private clients (web apps or native mobile applications) that have the capability to spawn a web browser. In that case, private clients establish a secret with the OAuth server. The secret will be used to authenticate the client during the access token redemption.

The access tokens expire and need to be refreshed with refresh tokens, and each of them has their own lifetime and can be stored for a longer term. A refresh token can also be used to redeem a new access token later.

The following example shows the *Authorization Code Grant Type*:

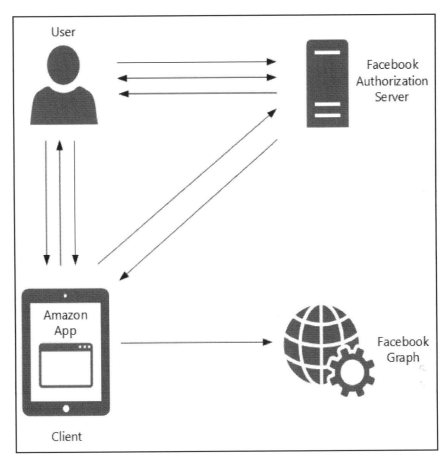

1. The user clicks the button to `Post this purchase.`
2. The client redirects the user to OAuth Server.
3. The user authenticates and grants consent.
4. The OAuth Server redirects the user to the client with the Authorization Code.
5. The client requests an Access Token from the Authorization Server.
6. The OAuth Server returns the Access Token to the client.
7. The client uses the Access Token to authorize to the Resource.

# Client credential flow

The main concept of this flow is application authentication and not user authorization, where the application establishes a secret. The application authenticates with the secret and receives an access token. Users are not involved in this flow and the client can perform this flow out of band.

The following example shows the *Client Credential Grant type*:

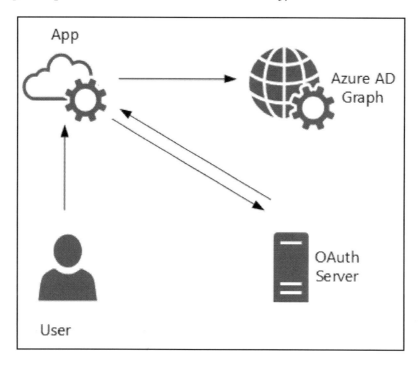

1. The user uses the client (through the address book app).
2. The client authenticates to the OAuth Server (Azure AD).
3. The OAuth Server provides an access token to the client.
4. The client calls Resource (Web Service) with the access token in the header.

# Implicit grant flow

When acquiring an access token, this flow is mostly used by JavaScript clients running in the web browser. Also important to note is that there is no authentication requirement for the JavaScript client. The difference between this and the Authorization Code flow is that the access token will be received in the grant request.

The following example shows the *Implicit Grant type*:

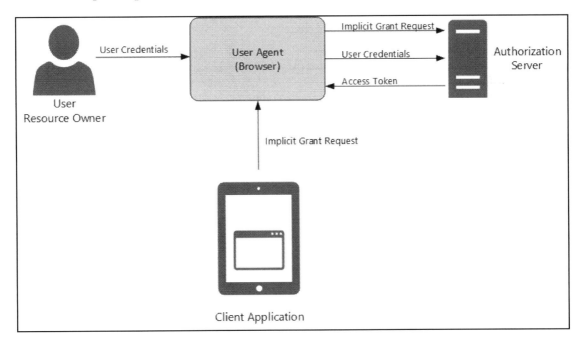

# Resource Owner Password Credentials flow

The main concept in this flow is that the resource owner must trust the client application. This means that the resource owner has to give its credentials directly to the client application.

The following example shows the Resource Owner Password Credentials Grant type:

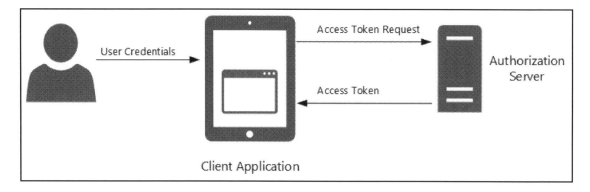

 In summary, we can say that the specification of OAuth 2.0 was published in October 2012 and is commonly used in rich client and modern application scenarios and with RESTful Web API access. The token format is agnostic but JWT is primarily used.

# OpenID Connect

OpenID Connect was established as a standard by its membership in February 2014. OpenID Connect provides a lightweight framework for identity interactions in a RESTful manner. The specification was developed under the OpenID Foundation and has its roots in OpenID; it was greatly affected by OAuth 2.0 because that specification was not intended for authentication. Microsoft was also a co-author of the OpenID Connect specification.

It defines the following identity layer on top of OAuth 2.0:

- It uses two OAuth 2.0 flows:
    - Authorization Code flow
    - Implicit flow
- Adds an ID Token to OAuth 2.0 exchange
- Adds the ability to request claims using an OAuth 2.0 access token

The following example shows the Authentication (AuthN) process with the *Authorization Code flow*:

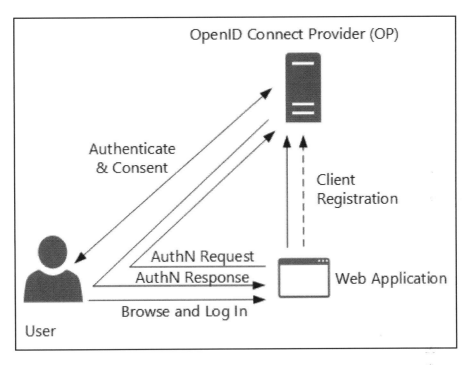

1. A client registers with the **OpenID Connect Provider (OP)**.
2. The user browses to the Web App and initiates Log IN.
3. The Web App redirects the user to the OP.
4. The user authenticates to the OP and gives consent for the Web App to use his identity.
5. OP builds the Authorization Code.
6. OP redirects the user back to the Web App with the Authorization Code.
7. The Web App sends the Authorization Code to OP.
8. OP creates the ID Token and Access Token and sends back to the Web App.
9. The Web App verifies the ID Token.

The specification also uses a *UserInfo EndPoint* with the following characteristics:

- Returns additional claims about a user
- REST-based endpoint
- Authenticates with Access Token received from OPx
- Response returned in JSON

 In summary, we can say that the specification was released in February 2014, was co-authored by Microsoft, and is used for Web Sign-In when consent is needed. The token format is JWT.

# Azure Active Directory Domain Services

Azure AD Domain Services helps you to move your on-premises applications, depending on traditional authentication methods like Kerberos and NTLM, to the cloud. This cloud-based service allows you to join your IaaS virtual machines to a managed domain without the need to provide domain controllers on virtual machines. With this solution, you can integrate directly in your Azure Active Directory services and benefit from the rich feature set. The following figure shows the integration scenario from the perspective of an application installed on an IaaS virtual machine:

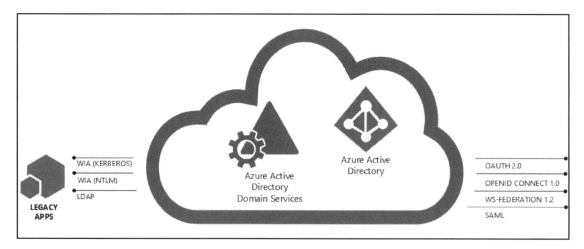

Actually, this service provides a flat organizational unit structure for managing the domain joined server systems. Generally, it's not an idea to join client computers in this directory. Hierarchical organizational units are not supported in the current version. You can also benefit from simple group policies for managing your server systems. It's not allowed to create your own GPOs at the moment. Furthermore, the extension of the computer object's schema is not possible. The following figure gives you an idea:

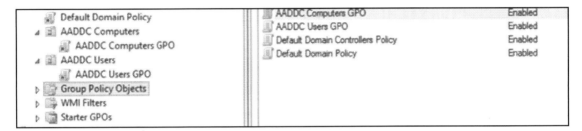

The following points represent the current feature set:

- Domain join – joins your servers to AAD DS
- User attributes and group memberships sync with Azure AD
- Usernames/passwords are synced with Azure AD
- GPOs for the built-in users and computer containers
- High availability – two Domain Controllers are provisioned

# Azure Active Directory B2B

The Azure AD B2B feature set mainly addresses the need to share applications with your business partners. Normally, you need to do it the hard way and federate with your business partner or create and manage a shadow user in your Active Directory. If you go to federate, you need to exchange information about the planned protocols, certificates, and claims and this is, most of the time, a burden for smaller or medium-sized companies, particularly if the business partner doesn't have a federation services infrastructure. Microsoft simplifies this process with the Azure AD B2B feature.

The following figure shows the process of enabling business partners to access your applications:

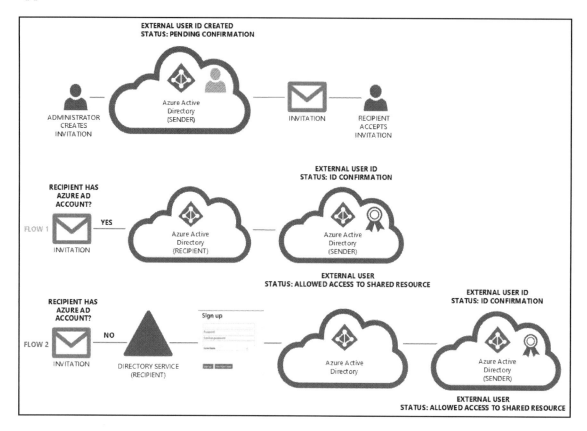

In the case of **FLOW 2**, the user signs up for his own Azure Active Directory and will be added to the Azure AD from which the invitation process was started. To get more information about the process, we recommend referring to the following resource http://b it.ly/2axgUjM and watching the following video http://bit.ly/2apLrB.

The high level workflow is based on an invitation process based on a CSV file imported to your Azure Active Directory. The file contains the following fields:

| Field | Example |
|-------|---------|
| E-mail | `jochen.nickel@idam.ch` |
| DisplayName | Jochen Nickel |
| InviteAppID | cd3ed3de-93ee-400b-8b19-b61ef44a0f29 |
| InviteReplyUrl | `http://identityplus.sharepoint.com/SitePages/Home.aspx` |
| InviteAppResources | cd3ed3de-93ee-400b-8b19-b61ef44a0f29 |
| InviteGroupResources | 8cd678e5-6ef7-48dd-b178-2af0798778ef |
| InviteContactUsUrl | `https://de.linkedin.com/in/nickeljochen` |

 With this file you define which users get access to which applications.

To get the relevant information for the file, you can use the following commands:

```
Get-MsolServicePrincipal | fl DisplayName, AppPrincipalId
Get-MsolGroup | fl DisplayName, ObjectId
```

After importing the CSV file, the invitation process starts and can go in two directions:

- The user has an Azure Active Directory account
- The user doesn't have an Azure Active Directory account

 The two directions you see in the preceding figure are described as **FLOW 1** and **FLOW 2**.

# Azure Active Directory B2C

The Azure AD B2C feature set allows you as a developer to work on the application functionality while Azure Active Directory provides the whole identity management framework around your application.

Azure AD B2C provides you with the following five main topics:

- Usage of social and local accounts
- Usage of multi-factor authentication
- Sign up, sign in, password reset, and profile editing
- User experience customization
- Seamless integration for development

The following figure shows you the *Sign up* process as an example:

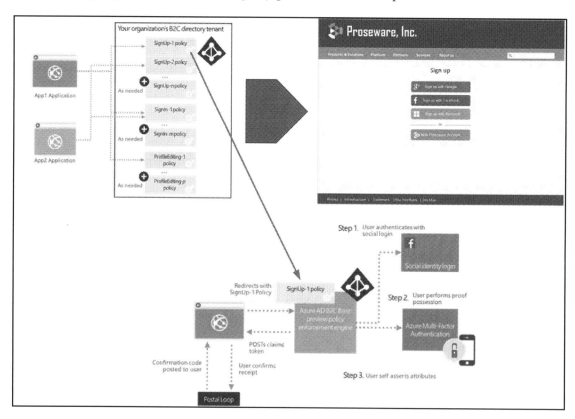

**Reading Note**:

Azure AD B2C will be addressed in more detail in the hybrid identity complex section. For now, it's helpful to just get an idea about the different capabilities you can use to design authentication and authorization with Microsoft Azure. There is also an Azure B2C Premium in preview with limited information at the time of writing this book.

# By example – SharePoint claims-based authentication

SharePoint 2013 provides a full set of authentication mechanisms, including claims-based authentication. The following schema shows the capabilities and the flow in SharePoint.

The claims-based authentication is particularly relevant to an effective collaboration solution:

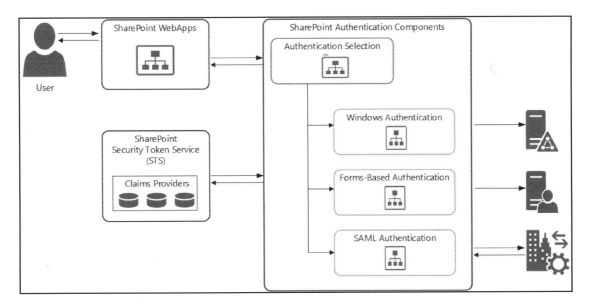

SharePoint also supports authentication using OAuth 2.0, particularly for external authentication in the Office 365 environment. The Azure **Access Control Services** (**ACS**) are required and the access tokens are passed to the SharePoint in CSOM calls and REST API calls. The next section shows this scenario.

## SharePoint Online use case using OAuth 2.0

When using OAuth 2.0 with SharePoint Online, the Azure ACS is required in order to implement the solution. The ACS acts as the authentication server in this scenario and Office 365 needs to be trusted to the ACS. The client application will communicate with the ACS to acquire the access tokens. The following terms need to be adopted to the solution:

- The content owners are SharePoint users who can grant permissions to site content

- The content server is the SharePoint web server that hosts the sites with the content
- The client application is a remote application that needs permissions to access the requested site content
- The authentication server is a trusted service that provides applications with the necessary access tokens

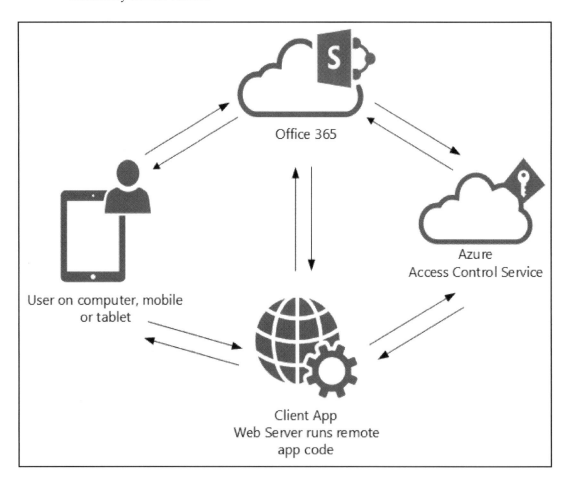

1. The User accesses the SharePoint application and authenticates using claims.
2. SharePoint requests the context token for the user.
3. ACS returns the context token.

4. SharePoint passed the context token to the user.
5. The user POSTS to the application and passes the context token.
6. The client application extracts the refresh token from the context token and passes it back to the ACS to request the access token.
7. ACS returns the access token to the client application.
8. The client application makes CSOM/REST calls to the SharePoint Site passing the OAuth token.
9. SharePoint authenticates the application and processes CSOM/REST calls and returns the content to the application.
10. The client application returns HTML to the user device.

# User and group-based application access management

For authorization, Azure Active Directory delivers many methods. As we already discussed in `Chapter 2, Planing and Designing Cloud Identities` groups are a preferred way of providing users with the correct permissions and access to their applications. It's good practice that users work with the Access Control Panel UI and access their applications, change the password, and add verification options. With this option, you can also allow the user to build his own preferred workplace. For example he can add his own applications and leave the passwords secure in Azure Active Directory, benefitting from SSO.

Generally, Azure Active Directory provides three main concepts for authorization:

- **Direct**: The user will be directly authorized
- **Group-based**: Rule based or Delegated
- **Role-based**: The developer can publish his own application roles

The following figure shows the complete context:

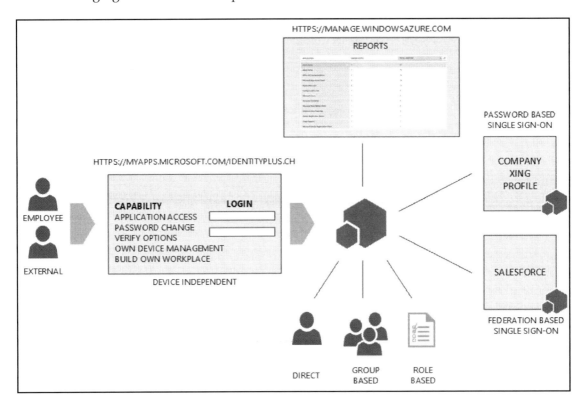

The following section describes the different methods for these concepts.

# User directly assigned

Access to an application can be granted either manually or through security groups from the Azure Management Portal. When granting access per user, the administrator has to select a specific user account from the ones available in Azure AD.

Currently, user access management is supported only for applications that have automatic user provisioning or password-based SSO enabled. Always assign permissions through groups.

# Group-based

For group-based access control you can use three concepts to provide a flexible authorization framework:

- **Rules-based**: Mainly used for organizational groups or roles
- **Delegated**: Mainly used for project or resource groups
- **Rules-based (EXT)**: Able to provide a simple segregation of duty scenario

The following section discusses the first two from the list.

# Rules-based

This method can be used to build organizational groups or roles based on user attributes, such as `department=Sales` or `job title=Sales Manager`. This is a good way to provide access to applications based on the department or the business role of the employee. The following figure shows the concept in a graphical way to provide a better understanding:

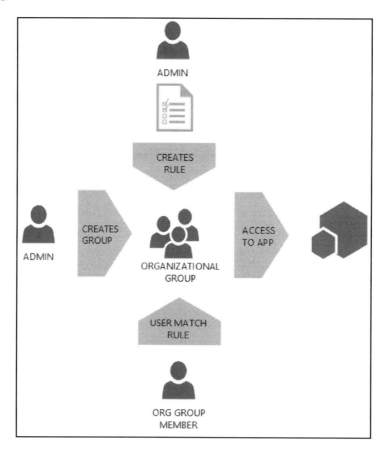

# Data owner

This method is mainly used to provide access to a specific subject or context, which group the employees together, for example, in projects or a product they work for. To provide this concept, you need to allow the project, product, or process owners the create security groups in Azure Active Directory. They are the data owners for those groups and can define which users are directly in a group or who can join with or without approval. The following figure shows the concept in a graphical way to provide a better understanding:

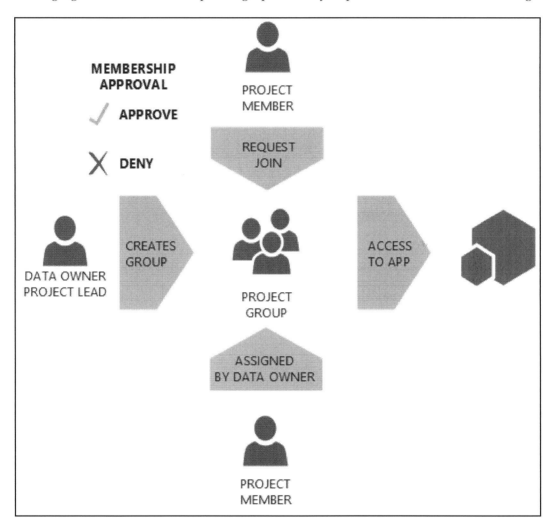

# Application Roles-based

This method provides the capability of using RBAC. Simply put, a role is a collection of permissions. Roles can be granted to users or groups. The developer defines a set of roles for the application, and the security administrator, for example, assigns the roles to manage access to the application. The following figure shows the concept. You will find more in depth information on this topic in the hybrid identity section of this book:

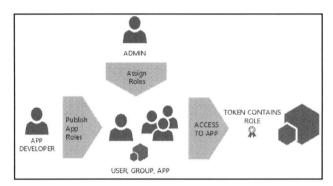

The developer can download the manifest of the `application, locate` the `appRoles` settings and is able to insert his own definitions in the array and upload the new manifest.

The following fields are available: `ID`, `displayName`, `description`, `value`, `allowedMemberTypes`, `IsEnabled`, and `Origin`.

The user experience looks as follows:

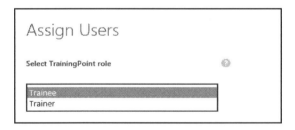

# Managing authentication reporting capabilities

You can use access and usage reports to gain visibility into the integrity and security of your organization's Azure Active Directory tenant. With this information, you can identify security risks and be able to adequately plan for mitigating those risks.

In the Azure Management Portal, reports are categorized in the following ways:

- **Anomaly Reports**: Contains sign-in events that were found to be anomalous
- **Integrated Application Report**: Provides insight into how cloud applications are being used in your organization
- **Error Reports**: Indicates errors that may occur when provisioning accounts to external applications
- **User-specific Reports**: Displays device/sign in activity data for a specific user

 Some advanced anomaly and resource usage reports are only available when you enable Azure Active Directory Premium and Basic. Advanced reports help you improve access security, respond to potential threats, and gain access to analysis on device access and application usage.

There are currently a few new reports available. When you enable Azure RMS as part of the EMS suite, you will receive an RMS section with four reports available. When you enable Azure B2B, you will receive an External Access section including an invitation summary report. And finally, the Integrated Applications.

# Azure AD free monitoring capabilities

The following reports are available for free in Azure for monitoring:

- **Sign-ins from unknown sources:** Successfully signed-in users with a client IP address
- **Sign-ins after multiple failures**: Successfully signed-in users after multiple failed sign-in attempts – hacker has been trying to guess the password of a user and finally succeeded

- **Sign-ins from multiple geographies**: Shows all successful sign-in activities from a user where two sign-ins appeared to originate from different countries where the time between sign-ins makes it impossible for the user to have traveled between those countries – hacker has signed in to the account of a user from a different country

The Premium offering adds the following machine learning-based anomaly reports:

- Sign-ins from IP addresses with suspicious activity
- Irregular sign-in activity
- Sign-ins from possibly infected devices
- Users with anomalous sign-in activity
- Users with leaked credentials

The following usage, error, and activity reports are free for monitoring user provisioning to external SaaS applications:

- Application usage
- Account provisioning activity
- Account provisioning errors

In addition to the above reports, the following new activity log reports are now available in Azure Active Directory Free and Basic to give you very detailed views of user activity:

- **Audit**: You can use this report when you want to view and audit all the key changes in the directory, for example, role membership changes, credential updates, and domain, user, license, and application management
- **Password reset activity**: Use this report when you want to view the history of resets done
- **Password reset registration activity**: Use this report when you want to view which users have registered their methods for password reset and which methods they have selected
- **Group activity**: Use this report when you want to view the history of changes to the groups that were initiated in the Access Panel

# Summary

After reading this chapter you should be able to explain and design the authentication and authorization capabilities of Azure Active Directory. You should know which functions, protocols, and interfaces Azure AD provides as an identity provider and you should be able to design a flexible and secure application workplace for the business to improve its productivity. Additionally, you will have seen the different reports for monitoring your solution. This will help you to design a proactive security solution and to mitigate security issues. Let's move on to implementing a designed example solution – see you in the next chapter!

# 4
# Building and Configuring a Suitable Azure AD

This chapter explains how to configure a suitable Azure AD tenant based on the decided cloud identity architecture. You will learn how to configure and manage users, groups, roles, and administrative units in order to provide a user and group-based application and self-service access, including audit functionality.

In this chapter we are going to cover the following topics:

- Implementation scenario overview
- Implementing a solid Azure Active Directory
- Creating and managing users and groups
- Assigning roles and administrative units
- Providing user and group-based application access
- Activating password reset self-service capabilities
- Using Standard Security Reports
- Integrating Azure AD join for Windows 10 clients

# Implementation scenario overview

After completing the following configuration tasks, you will see the rich functionality of Microsoft Azure in the field of IAM for cloud identities. You will be able to demonstrate the different capabilities in your own Microsoft Azure environment. This guidance will focus on the most important feature sets to give you an idea of how to improve your design considerations. We will use the default directory, which we call `domain.onmicrosoft.com`, from now on. Domain stands for your desired name. Be aware that this name will be visible in various applications, such as SharePoint online and Skype for business, to the end user. We recommend using the company name without the company form, for example `inovit GmbH` will be `inovit.onmicrosoft.com`. The configuration will be the base for additional, different scenarios in this book. For this reason, we will use an Azure, Enterprise Mobility Suite, and an Office 365 subscription so as to use all the available features. The following figure shows the different main areas we will focus on:

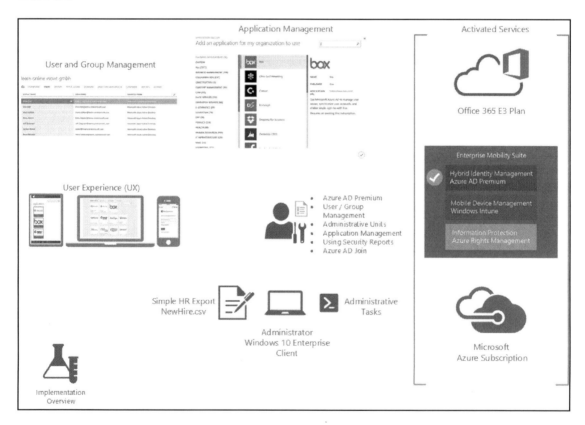

# Implementing a solid Azure Active Directory

The first step we need to do is to get an Azure Active Directory tenant. There are many ways to reach this target. The following four examples build the main entry points:

- Start with an Office 365 subscription, `http://bit.ly/1RVpFXe`

- Use an Azure subscription associated with a Microsoft Account:
- A typical start from an MSDN subscription:

- Use an Azure subscription associated with an organizational account:

- Starting from scratch, `http://bit.ly/1R2oIfx`

We will start with the last option. Let's go on and configure our personal Azure AD tenant.

# Configuring the requirements

First of all, we need to configure the prerequisites to work through this guide. You need to have a Windows 10 Enterprise client machine in a workgroup configuration. We recommend using a freshly installed Windows 10 Enterprise virtual machine. We need a Windows 10 device to use the Azure AD Join mentioned later in the book. If you are not able to access the Volume Licensed or MSDN versions, you can use the Enterprise Evaluation version at `http://bit.ly/1P6o8Yc`.

In the code section for this chapter you will find the following software to install on the client machine: the Azure AD PowerShell module and the required Microsoft Online Sign-In Assistant.

| Name ⌃ | Date modified | Type | Size |
|---|---|---|---|
| AADPowerShellModule_64.msi | 29.12.2015 12:11 | Windows Installer ... | 752 KB |
| MSOLSignInAssistant_32.msi | 29.12.2015 11:58 | Windows Installer ... | 4'178 KB |
| MSOLSignInAssistant_64.msi | 29.12.2015 11:58 | Windows Installer ... | 6'035 KB |

On the Windows 10 Client, you will need to extract the demo files, navigate to the `C:\Configuration\AdminTools` directory, and install the following modules:

- `MSOLSignInAssistant_(32/64)`: Microsoft Online Services Sign-In Assistant for IT Professionals RTW from `http://bit.ly/1TugAlN`
- `AADPowerShellModule_64.msi`: Azure Active Directory Module for Windows PowerShell from `http://bit.ly/1peKv6A`.

 Azure Active Directory Module for Windows PowerShell (32-bit version) is discontinued. There is no support for the 32-bit version.

With the following `cmdlet`, you can determine the currently installed version:

```
(get-item
C:\Windows\System32\WindowsPowerShell\v1.0\Modules\MSOnline\Microsoft.Onlin
e.Administration.Automation.PSModule.dll).VersionInfo.FileVersion
```

The `C:\Configuration\HRExports` directory contains the required HR import and group creation scripts for configuring your Azure AD tenant with some test data:

| Name | Date modified | Type | Size |
|---|---|---|---|
| AddOrgGroups.ps1 | 29.12.2015 21:48 | Windows PowerS... | 1 KB |
| HRImportToAAD.ps1 | 29.12.2015 21:57 | Windows PowerS... | 2 KB |
| NewHire.csv | 01.01.2016 20:24 | Microsoft Excel C... | 1 KB |

In the `HRImportToAAD.ps1` script, the following important variables will be used:

```
$domain = Get-MsolDomain | where {$_.Name -notlike "*mail*"}
$dir = "C:\Configuration\HRExports"
```

The `domain` variable will contain the `domain.onmicrosoft.com` name of your Azure AD default directory. We will use this directory and not a registered domain name for the different steps, so as to limit the requirements for these guidelines. To be productive, we recommend using a registered domain name. As you can see, the `dir` variable contains the path to the scripts and the simple HR export file called `NewHire.csv`. The `contoso.com` domain in the file will be replaced with your domain name, which is stored in the `domain` variable.

The `NewHire.csv` file contains the following demo user set, which will be used in further configurations to demonstrate the different functionalities:

```
userPrincipalName,DisplayName,FirstName,LastName,password
Don.Hall@contoso.com,Don Hall,Don,Hall,Pass@word1
Ellen.Adams@contoso.com,Ellen Adams,Ellen,Adams,Pass@word1
Jeff.Simpson@contoso.com,Jeff Simpson,Jeff,Simpson,Pass@word1
Brian.Cox@contoso.com,Brian Cox,Brian,Cox,Pass@word1
Doris.Sutton@contoso.com,Doris Sutton,Doris,Sutton,Pass@word1
Petro.Mitchell@contoso.com,Petro Mitchell,Petro,Mitchell,Pass@word1
```

# Azure Active Directory deployment

We will start the implementation by registering an Office 365 E3 plan:

1. Open your browser and navigate to `http://bit.ly/1aZa9Xk` and subscribe to the free Office 365 Enterprise E3.
2. Start to follow the registration process and define your user ID, such as `admin@domain.onmicrosoft.com`. We recommend using a non-personal ID.

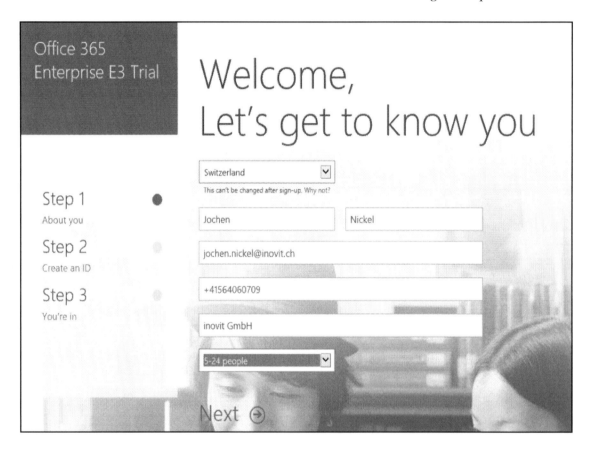

3. Next, you need to enter a new user ID and password.

4. Prove your identity with a text message or a phone call.
5. Enter the received code. Next, click **Create my account.**

6.  The provisioning process takes a few minutes and should end with a success message.

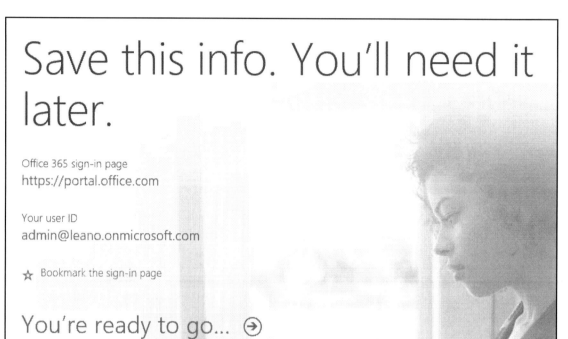

Save this info. You'll need it later.

Office 365 sign-in page
https://portal.office.com

Your user ID
admin@leano.onmicrosoft.com

☆  Bookmark the sign-in page

You're ready to go... ⊖

7. Next, you will log in to `https://manage.windowsazure.com` with your newly-created user ID.

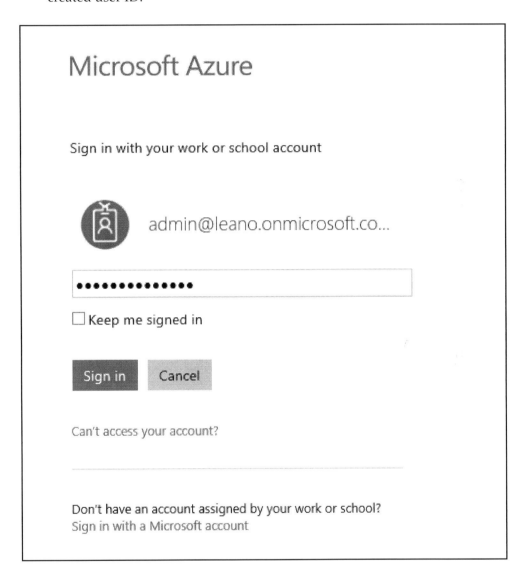

8.  Next, you will receive a message saying that no subscription is found for your account.

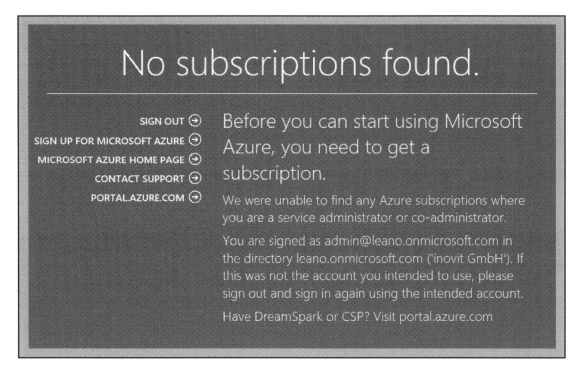

9.  We will receive the correct message, that is, we have no active subscription assigned to this user ID. Next, click Sign up for a Microsoft **Azure** subscription.
10. After we have signed up successfully for the Azure subscription, we will see our default directory `domain.onmicrosoft.com`, which we have already provisioned with the Office 365 E3 plan.

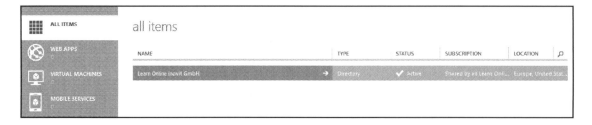

11. Extend the default directory and navigate to **Licenses**. Activate the **Enterprise Mobility Trial**.

12. After a successful activation, you should see something resembling the following:

13. With the next step, we will assign the first Azure AD premium license to our global administrator `admin@domain.onmicrosoft.com`.

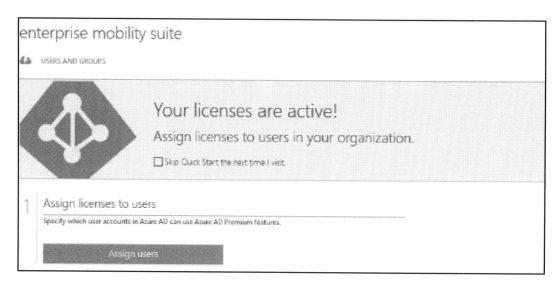

14. Assign the license with the **Assign users** button. See the following link for automatic assignment: `http://bit.ly/2axiHW1`.

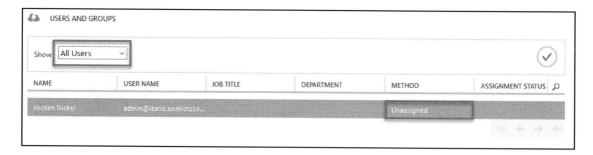

As a different option, you could start with your MSDN subscription account or use a demo with the amount of money specific to your subscription and country after the trial period. Log in to your MSDN subscription. Under **My Account,** you will find the option to **Activate Microsoft Azure**. You are also able to add a subscription at a later date. For now, just add your MSDN account as a Co-Administrator to your Azure **Settings**.

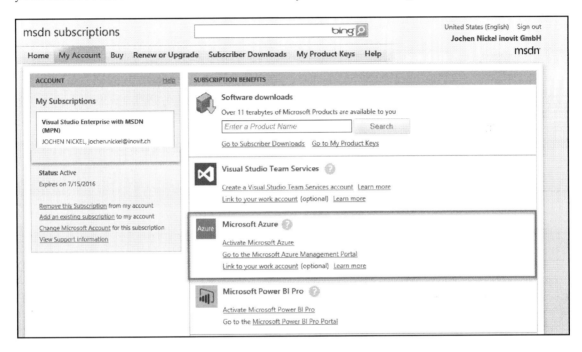

# Custom company branding

Most companies like to see how they can apply their corporate identity to Azure services. With a few easy steps, you can demonstrate the most important capabilities. The following simple example will show you what you can customize. These configuration tasks are always a good starting point in a demo or proof of concept. You are free to use your own pictures and designs for this setup.

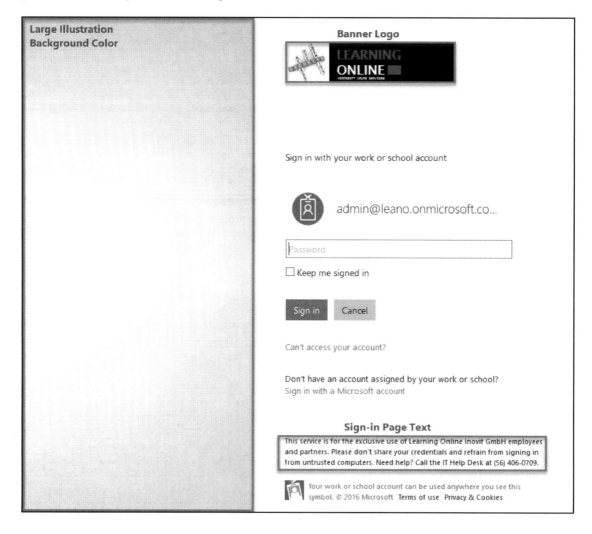

1. The first thing we are going to change is the **NAME** of the directory in the **CONFIGURE** section. Just enter your desired name. We used `Learn Online inovit GmbH`.

2. Next, click **Customize Branding** and you will see the following options. That you can prepare your pictures and brands we summarized the help information provided in Microsoft TechNet.

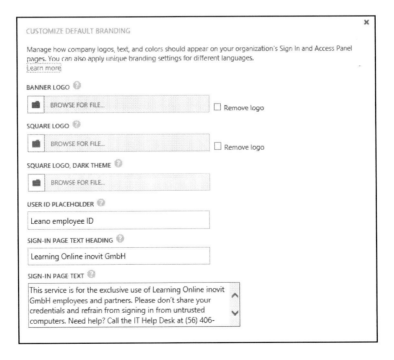

## Summary and recommendations of the help information

The following section provides you with several capabilities to customize your environment:

For the **BANNER LOGO** (60×280 pixels / PNG), choose between the following options:

- Displayed on the Azure AD sign-in page and `myapps.microsoft.com`
- Max. size: 60×300 pixels with a file size of: 5-10kb
- Recommended file type: PNG with transparent background (JPEG support)

For **SIGN-IN PAGE TEXT** body, choose between the following options:

- Appears at the bottom of the Azure AD sign-in page and in the Azure AD Join process for Windows 10
- Plain text only with a recommended length of 250-300 characters (max. 500 characters)
- Visible to everyone

For **SIGN-IN HEADING** (1420×1200 / PNG, JPEG, GIF), Choose between the following options:

- Displayed on the side of the Azure AD sign-in page
- Recommended 1420×1200 with a recommended file size of 300kb (max. 500kb)
- Keep the interesting part in the top-left corner (image is resized and cropped)

## Further customization options

You are also able to do some extended customization with the following options:

For **SQUARE LOGO** (240×240 / PNG) and **DARK THEME**, Choose between the following options:

- Represent user accounts in your organization on the Azure AD web UI and in Windows 10
- Dark theme option for dark backgrounds like the Windows 10 Azure AD Join screens

For **USER ID PLACEHOLDER**, Choose between the following options:

- Replacement of the hint `someone@example.com` in the user ID input field on the Azure AD Sign-In Page
- Sign-In Page Text Heading
- Recommended length of 30 characters of plain text

In Sign-in Page Background Color (RGB), choose between the following options:

- Recommended for high latency connections if the sign-in page illustration does not load
- Hide **Keep Me Signed In (KMSI)**
- Be aware that some features need this checkbox (for example, SharePoint Online and Office 2010)

In the Post-logout link (Plaintext Label/URL), choose between the following options:

- After users sign out, a link to a web site can be displayed
- Always configure both the label and the URL
- Language-specific information

 You will find more information on this at: `http://bit.ly/1O4HHQC`.

1. You are also able to configure language-specific branding content with the **ADD BRANDING SETTINGS FOR A SPECIFIC LANGUAGE** option, after you configure the default branding settings.

2. Next, we will configure the **CONTACT YOUR ADMINISTRATOR** link.

Now that we have provided a basic company branding, we will start with creating and managing users and groups.

# Creating and managing users and groups

In the next steps, we will connect to our Azure AD and create test users and groups.

1. Start the Azure AD PowerShell console.
2. Connect to Azure AD.
3. Type `$msolcred = get-credential` and enter your fresh user ID.
4. Type `connect-msolservice -credential$msolcred`.
5. Start the script `C:\Configuration\HRExports\HRImportToAAD.ps1`.

> Remember the Execution Policy settings of your PowerShell. More information can be found at: `http://bit.ly/1EWLG3`.
> Alternatively, you can also use `connect-msolservice` to connect.

After starting the script, go directly to `https://manage.windowsazure.com` with your `admin@domain.onmicrosoft.com` credentials. Select the user's section under your Azure Active Directory. You should find the users from the `HireUsers.csv` file.

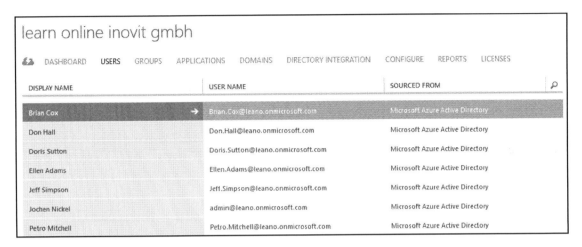

6. Next, we will create three example groups to represent the company organization with the script `C:\Configuration\HRExports\AddOrgGroups.ps1`.

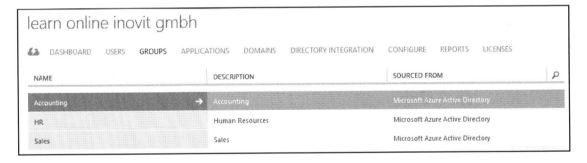

7. Open `https://portal.office.com` and navigate to **Admin | Active Users;** you will see your users with active licenses in Office 365.

8. You will also see the groups you created.

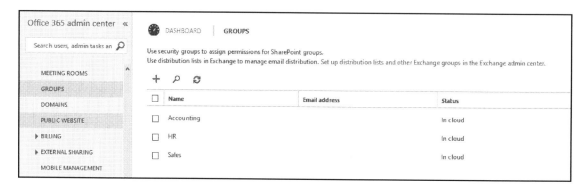

9. Test your configuration by opening `https://myapps.microsoft.com` and logging in with the user `Don.Hall@domain.onmicrosoft.com`; you should see Office 365 SharePoint and Exchange in the Access Panel UI. Click **Exchange** and you should be able to open the app without entering any additional login information to access your mailbox.

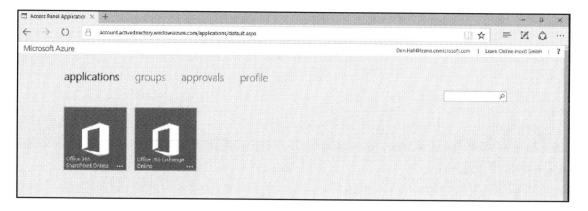

# Setting group owners for organizational groups

To provide group management by the department manager, we will confirm the following users as owners of their department group.

- **Accounting**: Brian.Cox@domain.onmicrosoft.com

- Do the same for **HR**: Don.Hall@domain.onmicrosoft.com
- Delete the figure for **Sales**: Doris.Sutton@domain.onmicrosoft.com

# Delegated group management for organizational groups

To allow a principal data owner, we activated the delegated group management feature. You will find it under the **CONFIGURE** section in your brand new Azure AD. Scroll down to **group management**. Log in as admin@domain.onmicrosoft.com on on https://manage.windowsazure.com.

1. Enable **DELEGATED GROUP MANAGEMENT**.

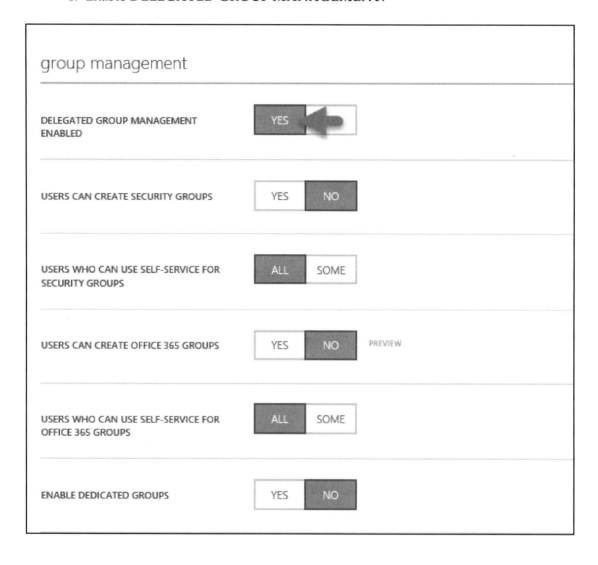

2. Log in as `Don.Hall@domain.onmicrosoft.com` on `https://myapps.microsoft.com`. Click on the **HR** group.

3. Add `Ellen.Adams@domain.onmicrosoft.com` to the **HR** group.

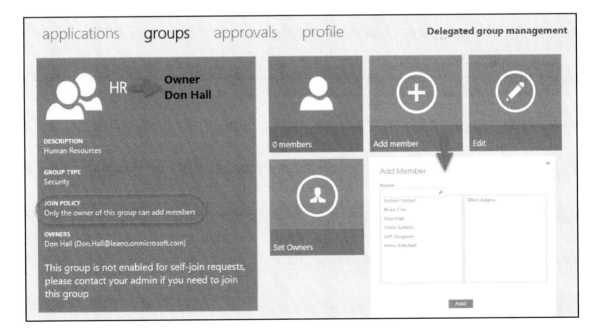

4. Review the **JOIN POLICY**.

# Configuring self-service group management

Another request might be from users who want to create groups, for example for projects or distribution groups. For this, they need the capability of an approval process. You can provide this functionality by activating the two shown options under **group management**.

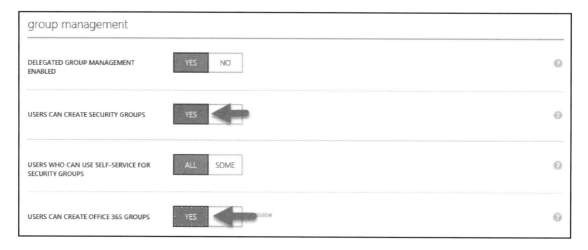

**Office 365 groups Note**
An Office 365 group includes a distribution list but also includes a shared:

- Inbox for group email communication
- Calendar for scheduling group meetings and events
- Library for storing and working on group files and folders
- OneNote notebook for taking project and meeting notes
- Planning tool for organizing and assigning tasks and getting updates on project progress

1. Log in as `Doris.Sutton@domain.onmicrosoft.com` (HR manager) on `https://myapps.microsoft.com`.

**Practical note**:
Use a different browser or the private browsing option to handle the different user sessions. We recommend one session on `https://manage.windowsazure.com` as `admin@domain.onmicrosoft.com` and another session as the explicit user under `https://myapps.microsoft.com`.

2. Create the group `Sales Internal News` as an `O365` (`Distribution group`).
3. Check **Group policy** as `This group is open to join for all users` as `No Approval`.

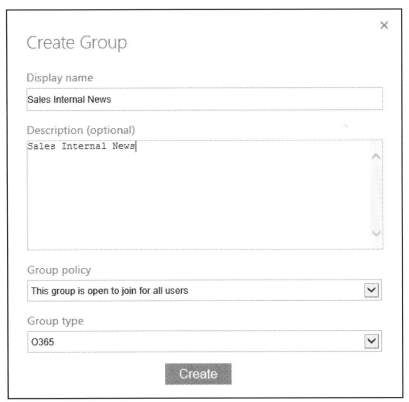

4. Review the **JOIN POLICY** of your newly-created group.

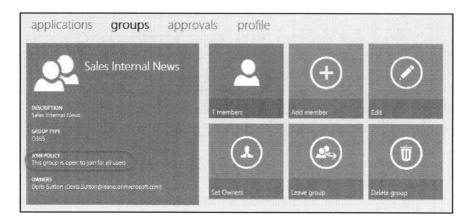

5. In your Azure AD, under **groups**, you will also find the newly-created group.

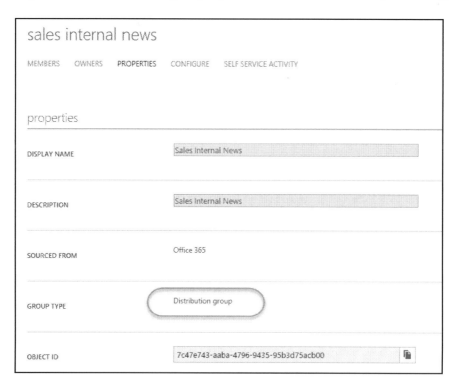

6. Now, as the group owner, you can change the group to request manager approval.

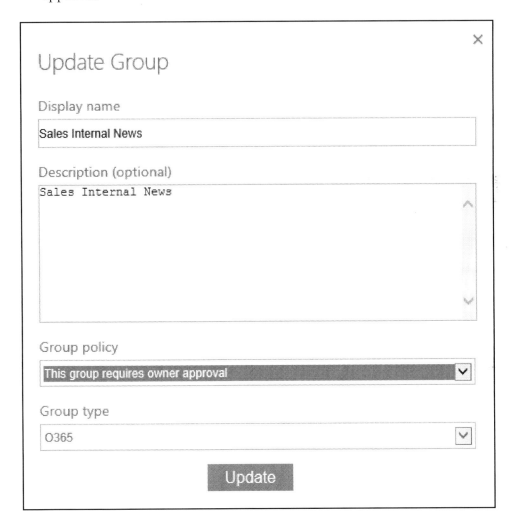

7. Test the new configuration and log in as `Don.Hall@domain.onmicrosoft.com` on `https://myapps.microsoft.com`. Navigate to **groups**. Choose **Sales Internal News**.

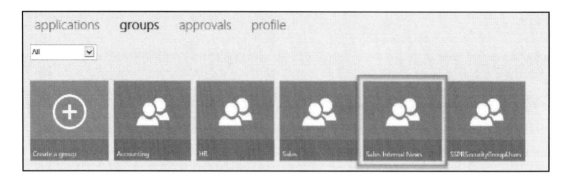

8. Join the **Sales Internal News** group.

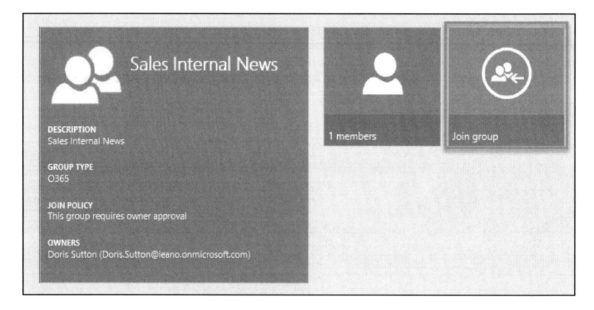

9. Type a Business justification, click **Request,** and the request should be started.

10. Log in as `Doris.Sutton@domain.onmicrosoft.com` on `https://myapps.microsoft.com`.

11. Check your Inbox. You should have received the join request mail.

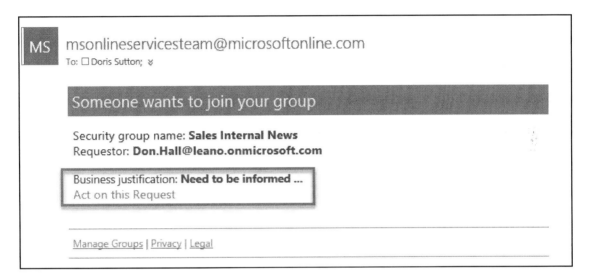

12. Click on **Act on this Request** and **Approve** the request.

Next, you will see the group members of the **Sales Internal News** group.

13. Log in as `Don.Hall@domain.onmicrosoft.com` on
    `https://myapps.microsoft.com`.

14. Check your inbox; you should have received the approval message.

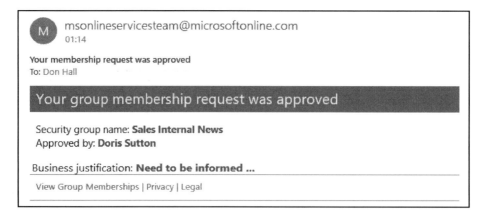

Check your group membership. Next, we will configure dynamic group memberships.

# Configuring dynamic group memberships

In the next section, we will configure simple dynamic group memberships to use the department attribute to automatically add users to their department group.

 When enabling dynamic groups, current memberships will be lost.

1. As `admin@domain.onmicrosoft.com`, choose the accounting group and navigate to **CONFIGURE.**
2. Check **ENABLE DYNAMIC MEMBERSHIPS** as `YES`.
3. Create a simple rule: `department Equals(-eq) Accounting`.

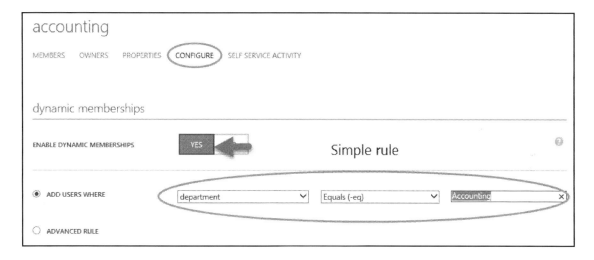

4. Set the **DEPARTMENT** attribute on the accounting users for `Brian Cox` and `Jeff Simpson` to `Accounting`.

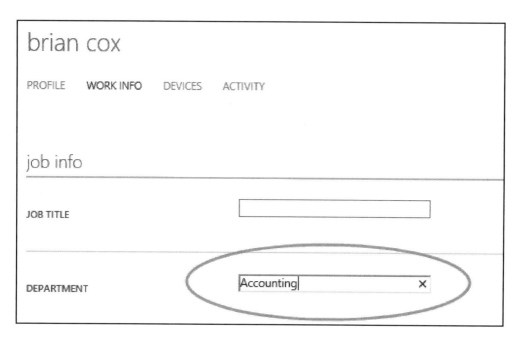

5. The member should be added automatically. Check the group membership.

# Assigning roles and administrative units

Top delegate tasks are used to create administrative units and assign roles for specific tasks. In this configuration, we will generate an HR and we will assign the role of managing user accounts to manager of the HR department.

# Connecting to Azure Active Directory

First of all, we need to connect to our Azure AD with the PowerShell `cmdlet Connect-MsolService` with the `admin@domain.onmicrosoft.com` user.

# Creating an administrative unit

Type `New-MsolAdministrativeUnit- DisplayName'HR' -Description'HumanResourcesUsers'` to create the HR.

```
PS C:\> Get-MsolAdministrativeUnit

ExtensionData                                        Description          DisplayName ObjectId
-------------                                        -----------          ----------- --------
System.Runtime.Serialization.ExtensionDataObject Human Resources Users HR          1ae30ead-b1d3-4414-8d86-73861db3f0de
```

# Adding users to an administrative unit

Next, we need to add the users of the HR department to the HR.

1.  Type the following commands;

    ```
    $au = Get-MsolAdministrativeUnit -searchstring 'HR'
    $user1 = Get-MsolUser -UserPrincipalName
    'don.hall@domain.onmicrosoft.com'
    $user2 = Get-MsolUser -UserPrincipalName
    'ellen.adams@domain.onmicrosoft.com'
    ```

2.  Test your variables, for example:

    ```
    PS C:\> Write-Host $au.ObjectID
    1ae30ead-b1d3-4414-8d86-73861db3f0de
    PS C:\> Write-Host $user.ObjectID
    6a6ddd21-b151-4e19-b319-5204fbf36690
    ```

3.  Type the following commands to add the users to the HR:

    ```
    Add-MsolAdministrativeUnitMember -AdministrativeUnitObjectId
    $au.ObjectId -AdministrativeUnitMemberObjectId $user1.ObjectId
    Add-MsolAdministrativeUnitMember -AdministrativeUnitObjectId
    $au.ObjectId -AdministrativeUnitMemberObjectId $user2.ObjectId
    ```

4.  Test your configuration with the following command:

```
Get-MsolAdministrativeUnit -UserObjectID $user1.ObjectId
Get-MsolAdministrativeUnit -UserObjectID $user2.ObjectId
Get-MsolAdministrativeUnitMember -AdministrativeUnitObjectId
$au.ObjectId
```

```
PS C:\> Get-MsolAdministrativeUnit -UserObjectID $user.ObjectId

ExtensionData                                    Description            DisplayName ObjectId
-------------                                    -----------            ----------- --------
System.Runtime.Serialization.ExtensionDataObject Human Resources Users  HR          1ae30ead-b1d3-4414-8d86-73861db3f0de


PS C:\> Get-MsolAdministrativeUnitMember -AdministrativeUnitObjectId $au.ObjectId

ExtensionData                                    DisplayName EmailAddress                         ObjectId
-------------                                    ----------- ------------                         --------
System.Runtime.Serialization.ExtensionDataObject Don Hall    Don.Hall@leano.onmicrosoft.com       6a6ddd21-b151-4e19-b319-...
```

# Scoping administrative roles

In the next step, we need to assign the **User Account Administrator** role. Verify the available roles with `Get-MsolRole`.

```
PS C:\> Get-MsolRole

ObjectId                              Name                           Description
--------                              ----                           -----------
17315797-102d-40b4-93e0-432062caca18  Compliance Administrator       Compliance administrator.
29232cdf-9323-42fd-ade2-1d097af3e4de  Exchange Service Administrator Exchange Service Administrator.
2b499bcd-da44-4968-8aec-78e1674fa64d  Device Managers                Allows access to read and edit device proper...
4ba39ca4-527c-499a-b93d-d9b492c50246  Partner Tier1 Support          Allows ability to perform tier1 support tasks.
62e90394-69f5-4237-9190-012177145e10  Company Administrator          Company Administrator role has full access t...
729827e3-9c14-49f7-bb1b-9608f156bbb8  Helpdesk Administrator         Helpdesk Administrator has access to perform...
75941009-915a-4869-abe7-691bff18279e  Lync Service Administrator     Lync Service Administrator.
88d8e3e3-8f55-4a1e-953a-9b9898b8876b  Directory Readers              Allows access to various read only tasks in ...
9360feb5-f418-4baa-8175-e2a00bac4301  Directory Writers              Allows access read tasks and a subset of wri...
9b895d92-2cd3-44c7-9d02-a6ac2d5ea5c3  Application Administrator      Application Administrator role has access to...
9c094953-4995-41c8-84c8-3ebb9b32c93f  Device Join                    Device Join
9f06204d-73c1-4d4c-880a-6edb90606fd8  Device Administrators          Device Administrators
b0f54661-2d74-4c50-afa3-1ec803f12efe  Billing Administrator          Billing Administrator has access to perform ...
c34f683f-4d5a-4403-affd-6615e00e3a7f  Workplace Device Join          Workplace Device Join
cf1c38e5-3621-4004-a7cb-879624dced7c  Application Developer          Application Developer role has ability to cr...
d29b2b05-8046-44ba-8758-1e26182fcf32  Directory Synchronization Acc... Directory Synchronization Accounts
d405c6df-0af8-4e3b-95e4-4d06e542189e  Device Users                   Device Users
e00e864a-17c5-4a4b-9c06-f5b95a8d5bd8  Partner Tier2 Support          Allows ability to perform tier2 support tasks.
f023fd81-a637-4b56-95fd-791ac0226033  Service Support Administrator  Service Support Administrator has access to ...
f28a1f50-f6e7-4571-818b-6a12f2af6b6c  SharePoint Service Administrator SharePoint Service Administrator.
fe930be7-5e62-47db-91af-98c3a49a38b1  User Account Administrator     User Account Administrator has access to per...
```

1. Set the variables to assign a user to a role. Type the following command:

```
$role = Get-MsolRole -RoleName 'User Account Administrator'
$user = Get-MsolUser -UserPrincipalName
'don.hall@domain.onmicrosoft.com'
```

2. Assign the role. Type the following command:

```
Add-MsolScopedRoleMember -RoleObjectId $role.ObjectId
-AdministrativeUnitObjectId $au.ObjectId -RoleMemberObjectId
$user.ObjectId
```

# Testing your configuration

Open a new PowerShell and connect with the command `Connect-MsolService` to the Azure AD and log in with the `Don.Hall@domain.onmicrosoft.com` credentials.

1. Modify a user account assigned to the HR administrative unit with the following command:

```
Set-MsolUser -UserPrincipalName ellen.adams@domain.onmicrosoft.com
-Department HR
```

2. Verify your modification using the following command:

```
Get-MsolUser -UserPrincipalName ellen.adams@domain.onmicrosoft.com | fl
```

```
PS C:\> Set-MsolUser -UserPrincipalName ellen.adams@leano.onmicrosoft.com -Department HR
PS C:\> Get-MsolUser -UserPrincipalName ellen.adams@leano.onmicrosoft.com | fl


ExtensionData                          : System.Runtime.Serialization.ExtensionDataObject
AlternateEmailAddresses                : {}
AlternateMobilePhones                  : {}
AlternativeSecurityIds                 : {}
BlockCredential                        : False
City                                   :
CloudExchangeRecipientDisplayType      : 1073741824
Country                                :
Department                             : HR
DirSyncProvisioningErrors              : {}
DisplayName                            : Ellen Adams
```

# Providing user-and group-based application access

In the next section, we need to configure a typical workplace that a user can access under the **Access** panel UI (`myapps.microsoft.com`). We will assign the applications to users and groups to see the different capabilities. These steps don't contain a scenario with user provisioning.

 Use the following links to integrate Salesforce at the end of this section:
Tutorial: `http://bit.ly/1fQer6q`
Video: `http://bit.ly/1WCpf7V`
Salesforce Sandbox: `http://sforce.co/1O5XPS6`

# Adding several applications from the application gallery

In the first step, we will add some example applications for a typical workplace in Azure AD under the **APPLICATIONS** section. After adding the application, we will assign the accounts to provide the access.

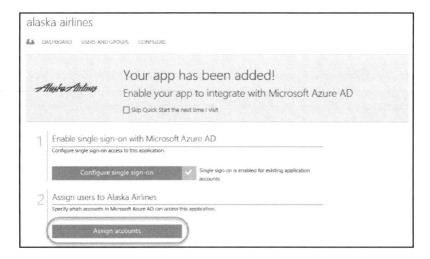

1. Build a list of applications, such as the following, and assign all groups to access the applications, except the one with user provisioning.

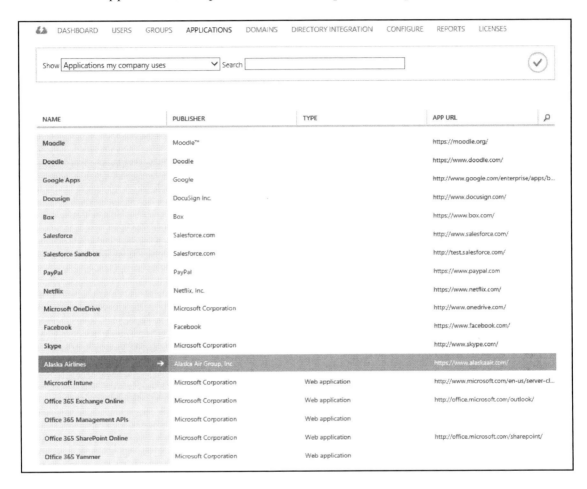

2. Note the formatting differences depending on whether it is with or without user provisioning.

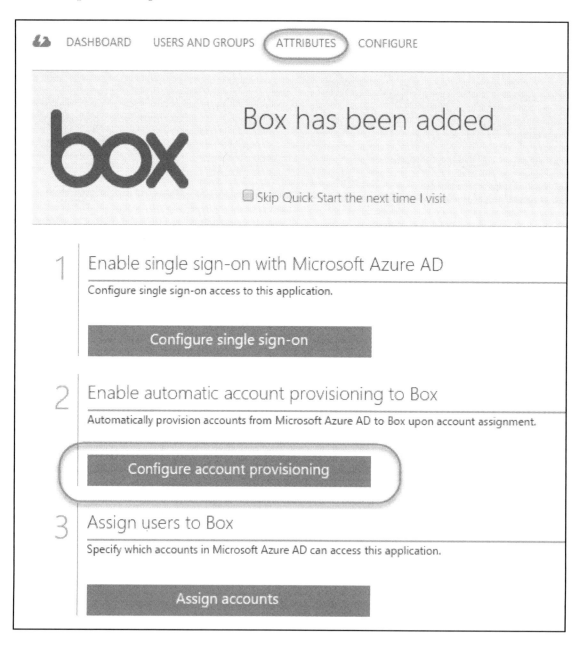

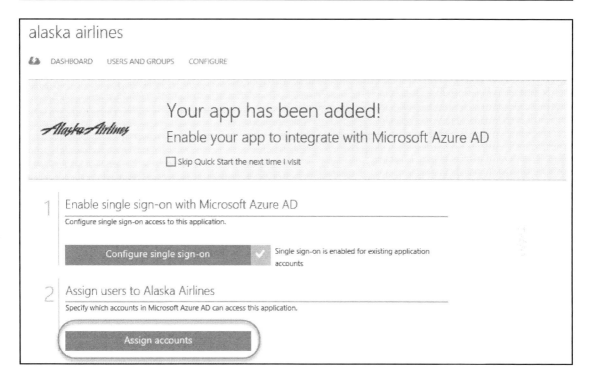

3. Test your newly-configured workplace and log in as
   `Don.Hall@domain.onmicrosoft.com` on `https://myapps.microsoft.com`.

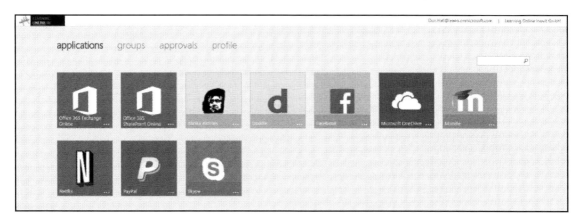

4. Also test the user experience on Office 365 and log in as
   `Don.Hall@domain.onmicrosoft.com` on `https://portal.office.com`.

5. Jump back to `https://myapps.microsoft.com` as `Don Hall` and click on **Microsoft OneDrive**; you will receive an **Update Now** message.

6. You need to install the Access Panel Extension add-on for Internet Explorer:

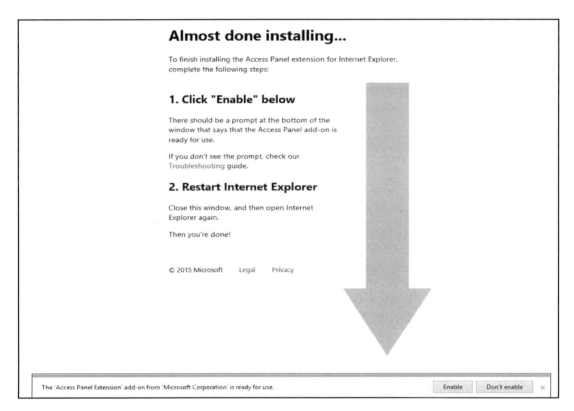

# Assigning applications to users and defining login information

In the next step, we will provide `Don Hall` with the LinkedIn application with company credentials. `Don Hall` will not be able to see the credentials, so if he leaves the company the credentials are still protected.

1. Add the LinkedIn application from the **application gallery.**

2. Next, we need to assign `Don Hall` to access this application.

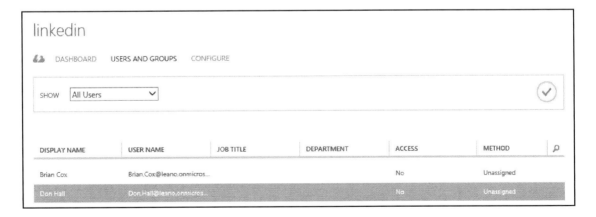

3. Next, we provide valid LinkedIn credentials. If you don't have any, just register as a demo. Don't check **I want to enable automatic password rollover**. For more information on this feature, visit: `http://bit.ly/1vriiwU`.

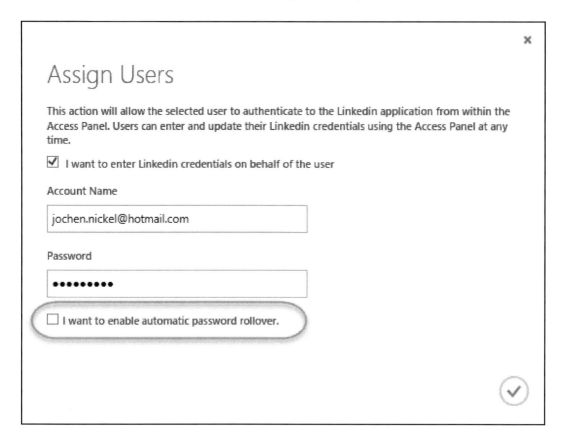

 If you assign an application to a group, you can decide whether the credentials will be shared.

- **View with shared credentials**: The user can view this for just a few seconds after clicking on the application. Test it with the Twitter app.

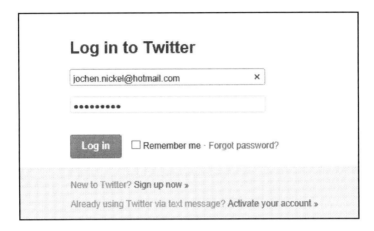

- **View with no shared credentials**: The user needs to add the preferred credentials once. Test it with the Twitter app. You should see the following result.

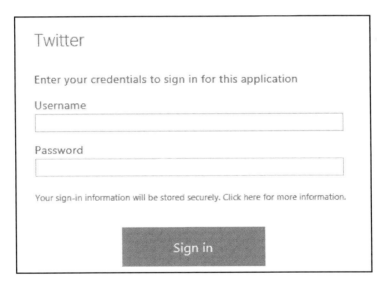

You will receive the same behavior if you as the administrator don't provide the credentials.

4. Test this behavior with the user account you used.

# Assigning applications to groups and defining login information

In the next steps, we will do the same for groups. In this example, we'll use an HR group that uses groups to get news from a dedicated Twitter feed.

1. Add the Twitter app from the application gallery.
2. Assign the **HR** group.

3. Enable the **sharing option** and don't check the **I want to enable automatic password rollover** feature.

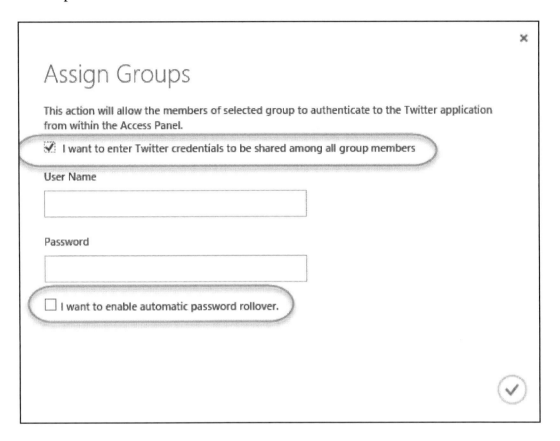

4. Check the application on `https://myapps.microsoft.com` with a user of the **HR** group.
5. Read the article on the **I want to enable automatic password rollover feature** at: `http://bit.ly/1vriiwU`.
6. Activate the password rollover and test the configuration.

# Self-service application management

In the next section, we will allow users to add their own applications to their workplace under https://myapps.microsoft.com so as to enjoy the SSO behavior. Under your Azure AD in the **CONFIGURE** section, navigate to **integrated applications**. Activate the shown feature.

1. Log in as Ellen.Adams@domain.onmicrosoft.com on https://myapps.microsoft.com.
2. Click **Get more applications** and add MailChimp.
3. After you have added MailChimp, click **manage applications** and choose MailChimp.

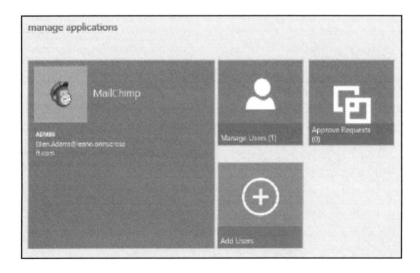

4. As `admin@domain.onmicrosoft.com` on `https://manage.windowsazure.com`, you will be able to see the newly-added application under the **Applications** section of your Azure AD.

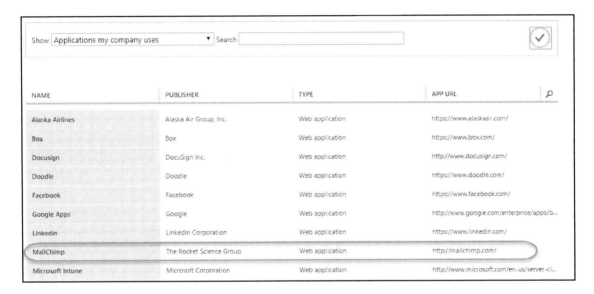

5. Configure the application, add some users, and test it!

# Activating password reset self-service capabilities

In this section, we will configure the password reset capabilities of Azure AD to reduce support costs and introduce 24/7 availability. We add no restrictions to the service, and we only require **one verification option** to reset the password. To verify the reset, we will use the **Mobile Phone** and **Alternate Email Address** methods.

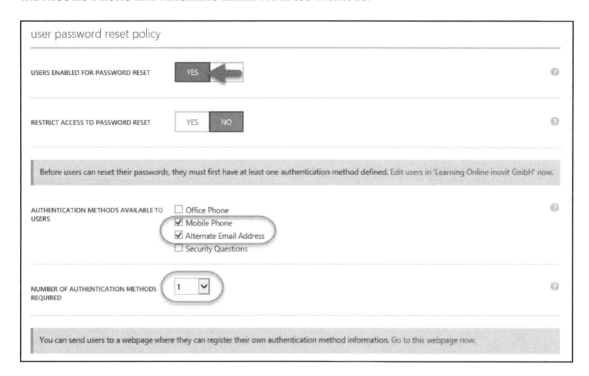

1. The next option we will activate is that the user will be forced to register their mobile phone number or an alternative e-mail address.

2. We can also activate an option so that a user can unlock his account over this functionality.

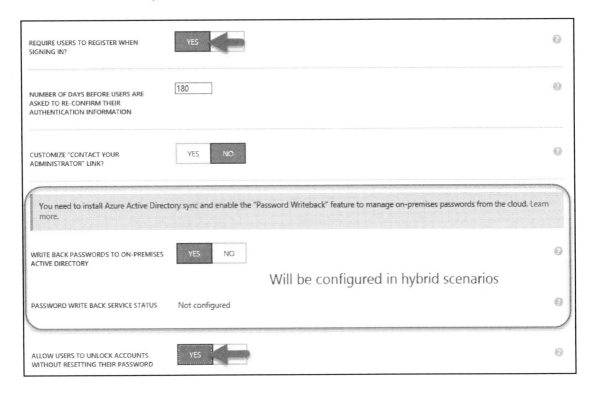

# Configuring notifications

In this section, we will configure notification options so that the administrator will be notified if anomalous sign-ins or administrator password resets happen. Configure the notifications as in the following screenshot:

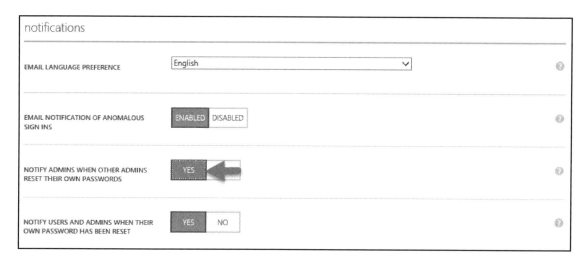

# Forcing password reset information

In this section, we will test our newly-configured feature and will see the required registration scenario for your verification options.

Next we will test the password reset

1. Test the newly-configured settings and log in as Don.Hall@domain.onmicrosoft.com on https://myapps.microsoft.com.

2. You will receive a message saying that you need to register for a password reset.

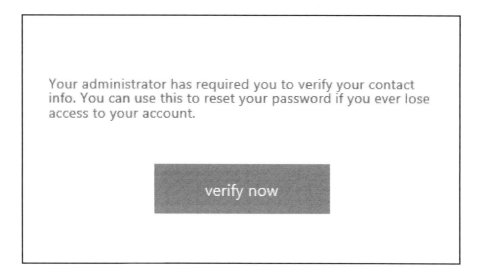

3. Add your preferred method for `Don Hall`.

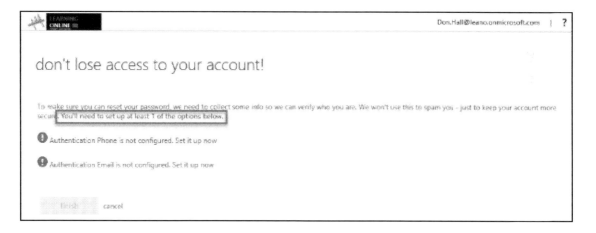

4. You will receive an SMS text message or a mail to your mailbox.

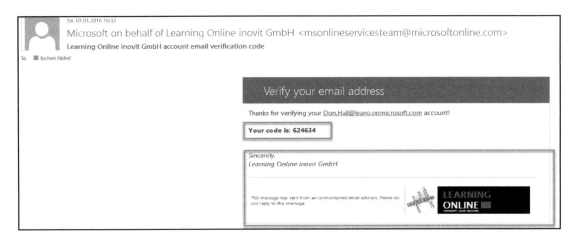

Log in as `admin@domain.onmicrosoft.com` on `https://myapps.microsoft.com` and you will see the request for two verification options.

Administrative users need two verification options by default.

# Testing the password reset process

1. Open `https://myapps.microsoft.com` and enter `Don.Hall@domain.onmicrosoft.com`.

2. Click **Can't access your account?** or use the following link:
   `https://passwordreset.microsoftonline.com`.

3. You will enter in the verification process and you will also need to follow the relevant tasks.

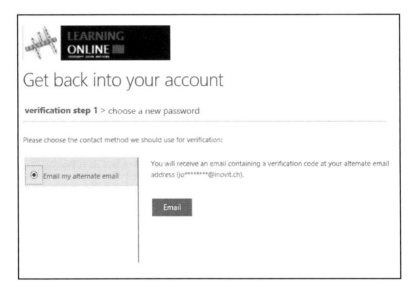

4. Finish the process and log in with the new password.

# Using standard security reports

In this section, we will configure and simulate some typical events that get reported in the Azure AD **Reports** section.

## Configuring – sign-ins after multiple failures

1. Configure in **sign ins after multiple failures** to 10.

2. Lock out a user account with a limit of 10 wrong login warnings.
3. You should receive the following message:

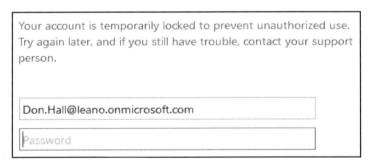

4. Next, we need to unblock the user account

## Possible ways to unblock a blocked user account

The following are two methods to unblock a user:

- Method 1: Wait 15 minutes
- Method 2: Unlock your account with the password reset process

## Possible ways to unblock a blocked user account for administrators

- Method 1: Reset the user's password; as an Office 365 or Azure AD admin, perform a password reset for the user.
- Method 2: Make sure that the user is allowed to sign in. Sign in to the Office 365 portal as an admin.
    - Locate the user and then open the settings for that user
    - Under Set sign-in status, click Allowed and then click Save
- Method 3: Reset the user's sign-in status

 Change the sign-in status of the user from **Allowed** to **Blocked** and then change it back to **Allowed**.

To do this, follow these steps:

1. Sign in to the Office 365 portal as an admin.
2. Locate the user and then open the settings for that user.
3. Under **Set sign-in status**, click **Blocked** and then click **Save**.
4. Under Set **sign-in status**, click **Allowed** and then click **Save**.

# Unlocking the user account

Perform the following steps to unlock a user account:

1. Unlock user accounts as an administrator (Azure).

2. Unlock user accounts as an administrator (Office 365).

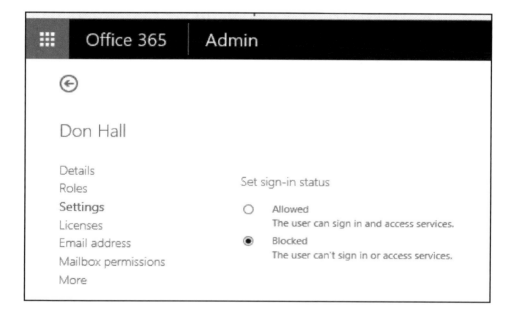

3. Log in as `Don.Hall@domain.onmicrosoft.com` several times without blocking the user on `https://myapps.microsoft.com` and perform a successful login.

4. Check the **Sign ins after multiple failures** report to see the activity.

# Configuring – sign-ins from multiple geographies

1. Log in with an account between geographic regions that are far apart. This requires a remote machine from your location and in a different time zone. Make sure the logins are as close together as possible.

    - Log in to `https://myapps.microsoft.com` as `Don.Hall@domain.onmicrosoft.com` from your local PC.
    - Log in to `https://myapps.microsoft.com` as `Don.Hall@domain.onmicrosoft.com` on a machine in a different time zone to your original PC.

 You can simulate such login activity with the simulation software `CyberGhost`.
Download: `http://bit.ly/1wVSqc5`

2. Select **REPORTS** from the top menus.
3. Select **ANOMALOUS ACTIVITY**.

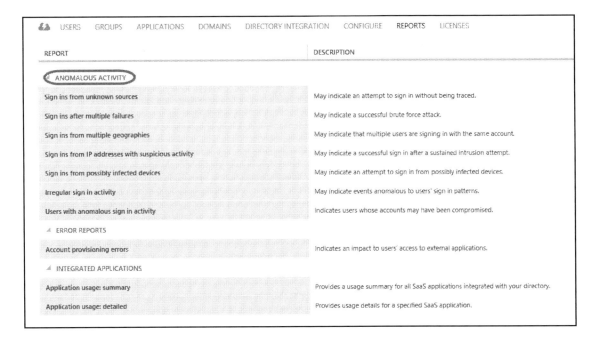

4. Review the different reports:

- Sign-ins from unknown sources
- Sign-ins after multiple failures
- Sign-ins from multiple geographies
- Sign-ins from IP addresses with suspicious activity
- Sign-ins from possibly infected devices
- Irregular sign-in activity
- Users with anomalous sign-in activity

5. Select a report and click on **DOWNLOAD** at the bottom of the page.

# Configuring users with anomalous sign in activity

1. Utilize an anonymous browsing tool such as Tor.
2. Download: `http://bit.ly/1dhroym`.
3. Download the secure Tor Browser.
4. Open the Tor browser and go to `https://myapps.microsoft.com` and logon as `Don.Hall@domain.onmicrosoft.com`.

5. Check the report **users with anomalous sign in activity.**

# Integrating Azure AD join for Windows 10 clients

In this section, we will configure the Azure AD join functionality and join our first Windows 10 client to Azure AD, with a maximum of five devices per user.

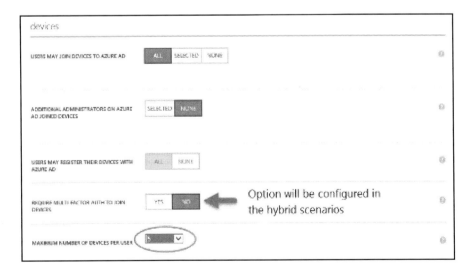

# Join your Windows 10 client to Azure AD

1. Log in to your newly-installed Windows 10 client machine and navigate to `Settings`.

2.  We will sign in with `Don.Hall@domain.onmicrosoft.com`. Check your branding information.

3. Click through the next section and join the client.
4. Check the new status **Organization** as your Azure AD Directory name.

# Verifyng the new joined Windows 10 client

Log in to `https://manage.windowsazure.com` as `admin@domain.onmicrosoft.com` and view under the **User | Devices** section the newly joined Azure AD device.

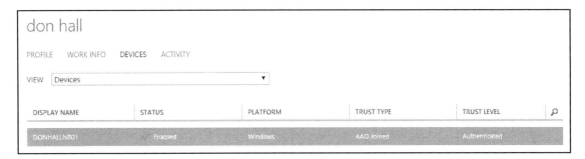

# Login and adopt security policies

1. Log in to the Windows 10 client with the credentials of `Don.Hall@domain.onmicrosoft.com` and click through the security policy configuration. Click **Enforce these policies**.

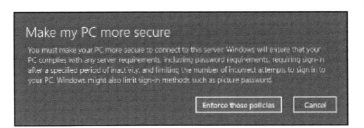

2. Click through the PIN setup and finish the process

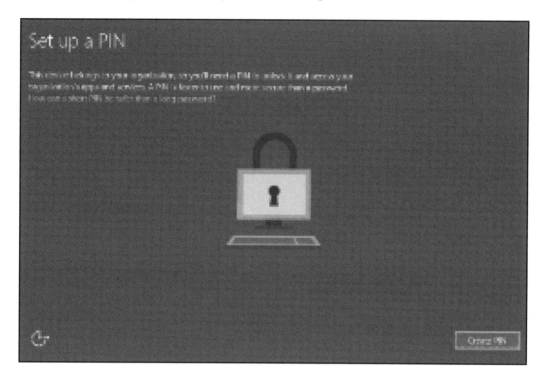

# Testing the user experience

Now we will test the newly-provided Single Sign-On capabilities.

1. Open the **Mail** application, and you will see that the system recognizes your User ID and Single Sign-On is provided.

2. Also, if you open `https://myapps.microsoft.com`, you will be directly logged in to the Access Panel UI.

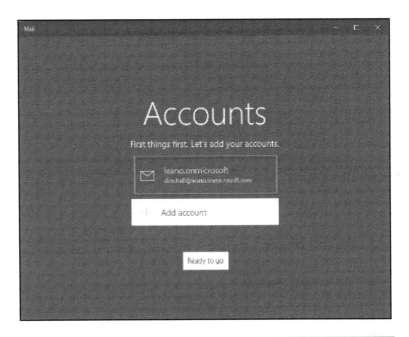

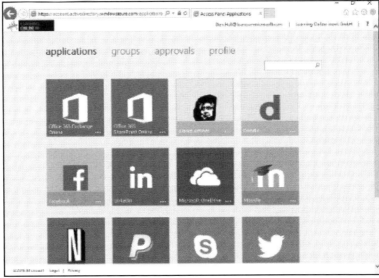

# Configuring a custom domain

After configuring the most relevant feature sets of your Azure AD tenant. We will prepare a registered domain name to set the configuration to a productive environment.

 This step is optional, because you need to register an official domain at a registrar in your country.

1. Click **ADD A CUSTOM DOMAIN** and see the verification options; note that you are the owner of the domain.

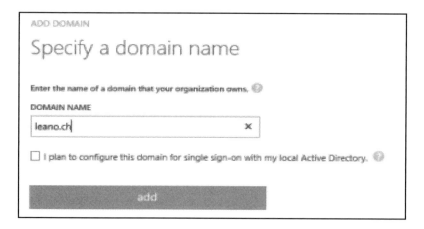

2. Add a TXT entry to your DNS zone to verify the domain.

3. Click the **Verify** button on your Azure portal.

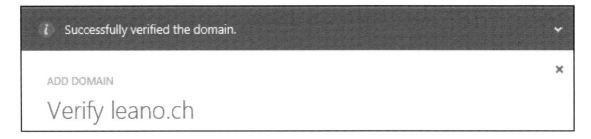

4. After a successful verification the new **DOMAIN NAME** will appear under **DOMAINS**.

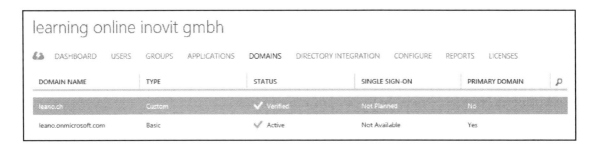

# Configuring Azure AD Domain Services

To integrate a legacy application based on NTLM and Kerberos authentication in an Azure IaaS scenario, we need to configure the Azure AD Domain Services. In this section, we will configure only the basic service and will integrate an active example application in a hybrid scenario.

The first step is to create a new group called `AAD DC Administrators`; the group needs to have this exact name. Afterwards, you need to add your administrator account `admin@domain.onmicrosoft.com` to the newly-created group.

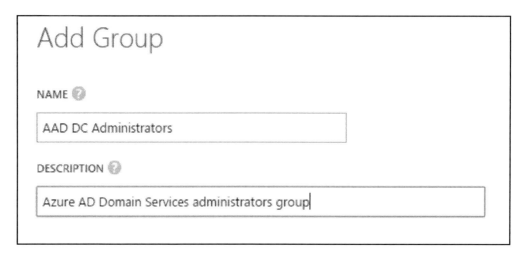

Add the admin account as a member of the group.

# Creating a virtual network

When enabling Azure AD Domain Services, you will need to specify which Azure virtual network is being used. We use the name **LeanoAzureNet** and a **192.168.x.x/20** as the range to configure the network.

Please note that you must satisfy the following criteria:

- The virtual network belongs to a region supported by Azure AD Domain Services. See the region page for details.
- Ensure the virtual network is a regional virtual network and doesn't use the legacy affinity groups mechanism.
- Ensure your workloads deployed in Azure Infrastructure services are connected to this virtual network.
- Create the network and make a note of the virtual network's name.

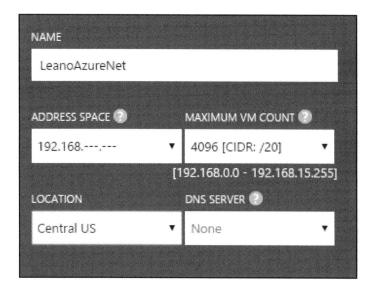

Verify the result.

# Enabling Azure AD Domain Services

You will notice the IP addresses for Azure AD Domain Services start to appear on the page as they come online. In our configuration, that is **192.168.0.4** and **192.168.0.5**.

 Azure AD Domain Services provide high availability and you should expect to see two IP addresses when the services are fully provisioned for your domain. It can take a while for the first IP address to be displayed and a bit longer for the second.

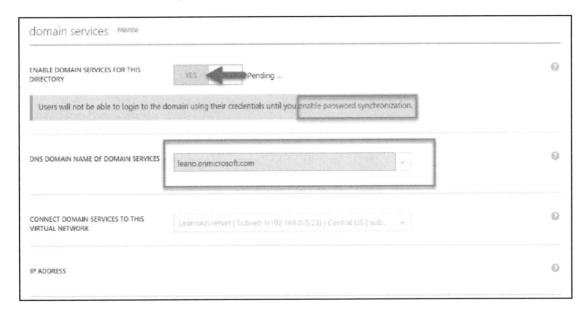

After successfully activating the Azure AD Domain Services, we need to update the DNS servers in the virtual network configuration.

1. Edit the `LeanoAzureNet` virtual network.
2. In the DNS servers section add the two IP's as DNS servers for the new environment.

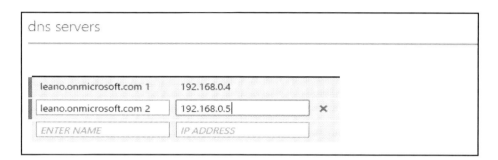

# Enabling password synchronization

The last important step that you will need to complete in order to use the domain you have just created is to enable password synchronization.

 By default, Azure AD does not store the credential hashes required for NTLM and Kerberos authentication. You need to populate these credential hashes in Azure AD so that users can use them to authenticate against the domain.

The steps involved in populating these hashes in Azure AD Domain Services are different for cloud-only and synced tenants.

If your organization is a cloud-only Azure AD tenant, users that need to use Azure AD Domain Services will need to change their passwords. This step causes the legacy credential hashes required by Azure AD Domain Services for Kerberos and NTLM authentication to be generated in Azure AD and populated into Azure AD Domain services.

You can either expire passwords for all users in the tenant that need to use Azure AD Domain Services or instruct these end-users to change their passwords.

Users can use Azure AD's self-service password change mechanism from the Azure AD Access Panel page in order to change their passwords.

For more information about this task, visit: `http://bit.ly/1PFDjwe`.

# Testing and verifying your new Azure AD Domain Services

Testing your Domain Services is an optional task for the moment. We will perform a complete integration in the complex hybrid identity scenario of this book. If you can't wait:

- Install a virtual Windows Server in your Azure IaaS environment
- Install the administrative tools for Active Directory
- Connect to Active Directory Users and Computers and the Group Policy Management console to verify your configuration

# Summary

After working through this implementation scenario, you will be able to configure and manage a suitable Azure AD tenant with the most important tasks. You will also be able to integrate Windows 10 and Office 365 to build a productive workforce for your users. Do not worry about the absence of functionalities such as MFA or other capabilities. We will integrate them in the following chapters, as they need to be explained in the context of their role in a hybrid identity infrastructure. In the next chapter, we will discuss the concepts required for providing an effective way to transition in an advanced scenario.

# 5
# Shifting to a Hybrid Scenario

After discussing and implementing a cloud-only identity strategy we will explore some necessary information for a transition process into a hybrid IAM architecture with a single or multi forest On-Premise Active Directory environment. In this chapter, we describe the architecture changes and relevant tasks that need to be applied to provide a successful solution shift. This chapter provides you with the big picture; it will be filled with these details in related chapters:

- Identifying the business drivers and changes for a hybrid move
- Special handling for moving to a multi forest Active Directory environment
- Describing the architecture and needed changes

## Identifying business drivers and changes for a hybrid move

There are many reasons why a company needs or wants to move to a hybrid IAM strategy. The first relevant argument is that such a strategy builds the base infrastructure to support all other cloud solutions by providing authentication and authorization over company borders. Another very important side-effect is that you start to support new services and workloads. Furthermore, to be realistic, most companies drive their own On-Premise infrastructure, which needs to be integrated and added with additional functionality to support different cloud scenarios. Typical questions you will receive are:

- Does the company need to support different cloud delivery models such as SaaS or PaaS?
- Does the company need to support legacy applications or do they try to move them to the cloud?

- Does the company need a central solution to manage On-Premise and cloud services at the same time?
- Does the company need to integrate external identities to work with them On-Premise and does it need cloud services?

Additionally, you need to handle the following typical challenges from developers and the company's operation team:

| Role | Challenge |
|---|---|
| Developer | • Knowledge about several security standards and protocols<br>• Requirements are quickly changing<br>• Move to other identity providers will be complex |
| Operation | • Bad usability (per application – identity provider and help desk)<br>• Different password policies<br>• Password Reset and User unlock<br>• Users collecting permissions because of missing processes such as on-boarding, change, and termination<br>• Replication of identities<br>• Complex support to provide a central access platform to SaaS, partners, or On-Premise applications<br>• Complex support to provide a central authentication and authorization platform |

To illustrate the challenges also from the perspective of a department, we look at the following example:

- Employee John works at company *A* and uses an ordering system of company *B*.
- Employee John does not use the identity provider of company *A* rather the identity provider of company *B* to log into the ordering system.
- In principle, this process works until employee John decides to leave company *A*.
- Employee John will be deleted from the identity provider of company *A*, but often remains in the identity provider of company *B*. This is still active and he can access the systems.

For this reason, some additional aspects of the On-Premise IAM system, to use efficient partnerships or SaaS applications, need to be available:

- Extension of identity classification for sensitive identities – their personal data may not be transferred or synced to the cloud

- Expansion or replacement of existing remote access (for example, VPN) and the authentication and authorization process

- Use of standardized interfaces that support a hybrid approach
- Providing a central authentication and authorization point in combination with a user portal
- Providing a synchronization and federation with SaaS providers

To provide a central and transparent user authentication and authorization service, Microsoft brings the necessary technology components with hybrid identity feature sets. The following screenshot shows the schema of a hybrid IAM architecture:

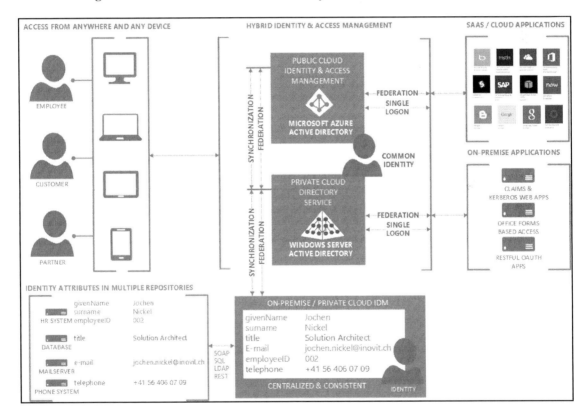

The architecture uses the investments already made in the area of On-Premise IAM and builds on it. Microsoft provides MIM 2016 for On-Premise identity management solutions (On-Premise/Private cloud IDM).

# Identity On-Premise integration

In particular, the results from the identity classification have to be considered. These include, for example, sensitive identities or attributes that cannot be synchronized to the cloud. Another result can be that password hashes are synchronized (or not). The hybrid construction and the provision of cloud identities in Microsoft Azure Active Directory will be achieved through synchronization or federation. To synchronize identities, the Microsoft Azure Active Directory Connect tool will be used, and for federation, Active Directory Federation Services 3.0/4.0 are included in the Windows Server 2012 R2/2016 operating system.

In principle, a decision must be made whether the central authentication service is provided in the cloud or On-Premise . In the proposed architecture, both options are possible. Depending on the choice, synchronization or federation will be configured accordingly.

The integration can be extended at any time and can be flexibly adapted to your needs. The following screenshot shows the **Configuration** tab in the Azure Active Directory:

## integration with local active directory

| | |
|---|---|
| DOMAINS VERIFIED FOR DIRECTORY SYNC | 2 |
| DOMAINS PLANNED FOR SINGLE SIGN-ON | 0 |
| DOMAINS CONFIGURED FOR SINGLE SIGN-ON | 1 |
| DIRECTORY SYNC | ACTIVATED DEACTIVATED |
| LAST SYNC | 2 hours ago |

With this integration you provide more transparent access for the end user to their own cloud applications, SaaS, and/or On-Premise partner applications with a single identity.

For the user, is it possible to access their business applications with any device, centrally authenticated and authorized in compliance with the security requirements of the company? In the area of federation, Microsoft Azure Active Directory supports the following excerpt from the Standards for Identity (Federation) provider and authorization servers.

The following table shows the differences between the Azure Active Directory and Microsoft **Active Directory Federation Services** (**ADFS**) 3.0 in Windows Server 2012 R2. In a later chapter, we will explore the new features of the Windows Server 2016 and ADFS 4.0.

| Azure Active Directory | Active Directory Federation Services 3.0 |
|---|---|
| SAML-P | SAML-P |
| WS-Federation / WS-Trust | WS-Federation / WS-Trust |
| OAuth2 | OAuth2 |
| OpenID Connect | |
| Graph Web API | |

The result of the whole integration is that a consistent identity can be used On-Premise and in the cloud. The following screenshot shows the results of the integration in the Azure Active Directory management portal:

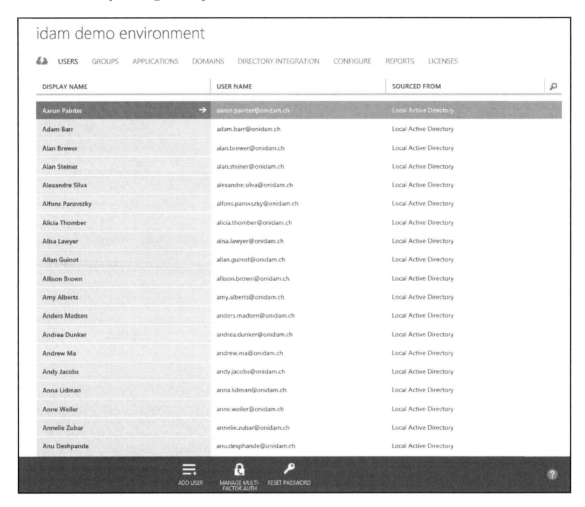

# Application detection and analysis

For a future-proof application ecosystem, it is important to know the exact state of the applications used in the company. Often there are several applications that could be already outsourced as a SaaS application. Another aspect we already discussed in *Chapter 1*, *Getting Started with a Cloud-Only Scenario* is shadow IT's, which occur when the requirements of the department cannot be met by IT. This way, an uncontrolled outflow of sensitive information can happen.

For this reason, Microsoft provides the Cloud App Discovery tool. This tool helps you to collect the following information for analysis:

- Information transmitted over HTTP/HTTPS
- Destination URL's – sites/applications
- HTTP header and metadata
- Name of the user
- Name of the computer

A selection of the application categories to be collected can be centrally configured. With these capabilities you are able to plan your hybrid environment. Identifying SaaS applications in an improved UX helps you to provide single sign-on for these applications. The following screenshot shows the concept of the Cloud App Discovery tool:

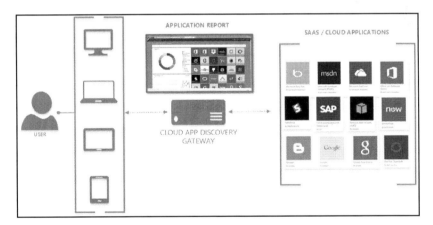

 Limitation – only application-relevant information categories is listed in the application gallery to protect the user's privacy. Azure AD Cloud App Discovery is currently only available for full Windows operating systems.

Looking at the IAM in this overall context, it is noted that these functions constitute the foundation not only for mobility, but also for the security of sensitive corporate data in the processing cycle.

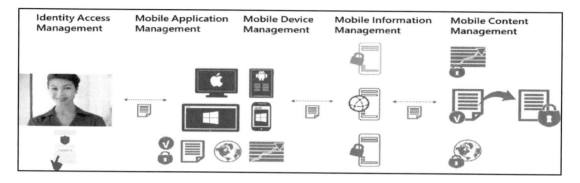

# Special handling for moving to a multi-forest Active Directory environment

Microsoft provides three main integration scenarios that can be used standalone or combined in a hybrid IAM architecture. The first scenario builds the cloud identity scenario which we have already discussed and implemented in the first chapters of the book. The next two scenarios are:

- **Synchronized Identities**: Azure AD Connect with password synchronization
- **Federated Identities**: Azure AD Connect and ADFS for federation and local passwords will be used

As you can see, the Azure AD Connect tool is always required for any hybrid scenario you drive. So we need to start the supported topologies so that you can move to a single or multi forest scenario combined with single or multiple Azure Active Directories.

## Supported topologies

The following topologies are supported by Microsoft:

- Single Forest mapped to single Azure AD
- This scenario is a commonly used one. Single forest and a single instance of Azure AD. For this scenario, the express settings of the tool can be used.

We recommend filtering objects so that service accounts, computers, or other objects will not be synchronized to the cloud.

- Single forest filtering scenario to multiple Azure AD's:

  The following decisions must be borne in mind:

    - Azure AD Connect must be configured for filtering
    - DNS domain registration is only possible in a single Azure AD
    - UPNs of the users On-Premises must use separate namespaces
    - One Azure AD directory can enable an Exchange hybrid with the On-Premises Active Directory
    - Group and device write-back scenarios are possible

**Practical Tips**
It is not possible to sync the same user to multiple Azure Active Directories.
It is not possible to modify Azure AD Connect to connect to multiple Azure Active Directories.

- Multiple forests to single Azure AD:

  The following must be borne in mind:

    - Users have only one identity across all On-Premise Active Directory forests
    - UPN and Source Anchor will be provided from the forest
    - Users have only one mailbox
    - There is no need to use Azure AD Connect on a domain joined server

Remember that multiple forests and multiple Azure AD Connect Tools on one Azure Active Directory are not supported. The only exception is the usage of a staging server. A staging server can be configured for High-Availability scenarios (active/passive). In this scenario, the staging server doesn't export information to the target system.

- Multiple forests to multiple Azure AD's

  For each Azure AD directory, you will need one Azure AD Connect installation.

 Azure AD directory instances are isolated by design!

Users in one Azure AD will not be able to see users in the other directory. You can also use the same design principles, such as the single forest to single Azure AD scenario. The following screenshot shows the different scenarios as a small summary. Be aware that we discuss these scenarios in depth in upcoming chapters.

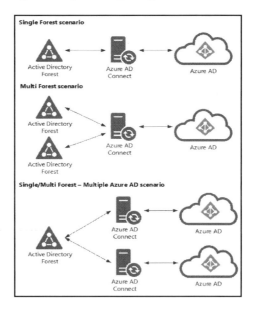

# Describing architectures and needed changes

In this section, we will describe different architectures including the needed changes in big picture scenarios. In particular, we will discuss the integration of On-Premise applications with the whole authentication and authorization strategy. Furthermore, we start to take the first steps in the hybrid usage of MFA and **Azure Rights Management Services** (**RMS**) with typical examples.

## Authentication integration

Azure AD provides the capability to integrate On-Premise applications with the Azure Active Directory Application proxy service. To use these capabilities, you just need to install the dependent module, the application proxy connector on your existing Windows Server 2012 R2 Web Application proxy server. With this installation and the necessary configuration, you have taken the first step in this hybrid authentication solution. The following figure shows this scenario to provide you with a better idea about this concept:

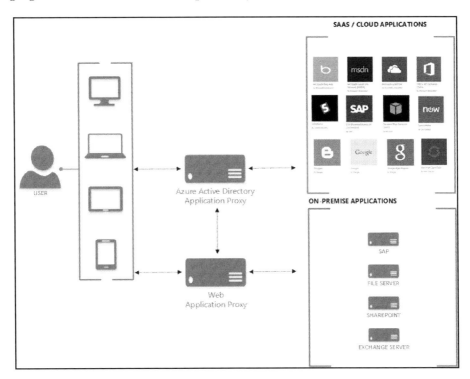

The Azure Active Directory proxy can publish On-Premises/Cloud applications. In the preceding figure, you see an example where the connector is centrally installed on the On-Premise Web Application proxy. You can also install the connector on the application itself and completely work without a local Web Application Proxy.

You are also able to add `Conditional Access Controls` to this scenario. The following parameters can be used:

| Dependencies | Parameter |
|---|---|
| Properties of the user | Identity of the user<br>Group memberships<br>Policies for authentication |
| Device | Ownership<br>Managed by the organization<br>Policy compliant<br>Not stolen or lost |
| Application | Sensitive business applications<br>Access restrictions<br>Actuality and strength of authentication |
| Network | Inside or outside the corporate network |

To get a better idea and to give an example of a conditional access scenario, we provide the following access control matrix:

| Application | Policies |
|---|---|
| On-Premise<br>SharePoint<br>Exchange | Allow Access in the event of:<br>• Employee Access<br>• Personal device joined to domain<br>• Managed by MDM<br>• Compliant with device policies |
| Cloud<br>Amazon S3<br>SAP<br>Service Now | Employee Access<br>• Access from unknown device<br>• Access from outside Corp Network<br>• Azure MFA satisfied |

Other examples that are often included in the security requirements are:

- Exchange Active Sync (EAS)
- One Drive for Business (OD4B)
- SharePoint MySite

Not only end users, but also administrators must meet certain requirements to work on the corporate services. For this, administrators are often limited through the conditional access controls to perform technical tasks from a non-protected terminal or from an unsafe defined network location.

# Multi-Factor Authentication (MFA)

Very often we find it to be a security requirement that access over the Remote Desktop Services need to be protected. With this example we want to start to explain the hybrid approach of the Azure MFA services (more information about the service itself can be found here: `http://bit.ly/1pXcbyh`). The following figure shows an example where the user needs to provide an additional verification to get access for the corporate On-Premise Remote Desktop Services.

 This scenario also works very nicely with any other On-Premise service and obviously with a Citrix configuration. However, DirectAccess is not supported for this scenario.

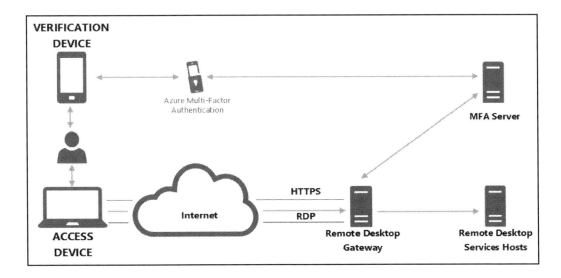

The following integration modules are needed to provide this functionality:

- The On-Premise setup and configuration of the Azure MFA server
- Configuration of the Network Policy server to provide the correct access rules

In the following section, the essential components and processes involved in the integration with the ADFS are shown. The common functionality and basic description of ADFS are not included in this section.

When integrated with ADFS, there are three major components that are required for the solution. Besides the ADFS services, even the ADFS MFA adapter and the MFA Provider (server) of the Azure Active Directory need to be downloaded from the management side and linked by a code with the online component. In the following figure you can see the interaction between the On-Premise components:

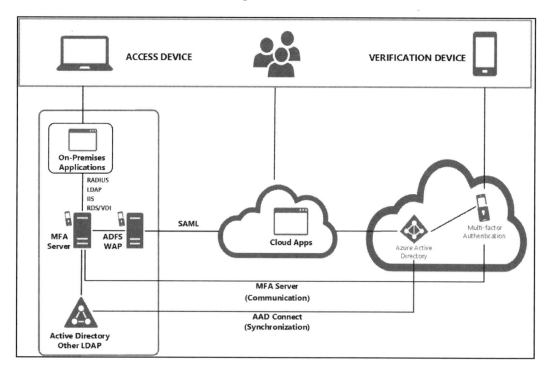

In order to make the interaction more understandable, we explain the AuthN flow with a typical application in the next figure. If we assume that the reliant party is a typical SaaS application such as Outlook Web Access with Office 365, the browser opens and `https://portal.office.com` will be opened. Since it is no cloud user, a redirect is triggered to the On-Premise ADFS server and the user is prompted to authenticate. If authentication is successful, and the Application MFA is activated, it starts with the verification. The data is processed through the server adapters and completed in the best case as successful. Thereafter, a POST is triggered on the actual application, the authentication is performed with the token, and the user can use the application.

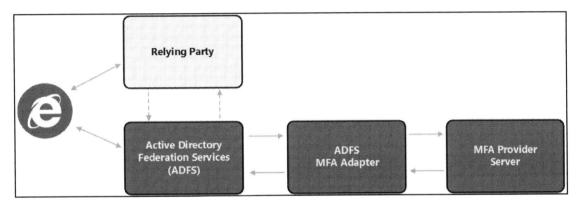

The following figure shows the process of integration with further details:

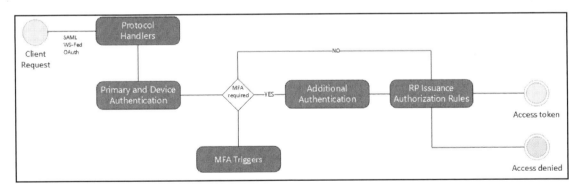

The cloud components in the following solution architecture are purely used for licensing and required for the registration of verifying devices or applications. The configuration and management of the individual functions for the integration of the On-Premise infrastructure are consistently performed in the corporate infrastructure.

The solution infrastructure does not differ greatly from a standard ADFS architecture. The reasons are very simple as to install the server component for MFA on current ADFS servers. This results in a reduction in complexity and improves the manageability of the solution. Furthermore, a second MFA server can be added quickly and efficiently to map a redundant solution in this area. The second change is the installation of the adapter on the ADFS servers and the basic structure of MFA Claim Rules results, defining when, how, and if a MFA is required.

The following core principles are the most important ones in the solution:

- Authentication
- Alarms and reports
- One-Time Bypass
- Custom voice messages
- Contact methods

This diagram shows the required communication paths of the solution and the required installations on the ADFS components:

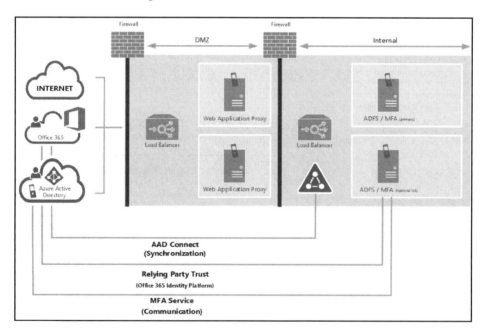

# Rights Management Services

With the integration of Azure RMS, we can deal with the need for information protection and partially sensitive access to security zones based on the data classification. Rights Management Services provide the technology for such a solution. Microsoft also provides a hybrid approach to use this service. Maybe because of security requirements you need to have special protection mechanisms for the master key material; for example, they must be stored and managed within the corporation and protected by a **Hardware Security Module (HSM)**. Azure RMS allows you such a scenario. The Azure Rights Management Service accesses the key to enable the encryption process. Furthermore, the cloud service can integrate local server systems such as SAP, File Server, SharePoint, and Exchange to allow encryption with RMS in the applications.

The following figure shows the architecture schematically:

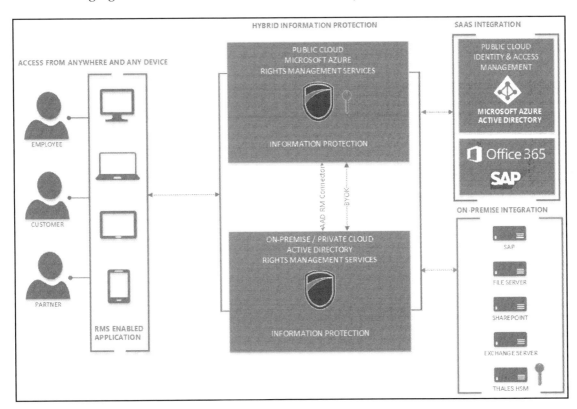

# Summary

Now that you have finished working through this chapter, you will be able to identify some business drivers, feature sets, and architecture changes involved in stepping into a hybrid IAM scenario. You are also in a position to handle the special requirements of a hybrid approach with a single or multi forest On-Premise Active Directory. Remember that this chapter just provides overview information. However, don't worry, as we will get into all the details in the next couple of chapters.

# 6
# Extending to a Basic Hybrid Environment

With this chapter, we will start to jump into our first hybrid identity and access management scenario. You will be guided through business-relevant information to plan and make the right decisions for a hybrid approach with a single On-Premise Active Directory forest. You will learn to adopt the relevant features, licensing models, and a common security strategy for typical legal requirements. Furthermore, you will also be in a position to build the first basics for the special requirements of a hybrid approach with a multi forest On-Premise Active Directory.

- Identifying business needs for a hybrid approach
- Choosing the correct features
- Getting the benefits and costs
- Applying the right security strategy for legal requirements

## Identifying business needs for a hybrid approach

First, we will start to discuss important and relevant business needs of the hybrid identity and access management approach. We will divide this section into three parts:

- **Typical business needs** – common use case and challenges
- **Enterprise Mobility context** – supporting Enterprise Mobility with hybrid identity and access management

- **Enterprise cloud suite context** – supporting Office 365 and Windows 10 clients on top of Enterprise Mobility

# Typical business needs

As already touched upon in previous chapter's, companies usually have Active Directory as their local identity provider to authenticate users with a single sign-on scenario to access their applications. Larger companies have also made investments in On-Premise identity and access management tools to provide the capabilities for user provisioning, automation, and data integrity. In terms of Microsoft technologies, MIM 2016 or earlier versions of the product could be in place. But it doesn't really matter which tool is in place. So until last year, the main focus was on the On-Premise world. With the area of cloud services and other identical scenarios such as hosting, they need to think about managing both the On-Premise and the services outside the company network.

With these changes, companies need to extend their strategies for managing both scenarios including many other different challenges that come up, such as integrating external users for collaboration, building their own apps with a rich set of identities, and access management functionality facing customers.

So the biggest need is to build a flexible and standardized identity bridge to integrate cloud services and external partners. Microsoft provides different tools and architectures to fulfill the existing requirements, and we will discuss them in upcoming chapters.

# Enterprise Mobility context

Today companies face the challenge of building the foundations for the further usage of cloud technologies to create and develop an effective and sustainable strategy for a manageable and overall secure infrastructure.

The most important aspects are:

- Development of a hybrid cloud strategy for a secure and phased implementation of cloud services (2800+ in Azure Marketplace) such as Office 365
- Providing a modern workplace by an Enterprise Mobility Management solution supported by Microsoft Intune
- Optimization of IAM for the use of standardized authentication, and authorization protocols

- Reduction of fractures in the area of authentication, and double identity management and related services
- Optimization of resource your access concerning usability/security

These development steps are currently going through a number of companies in different sizes and sectors. Looking at the developments and trends, which are shown by Gartner, you find yourself very quickly thinking of ideas and strategies for your own company. The following figure shows the relevant information based on the hype cycle from 2015:

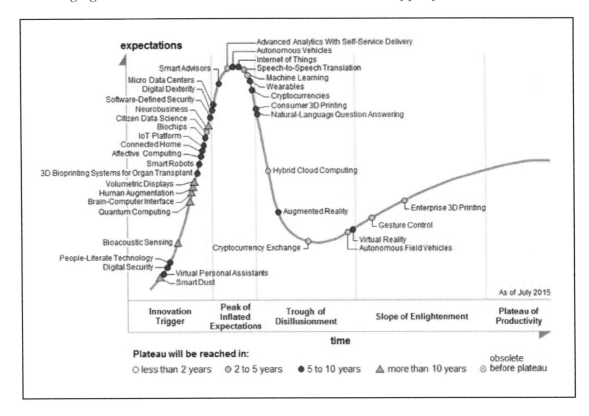

For the construction of a hybrid cloud strategy, individual manufacturers offer a large number of functions and the appropriate solutions and products. Also does this as we already know? Microsoft's global approach, in addition to the cloud-first strategy, is to support all major cloud models such as public, private, and hybrid. This approach enables a differentiated and specific use of cloud services for different application scenarios and security requirements of an enterprise.

The three basic cloud services of Microsoft in the field of IAM and Enterprise Mobility are represented by the following products:

- Microsoft Azure Active Directory Premium
- Microsoft Intune
- Microsoft Azure Rights Management

The following figure shows the main themes in strategically building a hybrid cloud strategy:

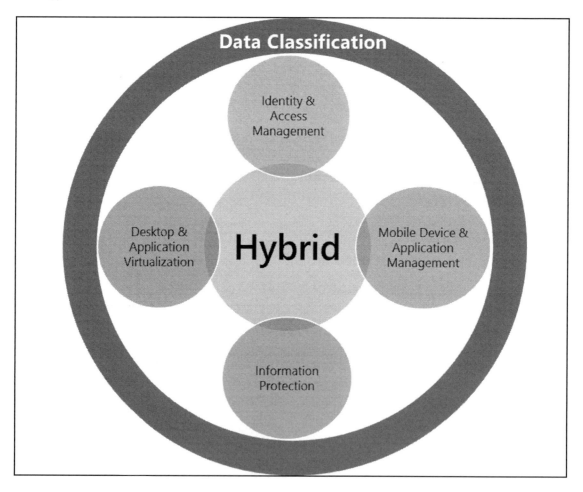

To gain a better understanding, we provide the main technology objectives or functions to support an Enterprise Mobility initiative based on solid identity and access management.

# Data classification

The classification of data, such as business information or personal data, is not only used for On-Premise infrastructures as a basis for providing secure business-critical information and the fulfilment of compliance with official requirements , it is also even more pertinent to the use of cloud services or solutions for a company. As they use a controlled transfer of data in a region in which responsibilities need to be defined, contracts must be regulated. Security requirements do not stop at the private cloud, maybe the responsibility for the technical and organizational implementation and control of security settings.

Subsequent objectives are:

- Construction, extension, or adaptation of data classification schemas for cloud integration
- Data classification as a basis for encryption or the usage of isolated security silos
- Data classification as the basis for authentication and authorization

In principle, data classification is the categorization of data in document classes. These document classes define the level of control over how the data needs to be protected against theft, compromise, or inappropriate usage.

 By classifying data, managing information security is greatly increased in its maturity.

Data classification is an important component in the implementation of audit and compliance activities in an enterprise. For a successful data classification, you need to know where and with which security criteria information needs to be stored, and what the impact is when data loss occurs. In principle, information can be in three different states:

- Saved state (at rest, for example, a file server)
- In process
- On the move (transport)

The following figure shows the different states in an enterprise:

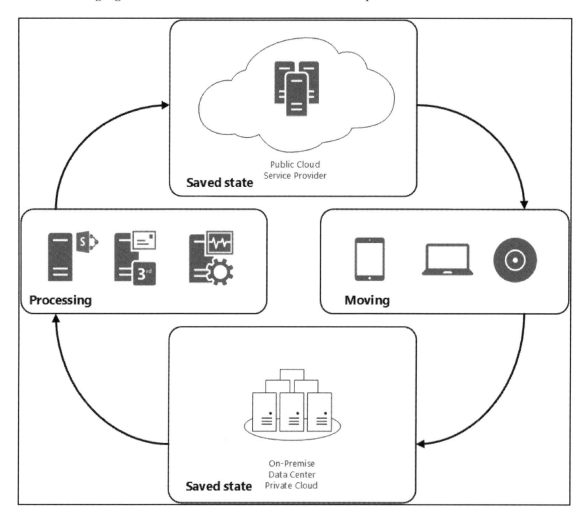

 The classification of unstructured data such as documents or e-mail messages is a more complicated and expensive process than structured data.

The classification of data should be a prerequisite for the use of common initiatives such as **Bring Your Own Device (BYOD)**, Consumerization of IT, or a cloud solution. *Only,* if it's clearly defined what information can be at what location and which safety measures need to be taken or processed, can these be used safely and efficiently used.

Typical needs of data classification for cloud applications are:

- Meeting compliance requirements
- Optimization of storage management
- Compliance and definition of security requirements in the area of access protection
- Compliance and definition of security requirements in **Data Leak Prevention (DLP)**

# Hybrid IAM

As a cloud service for this area, the Microsoft Azure Active Directory, which is built on the context of SaaS and Cloud IAM, plays a central role in hybrid deployment. Azure Active Directory also serves as a central platform for each SaaS application from Microsoft.

The service provides the following main objectives:

- Synchronization of identities with the On-Premise Active Directory
- Group and role-based access control for SaaS applications
- Management of security and distribution groups (managed/self-service)
- Reduction of risks
- Compliance with safety reports and MFA
- Providing a Self-Service Password Reset and Change functionality

# Mobile Device and Application management

The cloud service for this area is Microsoft Intune (standalone) and it includes On-Premise System Center Configuration Manager infrastructure (an Intune hybrid) through a specific connector. The identities of the user-controlled distribution of applications and security settings are provided with the Azure Active Directory.

This service provides the following functions:

- Controlling resource access using registration of the device and configuring compliance policies
- Central overview and administration of all devices to be managed from servers to smart phones via one central management console
- Application delivery for all current platforms such as IOS, Android, and Windows

- Seamless integration in the deployment and management of Office Mobile applications
- User-Oriented Applications and Safety administration

# Information protection

Azure Rights Management provides a solution for the protection of information on the basis of digital rights management. Identities are also provided by the Microsoft Azure Active Directory. The hybrid approach is carried out by the integration of the On-Premise infrastructure through a connector and the provision of the master key material by a HSM.

- Data security for all current platforms such as IOS, Android, and Windows
- Support for all file formats
- Support for current identity federation
- Providing B2C by *RMS for individuals*, the user can consume protected documents

Microsoft RMS can help you to fulfill nearly all the actual challenges out-of-the-box. RMS protects sensible information such as:

- The information can only be consumed by the right person
- The information can only be modified with very detailed rights
- The protection level moves with the data
- The information is always under the control of the company
- Documents can be tracked and revoked

The following figure shows the functionality of RMS:

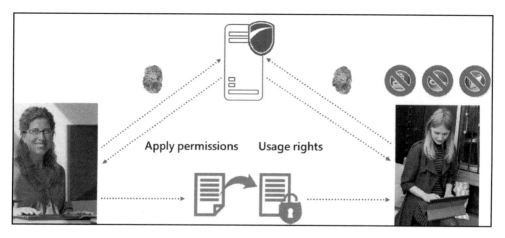

The process starts with protecting information and ends with consuming it with the applied permissions from the data owner or the classification level.

1. **Applying permissions**: The document will be created and protected with RMS – for this we need to be authenticated against the RMS by SSO.
2. We define the rights, and the key material will be requested transparently to the user.

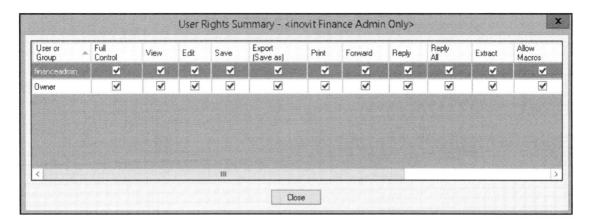

| User or Group | Full Control | View | Edit | Save | Export (Save as) | Print | Forward | Reply | Reply All | Extract | Allow Macros |
|---|---|---|---|---|---|---|---|---|---|---|---|
| financeadmin. | ✓ | ✓ | ✓ | ✓ | ✓ | ✓ | ✓ | ✓ | ✓ | ✓ | ✓ |
| Owner | ✓ | ✓ | ✓ | ✓ | ✓ | ✓ | ✓ | ✓ | ✓ | ✓ | ✓ |

3. The key material will be received transparently by the user.
4. The document will be protected with the chosen rights.
5. The document will be distributed to the required recipients.
6. **Usage rights**. The document will be received from the recipient – the recipient need to be authenticated against the Rights Management Service by SSO or Single Logon.
7. The key material and the usage rights will be requested transparent to the recipient.
8. The key material will be received and the recipient can access the information with the appropriated rights – or the user will get an access denied message.

# Desktop and application virtualization

By Microsoft Azure RemoteApps or the operation of a Remote Desktop Services infrastructure such as Azure IaaS, desktop and application virtualization can be achieved within a hybrid approach. In the area of IaaS, virtual Remote Desktop Services are instances integrated in the On-Premise Active Directory of the company and can be equipped with local security configurations.

The following main objectives will be provided:

- Desktop and application virtualization for all current platforms such as iOS, Android, and Windows
- Scale up or scale down/scale out/scale in – for example, in mergers for quick and efficient delivery of relevant business applications
- Providing an access solution for certain security silos
- Integration of multi-factor authentication through the Azure Active Directory

**Practical Note**:
Azure Remote Apps don't provide a real desktop virtualization and are positioned to bring current (legacy) Windows 32 applications to mobile devices such as iOS, Android, Windows (phone/mobile) and Mac OS.

## Requirements for expansion – identity classification

First, it must be determined whether the standard information may be synchronized by an employee within the enterprise to the cloud. In the following example, there are default attributes that are synchronized for the use of Office 365 with all of its functions:

| Attribute Name | Value | Contributing MA | Sync Rule | Type |
|---|---|---|---|---|
| countryCode | 0 | onidam.ch | In from AD - User ... | number |
| department | Sales | onidam.ch | In from AD - User ... | string |
| displayName | April Stewart | onidam.ch | In from AD - User ... | string |
| domainFQDN | onidam.ch | onidam.ch | In from AD - User ... | string |
| domainNetBios | ONIDAM | onidam.ch | In from AD - User ... | string |
| forestFQDN | onidam.ch | onidam.ch | In from AD - User ... | string |
| forestNetBios | ONIDAM | onidam.ch | In from AD - User ... | string |
| givenName | April | onidam.ch | In from AD - User ... | string |
| objectSid | 01 05 00 00 00 00 00 05 15 00 00 00 ... | onidam.ch | In from AD - User ... | binary |
| objectSidString | S-1-5-21-1323180023-1460257248-12... | onidam.ch | In from AD - User ... | string |
| pwdLastSet | 20140912112941.0Z | onidam.ch | In from AD - User ... | string |
| sn | Stewart | onidam.ch | In from AD - User ... | string |
| sourceAnchor | XurqhcNW+0OR7wpaoHIXdg== | onidam.ch | In from AD - User ... | string |
| sourceAnchorBin... | 5E EA EA 85 C3 56 FB 43 91 EF 0A 5... | onidam.ch | In from AD - User ... | binary |
| sourceObjectType | User | onidam.ch | In from AD - User ... | string |
| telephoneNumber | (312) 555-5454 | onidam.ch | In from AD - User ... | string |
| thumbnailPhoto | FF D8 FF E0 00 010 4A 46 49 46 00 0... | onidam.ch | In from AD - User ... | binary |
| title | Sales Manager | onidam.ch | In from AD - User ... | string |
| userPrincipalName | april.stewart@onidam.ch | onidam.ch | In from AD - User ... | string |

Attributes such as the job title or phone number do not necessarily have to be synchronized. Private information is very rare in this process, and if it is present, it's then taken specifically with the consultation of the employee. A typical example could be a MFA solution such as Azure MFA using a private e-mail address or cell phone number for a Self-Service Password Reset or user unlock.

# Enterprise cloud suite context

The last context you should know is the **Enterprise Cloud Suite** (**ECS**). Just remember the basics: all the products in the ECS, and also the **Enterprise Mobility Suite** (**EMS**) within the ECS, are available separately. So ECS and EMS are new license bundles; they are licensing suites to put different use cases together to match customer needs in a simple and cost-effective way. Yes, it is cheaper to buy the suite than individual products.

The following figure shows the included products in the ECS:

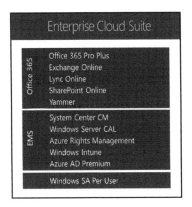

So, when can you use ECS?

As you see, the products inside this licensing model help you save money if you use a combination of *Office 365, EMS*, and user-associated clients such as a *Windows 10* Notebook. For this very use case, Microsoft has designed ECS to give users the productivity they want and IT the security and control they need to enable this.

In detail, you may well be familiar with the components of this suite:

- Office 365 E3 plan
- EMS
- Windows Enterprise

In this usage scenario, Office 365 E3 gives you access to all the productivity services and Office 365 Pro Plus. Coming from the EMS, you get some additional licenses:

- Windows Server CAL
- System Center Configuration Manager CAL
- System Center Endpoint Protection CAL
- Windows 8.1 Enterprise edition (or higher) of the client operating system

With this combination, the licensing has been updated to **User Subscription License** (**USL**).

 The biggest change here is that Windows Enterprise has always been licensed per-device, but now it will also be available on a per-user basis.

# Choosing the correct features

In this section, we will provide you with an overview of the most important features to provide a suitable hybrid identity and access management platform. We will divide this section into the following feature parts:

- MIM – On-Premise Identity Management
- Azure AD Connect – First part of the identity bridge
- Azure Active Directory Connect Health (part of Azure AD Connect binaries)
- Active Directory Federation Services – second part of the identity bridge
- Azure MFA Server
- Azure Rights Management Connector
- Bring Your Own Key (BYOK)

# MIM 2016

MIM 2016 is the On-Premise IAM product. So if you want to integrate a native solution with the following capabilities it will be a good choice to take:

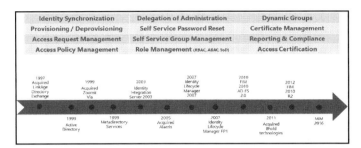

The following are new features is in MIM 2016:

- Licensed with Azure AD Premium – remember Azure AD premium is part of EMS and ECS
- Windows 10 support
- **Privileged Access Management (PAM)** – also management of Windows Server 2016 in the near future
- More self-service capabilities such as user unlock or privileged access requests
- A brand new certificate management
- New hybrid identity management
- A cloud-ready solution – the next steps in the roadmap are to merge the MIM 2016 synchronization engine with Azure AD Connect, which we will describe soon in this chapter

# Azure Active Directory Connect

Azure AD Connect is the first part of the identity bridge (hybrid identity) to integrate the cloud IAM. The main functionality of this tool is to synchronize On-Premise identities to the cloud. MIM 2016 is also able to do this with the Azure AD Management Agent. Be aware that this will only be supported until the merger of the synchronization engine is done.

Also, another question we always get is: *Can I use another tool to synchronize identities to Azure AD?*

Yes. But keep the following in mind:

- Supportability
- You need to develop all the rules and functions in your tool
- Some functions will not be available such as password re-hashing/synchronization
- Why you should not use two tools – separate the workloads, rules, and functions

 Azure AD Connect is able to install and configure the whole identity bridge. This means that you can also install and configure your ADFS infrastructure for federation reasons with this tool.

# Azure Active Directory Connect Health

Azure AD Connect Health it offers you the ability to view alerts, performance, usage patterns, and configuration settings; it also enables you to maintain a reliable connection to Office 365, and much more. This is accomplished by using an agent that is installed on the targeted servers.

Azure AD Connect Health for AD FS supports AD FS 2.0 in Windows Server 2008/2008 R2, and AD FS in Windows Server 2012/2012R2. These also include any AD FS Proxy or Web Application Proxy servers that provide authentication support for extranet access. Azure AD Connect Health for AD FS provides the following set of key capabilities:

- View and take action on alerts for reliable access to AD FS-protected applications including Azure AD
- E-mail notifications for critical alerts
- View performance data to determine capacity planning
- Detailed views of your AD FS login patterns to determine anomalies or establish baselines for capacity planning

### Installation notes

 The Azure AD Connect health agent is natively integrated from Azure AD Connect (1.0.9125.0) and has to be manually installed on your AD FS/WAP servers. Azure AD Connect Health requires an Azure AD Premium assigned to the relevant Azure administrator in order to be pinned to your Azure Portal dashboard. Actually, as a preview, you will also be able to monitor your local Active Directory in future (http://bit.ly/2aAtRtr).

The following figure shows an example of the Azure portal:

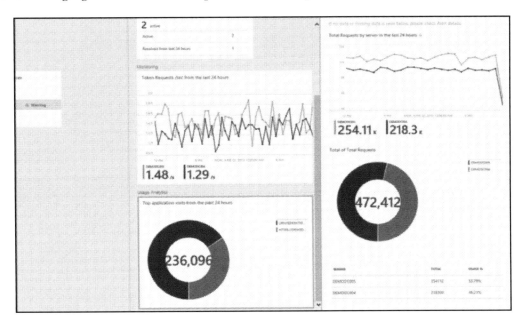

# Active Directory Federation Services

AD FS are the second part of the identity bridge, and the main capability they provide is federation. This service is required to build single sign-on to your Azure AD and associated SaaS applications. ADFS can also be used to integrate partners or social identities without Azure AD and a lot more.

# Azure MFA Server

The Azure MFA server is the On-Premise component of the Azure MFA service. With this server installation, you are able to integrate On-Premise applications into a multi-factor authentication scenario. Very common use cases are:

- ADFS Integration
- Remote Desktop Services or Citrix landscapes

- On-Premise SharePoint or Exchange
- On-Premise IIS applications
- VPN's or other local applications

 DirectAccess is not supported because of technical reasons.

# Azure Rights Management Connector

With Rights Management Connector, you will be able to include On-Premise Exchange, SharePoint, and Windows File Server to use the Azure RMS service. This gives you the capability to use the File Server Resource Manager to protect your local stored information on a Windows Server 2012 R2 file server. The following screenshot shows a use case with integration in a `Work Folders` scenario:

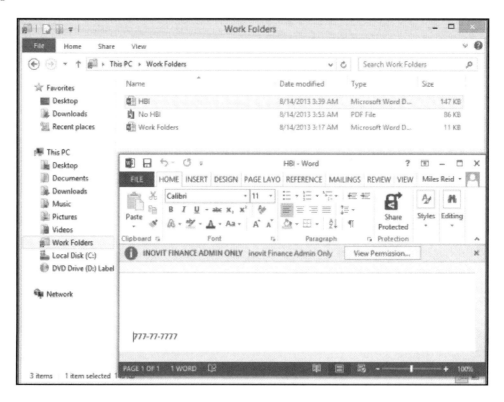

The main benefit in the case of a file server is that you use the classification engine and a fully integrated scenario with the Azure RMS services. The following figure shows this integration from a technical perspective:

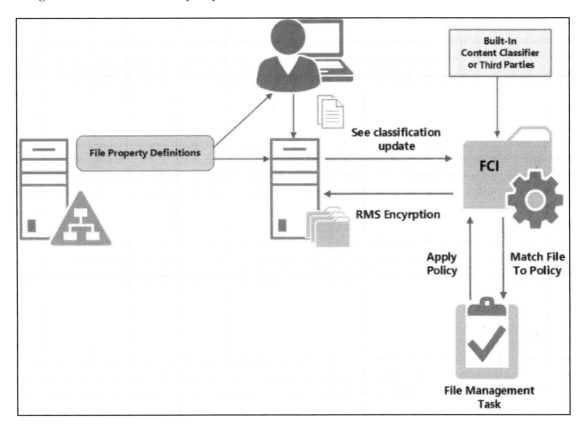

# Bring Your Own Key

An additional component to the hybrid approach of Azure RMS is that you are able to create and protect the sensitive key material of Azure RMS on a local **Hardware Security Module (HSM)**. This helps companies with very restrictive security controls to use cloud services to protect sensitive information. The following figure shows the relevant concept:

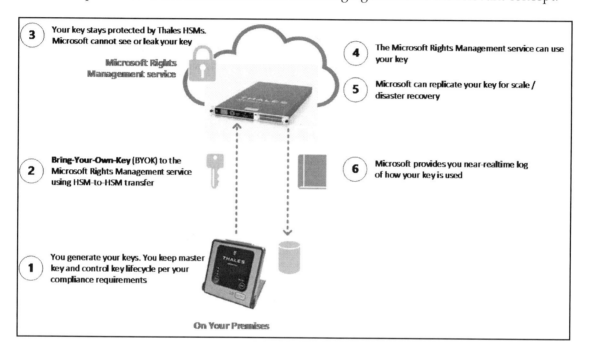

 This scenario is not supported for Exchange online. Exchange Online will be supported at the end of 2016.

# Getting the benefits and costs

In this section, we give you an idea about the different possibilities to buy the discussed licenses of the services. If you remember the tables from *Chapter 1, Getting Started with a Cloud-Only Scenario*, it will be clear that with a hybrid approach it makes sense to invest in Azure AD Premium, as you see in the following table:

| Features | Azure AD Premium |
|---|---|
| Self-Service Password Reset with On-Premises write-back | X |
| MIM server licenses | X |
| Advanced anomaly security reports | X |
| Advanced usage reporting | X |
| MFA (cloud users) | X |
| MFA (On-Premises users) | X |

So, if you also use Office 365 and want to use other hybrid services, it would be great to take a look at EMS and ECS. To be up-to-date, use the following link: `http://bit.ly/2atHFe1`.

The following list shows you Microsoft's different sales models:

| Product | EA/VL | Open | CSP | MPN use rights | Direct purchase | Trial |
|---|---|---|---|---|---|---|
| Enterprise Mobility Suite | X | X | X | X | | X |
| Azure AD Premium | X | X | X | | X | X |
| Azure AD Basic | X | X | X | X | | |

 Remember to use the licensing tools from *Chapter 1, Getting Started with a Cloud-Only Scenario*! Azure RMS and Microsoft Intune can also be licensed on a standalone basis.

# Applying the right security strategy for legal requirements

In this last section, we want to briefly explore the most important topics about Azure and security, so that you can get a toehold in this area to provide a suitable strategy for a hybrid approach. We start with service regions and finish with an overview of Microsoft certifications.

## Service regions

To decide the correct strategy it's very important that you know that the core Azure Active Directory service is a global service. So your identities will be replicated over the whole world. For example, with Office 365 you can define in which location/datacenter the service should run. You say *YEAH!* – But what about the identities! Be aware that you need to be sure that your identities and the associated attributes are allowed to be replicated to the US.

| | Global | Central US | East US | East US 2 | US Gov Iowa | US Gov Virginia | North Central US | South Central US | West US | North Europe | West Europe | East Asia | Southeast Asia | Japan East | Japan West | Brazil South | Australia East | Australia Southeast |
|---|---|---|---|---|---|---|---|---|---|---|---|---|---|---|---|---|---|---|
| **IDENTITY & ACCESS MANAGEMENT** | | | | | | | | | | | | | | | | | | |
| Azure AD | ● | | | | | | | | | | | | | | | | | |
| Azure MFA | ● | | | | | | | | | | | | | | | | | |
| Azure AD B2B | | ● | ● | ● | | | ● | ● | ● | ● | ● | ● | ● | ● | ● | ● | ● | ● |
| Azure AD DS | | ● | ● | ● | | | | ● | ● | ● | ● | ● | ● | | | | | |

# Microsoft certifications

Microsoft invests a lot of money in governance, risk, and compliance to provide the best security strategies and controls for their customers. They have already reached a very high certification standard level around the world. An important one is the ISO/IEC 27000 family of standards, which helps organizations of any type and size keep information assets secure. ISO adopted ISO/IEC 27018:2014 in 2014, the first international code of practice for cloud privacy. Based on EU data-protection laws, it gives specific guidance to cloud service providers acting as processors of **Personally Identifiable Information** (**PII**), on assessing risks and implementing state-of-the-art controls for protecting PII.

By following the standards of ISO/IEC 27001 and the code of practice embodied in 27018, Microsoft demonstrates that its privacy policies and procedures are robust and in line with its high standards.

The following figure shows Microsoft's actual standards:

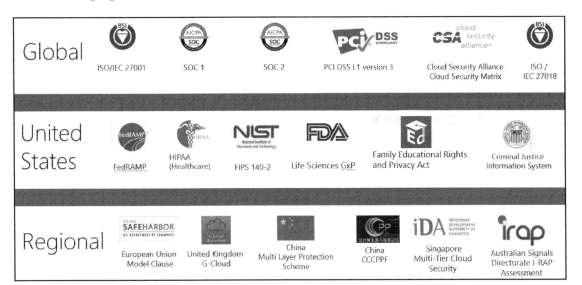

The following link will provide you with information about different standards based on different services:

- Microsoft Trust Center `http://bit.ly/1JXTGU4`

You can also review ISO/IEC 27001 certificates:

- Reference BSI Azure `http://bit.ly/1d3jnCn`

# Summary

After working through this chapter, you will be able to make the right business decisions and apply the key concepts about features, licensing, and security to planned basic hybrid infrastructure. Furthermore, you can now describe the basic need for data and identity classification. Additionally, you have taken first steps in mapping existing use cases and to providing good project marketing.

In the next chapter, we will start to design our hybrid identity architecture. We will focus on key design concepts with several capabilities. As an extra, we will start to enable strong authentication scenarios and advanced identity and authentication reporting features.

# 7
# Designing Hybrid Identity Management Architecture

After reading the business-relevant aspects for hybrid identity management architecture, we will start to take advantage of managing common identities with Microsoft Identity Manager 2016 and build the cloud identities with the Azure AD Connect utility. We will also explore all the various functions of identities building a solid hybrid identity management solution. Additionally, we will discuss the bigger picture of hybrid architecture, and all its relevant features, at the beginning of this chapter to get a better overview and understanding. We will also use this architecture throughout the following chapters as a reference. The key points that we are going to go through in these chapters are:

- Key design concepts
- Management of common identities with Microsoft Identity Manager and Active Directory
- Choosing the best directory synchronization scenario for cloud identities
- Delivering password management capabilities
- Using multiple identity providers and authentication scenarios
- Enabling strong authentication scenarios
- How advanced identity and authentication reporting works

# Key design concepts

As promised in the chapter overview, we will start with a bigger picture of the hybrid identity and access management features that are provided by Microsoft. From talking to customers, we found that many of the features in this technology field are not known of or not assigned correctly. This is not surprising, because the speed and breadth of this specialized area is extremely high and large. This led us to create a blueprint with all the actual features and relations to provide users with a better understanding.

In the following figure, you will find our ideas and the key components of a hybrid environment.

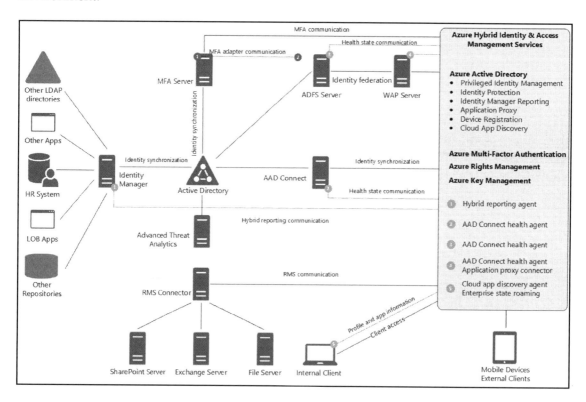

The blueprint consists of two main actors: your on-premises infrastructure and the Azure hybrid identity and access management services in the right box of the blueprint. Let us briefly discuss the main actors in the following section.

# On-premises features overview

*Active Directory* is your core directory service and mostly your primary identity provider. With this service, the reality is single sign-on based on Kerberos and NTLM in your own infrastructure. An Active Directory forest is used as the main security boundary. To work between two or more forests, a trust relationship will be used to provide access to the relevant resources. This environment stores your everyday user account. There are also different scenarios to consider, including a common three forest model made up of a fabric forest, a service forest, and an account forest. Another service model that is commonly used is a resource and account forest scenario.

*Microsoft Identity Manager* is the main identity and access management product of Microsoft that integrates with all the different server roles and components provided in this field of technology. MIM 2016 is mainly used to provide a sanitized and central identity in on-premises environments. In the context of hybrid architecture, it plays a key role in connecting any kind of repository to manage identities in different repositories. Furthermore, complex identity management scenarios are provided with this component. This also includes the management of Azure Active Directory, as well as many SaaS applications available in today's market. A practical example is its usage for licensing Office 365, which can be done by a MIM PowerShell connector or the MIM Workflow Activity Library (WAL) (`http://bit.ly/1Vbw3dlv`), because the actual directory synchronization tools do not automate license provisioning in Office 365 or other services.

| details | Assign licenses | |
|---|---|---|
| settings | ☐ Microsoft Office 365 Plan E3 | 22 of 25 licenses available |
| licenses |    Yammer Enterprise<br>   These licenses do not need to be individually assigned | Buy more licenses |
| more | ☐ Windows Azure Active Directory Rights | |
| | ☐ Office 365 ProPlus | |
| | ☐ Lync Online (Plan 2) | |
| | ☐ Office Online | |
| | ☐ SharePoint Online (Plan 2) | |
| | ☐ Exchange Online (Plan 2) | |
| | Compare the various license options | |

This is a feature planned for future release for AAD Connect, which we will describe in the next section. Additionally, Microsoft has a plan to merge the different synchronization tools into one that can be used for every scenario. The following main feature sets are provided by MIM 2016:

- Identity Synchronization, including provisioning/de-provisioning
- Access Request and Access Policy Management
- Delegation of Administration
- Self-Service Password Reset
- Self-Service Group Management
- Role Management (RBAC, ABAC, SoD)
- Dynamic Groups
- Certificate Management
- Reporting & Compliance and Access Certification

If you want to use MIM 2016 as your central identity management system, we highly recommend that you take a look at the described WAL. The combination of newly-integrated privileged access management solutions in Windows Server 2016 and MIM 2016 provides an effective way of managing and limiting security issues with administrative accounts.

*AAD Connect* is the most commonly used synchronization tool between local Active Directory and Azure Active Directory core services. The tool provides users all the necessary functionality for supporting exchange co-existence scenarios, and combined with ADFS is the best out-of-the-box option for federation and synchronization. Using the installation wizard, you can build the whole identity bridge, which also supports password hash synchronization.

*Identity Bridge = AAD Connect + ADFS*

MIM 2016 doesn't provide password hash synchronization to the cloud and back. The password will be re-hashed in the synchronization process. The password sync is provided directly through a special service, which we will explain later on in this chapter.

To give you more of a differentiator to MIM 2016 to assist you in designing hybrid architecture, be aware that MIM is commonly used for the following scenarios:

- Connecting different repositories like SAP HR/OM, Oracle, or others
- Complex multi-forest AD scenarios with more than one Exchange organization
- Usage of non-AD synchronization, such as entitlement databases or other authentication repositories

Another important thing to note is that PowerShell-managed Azure Active Directories are suitable for small or medium sized organizations with or without Active Directory. However, there are performance and functionality limitations inside the provisioning and management process. Instead, use PowerShell for writing wrappers. Keep in mind support from Microsoft!

Under the hood, AAD Connect is a packed version of the FIM/MIM Synchronization Service and covers the following central options:

- Metaverse, Management Agents and run profiles, and everything you know from Forefront Identity Manager and Microsoft Identity Manager
- Can be installed with SQL Express, and if you have more than 100K objects in your Active Directory you should move them to an SQL Server – keep in mind that *high availability is only available with SQL Cluster*
- Provides the following enhanced functionality:
    - Exchange Hybrid Deployment
    - Azure AD app and attribute filtering for providing a minimal footprint in limiting attribute sets
    - Password Synchronization and write-back
    - Group and Device write-back
    - Directory extension attribute sync for providing special attributes

*ADFS Server*, the **Active Directory Federation Services** (**ADFS**), builds the second component of the identity bridge and provides the capabilities of federation-based authentication. Federation-based single sign-on enables the users in your organization to automatically sign in to a third-party SaaS application by Azure AD using the user account information from Azure Active Directory. This means, when you are already logged into Azure Active Directory, and you want to access resources that are controlled by a third-party SaaS application, federation will eliminate the need for a user to be re-authenticated. Federated SSO is available for end-user browsers which support JavaScript and CSS.

Another option is to use password-based single sign-on, which enables an organization to automatically sign in to a third-party SaaS application by Azure Active Directory using the user account information from the third-party SaaS application. When you enable this feature, Azure Active Directory collects and securely stores the user account information and the related password.

A new era in modern authentication has begun; in the past we could only use ADFS to provide SSO to web-based Office 365 applications such as Outlook Web Access. Now with modern authentication, **Active Directory Authentication Library** (**ADAL**)-based sign-in comes into play, providing SSO to Office client apps across different platforms. The following figure shows ADAL in combination with the Office 2013 client:

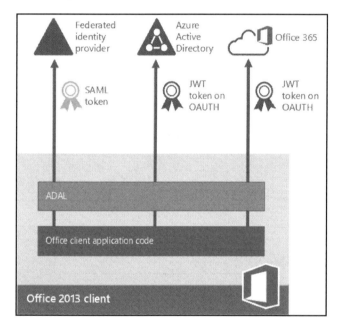

Source: Microsoft

The following features will be enabled:

- Multi-Factor Authentication (MFA)
- SAML-based third-party Identity Providers with Office client applications
- Smart card and certificate-based authentication
- Removes the need to use the basic authentication protocol

 You can find similar design options by visiting the following link:
`http://bit.ly/1RPZJNZ.`

*The Web Application Proxy* role was first established in the Remote Access role service in Windows Server 2012 R2. The Web Application Proxy provides reverse proxy functionality for web applications inside your corporate network, which allows users on any device to access apps from outside the corporate network and functions as an AD FS proxy.

The following key functionality will be provided by this role:

- Secure access to on-premises line of business applications
- Application publishing with the reverse proxy functionality
- Clients include a standard browser, an Office client, or a rich client using OAuth
- Deployment with ADFS, replacing the typical ADFS proxy role
- Supports applications using claims-based authentication and Integrated Windows authentication using Kerberos Constrained Delegation – the authentication capabilities will be extended with Windows Server 2016, which we will discuss in further chapters
- Integrated Windows authentication-based applications can be defined as relying party trusts
- External threat protection to protect applications

*Advanced Threat Analytics* provides the capabilities for identifying breaches and threats using behavioral analysis against your directory and authentication services. This component helps you to protect your identities in a proactive way, because cybersecurity is also knocking on your data center door. **Advanced Threat Analytics (ATA)** provides deep packet inspection technology and integrates in your **Security Information and Event Management (SIEM)** and Active Directory. The following attacks and behaviors can be detected:

- Pass-the-Ticket (PtT), Pass-the-Hash (PtH), and Overpass-the-Hash
- Forged PAC (MS14-068), Golden Ticket, Skeleton key malware, and Reconnaissance
- Brute force, remote execution, anomalous logins, unknown threats, and password sharing
- Lateral movement, broken trust, weak protocols, and known protocol vulnerabilities

This functionality helps you to secure your hybrid identity and access management architecture and assists you in protecting against highly personalized phishing emails and sophisticated social engineering techniques that trick users into providing their sensitive access information.

*Rights Management Connector* is the connector to the Azure RMS service that integrates on-premises file servers, exchange servers, and SharePoint servers. The connector acts as a relay. With on-premises tenant key management (BYOK), the RMS connector and the on-premises server do not need access to the **Hardware Security Module (HSM)**. The connector can also be used in a hybrid scenario, for example with Exchange Online and Exchange On-Premise. Typically, we will need to install two load-balanced connectors to provide high availability. We highly recommend an AAD RM Role-Based Administrator with the role **ConnectorAdministrator** for the configuration.

The following servers can be connected:

- Exchange 2016 and Exchange 2013: Client access servers and mailbox servers
- Exchange 2010: Client access servers and hub transport servers
- SharePoint: Front-end SharePoint webservers, including those hosting the Central Administration server
- File Classification Infrastructure: Windows Server computers that have File Resource Manager installed

Finally, there are different agents installed to provide the connection to Azure services. We will discuss these agents in the following section in combination with the services.

# Azure services features overview

After discussing the on-premises components, we now need to change focus to Azure identity and access management services.

*The Azure Active Directory core* is your tenant directory and the key component of every Azure subscription and Office 365 plan. However, it's not just an Active Directory in the cloud, as we already know from `Chapter 2`, *Planning and Designing Cloud Identities*. It's much more than that, and includes many identity management options as a service, as well as many subordinated features. It's able to provide a suitable solution for almost all environment and organizational needs. The following solutions and services work in direct ways with Azure Active Directory.

- Privileged Identity Management: the cloud version of the on-premises Privileged Access Management (PAM) of Windows Server 2016 and MIM 2016.
- Identity Protection: the adoption of ATA for protecting your cloud identities.
- Identity Manager Reporting: a hybrid reporting feature providing relevant reports from the On-premise MIM 2016 solution in the Azure Active Directory management portal.
- Application Proxy: the Azure AD Application Proxy is similar to the On-premise Web Application Proxy role in Windows Server 2012 R2. With this service you can enable external access for On-premise applications. Azure AD Application Proxy requires an Azure AD Basic or an Azure AD Premium subscription. The connection is made directly with Azure and done through proxy into the private network with an application proxy agent installed on the On-premise Web Application Server.
- Device Registration: also known as Azure AD Join. With this service you are able to join Windows 10 and other devices in Azure Active Directory to use device information for access control or management of the device. Additionally, you can gain SSO to the SaaS applications used by your company based on device authentication. The registered device information can also be synchronized back to the On-premise Active Directory via the AAD Connect tool. In such a use case, your local ADFS infrastructure can use the device information, for example, for conditional access.

- Cloud App Discovery: this service helps you to discover cloud applications used in the On-premise environment. To gain information, the cloud app discovery agent needs to be installed on local computers. Unauthorized access to corporate data, possible data leakage, and other security risks can be avoided if you know which applications are used by your employees.

*The Azure Multi-Factor Authentication* service adds the capability of a secondary authentication prompt when a user signs in to an application integrated in Azure AD or your local infrastructure. For a hybrid use case, a server component needs to be installed in your environment. There are exactly two deployment models of the service: activated as an Azure feature or combined with the local instance of the Azure MFA server. We have already discussed the cloud service functionality in previous chapters, so this chapter focuses on the local instance.

The following list provides a short overview of the key facts:

- Secure cloud applications use Microsoft **Azure Active Directory** (**AAD**).

 You can have one MFA provider per tenant

- Secure on-premises resources and Active Directory Domain Services (AD DS) use the Azure MFA Server.
- Secure custom applications are used with the MFA Software Development Kit (SDK).
- Secure Microsoft Office 365 Applications: actually, there is no way of separating the different Office 365 applications; this means all or nothing. Microsoft plans to change this behavior in the near future.

- MFA used for Microsoft Azure Administrators and access to the Azure Management Portal

We recommend using the On-premise Azure MFA server if you need:

- MFA to On-Premises devices, such as VPN devices or for securing your Remote Desktop connections like RDS and Citrix with the usage of RADIUS

- MFA to applications that don't support identity federation protocols or are not integrated with Azure AD

- To integrate MFA with AD FS directly

If you want to use one of the following MFA methodologies: OAuth tokens or Two-Way SMS.

- *Azure Rights Management* helps you to protect data at rest or in transit. There are three available deployment models of the Rights Management services, as shown in the following table:

| Cloud Only with Azure RMS | Azure AD | Azure RMS |
|---|---|---|
| Hybrid Identity with Azure RMS | Azure AD, On-Premises AD, Azure AD Sync, and (optional) AD FS | Azure RMS |
| On-Premises only with AD RMS | On-Premises AD | On-Premises AD RMS |
| Cross-Premises with Azure RMS | Azure AD, On-Premises AD, Azure AD Sync, and (optional) AD FS | Azure RMS, RMS Connector |

Microsoft is planning to ship a special complex deployment model that should allow a parallel service installation On-premises and in the cloud. It's called Dual Server.
You will find a public beta with Azure Information Protection at `http://b it.ly/2aN4lpW`.

This will help organizations with high security requirements to use the full feature set for every use case and need.

From a design perspective, it's important to know that you can limit the synchronized attributes to a small subset that is needed to use Azure RMS. The following table shows that the only PII data included is the first name, last name, and the email address of the user:

| CN (common name) | tsmith |
|---|---|
| displayName | Tony Smith |
| Mail | tony.smith@idam.ch |
| proxyAddresses | SMTP: tony.smith@idam.ch |
| userPrincipalName | tony.smith@idam.ch |
| accountEnabled | True |
| objectSID (sync ID) | 01 05 … 00 05 15 00 00 E2 DB … AD A1 29 71 04 09 .. |
| pwdLastSet | 20151013171110.0Z |
| sourceAnchor (for Licensing) | MySourceAnchor…..== |
| usageLocation (for Licensing) | CH |

The implementation of the cross-premises deployment scenario provides a flexible and highly functional solution that can fulfill most requirements in a typical organization. To integrate On-premise files or exchange servers, the Azure RMS connector needs to be installed on a local server. Furthermore, there is the capability of using different scenarios for key management, which we will discuss in the following section on *Azure Key Management* and the **Bring your Own Key** (**BYOK**) scenario.

*Azure Key Management* is an Azure Key Vault that helps your organization to save cryptographic keys and secrets used by cloud applications and services on a **Hardware Security Module** (**HSM**). Azure Key Vault offers you different levels of control. The Key Vault server key becomes your key in Azure, and you can trade off the level of control you desire. By default, Azure generates and manages the lifecycle of your key. As an option, a unique BYOK capability lets you generate your key On-premises and gives you additional levels of security, such as near-real time usage logs that allow you to see exactly how and when your key is being used.

 The BYOK scenario is not actually supported for Exchange Online will be supported at the end of 2016.

HSMs provide organizations with the ability to securely manage their private keys On-Premises. The following table provides a summary of the benefits of implementing a Thales HSM in the Azure RMS deployment:

| Secure Key Storage | **HSMs provide a tamper-resistant environment for the storage of private keys. All Thales HSMs are certified to meet the highest security standards.** |
| --- | --- |
| Compliance | HSMs are FIPS 140-2 Level 3 Standard: the most widely accepted benchmark for hardware security in both enterprise and government environments. |
| Extensibility | Using a Thales HSM for key storage allows the Azure RMS environment to be extensible to on-premises per a future migration. Microsoft solely uses Thales HSMs for key storage in Azure RMS; therefore, a Thales HSM is required for Azure RMS. |

# Azure Active Directory design decisions

The most common starting point in any customer conversation is a question on how many Azure Active Directories an organization needs, or rather how many should they already own. A typical problem we always see is that, for example, productive environments are created and operated on MSDN subscriptions, and with the ease of creating a new subscription, they build more than one fully independent Azure Active Directory tenant. Usually, this situation arises when a company already uses Office 365 and an administrator, let's call him `John`, decides to sign up for Microsoft Intune or an Azure subscription. In this moment, he created a second Azure Active Directory which cannot be used for supporting the actual Office 365 environment. John could avoid this scenario if he signs up to Microsoft Intune or the Azure subscription with the global administrator account in Office 365.

As a general rule, we can say that an Azure subscription always includes Azure Active Directory. So, if an organization wants to completely separate the administration and usage scenario between two Azure Active Directories, for example if you need a development environment for your developers separate from Azure Active Directory, then they need to create a second directory.

 We highly recommend that you design and create at least two isolated Azure Active Directories for development and productive usage. In the field of IAM, you always need the capability to test new processes.

The following figure presents the idea of having two Azure Active Directories for this case. Keep in mind that a public domain name and the UPN need to be unique over all Azure Active Directories, for example, you cannot use the same public domain name for two Azure Active Directories.

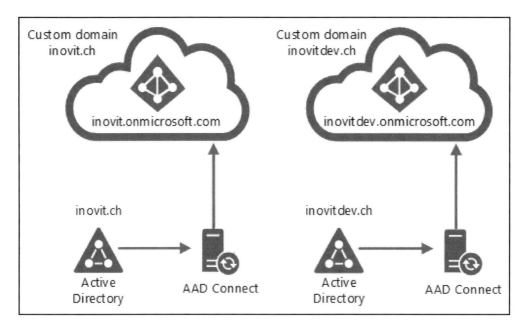

If you design this scenario, be aware of the following conditions:

- Is there a need for Azure AD premium features such as password reset or MFA? If so, you need to have an additional Azure AD premium subscription; Azure AD Premium is licensed per-directory. This is the same with Office 365 and other services.
- If you need to maintain twice: for example, both ADFS and Azure AD Connect.

The following figure illustrates this scenario in the Azure management portal. For this use case, we created an additional directory in the same Azure subscription. You can also work with two Azure subscriptions to completely isolate the administration without the usage roles and permissions.

# Azure subscription management

The next point of discussion comes from the previous section – subscription management. In the past, a subscription was the administrative security boundary inside of the Microsoft Azure ecosystem. Since Microsoft introduced the **Azure Resource Management** (**ARM**) capabilities, we now have two administrative models:

- Azure Service Management (classic)
- Azure Resource Management

 With the usage of Azure Resource Management and the granular RBAC model, a subscription is no longer required as an administrative boundary. You can find more details on this by visiting the following link: `http://bit.ly/1XJMpJ6`.

The usage of multiple Azure subscriptions as a security boundary is required if you want to design an Azure subscription-based model for separating the administration and Azure Active Directories, as discussed above. If you use such a model, clearly define naming conventions to prevent any misunderstanding.

The naming convention can be designed in the following format:

```
<Company><Department (optional)><Product or Project (optional)>
<Environment>
```

The following are some examples:

```
inovit GmbH - Engineering - BusinessApplication 1 - Development
inovit GmbH - Core Services - Business - Production
```

- `Company` – most of the time, this is the same for all subscriptions. However, if you have more companies in your organizational structure, or you need to be open for acquisitions, it's a good idea to use the company value.
- `Department` – this represents the department or team. This value is often used in bigger companies, not in small or medium ones.
- `Product or Project` – this represents, for example, a development of a new product or the project for a new app. This is commonly used to organize resources that are used. Also rarely used in small or medium organizations.
- `Environment` – this is the description of the environment used to adopt the management strategy representing the lifecycle.

To recap, we use the following subscription principles:

- The first container created
- Represents a billing unit
- Defines a logical limit of scale
- Is used as an administrative security boundary
- Supports **Role Based Access Control (RBAC)**

 The limits of the Azure subscription and its services can be found at the following link: `bit.ly/1LjBORA`.

Another important topic to cover is how to build the toolset and associated accounts. The management of your subscription can be done in several ways. The easiest way to view and manage your subscriptions will be through the Azure management portal, as shown in the following figure:

If you prefer to access your subscriptions with PowerShell, we recommend using the Azure AD authentication with the `Add-AzureAccount` and `Login-AzureRmAccount` (in ARM) `cmdlet` to enter your credentials in the provided window. If you want to go back to the management certificate method, you just need to use the cmdlets `Remove-AzureAccount` or `Remove-AzureRmEnvironment` (in ARM).

Azure AD authentication is the preferred mode if you work interactively. This method is also the primary authentication method for the new ARM deployment model.

Additionally, you will have the following options for managing your subscriptions:

- Azure Service Management Certificate Authentication
- The Publish Settings File (Azure Service Management)

With the following toolsets:

- Azure PowerShell (Microsoft devices)
- Software Development Kits (SDKs)
- XPlat-CLi (Cross-Platform)

You will find the necessary tools at the following link: `http://bit.ly/238wmbj`

Now that we have discussed the different authentication mechanisms and toolsets, we can dive a bit deeper into associated accounts, in particular the three most important accounts related to subscriptions:

- Service Administrator
- Co-Administrator
- Account Administrator

Let's use a brief example to explain the different accounts and their permissions. First of all, if you create a new subscription, by design, a service administrator will be assigned to the subscription and the default service administrator will also be the account administrator for the subscription. The account administrator can assign a different service administrator by editing the subscription:

Next, we add Co-Administrators that assist with the management of Azure Services. The Co-Administrators have the following characteristics:

- Requirement of a valid Microsoft Account or Organizational Account
- The first Co-Administrator must be added by the Service Administrator
- Additional Co-Administrators can be added by other Co-Administrators
- Co-Administrators can log in to the Azure Management Portal (view all services)

- Co-Administrators share the same rights as the server administrator, except the right to remove the service administrator

Using the ARM Portal, subscription owners share the same rights and permissions that the service administrator owns, except the right to remove the service administrator from the subscription

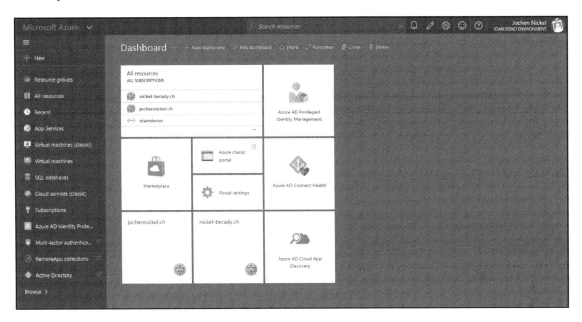

The following diagrams explain the different roles: the account administrator, the service administrator, and the co-administrators. These roles can be assigned to one or multiple identities.

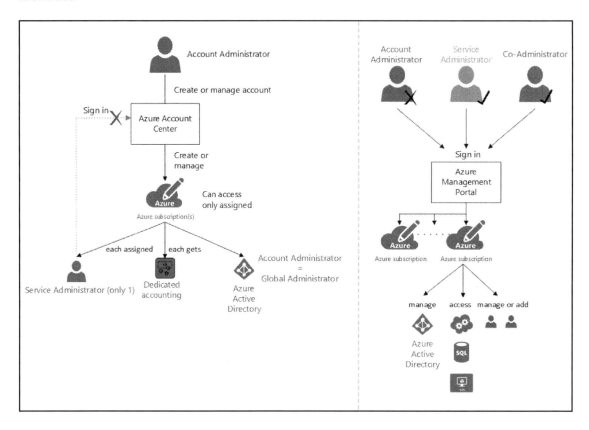

Now that we know you can use two administrative models to manage your subscriptions, keep in mind that if you choose the ASM classic option you will have multiple objects combined into a single manageable instance. Therefore, if you use the ARM resource manager you will receive the capability to manage each object separately.

 The resource manager model is where the development of Microsoft happens.

Obviously there are many other topics related to the key design concepts, but we have only described the most important ones. If you need further information, visit the following link to gather more information: `http://bit.ly/1On2Iq4`.

# Management of common identities with Microsoft Identity Manager and Active Directory

The classic Identity Management service deals with the life cycle of an identity within, or in conjunction with, an organization. Furthermore, it manages identities across different directories, databases, and applications in On-premise environments based on business processes and the employee lifecycle. **Microsoft Identity Manager** (MIM) 2016 is the latest Identity Management product from Microsoft that focuses on this field of technology. For hybrid identity and access management strategies, the management of On-premise identities becomes more and more relevant.

## General capabilities of MIM 2016 in a hybrid world

In particular, the usage of MIM 2016, or other Identity Management services, provides the capability to prepare identities stored in the local Active Directory for the cloud synchronization tool AAD Connect so it can be used in Azure Active Directory for SaaS application access. The main advantage MIM provides to this solution is help with domain/forest consolidations, attribute normalization, and obviously, complete On-premise identity management. Another important point to note is that you can prepare complex group management based on policies and workflows to control access to SaaS applications.

Other typical use cases are:

- Office 365 licensing
- Identity provisioning/de-provisioning to SaaS applications
- Azure Active Directory application role management
- Providing a rich policy framework for enforcing corporate security policies regarding identity and access

The following figure provides you with an in-depth look at the hybrid synchronization environment.

 Be aware that we have not discussed the On-premise identity management tasks in depth. We have just given you the first steps of making decisions so you can have a good basic understanding of MIM. *Packt Publishing* provides complete guidance books for this topic, such as the book and video series from *Kent Nordstrãg̈m, Microsoft Forefront Identity Manager 2010 R2 Handbook and Enterprise Identity Management with Microsoft Forefront Identity Management*. There is also an upcoming handbook about MIM 2016 where we actually review the writing process of this book.

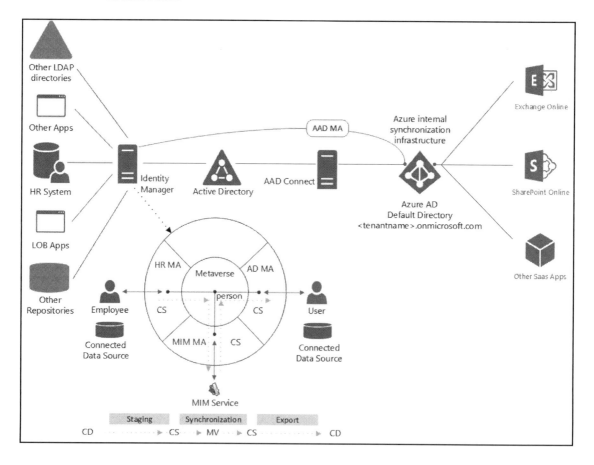

As you can see in the previous figure, MIM 2016 is also capable of synchronizing identities with the Azure Active Directory. So, the first question we always get is: *Which tool do we use for synchronizing identities with Azure Active Directory?* The short practical answer for a common scenario is the Azure AD Connect tool. The following figure shows you a small decision helper:

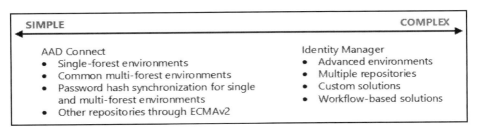

To give you an idea of when it makes sense to use MIM 2016 for synchronizing identities or identity information directly, we use the following two examples. There are many other scenarios available – we have just used the two most common ones.

# Use case – Office 365 license management

There is no functionality in the AAD Connect tool for assigning different Office 365 plans to a user or, like with Azure AD Premium licenses, over a group membership.

So, you have different options for solving this requirement:

- Licensing users after synchronization with a PowerShell script
- Adding a PowerShell Connector based on ECMAv2 in combination with AD extension attributes to the AAD Connect Tool – for example, FIM/MIM Granfeldt PowerShell Management Agent (`http://bit.ly/1N4bgla`), which is based on ECMAv2

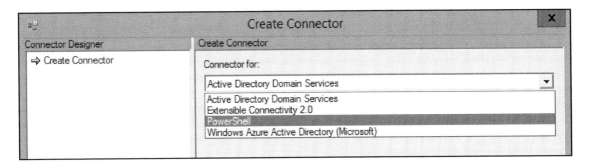

- Implementing a solution in MIM also based on a PowerShell connection, but with a clear integration in the identity management process without using Active Directory extension attributes

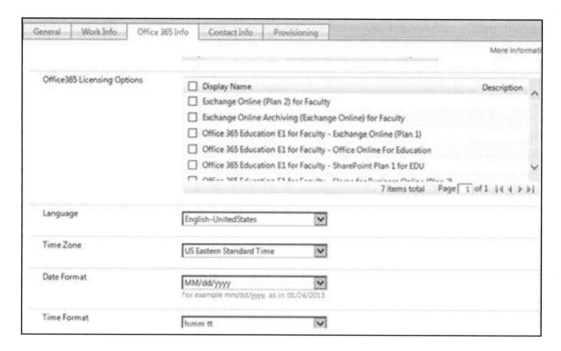

- This solution can be prepared with the MIM PowerShell MA or the Workflow Activity Library (WAL), as you can see in the following figure:

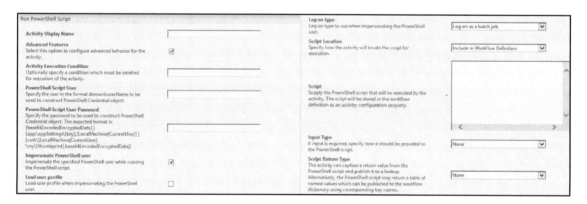

With these options, you should be able to design a suitable solution for different customer sizes and needs.

Microsoft plans to provide Office 365 based on group memberships in the future. But there will still be a need to integrate this in the employee lifecycle based on Azure AD Premium features or MIM 2016.

# Use case – provisioning in an SaaS application

In this use case, we will discuss the capability to provision SaaS applications.

This use case is not shown in the general capabilities architecture.

Azure Active Directory already provides automated provisioning for the following applications:

- Box
- Citrix GoToMeeting
- Concur
- DocuSign
- Dropbox for business
- Google apps
- Jive
- Salesforce
- Salesforce sandbox
- ServiceNow
- Workday (inbound provisioning)

This automated provisioning functionality is a nice starting point for providing users in your SaaS applications, but it's missing some very important functionality, such as inbound and outbound synchronization or other identity types such as groups or roles with complex advanced rule sets.

The actual functionality of Azure Active Directory can be seen in the following example of the Salesforce sandbox:

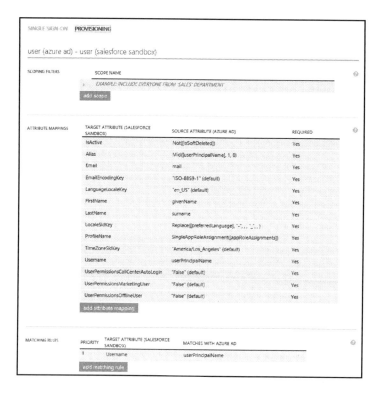

 Obviously, we know that there is a SCIM model for enabling the automatic provisioning of users and groups from Azure AD to applications. If you need more information about this topic, you can visit:
http://bit.ly/1VmMkMx.

From our experience, we often need to integrate MIM 2016 with SaaS applications for the relevant identity and management tasks, and then integrate them in the policy and workflow based on the on-premises environment.

# Small technical footnote about MIM 2016

The following section gives you a short overview of the key components and possible interactions that need to be included in the blueprint for a suitable architecture solution. We have also included some of these components in the provided implementation guides in this book.

## MIM 2016 components overview

MIM 2016 contains the following components:

- Synchronization Service: the core engine of MIM that connects different repositories

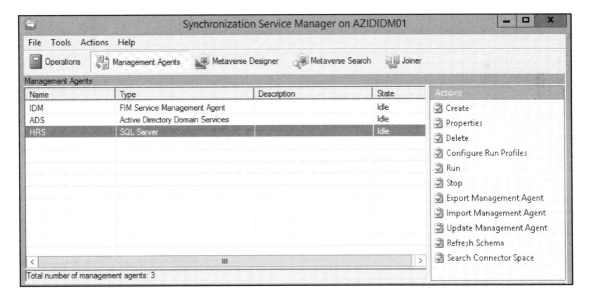

- Service and Portal: this provides management policies and workflows, including several activities

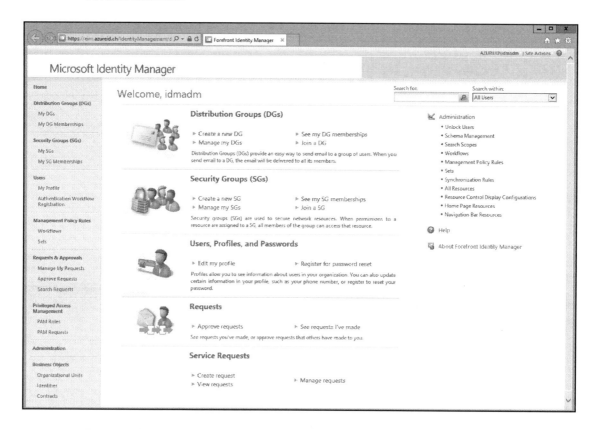

- Password Synchronization: this provides password synchronization to other repositories based on the Active Directory password change or reset

- Password and Account Self-Service: these are separate portals that provide self-service password reset and account unlock capabilities

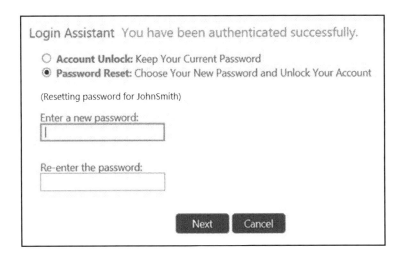

- Privileged Account Management: the management of administrative user accounts: JIT and workflow-based

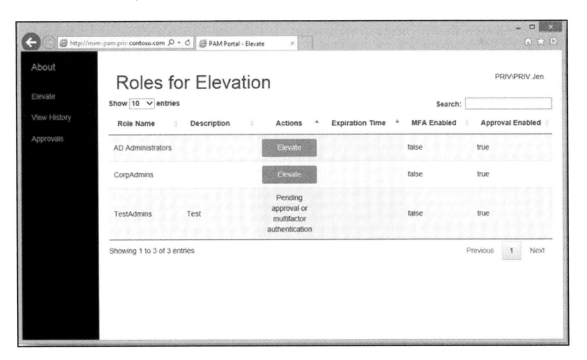

- Reporting: this provides central reporting in the System Center Service Manager data warehouse and others
- Role Management: this is a special BHOLD module that provides role mining, management, and different attestation campaigns

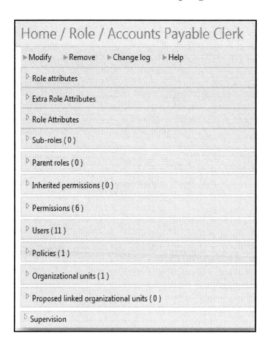

- Certificate Lifecycle Management: this is a workflow-based certificate management system for soft certificates and smart cards

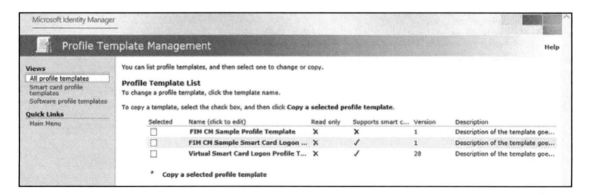

As you can see from previous figures, MIM 2016 uses technical terms inside the synchronization service, which we need to discuss. AAD Connect works in an almost identical way, with only a few differences.

# MIM Synchronization Service

A **Metadirectory (Metaverse MV)** is at the core of all identity management solutions. The Synchronization Service component of the MIM is a metadirectory. The purpose of a metadirectory is to collect information from different data sources throughout an organization and then combine all or part of that information into an integrated, unified view called the metaverse. This unified view presents all the information about an object, such as a person or network resource, that is contained throughout the organization. It provides an organization with a unified view of their identity information regarding users, groups, resources, applications, etc., but it also provides the basis for pumping identity information between data sources according to technical and business rules. The **Metaverse (MV)** is a set of tables within MIM 2016 that contains the integrated identity information from multiple connected sources. All identity information about a specific person or object, which is stored in multiple connected sources, is synthesized into a single entry in the MV.

Do consider the following design notes:

1. MIM Synchronization Service is a state-based system:

    - Imported data will be compared with previously imported data – a difference indicates modifications in source
    - Imported data will be compared with previously exported data – no difference indicates a successful export

2. MIM is not *real time*, it uses run cycles that can be configured.

## Connected Data Source

The **Connected Data Source (CD)** is a data source that can be represented by a repository, directory, database, or data included in flat files.

## Management Agent

The **Management Agent (MA)** is the connector to a CD and manages the data specific to the CD.

## Connector Space (CS)

The **Connector Space (CS)** represents a storage and staging area. It stores the states that indicate whether information has changed in the CD. Each CD has its own logical area in the connector space.

## Staging

If you run a Staged Import operation on a Management Agent, such as *Full/Delta Import (Stage Only)*, the data is imported from the CD into the CS but with no synchronization rule applied to it. Therefore, a staged Import does not affect the MV.

## Synchronization

This is the process of applying all the configured rules to the staged objects in the connector space. Synchronization can be divided into inbound and outbound.

## Export

This is the process of writing changes that occurred during synchronization from the CS back to the CD.

# MIM Service

The MIM Service provides all the necessary capabilities for policies and workflows. All users, groups, requests, workflows, and other resources used in MIM are stored as objects in the FIM Service database. These objects can be modified through **Create, Read, Update, and Delete (CRUD)** requests made to the FIM Service IDM Platform.

After working through this small introduction section for MIM 2016, you should now be able to interpret the basic functionality of MIM and to understand the overview figure. In the next section, we will walk through the different options for directory synchronization.

# Choosing the best directory synchronization scenario for cloud identities

To integrate or extend the local Active Directory to the cloud, we need a rich set of capabilities to address all the different requirements of our customers. In the following figure, we see the three most common synchronization and two extension scenarios we can use.

- Synchronization scenarios:
    - Directory and password synchronization
    - Federation and directory synchronization
    - Federation, directory, and password synchronization
- Extension scenarios:
    - Stretching your local Active Directory to Azure IaaS
    - Using Azure Active Directory Domain Services to bring legacy authentication LOBs to the cloud

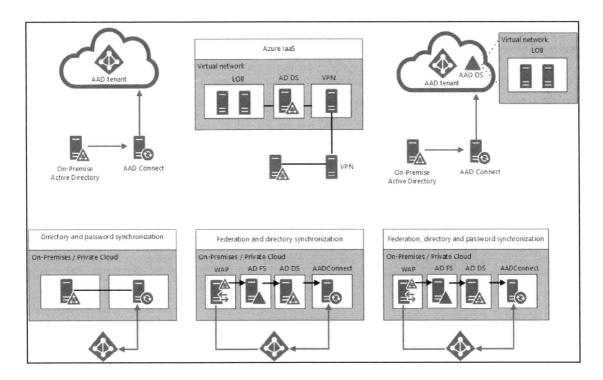

# Synchronization scenarios

With the creation of a new Azure Active Directory tenant, directory information is managed independently from the On-Premises Active Directory forest by default. A new on-board user must be created in both the Azure Active Directory and the local Active Directory. Unless you drive a cloud-only company, you always need to synchronize identities from the On-premise AD to the AAD tenant you own to provide a single identity. After the synchronization process is in place, AAD and AD can be viewed as one single identity service.

 In this chapter, we have discussed the usage of a single forest with a single Azure AD tenant. In complex hybrid scenario chapters, we will discuss the following scenarios: single forest with multiple domains, account/resource forest models, and multiple forests with unique and duplicate users. You can also synchronize your domain-joined Windows 10 devices; for more information, visit:
`http://bit.ly/2b1VuMv.`

# Directory and password synchronization

By synchronizing identities and the associated passwords from the On-Premise Active Directory to the Azure Active Directory, we build a basic scenario for smaller companies if they don't want to invest in an **Active Directory Federation Services** (**ADFS**) infrastructure. In addition, there is no SSO required. With this scenario, the same password can be used to authenticate the user either in the cloud or On-premise, depending on what resource is being accessed. Furthermore, the password reset and account unlock features are available with an Azure AD Premium license.

The requirements for this process are an AAD Connect with password hash synchronization enabled. Optional password write-back is enabled.

 For this process a re-hashing functionality is in place, which allows users to have two different hash values in the local AD and the Azure Active Directory. Additionally, multi-forest synchronization is supported.

# Federation and directory synchronization

With the implementation of federation, all authentication is retained On-Premises and all passwords are stored on-premises only. All authentication traffic is redirected from Azure Active Directory to the On-Premises ADFS, which authenticates the user against a trusted Active Directory domain. This scenario is commonly used in various company sizes if SSO is required and password hash synchronization is prohibited because of security reasons.

The requirements for this process are the usage of a federation service provider, such as the ADFS, in addition to AAD Connect.

# Federation, directory, and password synchronization

This combination relates to the usage of federation for SSO, the synchronization of identities, which is always required, and the usage of the self-service password reset and account unlock capabilities from the Azure Active Directory Premium feature set. This scenario is commonly used in all company sizes without any special security requirements for the password synchronization process.

The requirements for this process are the usage of a federation service provider, such as the ADFS, in addition to AAD Connect with password synchronization and write back enabled.

# Extension scenarios

Extending **Active Directory Domain Services (AD DS)** supports different use cases compared to the synchronization of identities using the AAD connect tool to Azure Active Directory. The following reasons are the key indicators for using an extension scenario:

- Required legacy authentication mechanisms, such as NTLM or Kerberos
- Domain joined virtual servers for management reasons
- Cross-platform support is needed

# Stretching your local Active Directory to Azure IaaS

Extending your local AD DS to Azure IaaS provides you with a very flexible scenario for using your line-of-business applications in the cloud. To realize this integration, you will need to build a VPN or express route connection to Azure.

Domain controllers are highly sensitive roles and will focus mainly on trusting the service. Many alternative solutions do not support seamless lift and shift migration to Azure like this one.

**Domain Controllers (RW)**
Will be the best choice for IaaS workloads; be aware of your replication considerations
**Domain Controller (RO)**
Normally used for scenarios with poor security; not a good choice for IaaS workloads
**Resource Forest scenarios**
Also not recommended in IaaS

# Using Azure Active Directory Domain Services

This service provides the capability to use AD DS as a service in Azure. It provides two domain controllers with a small footprint of management options. It integrates directly with your Azure Active Directory. It's a very good option for moving everything used on-premises to the cloud, providing smaller companies a way of functioning without a local infrastructure. In this case, a legacy main LOB can now be used in an Azure Active Directory integration scenario, with everything managed under service conditions. We have already discussed this new service in previous chapters.

# Source Anchor decisions

It's important to understand source anchor because it builds the basis for the relationship between AD DS users and Azure AD users. If a user account is to be migrated to another forest, you need to use a different source anchor; this is because `objectGUID` can't be migrated with the user. After migration, there will be multiple accounts in Azure AD for migrated users: one for the old forest and another for the new forest.

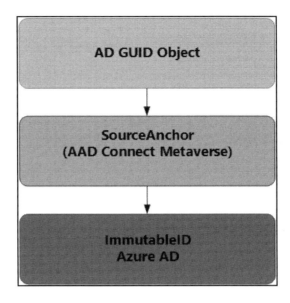

Other valid source anchors are the user's email address or UPN.

If you plan to migrate in the near future, plan to use another Source Anchor in your environment and be sure that it's unique in the other forests.
We will provide some synchronization examples in the complex hybrid chapters to provide you with a better understanding of this topic.

# IdFix error remediation tool

To prepare your Active Directory environment, you can also use the IdFix tool. This performs the discovery and remediation of identity objects and their attributes in an on-premises Active Directory environment in preparation for migration to Office 365. IdFix is intended for the Active Directory administrators responsible for AAD Connect with the Office 365 service. You can also use the tool for every synchronization scenario.

You can download the tool at: http://bit.ly/1VnsvVn.

# AAD Connect tool

After discussing Microsoft Identity Manager 2016 in the previous sections, we now want to start diving into the AAD Connect tool.

## General overview

The tool uses the following terms:

- Like in MIM, we have the CS. The CS can contain three kinds of objects: connector objects, disconnector objects, and placeholder objects.
- Connector objects – there are two types of connector objects: connectors and explicit connectors.

The connector is an object in the CS that represents an object in a connected data source that is currently linked to an object in the MV. All management agent rules will still be applied to this type of connector.

An explicit connector is an object in the CS that is linked to an object in the MV and cannot be disconnected by a connector filter. An explicit connector can only be created manually with Joiner, and it can only be disconnected by provisioning or by using Joiner.

Disconnector objects means:

There are three types of disconnector objects:

- **Disconnectors**: An object in the connector space that represents an object in a connected data source and is not currently linked to an object in the MV
- **Explicit disconnectors**: An object in the connector space that is not linked to an object in the MV and can only be joined by using Joiner
- **Filtered disconnectors**: An object in the connector space that is prevented from being joined or projected to an object in the MV based on connector filter rules in the associated management agent

The placeholder objects are objects in the CS that represent a single level of the hierarchy of the CD. For example, if you want to synchronize objects with an AD DS forest, you need to import the containers that make up the path for the Active Directory objects. A placeholder object can also represent an object in the connected data source to which an imported reference attribute value refers, for example, the object to which the manager attribute refers in a `User` object. Placeholder objects do not contain attribute values and cannot be linked to the MV.

**Run profiles:** One per forest, one step per domain:

- We import (stage) all objects into the CS (filtered by the connector filter)
- Full import: all objects
- Delta: only changed objects

The MV is the same as in MIM 2016.

When you create a management agent, you configure how the MV object types map to the object types in the data source. For example, a User object type in a data source might map to the Person object type in the metaverse, or a Distribution list object type in a data source might map to the Group object type in the metaverse.

- During sync, we handle either all objects (full) or only changed (delta)
- We search for a matching object in the MV (based on a join criteria) and join
- If there is no join, we first project one object in the MV, join the connector space to the MV object, and then run attribute the flow with join rules

The *Anchor attribute* works as a unique identifier for an object in the management agent's connector space. It can consist of a single attribute or a combination of multiple attributes from the connected data source. All attributes used for an anchor must be single-value attributes or multi-value attributes with only one value. Typical candidates for an anchor attribute are unique attributes, such as the employee ID or possibly a distinguished name (also known as DN) for directories where the distinguished name is not subject to change. The anchor attribute is configured in Management Agent Designer.

*Join rules* determine the linking of a connector space object with an existing MV object. Join rules can have two parts: search criteria and resolution. You use the search criteria to compare connector space object attribute values and MV object attribute values. The search criteria are listed in the join rules in order of precedence. When you run a management agent, a join search is applied to each object in the connector space, which attempts to find a corresponding object in the MV based on the search criteria:

- **Not one MV object is acceptable** – The next search criteria in the precedence list are evaluated. If there are no more criteria in the precedence list, processing proceeds to the projection rules, if they exist.
- **Exactly one MV object is acceptable** – If there is no rules extension for join resolution, the connector space object is joined, or linked, with the MV object. If you have configured a rules extension for join resolution, the rules extension will determine if the object can be joined.

- **More than one MV object is acceptable** – The connector space object is not joined with the MV object. If you have configured a rules extension for join resolution, the rules extension will attempt to determine which object to select. Alternately, you can use Preview to diagnose the reason for the multiple search results and then use Joiner to manually join the connector space object to the MV.

 **Best practices for join rules**
Join rules are evaluated in order from top to bottom until a single match is found. When you configure the order of join rules, start with the most significant first and work down to the least significant.

Now, we run:

- **Import Attribute Flow (IAF)**
- **Export Attribute Flow (EAF)** and their join rules

An attribute flow is the process of pushing changes to an object's attributes into and out of a connector space. Attribute flow rules are defined by the attribute mappings in the management agent.

- IAF rules from the connector space to the MV are applied when the connector space flows a change to the MV
- EAF rules from the MV to the connector space are applied when the MV flows a change to the connector space

We have joined and run the attribute flow. If an MV entry is modified, we call provisioning. Now, we provision a new object.

## Provisioning

When an authoritative source projects a new object into the MV, a new connector space object can be created in another connector representing a downstream connected data source. This inherently establishes a link, and the attribute flow can proceed bi-directionally. Whenever a rule determines that a new connector space object needs to be created, it is called provisioning. However, because this operation only takes place within the connector space, it does not carry over into the connected data source until an export is performed.

# AAD Connect Sync Flow

ISR is the abbreviation for Inbound Synchronization Rule; the following are the characteristics of an ISR:

- **Connector** – The code modules that are used to communicate with a connected data source are called connectors (formerly **Management Agents** (**MA**s)). These are installed on the computer running Azure AD Sync.
- **Attribute flow** – The MV is the consolidated view of all joined identities from neighboring connector spaces. Attribute flow occurs between the connector space and the MV bi-directionally when synchronization (full or delta) operations are scheduled to run. Attribute flow occurs only when these synchronizations are run. Attribute flows are defined in the synchronization rules. These can be inbound (ISR) or outbound (OSR).

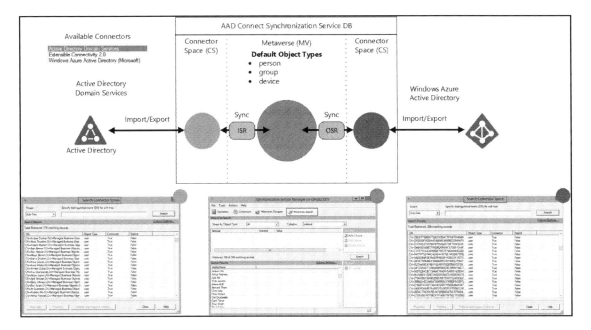

# AAD Connect high availability

For high availability, a new Azure AD Connect server can be re-built and re-synchronized in a couple of hours for a medium sized business. However, this is not an option for bigger organizations. Larger organizations with more than 100,000 users will take more time to synchronize. If there needs to be a faster recovery time, AAD Connect can be configured to use a dedicated SQL server deployment with SQL high availability. When the number of users is over 100,000, a SQL server is required because a large organization needs to have a low recovery time for the synchronization service.

Another method is to use another server with AAD Connect installed and configured in staging mode. This functionality reduces the recovery time. The following figure shows a staging mode configuration.

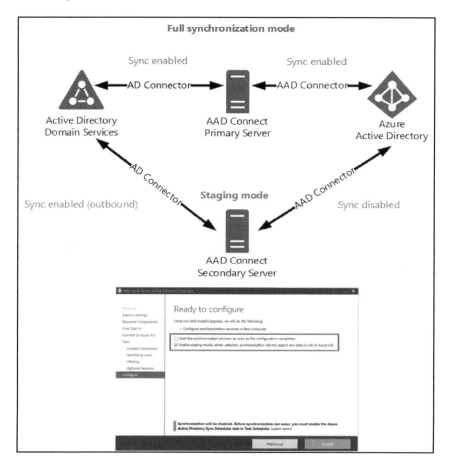

# Delivering password management capabilities

For providing password management capabilities, there are four main feature sets available in a hybrid scenario:

- Self-Service Password Reset and Account unlock, MIM 2016
- Password Change Notification Service to synchronize the actual AD password to different repositories, MIM 2016
- Password Update functionality, ADFS 3.0 and ADFS 4.0
- Password Self-Service Change, Reset and Account unlock, and AAD

The following figure shows the different capabilities in solution architecture:

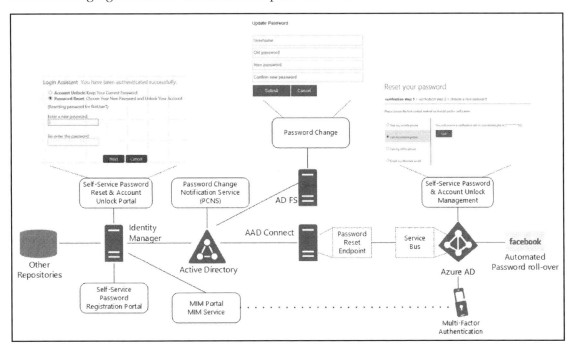

What happens when a user resets their password in the cloud?

1. Check if password write-back services are running. If yes, proceed

The service checks that a user has a valid license assigned.

2. The user reaches the password reset screen and then enters the new password
3. The password is encrypted with a public key created for the process
4. The password is sent through HTTPS to the tenant bus relay
5. The connector password reset endpoint looks for the user object in the AD Connector Space through the AAD Connector Space and the Metaverse; On-premise password policies will also be checked
6. Once the user is found, their password is reset in the appropriate forest; if a user account is enabled for password hash sync, the cloud password is reset simultaneously
7. The user is informed their password has been successfully changed

If you want to use the On-premise feature set of MIM 2016, you can use the following solution designs for your architecture

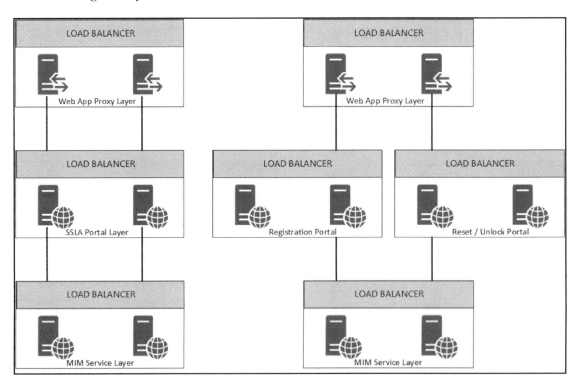

The figure shows the different scenarios in a highly-available manner, but obviously you can also use them as single instances. You can use the following verification modes for password reset and account unlock:

- Security questions over Q&A gate
- SMS notifications
- E-mail notifications
- Azure MFA

# Using multiple identity providers and authentication scenarios

Users can log into the accounts and access applications that are integrated with Azure AD.

## Using multiple identity providers

There are two options for signing users into Azure AD:

- Authenticating to Azure AD.
- Authenticating to an On-premises Identity Provider.

In the following figure, you can see a simple example of a combination of these two modes. If you are a user of `msazure.ch`, you use AAD as your identity provider and a user from `idam.ch` the local Active Directory with a configured ADFS infrastructure.

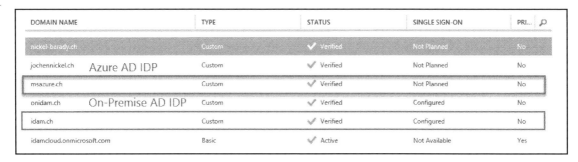

# AD FS architecture including the Web Application proxy (AD FS proxy)

The Web Application proxy, or the AD FS proxy in older versions, is used for the following reasons:

- Used to enhance the security and performance of the AD FS installation
- The proxy service is exposed over HTTPS and client connections terminate at the proxy
- When installing AD FS proxy, a trust is created between the proxy and the AD FS farm
- It is included in the web application proxy role for AD FS 2012 R2 and in AD FS 2.0 executable for AD FS 2.0
- A trust is established by issuing a proxy trust certificate that will be stored locally on each **Web Application** proxy/AD FS proxy
- A Web Application proxy:
    - Combines the AD FS Proxy and web publishing service
    - Should be located in the *perimeter network*/edge network
    - Is typically published to the Internet
    - Provides the ability to pre-authenticate or pass through HTTPS connections
    - AD FS 3.0 farm is required to set up the Web Application proxy

The following figure shows the authentication flow in an ADFS 3.0 and Web Application proxy configuration:

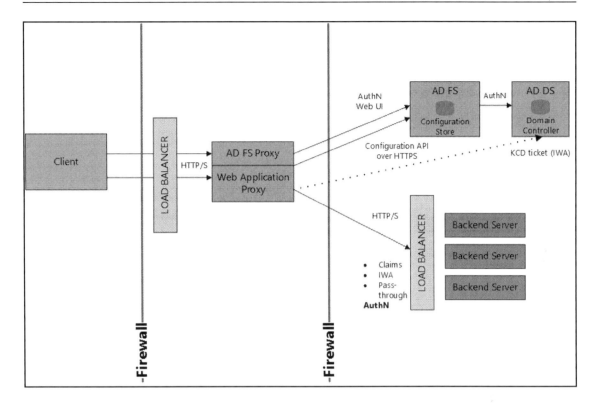

 We highly recommend using the Web Application proxy in medium and large environments.

With the integration of the Web Application proxy and the AAD application proxy, you will receive the following features and capabilities:

- End-user portal: The Azure Access panel at `https://myapps.microsoft.com`
- The Azure AD authentication capabilities are as follows:
    - Usernames and passwords synced from on-premises AD DS
    - Federated login to on-premises or other federation servers
    - MFA
    - Customized login screen
    - Authorization based on the user or groups
    - SSO to Office 365, thousands of SaaS applications, and all applications integrated with Azure AD
- Reports, auditing, and security monitoring are based on big data and machine learning
- All HTTPS traffic is terminated in the cloud, blocking most HTTP level attacks
- Unauthenticated traffic is filtered in the cloud, and will not arrive On-Premises
- There are no incoming connections to the corporate network – only outgoing connections to the Azure AD Application proxy service
- Internet-facing services are always up to date with the latest security patches and server upgrades
- Login abnormalities detection, reporting, and auditing by Azure AD
- SSO experience from Azure AD to On-Premises applications
- Connectors use the Azure AD token data to impersonate the end user to the backend applications using **Kerberos Constrained Delegation (KCD)**
- Support for any application that uses **Integrated Windows Authentication (IWA)** such as SharePoint, Outlook Web Access, and Microsoft Dynamics CRM
- There is no need to change the backend applications
- There is no need to install agents on backend applications
- There is no need to expose on-premises applications directly to the Internet

So, how does it work?

- Connectors are usually deployed on corpnet next to resources
- Multiple connectors can be deployed for redundancy, scale, multiple sites, and different resources

- The connector auto-connects to the cloud service
- The user connects to the cloud service that routes their traffic to the resources using the connectors

The following figure shows the different identity delegation modes and the scale to different datacenters.

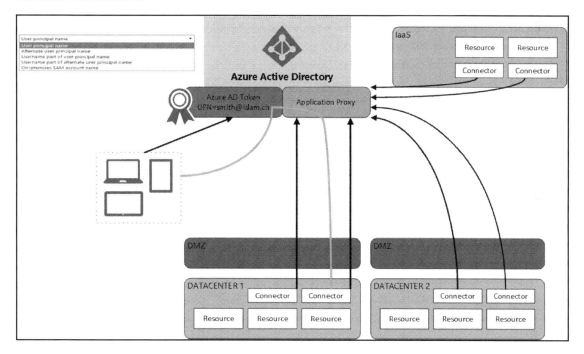

So, what do we need for identity delegation? Admin can now control the identity that is delegated to the backend application.

The identity enables the following capabilities:

- Alternate login ID for customers who have different cloud and On-Premises identities
- Applications that are in use
- Assignment of applications to a specific group of connectors

The following use cases can be fulfilled:

- Applications that are installed on isolated networks
- Multi-forest -different connector groups for each forest
- Applications installed on IaaS
- Optimized multi-data center experience
- Requirement of disaster recovery sites

You will also get the following capabilities:

- The selection of an external URL – your own public domain to publish the app by creating a `CNAME` entry pointing to the `mssappproxy.net` URL
- Allowing pass-through apps to hide from the portal, only showing them to specific assigned groups
- Disabling header translation
- Self-service application access

We highly recommend building a highly-available AD FS infrastructure that fulfills the security and availability requirements of your customer. We commonly use the following design with the Windows internal database. For larger customers, we use a dedicated SQL server in high availability mode.

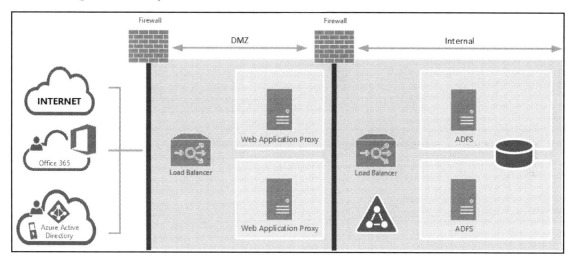

 The only requirement for joining the Web Application proxy in the Active Directory is KCD and the usage of the Workplace Join feature. You can also join devices to Azure AD and sync the devices back to your local Active Directory.

# Enabling strong authentication scenarios

Initially, a user signs in from any device using their existing account credentials. If a user is signing into an on-premises application, the Multi-Factor Server that is installed at the customer's site intercepts the authentication request.

 Authentication requests can be differentiated based on the location and the device trust level, such as managed (`isManaged`) or compliant (`isCompliant`).

First, it checks the username and password against the user directory. If the correct credentials are entered, a request is sent to the MFA cloud service. The service sends the authentication request to the user's phone. Once the user has been authenticated, they are instantly signed into the application. There are a number of ways to configure the service to secure cloud apps. First, the on-premises multi-factor server can be used with Active Directory Federation Services, or any other SAML application for single sign-in to cloud applications.

For apps that use Azure AD, the directory can call the MFA cloud service directly, or developers can build multi-factor servers into their custom apps using one of the Software Development Kits. The following figure shows the principal flow with the usage of Azure MFA.

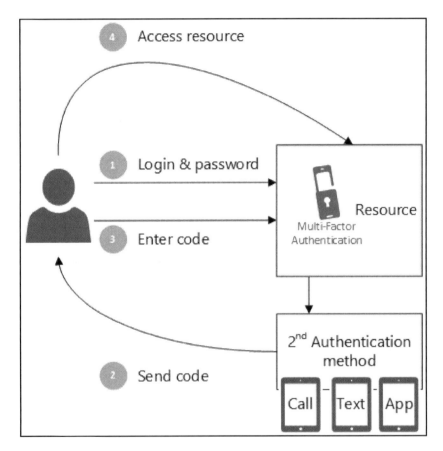

We have already discussed the Azure MFA functionality in the cloud-only scenario. We will dive into the On-premise feature set in the risk based access control section in the next chapter.

# What are app passwords?

Non-browser apps, such as Microsoft Outlook and Microsoft Lync, do not currently do support multi-factor authentication.

 Outlook 2013 and higher supports modern authentication, and the same applies for Skype (on Windows). Further information can be found at `http://bit.ly/2b1Wvo1`.

An app password is a password that is created within the Azure portal that allows the user to bypass the MFA and continue to use their application.

# Deployment models

As already discussed, the Azure MFA (`http://bit.ly/2aAIuNv`) functionality can be deployed in two models:

- Azure MFA cloud-only
- Azure MFA server On-premise

With the integration of the Azure MFA server On-premise, you will have the following capabilities to protect:

- AD FS
- IIS Authentication
- RADIUS Authentication
- LDAP Authentication

The *User Portal* section allows the administrator to install and configure the Azure MFS User Portal.

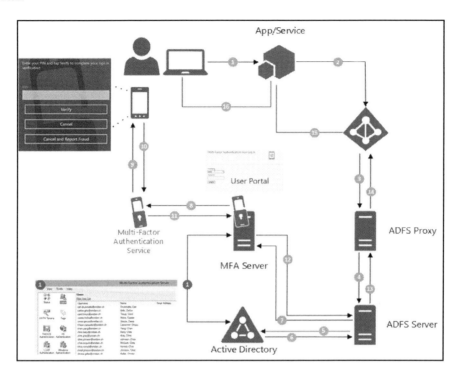

The previous figure shows the interaction between the components:

1. The user requests access to an application.
2. The application redirects to Azure AD for authentication.
3. Azure AD redirects to AD FS
    - A federated domain has been configured between AD FS and Azure AD
    - Microsoft loads the logon page
    - The user inputs their credentials, which executes home realm discovery
    - The home realm discovery uses a suffix to determine federated trusts and redirects users to your configured AD FS endpoint (AD FS Proxy)

4. The AD FS Proxy receives and validates the request and forwards it to the AD FS server.

5. AD FS performs Windows logon against the on-premises Active Directory.

6. The AD authenticates the user, the AD FS server validates the MFA policy and sees that MFA is required; the AD FS loads the installed MFA adapter.

7. The AD FS MFA adapter sends request to the MFA server. The MFA server finds that a user in its data store and looks up the user's MFA settings.

8. The MFA server sends a request to the MFA service.

9. The MFA service performs the call, text, or notification.

10. The device returns a result to the MFA service.

For one-way SMS or OATH tokens, the MFA AD FS adapter displays a textbox to the user into which they will then enter their OTP.

11. The MFA server receives the authentication result from the MFA cloud service.

12. The MFA server returns the result to the AD FS MFA adapter.

13. Upon successful validation, AD FS executes an issuance policy and generates a security token based on the claims and passes it to the AD FS proxy.

14. The AD FS proxy passes the security token to Azure AD.

15. Azure AD creates a new security token and sends this security token to the application with the appropriate claims.

16. The user has now gained access to Azure AD and is redirected to the application/service.

This procedure information is based on the following original article:
http://bit.ly/1qp8LoR

# How does advanced identity and authentication reporting work?

With MIM hybrid reporting, you receive a unified view of the most common identity management activities that happen in your Azure AD or in the on-premise identity management solution, from password self-service reset to group management. To include the On-premise data, you need to install the reporting agent on all the MIM Service servers that need to be included. The agent uploads data from service requests in the MIM service to the tenant-specific reporting service in Azure Active Directory. When using this scenario, there is no dependency to the MIM SCSM Reporting.

You will still need to implement a local reporting infrastructure if you want to hold data for auditing purposes for longer than one month. The Azure Active Directory reports are kept for no longer than one month. The hybrid reporting feature is an Azure AD Premium licensed feature.

Additionally, the reporting data uploaded to your Azure Active Directory can be turned off from the MIM Service configuration file. The following figure shows this process:

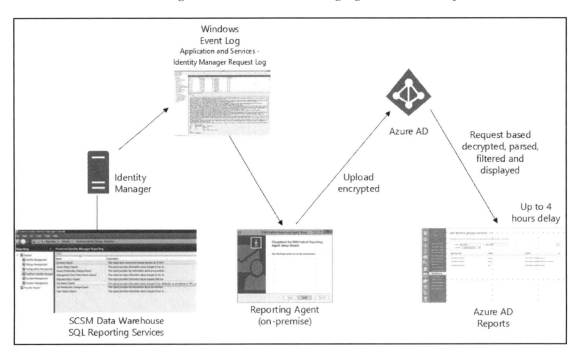

The main function here is that the reporting data will be written to the event log and will be viewable in the Event Viewer of the server system. This reporting data can also be forwarded to a **Security Information and Event Management** (**SIEM**) system for customization.

The events are stored under the following section in the **Event Viewer**:

**Application and Services logs | Identity Manager Request Log**

In the following format:

| Event type | ID | Event Details |
| --- | --- | --- |
| Information | 4121 | FIM event data that includes all the request data. |
| Information | 4137 | FIM event 4121 extension, in the case there is too much data for a single event. The header in this event is in the following form: `Request: <GUID>, message <xxx> out of <xxx>` |

The following figure shows an example report of the functionality:

The hybrid reporting feature integrates natively in the reports for authentication activities.

| REPORT | DESCRIPTION |
| --- | --- |
| ⊿ ANOMALOUS ACTIVITY | |
| Sign ins from unknown sources | May indicate an attempt to sign in without being traced. |
| Sign ins after multiple failures | May indicate a successful brute force attack. |
| Sign ins from multiple geographies | May indicate that multiple users are signing in with the same account. |
| Users with threatened credentials | Users with threatened credentials |
| Users with leaked credentials | Users with leaked credentials |
| Sign ins from IP addresses with suspicious activity | May indicate a successful sign in after a sustained intrusion attempt. |
| Sign ins from possibly infected devices | May indicate an attempt to sign in from possibly infected devices. |
| Irregular sign in activity | May indicate events anomalous to users' sign in patterns. |
| Users with anomalous sign in activity | Indicates users whose accounts may have been compromised. |
| ⊿ ACTIVITY LOGS | |
| Audit report | Audited events in your directory |
| Password reset activity | Provides a detailed view of password resets that occur in your organization. |
| Password reset registration activity | Provides a detailed view of password reset registrations that occur in your organization. |
| Self service groups activity | Provides an activity log to all group self service activity in your directory |
| Office365 Group Name Changes | Creations and name changes to Office 365 groups. |
| ⊿ INTEGRATED APPLICATIONS | |
| Application usage | Provides a usage summary for all SaaS applications integrated with your directory. |
| Account provisioning activity | Provides a history of attempts to provision accounts to external applications. |
| Password rollover status | Provides a detailed overview of automatic password rollover status of SaaS applications. |
| Account provisioning errors | Indicates an impact to users' access to external applications. |
| ⊿ RIGHTS MANAGEMENT | |
| RMS summary | Rights Management (RMS) usage summary |
| RMS active users | Top 1000 users who accessed content protected by Rights Management (RMS) |
| RMS device platforms | List of device platforms used to access content protected by Rights Management (RMS) |
| RMS application usage | Applications that accessed content protected by Rights Management (RMS) |
| ⊿ EXTERNAL ACCESS | |
| Invitation summary | Invitation summary |

# Summary

After having worked through this chapter, you will now be able to design common and cloud identities. Furthermore, you are in the position to build identity management architecture, including MIM 2016 and the Azure AD Connect utility with the necessary considerations. Additionally, you will be able to construct a blueprint with different authentication scenarios including MFA. You are also well-equipped to take the necessary decisions regarding reporting functionalities and usage scenarios. In the next chapter, we will go ahead with the planning of authorization and information protection. We will take an in-depth look into risk-based access control mechanisms and offer you insight into Microsoft rights management services.

# 8

# Planning Authorization and Information Protection Options

In this chapter, we will explore the various functions for authorization and information protection when building a solid hybrid Access Management solution. Furthermore, in this chapter you will get to know risk-based Access Control and the future functionality of Windows Server 2016. The following topics to be covered in this chapter include:

- Designing and applying risk based Access Control
- Delivering authentication and authorization improvements with Windows Server 2016
- Enabling advanced application Access Control
- Getting in touch with information protection
- How authorization and information protection reporting works

# Designing and applying risk-based Access Control

In the first section of this chapter we will discuss both the design required information for applying risk based Access Control. The main actor in this story is your ADFS and WAP infrastructure, which will help you to integrate such a solution in your environment. Obviously, there are many other technologies in the field, but we want to focus on the native components that are already in place with the use of an identity bridge. This will give you the opportunity to provide an efficient and flexible solution for providing Risk-Based Access Control. We will divide this section into the following topics to provide a better understanding:

- Managing device registration
- Managing authentication and authorization
- The magic of claims rules for application access

The main focus will be on how to support a risk matrix, like the following simple example:

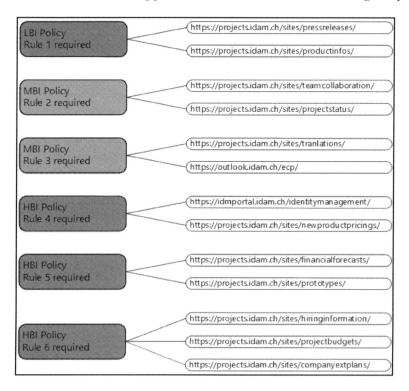

The terms of the matrix (HBI, MBI, and LBI) define the business impact:

**HBI** stands for High Business Impact (including additional Access Controls like Azure MFA).

**MBI** stands for Medium Business Impact (group, role, and device based Access Controls).

**LBI** stands for Low BusinessImpact (standard Access Controls).

# Managing device registration (AD FS DRS)

To include the device information for authentication and Access Control, Windows Server 2012 R2 provides the **Device Registration Service** (**DRS**), which is included in the AD FS role. With this functionality, a user is able to use the Workplace Join procedure to register the device in the on-premises Active Directory. DRS implements the server-side of Workplace Join. Azure AD Join is the cloud-based approach. You will find more information on this at `http://bit.ly/2b1ZM6K`.

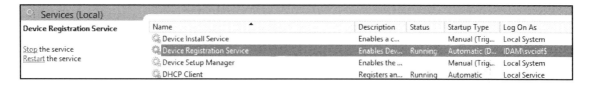

A Workplace-joined device can be a personal or corporate device and is in the second stage of the following managing and usage scenarios:

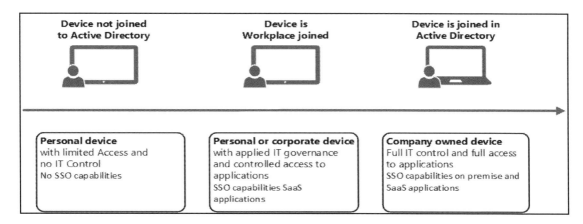

Workplace Join targets on premise environments, such as Windows 8.1. With the usage of Azure Active Directory, this process and feature is called Azure AD Join (we have already used this in previous chapters). Windows 10 is a requirement for AAD Join. The device write-back capabilities of the Azure AD Connect tool provide the synchronization of the device information back to your local Active Directory.

The following key scenarios will be enabled with the usage of this feature:

- Device-to-user mapping for domain-joined and non-domain-joined devices
- Workplace Join deployment of a user certificate to the device
- The certificate subject name is mapped to an object in Active Directory
- Provision of a second factor for seamless authentication
- Provision of additional authorization decisions
- Enabling of a better end-user experience with SSO
- Avoiding risks involved in saving passwords with each application
- Avoiding users repeatedly entering their credentials
- Relying Party Applications may also leverage Workplace Join, for example, Work Folders or the ADFS Update Password Portal

In addition to the ADFS requirements, the Device Registration Service requires the following configuration items:

- Windows Server 2012 R2 Active Directory Schema version 69 or higher
- The SSL/TLS Service Communication Certificate, which must include:
- SAN of `enterpriseregistration.<domain_name>` for each UPN suffix
- DNS CNAME record `enterpriseregistration.<domain_name>` pointing to the STS URL

From the client's perspective, you will need to fulfil the following requirements:

- Personal device support
- Microsoft Windows 8.1 or higher

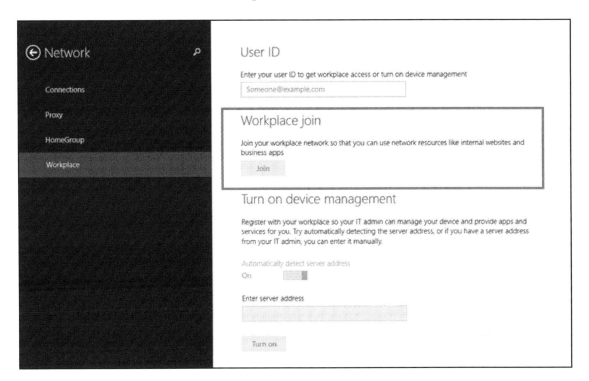

You can do the same with the following command line tool:
`%SystemRoot%\System32\AutoWorkplace.exe join`

- Microsoft Windows 10
- Apple iOS 6.0+
- Android 4.0+ only for Azure AD join

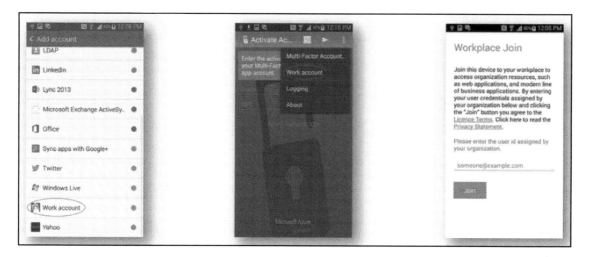

- Domain-joined device support
- Microsoft Windows 7 (with updates)
- Microsoft Windows 8.1
- Microsoft Windows 10

The process for joining a device is shown in the following figure:

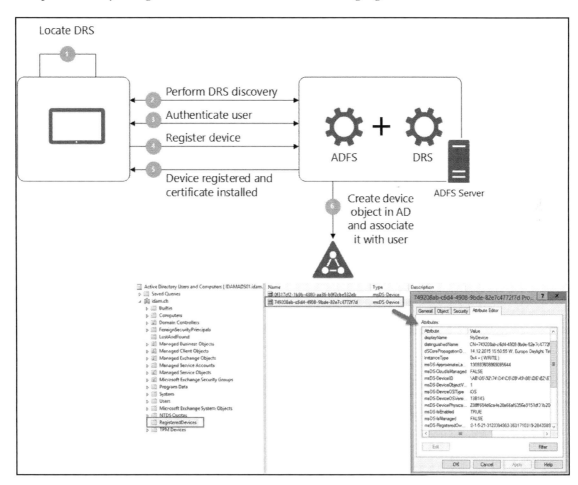

**Design note**
We recommend using MFA to use Workplace Join.

The following important device object properties are used:

| | |
|---|---|
| `DisplayName` | **Friendly name of the device. Windows devices use the host name of the computer.** |
| `DeviceID` | GUID generated by the DRS server in the join process. |
| `AltSecurityIdentities` | SHA 1 hash X509 certificate thumbprint. Certificate signed by the DRS server in the join process. |
| `OSType` | OS of the device. |
| `OSVersion` | OS version of the device. |
| `IsEnabled` | Boolean that represents the status of the device – `enabled/disabled`. |
| `ApproximateLastUseTime` | When the device was last used to access resources. This value will only be updated every 14 days to minimize replication traffic. |
| `RegisteredOwner` | SID of the user that joined the device. |

The DRS can be used with some limits and considerations. The first important factor is that you can only use one device/user combination, which means that you cannot register with different DRS instances. Obviously, you can register a computer multiple times with different user profiles. Another important point to note is that there is only one DRS configuration per forest. All your ADFS farms will use the same instance. With two DRS servers, you should be able to handle 200,000 user/device combinations – this represents no hard limit. Furthermore, you can use your ADFS/DRS farm in any trusted forest. To support this scenario, a forest level trust is required.

# Managing authentication and authorization

The ADFS in combination with the WAP role of Windows Server 2012 R2 is a very powerful solution not only for providing simply federation, but also for enabling risk based Access Control scenarios. One of the additional capabilities we now know from a registration perspective is your Workplace-joined device. To get a better understanding of how to design tasks, we will explain the main concepts of ADFS in relation to the different authentication and authorization capabilities.

The following figure illustrates how to receive a token to access resources and services:

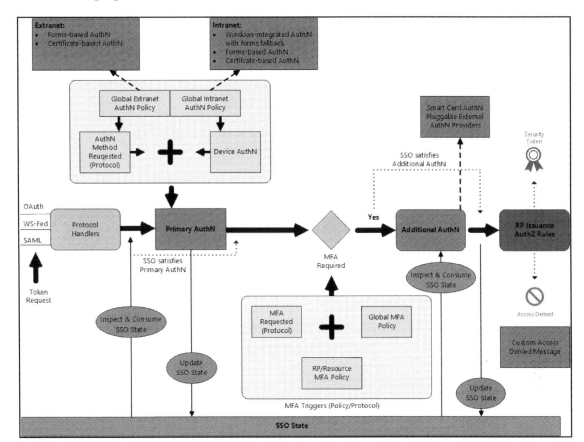

**Primary Authentication (Primary AuthN)** applies to all applications that trust AD FS. The authentication types are limited to what is supported by the AD DS. You can choose different authentication policies for intranet and extranet scenarios. The authentication methods for extranet include forms- and certificate-based methods. With the intranet configuration, you can use Windows-integrated authentication with a fall-back to forms-based authentication. On the other hand, you can also use the same methods used in the extranet configuration.

 **Windows Integrated Authentication (WIA)** for intranet and forms for extranet. The WIA fall-back to forms is used for a better user experience.

Typical configuration Windows Integrated Authentication (WIA) for intranet and forms for extranet. The WIA fall-back to forms is used for a better user experience.

The device authentication method is the usage of the Workplace-joined device object, which is always validated against directory information in Active Directory. This option builds the basis for SSO, seamless to a MFA.

Furthermore, you should also be aware that you have the option to force fresh authentication for sensitive apps. Typically, this option will be used for payroll or HR applications. The user is required to authenticate each time they try to access the application.

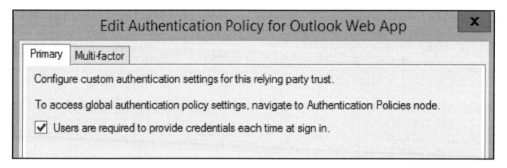

With Additional Authentication (MFA) Triggers, you add a second authentication factor to the process in order to fulfil restrictive security requirements and to protect your applications and information. You can use these options in the following manner:

- You can apply them to only your sensitive applications and resources
- You can trigger additional authentication based on the user, device, and location context, for example `Trigger additional authentication if the following statements are true ...`
- `...my users are coming from the extranet`
- `...the user is part of the finance group`
- `...the user is accessing from a non-workplace joined device`
- You can also apply this trigger for all applications to support broad organization policies and security requirements

- You can also use X509 Certificate Authentication, like smart cards or soft certificates

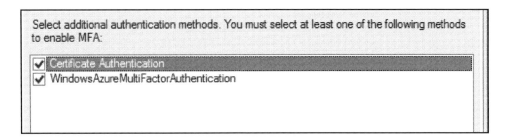

The Extensible Additional Authentication part includes the framework to support Web credential collection from any third-party MFA provider (for example, phone-based or OTP-based MFA systems). This supports challenge-response interaction, and the sign-in experience is consistent with the rest of the AD FS sign-in pages. Additionally, third-party MFA providers can provide additional data to the authentication context for the enrichment of the authentication process.

After discussing authentication methods, we will now jump into the authorization functionality of the AD FS. In AD FS, you can configure authorization policies per application. In detail, you get the chance to permit or deny access to applications based on the user, device, and network location. The following examples can be used:

- We only allow Workplace-joined devices from the extranet to this application
- Only users that are members of a specific security group from the extranet are allowed to access this application

The magic behind this gives you all the necessary tools for conditional Access Control capabilities with the issuance authorization rules.

The following figure shows the placement of the issuance authorization rules in the claims pipeline:

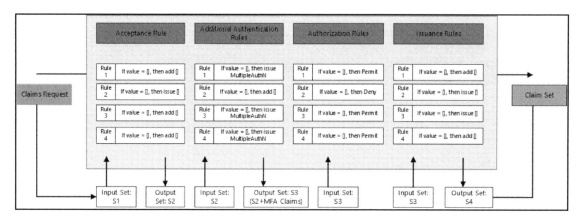

During the authorization process you are also able to provide custom access or deny messages, even per relying party application. This helps the user understand access deny and self-service guidance.

The following PowerShell commands give you an overview of the custom error messages that can be used in your planned environment:

```
Set-AdfsGloblaWebContent -ErrorPageDescriptionText "This is the
identityplus error page description."
Set-AdfsGlobalWebContent -ErrorPageGenericErrorMessage "This is a generic
error message. Contact identityplus IT for assistance. "
Set-AdfsGlobalWebContent -ErrorPageAuthorizationErrorMessage "You have
received an Authorization error. Contact identityplus IT for assistance. "
Set-AdfsGlobalWebContent -ErrorPageDeviceAuthenticationErrorMessage "Your
device is not authorized. Contact identityplus IT for assistance. Or
directly register your device. "
Set-AdfsGlobalWebContent -ErrorPageSupportEmail
"servicedesk@identityplus.ch"
Set-AdfsRelyingPartyWebContent -Name fedpassive -
ErrorPageAuthorizationErrorMessage "<p> You need to be a member of HR group
to access this site. Click <A
href='http://accessrequests.identityplus.ch/'>here</A> for more
information. </p> "
```

# The magic of claims rules for application access

Before we start investigating the different scenarios and configuration options, we will use a brief claims rule language example. If the claims pipeline includes a claim of type `firstname` and a claim of type `lastname`, concatenate them and issue the result as a claim of type `name`:

```
c1:[type == "http://example/firstname"] && c2:[type ==
"http://example/lastname"] => issue(Type = "http://example/name", Value =
c1.value+" "+c2.value);
```

**Practical note**

If you are not familiar with claim rules, we highly recommend visiting the following link at `http://bit.ly/1qAwjHt` to get an in-depth look into the claims rule language.

You can also use the claims rule wizard with the provided templates for common claim rules. Some scenarios require custom rules constructed with the claims rule language, which can permit the:

- Modification of claim values
- Concatenation of claim values
- Conditional claim issuance
- And much more

The following examples give you a starting point of practical usage scenarios:

- **Scenario 1:** Validating user identity with MFA

```
@RuleTemplate = "Authorization"
@RuleName = "UserValidationWithMFA"
c:[Type == "http://schemas.microsoft.com/claims/authnmethodsreferences",
Value =~ "^(?i)http://schemas\.microsoft\.com/claims/multipleauthn$"] =>
issue(Type = "http://schemas.microsoft.com/authorization/claims/permit",
Value = "PermitUsersWithClaim");
```

- **Scenario 2:** Validating a user via Workplace Join

```
@RuleTemplate = "Authorization"
@RuleName = "ValidateUserViaWorkplaceJoinedDevice"
c:[Type ==
"http://schemas.microsoft.com/2012/01/devicecontext/claims/isregistereduser
", Value =~ "^(?i)true$"] => issue(Type =
"http://schemas.microsoft.com/authorization/claims/permit", Value =
"PermitUsersWithClaim");
```

- **Scenario 3:** Permitting access with Workplace Join and MFA validation

```
@RuleTemplate = "Authorization"
@RuleName = "MFAOnRegisteredWorkplaceJoinedDevice"
c1:[Type == "http://schemas.microsoft.com/claims/authnmethodsreferences",
Value =~ "^(?i)http://schemas\.microsoft\.com/claims/multipleauthn$"] &&
c2:[Type ==
"http://schemas.microsoft.com/2012/01/devicecontext/claims/isregistereduser
", Value =~ "^(?i)true$"] => issue(Type =
"http://schemas.microsoft.com/authorization/claims/permit", Value =
"PermitUsersWithClaim");
```

- **Scenario 4:** Extranet access with MFA user validation

```
@RuleTemplate = "Authorization"
@RuleName = "MFAForExtranetAccess"
c1:[Type == "http://schemas.microsoft.com/claims/authnmethodsreferences",
Value =~ "^(?i)http://schemas\.microsoft\.com/claims/multipleauthn$"] &&
c2:[Type ==
"http://schemas.microsoft.com/ws/2012/01/insidecorporatenetwork", Value =~
"^(?i)false$"] => issue(Type =
"http://schemas.microsoft.com/authorization/claims/permit", Value =
"PermitUsersWithClaim");
```

You can also create a custom MFA trigger using PowerShell:

Consider a scenario where you want to trigger MFA based on a specific group.

First, we need to get the SID of the specific group. In our example, this is the **Sales** group.

```
Administrator: Windows PowerShell
PS C:\Users\administrator.IDAM> Get-ADGroup sales


DistinguishedName : CN=Sales,OU=Managed Business Objects,DC=idam,DC=ch
GroupCategory     : Distribution
GroupScope        : Universal
Name              : Sales
ObjectClass       : group
ObjectGUID        : 239271ad-1e63-4ccb-972f-b6936ca3a28a
SamAccountName    : Sales
SID               : S-1-5-21-3123384963-3601710319-2843089171-2145
```

```
$rp = Get-AD FSRelyingPartyTrust -Name "SharePoint"
$GroupMfaClaimTriggerRule = 'c:[Type ==
"http://schemas.microsoft.com/ws/2008/06/identity/claims/groupsid", Value
=~ "^(?i) S-1-5-21-3123384963-3601710319-2843089171-2145$"] => issue(Type =
"http://schemas.microsoft.com/ws/2008/06/identity/claims/authenticationmeth
od", Value = "http://schemas.microsoft.com/claims/multipleauthn");'

Set-AD FSRelyingPartyTrust -TargetRelyingParty $rp -
AdditionalAuthenticationRules $GroupMfaClaimTriggerRule
```

The last practical example we want to provide is very common for Office 365:

- Bring the relying party information in a variable:

```
$rp = Get-AD FSRelyingPartyTrust -Name "Microsoft Office 365 Identity
Platform"
```

  - Identify the group that triggers MFA, for example, this is the `Finance` group in our environment:

```
$groupMfaClaimTriggerRule = 'c:[Type ==
"http://schemas.microsoft.com/ws/2008/06/identity/claims/groupsid", Value
=~ "^(?i) S-1-5-21-3123384963-3601710319-2843089171-2188$"] => issue(Type =
"http://schemas.microsoft.com/ws/2008/06/identity/claims/authenticationmeth
od", Value = "http://schemas.microsoft.com/claims/multipleauthn");'
```

- Set the new rule:

```
Set-AD FSRelyingPartyTrust -TargetRelyingParty $rp -
AdditionalAuthenticationRules $groupMfaClaimTriggerRule
```

**Design note**
The default MFA behavior for federated Azure AD/Office 365 tenants is set to authenticate against the Azure MFA service and not to the on premise instance of your MFA server.

To perform MFA to your On-Premise MFA server, you need to fire the following PowerShell command:

```
Set-MsolDomainFederationSettings -DomainName <domain name> -SupportsMFA
$true
```

If `SupportsMFA` is set to true, Azure AD will redirect the user to AD FS for MFA if MFA is required and a claim of type `http://schemas.microsoft.com/claims/authnmethodsreferences` with the value `http://schemas.microsoft.com/claims/multipleauthn`, which is the so-called MFA claim, is missing.

We highly recommend activating additional risk mitigation features that will help you achieve the following functionality:

- Soft account lockout for extranet access
- Setting password lockout policy for extranet logins
- `Badpwdcount` count increase for bad passwords
- Users locked-out of extranet login until reset
- Independent of AD DS password lockout mechanism
- Protecting DOS or DDOS attacks from AD DS account lockout
- Protecting against extranet brute force password guessing

Set this protection level using the Windows PowerShell for the AD FS module:

```
Set-AdfsProperties -ExtranetLockoutEnabled: $true
Set-AdfsProperties -ExtranetLockoutThreshold 3
Set-AdfsProperties -ExtranetObservationWindows: (new-timespan - Minutes 30)
Get-AdfsProperties | Select-Object *extranet* | fl
```

Another valuable feature that you should think about is `Password Expiration Notifications`. You can enable a notification regarding expiring passwords within the Office Portal and its applications. The only thing you need to do is to add password expiration claims in the token. With the following issuance rule for Azure Active Directory/Office 365 relying party trusts, you will activate the function:

```
c1:[Type ==
"http://schemas.microsoft.com/ws/2012/01/passwordexpirationtime"]
=> issue(store = "_PasswordExpiryStore", types =
("http://schemas.microsoft.com/ws/2012/01/passwordexpirationtime",
"http://schemas.microsoft.com/ws/2012/01/passwordexpirationdays",
"http://schemas.microsoft.com/ws/2012/01/passwordchangeurl"), query =
"{0};", param = c1.Value);
```

Additionally, you can enable the `Password Update Feature` in AD FS so that users will be informed about the expiring state of their password. They can then change their password over the AD FS capabilities, which can be activated with the following tasks:

- AD FS – enables the Password Update function
- Restart AD FS on every node when enabled
- Restart WAP on every node when enabled at proxy

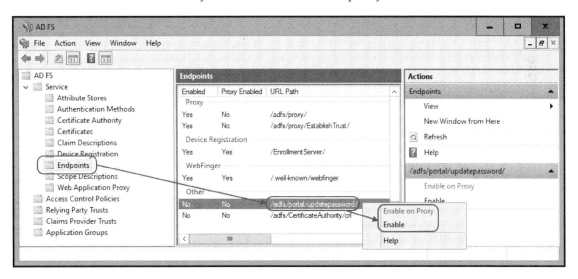

In the next section, we will discuss a few new AD FS 4.0 features in the new Windows Server 2016.

# Delivering authentication and authorization improvements with Windows Server 2016

For Microsoft, and the hybrid vision AD FS, Windows Server 2016 plays a key role in the whole IAM strategy. It's critical to the overall success of Azure Stack and the hybrid identity. This takes us to the point of the new feature sets of AD FS 4.0, which you can include in your design considerations. Additionally, we will provide more in-depth insights in a later, special chapter dedicated to the new features of Windows Server 2016.

## Features overview

The AF FS provides the following extensions to the identity and access management framework:

- Comprehensive Authentication, supporting multiple stores with additional security controls for MFA
- Enhanced Conditional Access, supporting MDM capabilities for conditional Access Control
- Modern applications – REST based services support with OAuth
- Enhanced Sign-In experience – a rich and flexible set of customization options in special per relying party
- Simplified deployment – more scripts and guidance, particularly in the rule sets

## LDAP authentication

One of the main changes or features that often come back is the authentication capability to LDAPv3 directories. The details are:

- Each LDAP directory is modelled as another CPT, like Active Directory
- Each directory shows up as another claims provider in the HRD for passive authentication

- They augment claims for a user after authentication by modifying claims provider rules
- They can restrict the scope of directory-based OU
- Login IDs can be of any attribute
- An untrusted AD forest can be modelled as an LDAP directory

# Azure MFA integration

Another feature that will also be directly included is the built-in Azure MFA adapter.

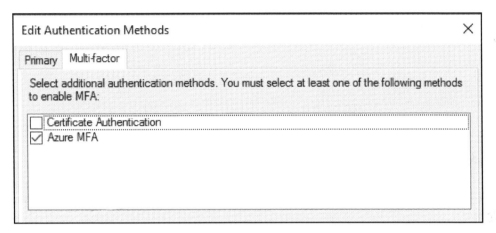

Following are features of Azure MFA integration:

- No requirement for deploying and managing MFA server
- Bootstrap with Azure AD Credentials
- Eliminate extranet passwords using MFA

You can gather or set the Azure MFA with the following PowerShell commands:

```
Get-AdfsAzureMfaConfigured
Set-AdfsAzureMfaTenant
```

In the case of device authentication, there has been an improvement: device authentication will be supported as primary authentication, in detail, this means:

- Simpler sign-in from compliant devices
- In Windows, the certificate is available from browser and store apps
- iOS browser apps due to app containerization
- Android devices will have prompting experience
- An elimination scenario for intranet username/password combinations

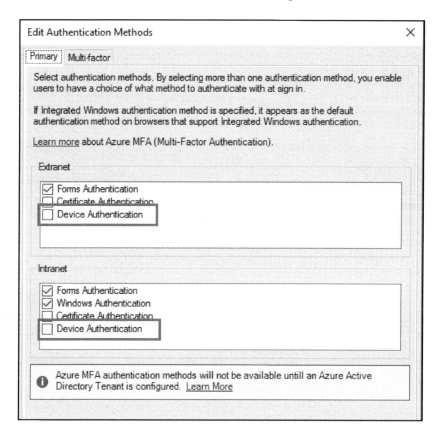

# AD certificate proxy authentication

The next improvement provides a usage scenario, which we were waiting for for a long time. That is, a complete single sign-on in a VM session is possible. AD FS 4.0 solves this issue with an AD certificate proxy authentication, which also enables:

- The usage of conditional access to VPN servers on Windows 10 devices
- Hybrid scenarios where cloud services can talk to on-premises services as the user with KCD requirement

So, how does it work?

- AD FS acts as a registration authority in two modes
- It integrates in an existing ADCS PKI infrastructure
- AD FS can act as a CA trusted by AD FS

---

⦿ **Standalone mode: AD FS issues certificates**

Certificates for user logon and VPN access are issued by AD FS. This option is suitable for organizations that do not have an enterpise public key infrastructure set up.

○ **Enrollment agent mode: AD FS requests certificates from Enterprise CA**

AD FS requests an enterprise CA running Active Directory Certificate Services (AD CS) to issue certificates for user logon and VPN access. This option is suitable for organizations that have an existing public key infrastructure and require all certificates to be issued by the CA.

---

- Specific certificate templates are provided:
- The client makes a call to AD FS through the OAuth extension to request a certificate

- Confidential clients provide an AD FS token for the user and gets back a certificate
- A public client logs in the user and gets a certificate as token response

# Access control policies

Furthermore, with AD FS 4.0 we also see big changes in the field of access control policies, which are a replacement for issuance authorization rules.

The following options can be used:

- Security groups
- Networks (inside, outside, and IP range)
- Device trust level (authenticated, managed, and compliant)
- Required MFA

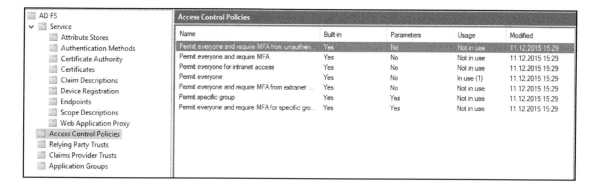

The new rule editor will help many administrators configure Access Control in a much easier way:

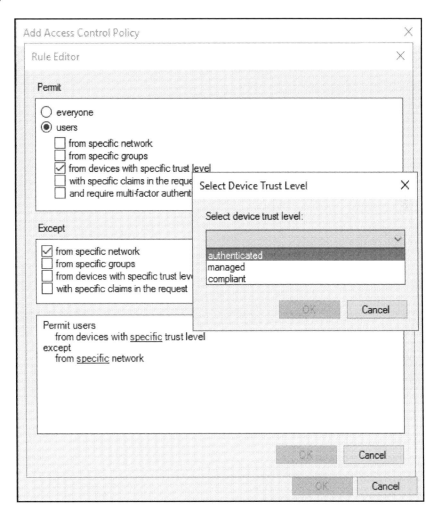

# OAuth 2.0 and Open ID Connect

Furthermore, AD FS 4.0 also now supports OAuth 2.0 and OpenID Connect in a highly-available manner to enable complete modern application development:

The following are OAuth 2.0 improvements:

- Windows Server 2012 R2 support
- Authorization code grant for public clients only

AD FS 4.0 provides the following additional profiles:

- Implicit flow to support single page applications (for example, Angular.js)
- Resource-owner passwords for scripting applications
- OBO Support
- Enabling of multi-tier applications to pass on user context to backend services
- Tokens
- ID token support
- Confidential clients
- Symmetric key, asymmetric key, and Windows accounts
- Secure device authentication Support using PKeyAuth
- Protection of tokens and refresh tokens against roaming attacks
- Avoidance of TLS where device certificate prompts are clunky

The following are the OpenID Connect improvements:

- Enabled apps (for example, MVC) now with web-frontend as well as Web-API backend
- Return of authorization codes to web applications, which are exchanged for tokens and refresh tokens
- Support for OpenID Connect Discovery
- Scopes, which defines a resource group within an application
- Permissions: assignment of scopes for 'client' to access 'service' application

Additional improvements are as follows:

- Mixed farm support for upgrading from 2012 R2 to 2016 AD FS
- Just *join* Windows Server 2016 to the farm and the farm acts in a *compatible mode*
- Validation of existing functionality and addition of more nodes as required
- Removal of legacy nodes and upgrading of the farm version
- Support of roll-back
- Configuration of new AD FS 4.0 features
- Delegated service management
- Audit enhancements
- AD FS support for Windows 10
- User Certificate Authentication: 443
- AD FS backlog
- And much more

**Reader note**
You will find more information at the following: `http://bit.ly/1RY7wUz`

# Web Application Proxy in Windows Server 2016

Now that we have given you a short introduction to the new AD FS 4.0 features, we need to take a look into the reverse publishing functionality of the WAP in Windows Server 2016 in order to close your design gaps with the full combination of AD FS and WAP. With Windows Server 2012 R2, we were limited in publishing applications in the case of the different AD FS pre-authentication mechanisms.

Windows Server 2016 provides the following additional AD FS pre-authentication types to Windows Server 2012 R2:

- **Web and MSOFBA**: Rich web applications and Microsoft Office clients
- **HTTP Basic**: Exchange ActiveSync
- **OAuth2**: Windows Store Applications and Microsoft Office clients

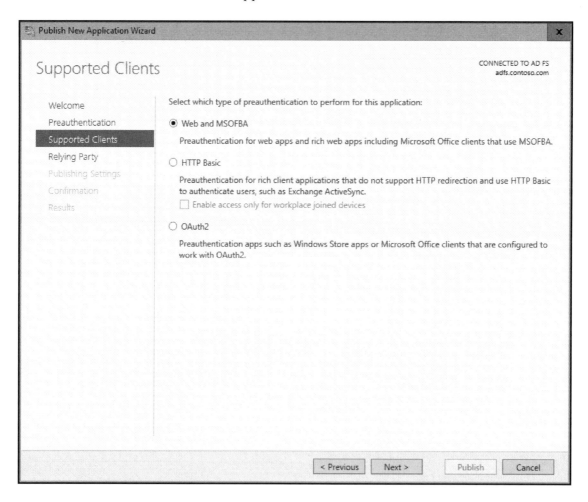

In addition to the new authentication types, we can now receive the HTTP to HTTPS redirect capabilities that were missing in Windows Server 2012 R2 in order to address a good user experience without typing `https://` in front of the application address.

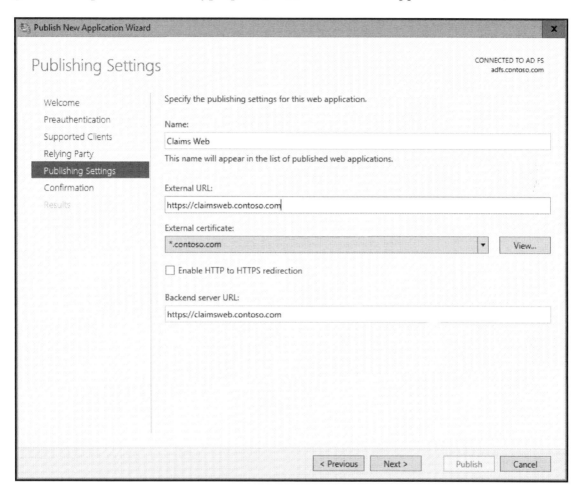

**Reader note**

We are still limited by pages and cannot describe every change in this book. You will find detailed information about this topic at the following link: `http://bit.ly/1peKv6A`. Furthermore, we will provide some more configuration examples in the following implementation chapters.

# Enabling advanced application Access Control

In the following section we will provide you with some design ideas to include in your on premise identity management system to prepare for an advanced application Access Control. We are often asked by our customers how they can manage access to applications both on premise and in the cloud, for example, SaaS.

## Usage of MIM 2016

For this reason, we will use the capabilities of MIM 2016 or earlier to provide the complex group building scenarios on premise. The groups are commonly based on roles derived from the contract or contracts of an employee. These can be business or application (technical) roles. Other models like **User** | **Role** | **Permission** or **User** | **Enterprise Role(s)** | **Application Role (s)** | **Permissions** are also representative examples of such models that provide the correct permissions to a user account.

We can also use the contract to define the representation of an employee in different repositories or applications with a special type of user account, for example, business user or administrator. The combination of MIM 2016 and the AAD Connect tool helps us to address many different scenarios when provisioning user accounts, managing them and also the associated permissions and groups for application access.

**Design note**
The AAD Connect tool is commonly used for Azure Active Directory-based SaaS applications like Office 365, Dynamics CRM, or others. Third party adoptions can be done directly from MIM 2016.

The following figure illustrates the schema of such a solution:

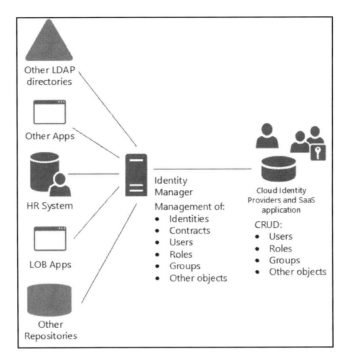

You can use MIM 2016 to manage distribution groups and security groups (whether mail-enabled or not), regardless of the scope: universal, global, or domain local. Furthermore, groups can be configured with more than one owner, and the ability to create groups can be delegated to any set of users within the MIM Portal.

Membership in groups can be managed in several ways:

- **Manual**: Members are manually managed
- **Manager**: Members are calculated based on the reporting relationship to a manager
- **Criteria-based**: This is evaluated after the result of any `Create/Update/Delete` operation if the updated resource falls within the scope of the group filter
- **MIM WAL**: Time-limited group membership

You will find a practical guidance at the following link:
`http://bit.ly/1oNsqNX` on how to use the MIM WAL scenario. You will
also find all the capabilities of the WAL at the following link: `http://bit.`
`ly/1Vbw3dl`, which will help you to design and implement many
scenarios.

# Group capabilities

The following figure illustrates the MIM Portal functionality. Often, the creation process is
done by a criteria based on a group builder method, but you are always able to create it
manually.

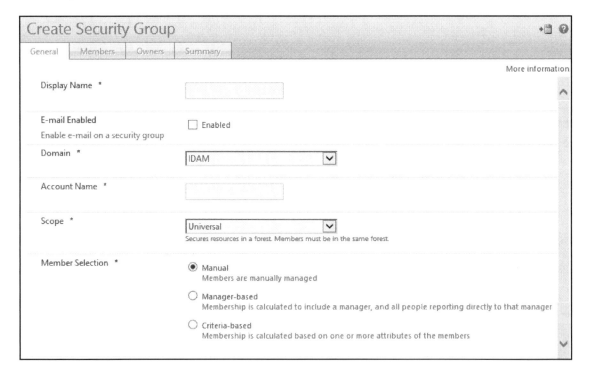

In a manually managed membership, the members are placed into manually managed
groups by the owners of the group, as shown in the following figure. Alternatively, users
can request to join a group. The request is either granted automatically or is subject to
owner approval. The owners are sent an e-mail asking them to approve or reject the request.

In a manager-based membership, a group can also be created that automatically maintains the membership based on who reports to a particular manager. This automatically adds all of the manager's direct reports. If a subsequent import from HR (or another authoritative data source) modifies someone's manager, they are removed from this group and possibly placed in another group. The following figure illustrates that the principal step is to select the manager upon which to base the group. The manager is included in the group as well as their direct reports.

In criteria-based membership, groups based on more advanced criteria can also be created. A criterion is based on attributes and is compared with literal values provided by the group owner. So, a group could be based on the following rule: *Department* is *Sales*. Additional rules can also be included, such as *Department* is *Sales* and *Manager* is not *John Smith*. The following figure illustrates how the filter builder can be used to set up these conditions. Criteria-based groups are one possible approach to RABC with MIM, although criteria-based groups are not by themselves considered as a RBAC solution; the combination of MIM Group Management and BHOLD can provide a more robust and complete solution. Criteria-based groups are extremely powerful methods for controlling group membership by ensuring only people that meet specific criteria receive sensitive emails, in addition to ensuring that only specific people have the necessary permissions to access resources in AD.

With this idea of bringing groups and user accounts based on roles to your identity repositories and applications, you can solve your whole application access requirements. For the following example, we will use a scenario with Azure Active Directory as the identity provider:

# Getting in touch with information protection

In the following section, we will dive into advanced Access Control for information on protection solutions.

## Overview and needs

There was an interesting presentation from Dan Plastina, a product manager at Microsoft, which asked a very important question: 'Why do you seek to protect information?' The following answers were given in an actual survey:

- 96% – Reduce leakage of data shared with others (B2B collaboration)
- 94% – Partitioning of sensitive data from unauthorized users
- 89% – Preventing malicious employees from leaking secrets
- 87% – Meeting compliance requirements

Exactly because of these needs, we need to think about an information protection strategy in our solution design in order to provide the following:

- Persistent protection level independent from your storage solution
- Permit all companies to authenticate and to enforce authorization policies
- Provide tracking and compliance with powerful logging for reporting, including end user use/abuse tracking
- The ability to remotely remove permissions on documents
- Enabling IT to reason over data
- Success across all platforms with a free content consumption
- Ease of use with a consistent user experience
- Integrated common apps/services
- The information protection solution from Microsoft or the RMS is an established product line available on premise and in the cloud as Azure RMS. The solution itself ensures security because sensitive data is never sent to the RMS server.

Typical use cases for RMS are as follows:

- Control of sensitive email flow, internally, across all devices
- Sharing an Office file with external users
- Board of Directors email communications
- Document use tracking, abuse detection, and revocation
- B2C secure email (and replies)
- Control over the downloading of files stored in SharePoint
- Securing reports generated from SAP
- Protecting files on a user's `Documents` folder and file share
- Sharing CAD drawings, redacted PDFs, and analyst reports

# Deployment models

- Microsoft provides the following deployment models for integrating the RMS in your environment:

| Deployment Scenario | Identity Components | RMS Components |
| --- | --- | --- |
| Cloud Only with Azure RMS | Azure AD | Azure RMS |
| Hybrid Identity with Azure RMS | Azure AD, On-Premises AD, Azure AD Sync, (Optional) AD FS | Azure RMS |
| On-Premises only with AD RMS | On-Premises AD | On-Premises AD RMS |
| Cross-Premises with Azure RMS | Azure AD, On-Premises AD, Azure AD Sync, (Optional) AD FS | Azure RMS, RMS Connector |

**Future planning**

In addition to these deployment scenarios, Microsoft plans to provide a parallel RMS Server model so that you can use your on premise and cloud rights management services at the same time. This will solve customer issues with security requirements and policies.

With RMS, you solve the issues with the changing perimeter in your environment, because with RMS the protection level of the information moves with your data, as you can see in the following figure:

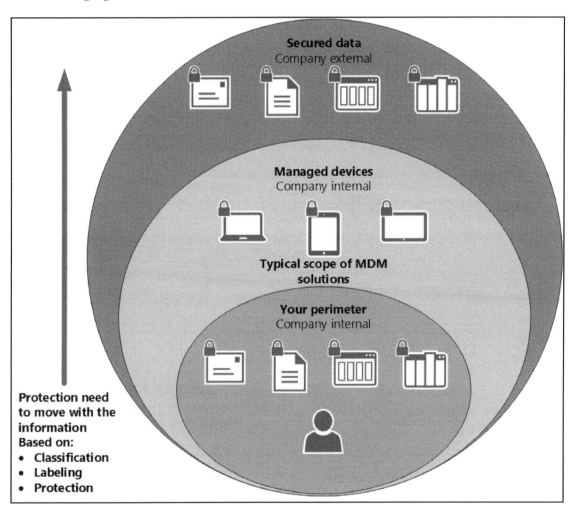

# On-Premise deployment model

The On-premise deployment model is often chosen to hold the complete security solution inside the own datacenter. Furthermore, the Solution Developer Kit allows third parties to extend the functionality with a rich set of features.

The On-Premises deployment scenario uses the AD RMS server role to provide the Microsoft RMS. The solution contains an RMS Cluster with RMS services and a database backend provided by an SQL Server instance normally deployed as cluster.

The following features are complex and sometimes require a third party:

- Extensible reporting
- Collaboration with third parties
- Mobile device support
- Document tracking
- Support for MFA

# Cross-premises deployment model

The cross-premises deployment model with Azure RMS combines flexibility and a rich set of functionality. In particular, the solution is based on a service with SLAs. Compared to the On-premise solution, the organization doesn't need to worry about the high availability of software components such as the RMS service cluster and the SQL database server. The missing capabilities from the On-Premises deployment scenario are already in place with the standard functionality of the Azure RMS service. It is exactly this deployment that we want to discuss as a starting point before moving into the RMA.

We will extend this solution with BYOK capabilities in later complex hybrid scenarios:

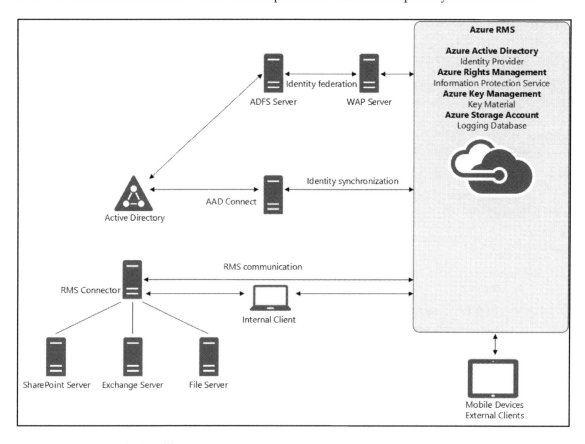

The following components are used in this integration scenario:

| Component | Description |
| --- | --- |
| Directory Service | Directory Service to authenticate users who participate in the RMS environment. |
| Azure AD Connect | Your organization must have an Azure AD to support user authentication for RMS. In addition, if you want to use your user accounts from your On-Premises directory (AD DS), you must also configure directory integration with the AAD Connect tool. |
| AD FS | To provide users with the most seamless authentication experience as they access Microsoft cloud services while logged on to the corporate network. In order to set up single sign-on, organizations need to deploy a security token service On-Premises, such as AD FS. |
| Microsoft Azure AD Premium | To use Azure RMS, you must have Azure AD Premium subscription. You can find more information on this at `http://bit.ly/1Niatxj` |
| Microsoft Azure Storage Account | RMS logging is enabled by default; for more information visit: `http://bit.ly/2atXZpd`. |
| RMS Enabled Application | Users must run applications that support RMS. For more information, see the applications that support Azure RMS section in this chapter. |
| RMS Client | Users must have a client device (computer or mobile device) that runs an operating system that supports RMS. For more information, see the client devices that support Azure RMS section in this chapter. One example is a client with the RMS sharing application installed. |

We often use the identity bridge to provide and implement these different components. An identity bridge contains the following components in a redundant way:

- **AD FS** – Provides federation to enable collaboration functionality
- **WAP including AD FS proxy** – Provides protection level for AD FS
- **AAD Connect** – Identity synchronization for collaboration and usage of Azure RMS
- **RMS Connector** – On-Premise Exchange, SharePoint, and Fileserver integration

To give you an idea of the infrastructure components in a high-availability scenario, we use the following figure:

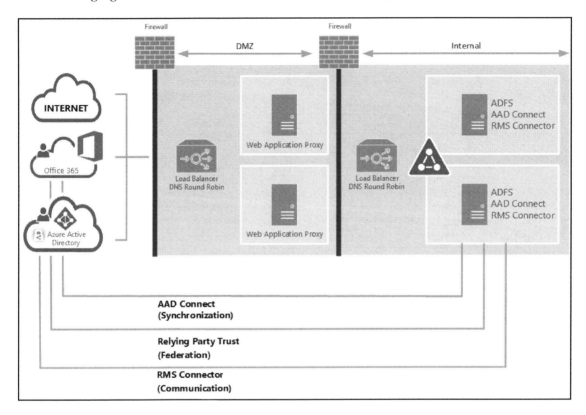

 The second AAD Connect instance is configured in staging mode.

# Important user attributes and information

In such a deployment, we are always asked which attributes are synchronized to the Azure Active Directory.

# Synchronization considerations

With the new features of the AAD Connect tool we can configure the minimum set of attributes that work with Azure RMS. The following attributes of a user will be synchronized in order to use Azure RMS:

| Attribute Name | User | Contact | Group | Comment |
|---|---|---|---|---|
| accountEnabled | X | | | Defines if an account is enabled. |
| cn | X | | X | Common name or alias. Most often the prefix of [mail] value. |
| displayName | X | X | X | A string that represents the name often shown as the friendly name (first name last name). |
| mail | X | X | X | full email address. |
| member | | | X | |
| objectSID | X | | X | mechanical property. AD user identifier used to maintain sync between Azure AD and AD. |
| proxyAddresses | X | X | X | mechanical property. Used by Azure AD. Contains all secondary email addresses for the user. |
| pwdLastSet | X | | | mechanical property. Used to know when to invalidate already issued tokens. |
| securityEnabled | | | X | Derived from groupType. |
| sourceAnchor | X | X | X | mechanical property. Immutable identifier to maintain relationship between ADDS and Azure AD. |
| usageLocation | X | | | mechanical property. The user's country. Used for license assignment. |
| userPrincipalName | X | | | This UPN is the login ID for the user. Most often the same as [mail] value. |

# User principal name considerations

You also need to be aware of your user principal name configuration in your environment. The following information is relevant to your UPN design:

- UPN requirements:
    - Must only contain letters, numbers, periods, dashes, and underscores
    - Must be known by users
    - Domain suffix must be under the domain chosen for SSO
- UPN alignment:
    - UPN domain selected to federate must be registered as a public domain
    - The required change of UPNs is in on premise Active Directory domains

An alternate login ID is a way of achieving UPN alignment without having to modify the UPN attribute of user accounts (AAD Connect – Synchronization scenario)

- Limitations of the alternate login ID are as follows:
    - No usage in an exchange hybrid online deployment
    - Current Azure AD Connect deploys with synchronized objects; this needs to change the UPN of every user account
    - Kerberos-based SSO no longer works for applications that rely on the Sign-in Assistant, for example, S4B or OD4B
    - Azure AD Application Proxy and Kerberos Constrained Delegation requires UPN match between Azure AD and on premise Active Directory

# Azure RMS

The Azure RMS core component feature provides the following functionality within the Azure Rights Management Service:

- Administration
- Account certification
- Licensing

Azure RMS Service is a web service providing the core RMS services and functionality, including administration, account certification, and licensing. Certification refers to the account certification and activation activities performed by Azure RMS. Each user must acquire a set of certificates that identity that particular user to be able to participate in the Azure RMS platform. Licensing refers to the set of operations by which the Azure RMS service grants access to protected content to authorized users. The Azure RMS service grants a use license for each document to authorized users. The Azure RMS service also exposes **Simple Object Access Protocol** (**SOAP**) interfaces used by clients to interact with Azure RMS. Azure RMS is an Azure service that provides information protection by using encryption and policy to help secure documents, files, and emails. The Azure RMS service provides the following functionality:

# Certification service

Certification refers to the account certification and activation activities performed by Azure RMS. Each user must acquire a set of certificates that identity that particular user to be able to participate in the Azure RMS platform.

# Licensing service

Licensing refers to the set of operations by which the Azure RMS Service grants access to protected content to authorized users. The Azure RMS Service grants a use license for each document to authorized users.

# Rights policy templates

Rights policy templates specify a predefined set of rights and conditions that can be applied to protected content, simplifying the RMS Protection for common or daily-use scenarios to the end-users. Azure RMS administrators create and manage rights policy templates. When publishing protected content, the author selects the rights policy template to apply from the templates that are available on the local computer. To make rights policy templates available for use, the administrator must deploy them to user computers or the client computer should have access to a shared folder. When a user attempts to consume content protected through a template, the Azure RMS Service retrieves the latest version of the rights policy template that was used to publish the content from the configuration database and issues a license based on that template.

# Azure RMS trusts

In Azure RMS, trust relationships are implied with any other organization supported by Azure Active Directory, including users with Office 365 or using RMS for individuals. Users can collaborate with external parties who have Azure Active Directory without the need to configure a trust relationship. Note that this trust relationship provides the ability to collaborate; it does not automatically grant external users access to protected content. External users must be explicitly mentioned in the permission policy.

# High availability

RMS Service – Azure RMS is delivered as a Windows Azure service and is therefore subject to the 99.9% uptime Windows Azure Service Level Agreement. Therefore, there is no action required to make the Azure Rights Management Service highly-available.

RMS Connector – For most purposes, joining one or more RMS Connector servers to a cluster is the recommended way to increase the availability and redundancy of your deployment. To achieve high availability, create two or more instances of the RMS Connector, define a connection URL server name and configure a load balancing system. The connector URL can be any name under a namespace that you control. There are no special requirements for this name and it does not need to be configured on the connector servers themselves. This name does not have to resolve on the Internet unless the Exchange, SharePoint, or FCI servers are going to be communicating with the connector over the Internet.

Once the name is created in DNS and is configured for an IP address, configure load balancing for that address. You can use any IP-based load balancer for this purpose, including the **Network Load Balancing (NLB)** feature in Windows Server. Use the following settings to configure the NLB cluster:

- Ports: 80 (for HTTP) or 443 (for HTTPS)
- Affinity: None
- Distribution method: Equal

AAD Connect – Azure AD Connect is the first part of the identity bridge to integrate the cloud identity and access management. The main functionality of this tool is to synchronize identities to the cloud. MIM 2016 is also able to do this with the Azure AD Management Agent. Be aware that this will only be supported until the merger of the synchronization engines is complete.

Azure AD Connect Health – This offers you the ability to view alerts, performance, usage patterns, and configuration settings and enables you to maintain a reliable connection to Office 365 and much more. This is accomplished using an agent that is installed on the targeted servers. Azure AD Connect Health for AD FS supports AD FS 2.0 in Windows Server 2008/2008 R2 and AD FS in Windows Server 2012/2012R2. These also include any AD FS proxies or WAP servers that provide authentication support for extranet access. Remember, for AAD Connect the agent is included in the installation binaries. Azure AD Connect Health for AD FS provides the following set of key capabilities:

- Viewing and taking action on alerts for reliable access to AD FS-protected applications, including Azure AD
- Email notifications for critical alerts
- Viewing performance data to determine capacity planning
- Detailed views of your AD FS login patterns to determine anomalies or establish baselines for capacity planning

AD FS – The AD FS is the second part of the identity bridge and the main capability it provides is federation. This service is required to build SSO to your Azure AD and the associated SaaS applications. AD FS can also be used for integrated partners or social identities without Azure AD.

# Azure rights management key material

By default, Azure RMS generates the tenant key and manages most aspects of the tenant key lifecycle. This is the simplest option with the lowest administrative overheads. In most cases, organizations do not even need to know that they have a tenant key. They just sign up for Azure RMS and the rest of the key management process is handled by Microsoft.

Alternatively, organizations might want complete control over their tenant key, which involves creating a tenant key and storing the master copy on-premises in an HSM. This scenario is often referred to as BYOK. BYOK is out of scope for the **Pilot** design and implementation.

# Hardware security modules

The following sections discuss the various considerations around the benefits of using HSM with Azure RMS in the BYOK scenario. HSM are physical devices that provide a hardened, tamper-resistant environment for management and secure storage for digital keys used in Azure RMS and other applications. Microsoft requires the sole use of Thales HSMs to guarantee compliance with Microsoft datacenters. Additionally, the use of HSMs at the outset of the Azure RMS deployment is required. HSMs provide organizations the ability to securely manage their private keys On-Premises. The following table provides a summary of the benefits of implementing a Thales HSM in the Azure RMS deployment:

| Benefit | Description |
|---|---|
| Secure Key Storage | HSMs provide a tamper-resistant environment for the storage of private keys. All Thales HSMs are certified to meet the highest security standards. |
| Compliance | HSMs are FIPS 140-2 Level 3 Standard, the most widely accepted benchmark for hardware security in both enterprise and government environments. |
| Extensibility | Using a Thales HSM for key storage allows the Azure RMS environment to be extensible to On-Premises per a future migration. Microsoft uses solely Thales HSMs for key storage in Azure RMS, therefore, a Thales HSM is required for Azure RMS. |

The following prerequisites are required to support the BYOK scenario:

| Requirement | Details |
|---|---|
| Thales HSM and associated components | Only Thales HSMs can be used in the BYOK scenario. The Thales nShield Connect, nShield Solo, or nShield Edge can be used in the BYOK scenario To deploy the BYOK scenario you should have basic operational knowledge of Thales HSMs. |
| A subscription that supports Azure RMS | Note that you cannot use BYOK with the RMS for individuals offering or exchange online. |
| Offline x64 workstation* | Not required if you travel to Redmond and transfer your key in person. Windows 7 or later. Thales nShield software version 11.50 or later. |
| Online workstation* | Not required if you travel to Redmond and transfer your key in person. Windows 7 or later. |

# Azure Rights Management Super User

The Azure RMS Super Users feature provides the following functionality within Azure RMS:

- Full control over all rights-protected content that is managed by Rights Management
- Full owner rights to Super Users for all use licenses that are issued by the subscriber organization
- Decryption of any rights-protected content file and removal of rights-protection from it for content previously protected within that organization

Typically, this level of access is required for legal eDiscovery and by auditing teams. This functionality needs to be manually enabled.

 Individual users and groups can be on the Super User list. RMS Super User can be configured with a PowerShell `cmdlet`. Find more information on this at `http://bit.ly/2aPopqD`.

# Azure Rights Management templates

RMS supports two protection options:

- Ad Hoc Protection with single-use permissions defined manually by the document author
- Right Policy Templates with centrally-defined policies

Rights policy templates specify a predefined set of rights and conditions that can be applied to protected content, simplifying the RMS Protection for common or daily-use scenarios to the end-users. Azure RMS administrators create and manage rights policy templates. When publishing protected content, the author selects the rights policy template to apply from the templates that are available on the local computer. To make rights policy templates available for use, the administrator must deploy them to user computers or the client computer should have access to a shared folder.

When a user attempts to consume content protected through a template, the Azure RMS Service retrieves the latest version of the rights policy template that was used to publish the content from the configuration database and issues a license based on that template.

Azure RMS contains two default Rights Policy Templates that are available to all end users in the tenant immediately upon the activation of the Azure RMS service. These rights policy templates are as follows:

- `tenant name - Confidential`: This template grants permission to view and edit content to internal users and denies the right to copy or print.
- `tenant name - Confidential Read Only`: This template grants permission to view content to internal users and denies the right to copy, edit, print, or save

For many organizations, the default templates might be sufficient.

Templates are typically defined to:

- Limit usage of protected information to different employee levels and roles
- Scope content to different organizations and departments
- Reflect different data classifications based on business impact
- Reflect different data classifications based on specific content such as PII or intellectual property
- Scope content to audiences such as full time employees, contractors, partners, etc.

The following usage rights are available:

| Option | Values |
|---|---|
| Rights | Viewer<br>Reviewer<br>Co-Author<br>Co-Owner<br>Custom (view content, save file, edit content, copy and extract content, view assigned rights, change rights, allow macros, export content (save as), print, forward, reply, reply all, and full control) |
| Content expiration | Content never expires<br>Content expires (date)<br>After the content is protected, content expires after the specified number of days |
| Offline access | Content is available only with an Internet connection<br>Content is always available<br>Number of days the content is available without an Internet connection |

**Recommendation**
Do not design policies with restrictions that are too granular. Instead, start with simple policies. The biggest business impact comes from preventing data leakage by applying the default rights policy template that restricts access to people in an organization. Start small and step by step, create new policy templates based on classification cards.

# Logging services

The Azure RMS logging service feature provides the following functionality within Azure RMS:

- Logging all user's activity in Azure RMS, including requests from users
- Logging actions performed by RMS administrators in the organization
- Logging actions by Microsoft operators to support RMS deployment
- Analyzing for business insights
- Monitoring for abuse
- Performing forensic analysis

**Security and compliance**
A special Microsoft Azure storage account stores all of the Azure RMS logging information. The information that is in this account is sensitive because its disclosure could affect user privacy. See more about the logging services at `http://bit.ly/1TJXNWp`.

# Azure rights management trusts

In Azure RMS, trust relationships are implied with any other organization supported by Azure Active Directory, including users with Office 365 or using RMS for individuals. Users can collaborate with external parties who have Azure Active Directory without the need to configure a trust relationship.

A trust relationship provides the ability to collaborate; it does not automatically grant external users access to protected content. External users must be explicitly mentioned in the permission policy.

# RMS for individuals

RMS for individuals is a free self-service subscription for users in an organization who have been sent sensitive files that have been protected by Microsoft Azure RMS, but they cannot be authenticated because their IT department does not manage an account for them in Azure. In short, with RMS for individuals you're allowing recipients outside your organization to consume RMS protected data.

 These users can sign up for a free work or school account to use with Azure RMS and can download and install the rights management sharing application. As a result, these users can now authenticate to prove that they are the person that the protected files were sent to and can then read the protected files on computers or mobile devices.

# RMS clients and application usage scenarios

The following clients and usage scenarios are ready to go out of the box:

- Windows Word, Excel, PowerPoint, Outlook 2010/2013/2016 – Consumption and protection
- Mac Word, Excel, PowerPoint, Outlook 2016- Consumption and protection
- Windows Universal Word, Excel, PowerPoint, Outlook – Consumption only
- Office 365 Web Word, Excel, PowerPoint, Outlook – Consumption and protection
- iOS Outlook – Consumption and reply
- iOS Word, Excel, PowerPoint – Consumption and protection
- Android Outlook – Consumption and reply

The following features are planned for the future:

- iOS Outlook – Protection, then native SDK usage
- Android Word, Excel, PowerPoint, Outlook – Consumption, then Protection
- Exchange Online – addition of HSM support via Azure RMS 'BYOK'
- SharePoint Online – improved "Maintain permission on download" behavior

# How does authorization and information protection reporting work?

For authorization, and especially for Azure RMS, there is a rich set of reporting capabilities. The full set of reports requires an Azure AD Premium license. The reports are shown in the following manner:

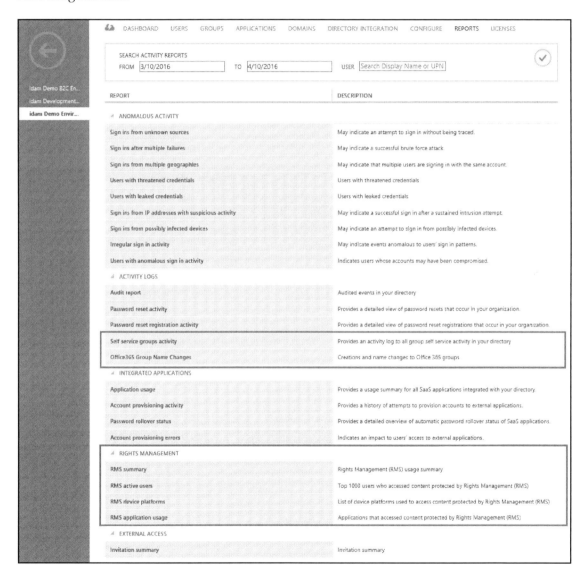

With the installed hybrid reporting agent on your MIM infrastructure, you can view all the details from your Azure AD and your local identity management infrastructure.

Another important feature in the usage of Azure RMS is the Azure RMS tracking website. On this website you can track the usage of your RMS-protected and shared information around the globe. You get also the capability to revoke permissions to a specific document. The Azure RMS tracking feature looks like the following figure:

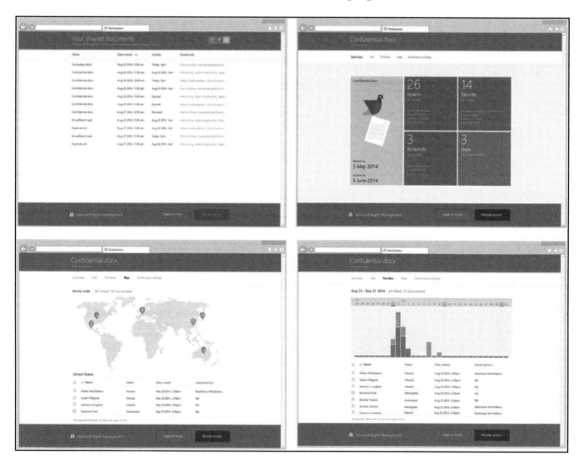

**Practical note**

For privacy considerations, organizations are able to disable the track feature if desired.

If you need to revoke permissions on a specific file, you can just select the option to revoke the permissions. You provide a reason that can be sent as a notification to the user, notifying them that they will not have any further access to the shared data. You will also see a summary declaring that the permissions have been revoked on the Azure RMS tracking website. The following figure illustrates the process:

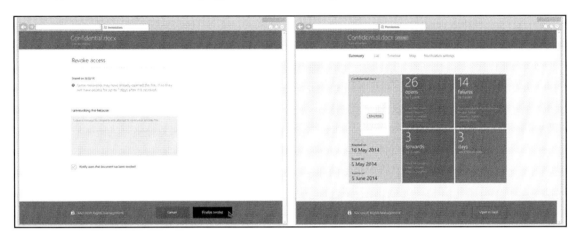

# Summary

In this chapter, we talked about the design of a hybrid access management solution, focusing on the key aspects of authorization and information protection. With this information, you can now apply the required design principles to a risk-based Access Control and information protection strategy, including Azure RMS and the future Windows Server 2016 system. In the next chapter, we will start to implement our own solution. We will focus on the synchronization and federation functionality, group management, and the activation of the MFA.

# 9
# Building Cloud from Common Identities

This chapter will focus on the implementation of a basic hybrid identity and access management solution. You will learn to configure and manage the Identity Synchronization and Federation environment. Furthermore, we will enable Azure MFA to protect cloud applications. Obviously there are many configuration options. We will try to focus at a beginner and professional level at the same time. So you will find some basic step-by-step instructions, and on the other hand configuration notes for advanced options to address the reader's experience. We will extend this lab with various feature configurations and additional virtual machines in the following chapters.

The following are the topics that we are going to go through in this chapter:

- Creating the basic lab environment
- Installing and configuring the Synchronization and Federation environment
- Creating dynamic groups
- Configuring self-service group management
- Implementing secure remote access and SSO for on-premise web applications
- Enabling and configuring Multi-Factor Authentication

# Creating the basic lab environment

At the beginning of the chapter we need to provide an example lab infrastructure to follow the steps we give you. You can use this lab configuration, or your own. If you use your own lab configuration, then it's up to you to make the necessary adjustments. For introduction purposes, we will use Azure IaaS to provide the lab environment, but you can also choose an on premise infrastructure based on your virtualization solution. In this chapter, we will use four virtual machines to demonstrate the installation and configuration steps.

> **Disclaimer**
>
> We will generate the lab on the Azure platform to help you perform tests with a *very cost* -effective solution. You just need a client, an Internet connection, and the trial versions. Obviously this configuration is not recommended for a production environment.

The following diagram shows the expected lab architecture:

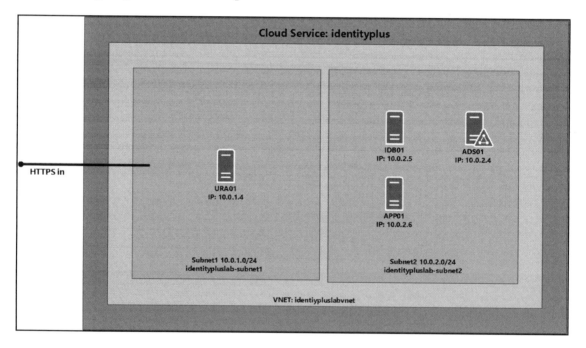

# Virtual machines

The lab contains virtual machines installed on a virtual network with two subnets based on a cloud service in Azure IaaS. The following table describes the virtual machines. We will install three machines by script and one manually so that you know how to extend the lab environment, also so that you are able to choose the method to provide additional machines yourself – by scripts or manually.

 `identityplus.ch` represents the demo suffix; replace it with your public domain name.

| Name | Role | OS | Subnet |
|------|------|-----|--------|
| **ADS01** | Domain Controller | 2012 R2 Data Center | identitypluslabvnet-subnet2(10.0.2.0/24) |
| **APP01** | Application Server | 2012 R2 Data Center | identitypluslabvnet-subnet2(10.0.2.0/24) |
| **IDB01** | Identity Bridge ADFS and AAD Connect | 2012 R2 Data Center | identitypluslabvnet-subnet2(10.0.2.0/24) |
| **URA01** | Unified Remote Access Web Application Proxy | 2012 R2 Data Center | identitypluslabvnet-subnet2(10.0.1.0/24) |

The first important task before starting the lab configuration script is to check the actual Azure subscription and define the default one to use. This task will be done on the virtual machine we used in *Chapter 4, Building and Configuring a Suitable Azure AD* . The next section will explain the additional installations on the Windows 10 client to manage your Azure environment.

# Cloud services

The following cloud services are already registered and used in *Chapter 4*, *Building and Configuring a Suitable Azure AD*. Double-check the services in the Azure Management and Office 365 Portal.

| Service | Purpose |
|---------|---------|
| Enterprise Mobility Suite | Azure Active Directory Premium<br>Azure Rights Management<br>Microsoft Intune |
| Office 365 E3 plan | SaaS applications |
| Azure MSDN or other subscription | IaaS for lab environment and access to the Azure Management |

**Practical note**
If you need to extend your Office 365 trial you can use the following link:
`http://bit.ly/1U7VRqk`.

# Public domain and Azure AD default directory

Before we jump into the installation process, double-check that you have already registered your custom domain. You should have registered the domain in *Chapter 4*, *Building and Configure a Suitable Azure AD*.

| Parameter | Value |
|-----------|-------|
| Public Domain | YourRegisteredDomain, for example, <identityplus.ch> |
| Azure AD Default Directory | YourDefaultDirectory, for example, <identityplus.onmicrosoft.com> |

# Administrative workstation

To prepare the administrative workstation, use the following steps:

1. Login to your Windows 10 client from *Chapter 4*, *Building and Configuring a Suitable Azure AD*.

2. Open an evaluated PowerShell.
3. Install the Azure Resource Manager modules from the PowerShell Gallery:

`Install-Module AzureRM`

4. Install the Azure Service Management module from the PowerShell Gallery:

`Install-Module Azure`

5. `Add-AzureAccount` – Provide your Azure Global Administrator credentials.

6. Next we need to view the actual subscriptions:

```
Get-AzureSubscription
```

7. Next we will use your MSDN or Azure Trial subscription:

```
Select-AzureSubscription -SubscriptionName "Your MSDN subscription" -
Default
```

Check that the subscription you want to use contains the following values: "**IsDefault = true**".

After choosing the correct subscription we will open the script `New-TestLabEnvironment.ps1` from the code package for the book and configure the correct parameters for your environment:

1. Check and modify the script for your needs.
2. Run the script with your customized parameters to start the installation process of the lab environment:

```
.\New-TestLabEnvironment.ps1 -ServiceName "identitypluslab" -Location
"Central US"`
```

The installation process runs approximately 30 – 45 minutes. The script is based on a Microsoft example script. Use the location nearest to you to get the best performance.

# Public SSL certificates

For this and further labs, we need to use public SSL certificate. We highly recommend you request a Wildcard or SAN SSL/TLS certificate. Before we start the certificate request with the following parameters, we need to create a new cloud user with a mailbox to receive the verification information from the certificate provider.

**Practical note**

Don't use **Cryptographic Next Generation** (**CNG**); use a Legacy Cryptographic Service Provider. More information can be found here: `http://bit.ly/2aAUmz5`

Perform the following tasks:

- `Administrator@yourpublicdomainsuffix`
- Enable an Office 365 E3 license

| Certificate property | Value |
| --- | --- |
| Subject | Yourdomainsuffix, for example, *.identityplus.ch |
| **Subject Alternative Name (SAN)** | login.yourdomainsuffix, for example, login.identityplus.ch |
| You need to enter the following additional entries based on your domain suffix: | enterpriseregistration.yourdomainsuffix, for example, enterpriseregistration.identityplus.ch (minimum) claims.identityplus.ch kerb.identityplus.ch workfolders.identityplus.ch mfa.identityplus.ch sps.identityplus.ch exs.identityplus.ch |

For the lab environment you can use an SSL Certificate from Comodo or another public certificate authority.

To create the certificate request you can use the DigiCert utility from the code package:

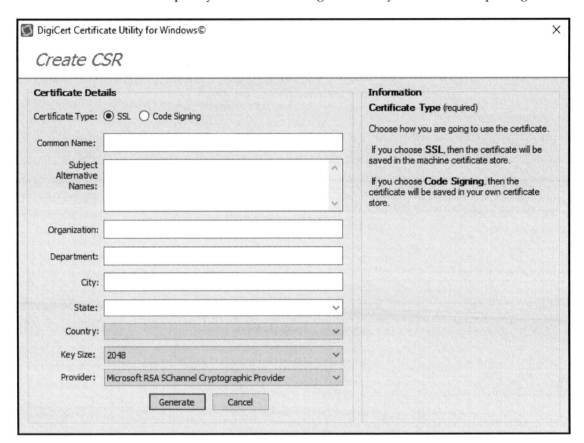

 You cannot use private SSL certificates to successfully enroll mobile devices. You must use a public SSL Certificate, such as one from DigiCert. Device enrollment will give an authentication error if a non-public SSL certificate is used.

After you receive the requested certificate we need to install the certificate in the local machine certificate store, `certlm.msc,` on all the servers in our lab environment.

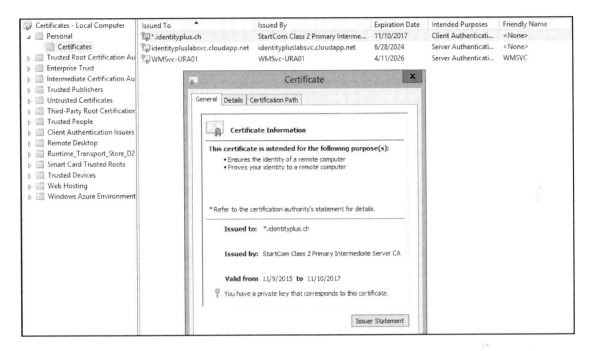

# Internal DNS entries

For the correct name resolution in the lab we need to configure the internal DNS entries:

Modify the values to use your DNS suffix.

```
Add-DnsServerResourceRecord -ZoneName "identityplus.ch" -A -Name "login" -
IPv4Address "10.0.2.5"
Add-DnsServerResourceRecord -ZoneName "identityplus.ch"
-A -Name "claims" -IPv4Address "10.0.2.6"Add-DnsServerResourceRecord -
ZoneName "identityplus.ch" -A -Name "kerb" -IPv4Address "10.0.2.6"
Add-DnsServerResourceRecord -ZoneName "identityplus.ch" -A -Name
"workfolders" -IPv4Address "10.0.2.6"
Add-DnsServerResourceRecord -ZoneName "identityplus.ch" -A -Name "mfa" -
IPv4Address "10.0.2.5"Add-DnsServerResourceRecord -ZoneName
"identityplus.ch" -A -Name "rmsconnector" -IPv4Address "10.0.2.5"
```

```
Add-DnsServerResourceRecord -CName -Name "enterpriseregistration" -
HostNameAlias "login.identityplus.ch" -ZoneName "identityplus.ch"
```

# External DNS entries

To use the different services in the lab you need to add the following DNS entries to your external DNS provider.

| Hostname | Type | Value |
|---|---|---|
| login.identityplus.ch | CNAME | yourservicname.cloudapp.net for example, identitypluslabsvc.cloudapp.net |
| enterpriseregistration.identityplus.ch | CNAME | yourservicname.cloudapp.net |
| claims.identityplus.ch | CNAME | yourservicname.cloudapp.net |
| kerb.identityplus.ch | CNAME | yourservicname.cloudapp.net |
| workfolders.identityplus.ch | CNAME | yourservicname.cloudapp.net |
| mfa.identityplus.ch | CNAME | yourservicname.cloudapp.net |

# Mobile applications

To configure and test the Multi-Factor Authentication and the Rights Management capabilities in *Chapter 10*, *Implementing Access Control Mechanisms* you need to install the following applications from your preferred store of your mobile device:

- Azure MFA Authenticator
- RMS Sharing application

# Adding additional virtual machines

The first virtual machine we add in the Azure Management Portal is the application server APP01 to access different capabilities:

1. Open the Azure Management Portal (classic):
   https://manage.windowsazure.com.
2. Login with your global administrator.

3. Go to **New** | **Compute** | **Virtual Machine** | **From Gallery**.
4. Use the **Windows Server 2012 R2 Data Center** image.
5. Enter the name APP01.
6. Choose the size **Small/A1 Standard**.
7. Provide the administrator credentials you used in the installation script.
8. Choose your cloud service, for example, identitypluslabsvc.
9. Choose your virtual network, identitypluslabvnet-subnet2.

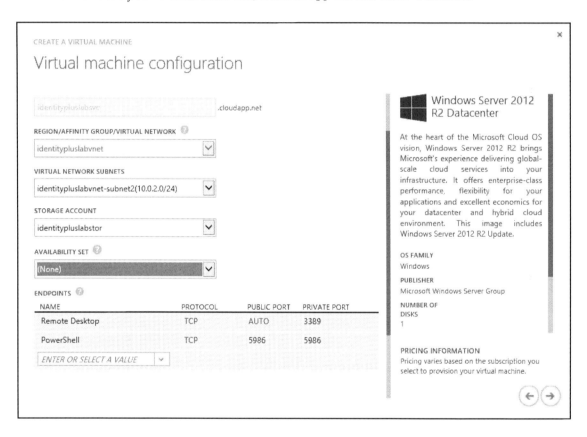

10. After the virtual machine is created – connect and login to the server.

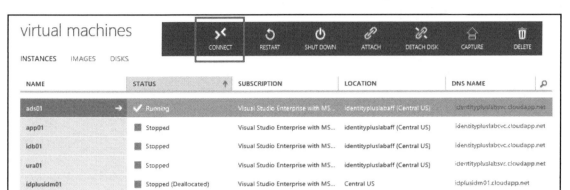

Download the RDP file and use it to connect in future.

11. Join the virtual machine to your domain environment.

# Installing and configuring the synchronization and federation environment

In this section, we provide guidance on implementing the basic synchronization and federation environment. We start with a simple infrastructure that just consists of the Identity Bridge, the Web Application Proxy, and small applications to show the main principles in practical use scenarios.

## Preparing the group management service account – GMSA

Use the following steps to prepare the group management service account:

1. Log on to the Domain Controller **ADS01** with the following credentials:

    - **Username**: Domain\AdminAccount
    - **Password**: YourPassword

2. Open a Windows PowerShell prompt with evaluated rights and enter:

```
Add-KdsRootKey -EffectiveTime (Get-Date).AddHours(-10)
```

# Installing AD FS on IDB01

The following are the steps to install ADFD on IDB01:

1. Log on to the server IDB01 with the following credentials:

   - **Username**: Domain\AdminAccount
   - **Password**: YourPassword

2. Open **Server Manager**.
3. Go to **Manage** | **Add roles and features**.
4. Click **Next** | **Next** | **Next** and select **Active Directory Federation Services**.

5. Click **Next** | **Next** | **Next**.
6. Click **Install**.
7. Wait for the installation to complete and then click **Close**.

**Practical note**
You can also use the following PowerShell commands to install ADFS:
```
Install-WindowsFeature ADFS-Federation -
IncludeManagementTools Install-AdfsFarm -
CertificateThumbprint <thumbprint of the cert> -
FederationServiceName login.identityplus.ch -
GroupServiceAccountIdentifier identityplus\svcfed$ -
FederationServiceDisplayName "IDPlus Login"
```

# Configuring AD FS on IDB01

Use the following steps to confrigure AD FS on IDB01:

1. Ensure that you are still logged on to **IDB01** with the Enterprise Administrator account.

2. Go to **Server Manager** | **Configure the federation service**.

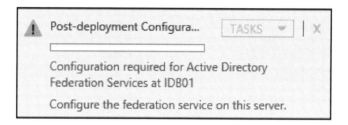

3. Ensure that the first federation server is selected and click **Next** | **Next**.

4. In SSL Certificate, select the **login.identityplus.ch** certificate.

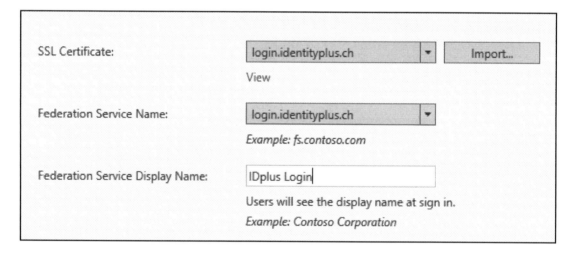

5. Type a preferred name, such as **IDplus Login,** in the **Federation Service Display Name:** field and click **Next.**

6. Create a Group Managed Service Account, enter `svcfed` in the **Account Name** field, and click **Next.**

7. Create the database on this server – click **Next.**

8. Click on **Next** and make sure the prerequisite checks pass.

> The warning about the root key is OK.

9. Click on **Configure.**

# Testing AD FS functionality

To test the AD FS functionality, use the following steps:

1. Ensure that you are still logged on to **IDB01** with the Enterprise Administrator account.

2. Open Internet Explorer.

3. Browse to `https://login.identityplus.ch/adfs/ls/idpinitiatedsignon.aspx`.

> Ensure that you don't see a certificate error. With ADFS 4.0 on Windows Server 2016 the `EnableIdpInitiatedSignonPage` is disabled by default.

4. Log on with the following credentials:

5. Click on **Sign In**.
   - **Username**: Domain\AdminAccount
   - **Password**: YourPassword

6. You will see a message saying **You are signed in**.

# Installing a Web Application Proxy on URA01

1. Log on to the server**URA01** with the following credentials:
   - **Username**: Domain\AdminAccount
   - **Password**: YourPassword

2. Go to **Server Manager** | **Manage** | and click on **Add roles and features**.
3. Click **Next** | **Next** | **Next** and select **Remote Access.**
4. Click **Next**| **Next** | **Next** and select **Web Application Proxy**.

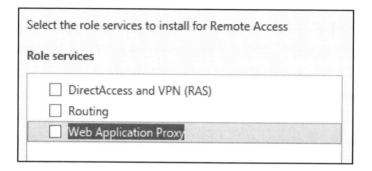

5. Click **Add Features**.
6. Click **Next** | **Install**.
7. After the installation completes, click **Close**.

5. **Practical note**
   You can also use the following PowerShell command to install the Web Application Proxy role:

   ```
   Install-WindowsFeature Web-Application-Proxy -
   IncludeManagementTools $credentials = Get-
   Credential Install-WebApplicationProxy -
   CertificateThumbprint <thumbprint of the cert> -
   FederationServiceName login.identityplus.ch -
   FederationServiceTrustCredential $credentials
   ```

# Configuring a Web Application Proxy on URA01

Use the following steps to configure the Web Application Proxy:

1. Ensure that you are still logged into **URA01** with the following credentials:

   - **Username**: Domain\AdminAccount
   - **Password**: YourPassword

2. Go to **Server Manager** and open the **Web Application Proxy Wizard**.

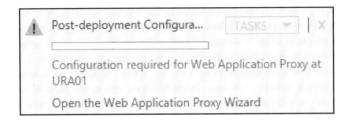

3. Click **Next** and type `login.identityplus.ch` in the **Federation service name**.
4. Use the following credentials:

   - **Username**: Domain\AdminAccount
   - **Password**: YourPassword

5. Click **Next**.
6. Select the **login.identityplus.ch** certificate and click **Next**.
7. Click **Configure**, ensure that the Web Application Proxy was configured successfully, and click **Close**.

# Testing Web Application Proxy functionality

1. Log on to your Windows 10 client.
2. Open Internet Explorer.
3. Browse to
   `https://login.identityplus.ch/adfs/ls/idpinitiatedsignon.aspx`.

 Ensure that you don't see a certificate error.

4. Click **Sign In**.
5. Log on with the following credentials:

   - **Username**: Domain\AdminAccount
   - **Password**: YourPassword

6. You will see a message saying **You are signed in**.

# Installing the Claims Web Application on APP01

Use the following steps:

1. Log on to the server APP01 with the following credentials:

   - **Username**: Domain\AdminAccount
   - **Password**: YourPassword

2. Open an evaluated PowerShell:

```
Import-Module ServerManager

Install-WindowsFeature NET-Framework-Core, AS-HTTP-Activation, NET-
Framework-45-Features, Web-Mgmt-Console, Web-Asp-Net, Web-Asp-Net45, Web-
Basic-Auth,Web-Client-Auth, Web-Digest-Auth, Web-Dir-Browsing, Web-Dyn-
Compression, Web-Http-Errors, Web-Http-Logging, Web-Http-Redirect,Web-Http-
Tracing, Web-ISAPI-Ext, Web-ISAPI-Filter, Web-Lgcy-Mgmt-Console, Web-
Metabase, Web-Mgmt-Console, Web-Mgmt-Service,Web-Net-Ext, Web-Net-Ext45,
Web-Request-Monitor, Web-Server, Web-Stat-Compression, Web-Static-Content,
Web-Windows-Auth, Web-WMI,Windows-Identity-Foundation

Configure-SMRemoting.exe -enable

Restart-Computer -Force
```

3. Log on to the server APP01 again with the same credentials.
4. Extract the `Configuration.zip` to `C:\Configuration`.
5. Run the following script:

```
.\deploy-testsite.ps1 -SourcePath
"C:\Configuration\ClaimsWebScriptAndSite\deploy" -SiteName "Claims Web
Site" -SitePhysicalPath C:\inetpub\claimsroot -ADFSServer idb01 -AppFQDN
claims.identityplus.ch
```

6. Open the `IIS Management` console.
7. Correct the website binding to your public certificate.

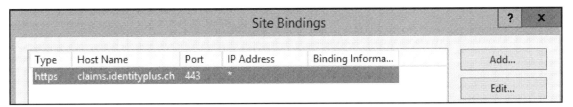

# Configuring the Claims website

1. Log on to the server IDB01 with the following credentials:

   - **Username**: Domain\AdminAccount
   - **Password**: YourPassword

2. Open an evaluated Windows PowerShell:

```
Get-ADFSCertificate
```

```
CertificateType : Token-Signing
IsPrimary       : True
StoreLocation   : CurrentUser
StoreName       : My
Thumbprint      : 9B578A4742B7E33354B2D9B741D7666D4723E05C6
```

**Practical Note**

The installation script automatically puts the thumbprint of the token-signing certificate in the `web.config` file of the Claims web application. If you renew the token-signing certificate you need to update the thumbprint in the application configuration.

3. Go to **Server Manager**, click **Tools |**, and open **ADFS Management**.
4. Expand **Trust Relationships** and select **Relying Party Trusts**.
5. Select **Actions |** add **Relying Party Trust** and click **Start**.
6. In the box, type `https://claims.identityplus.ch`.

○ Import data about the relying party published online or on a local network

Use this option to import the necessary data and certificates from a relying party organization that publishes its federation metadata online or on a local network.

Federation metadata address (host name or URL):

`https://claims.identityplus.ch`

Example: fs.contoso.com or https://www.contoso.com/app

7. Click **Next**.
8. Type the display name as **Claims Demo Web Site**.
9. Click **Next**.
10. Select **I do not want to configure multi-factor authentication settings for this relying party trust at this time** and click **Next**.
11. Select **Permit all users to access this relying party**.
12. Click **Next | Next**.

13. Clear the **Open the Edit Claim Rules dialog box for this relying party trust when the wizard closes** and click **Close**.

14. Verify the new app with Internet Explorer by typing:
    `https://claims.identityplus.ch`.

15. Log on with the following credentials:

    - **Username**: Domain\AdminAccount
    - **Password**: YourPassword

16. You should see a result like the following screenshot:

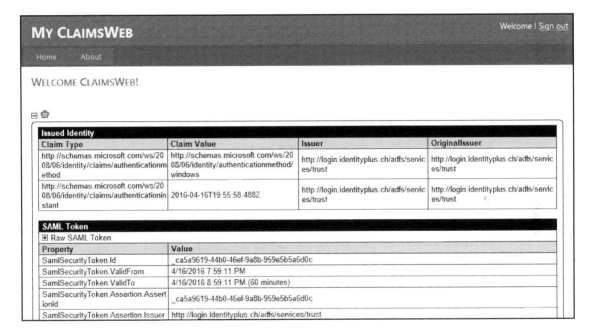

# Configuring the Kerberos website

Log on to ADS01 and create a service account to run the application pool with the name **svckrb** and with the option **password never expires** selected. Note the password so you can provide it in the following configurations:

1. Open an evaluated PowerShell and type:

```
setspn –S http/kerb.identityplus.ch identityplus\svckrb
```

2. Configure the Kerberos delegation on APP01 with the **svckrb** user account.

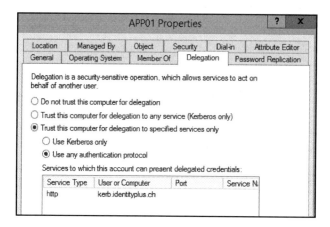

3. Log on to APP01 with the following credentials:

- **Username**: Domain\AdminAccount
- **Password**: YourPassword

4. Create the Kerberos Demo Web Site

```
New-Item C:\inetpub\kerbroot -type Directory

Import-Module Webadministration

cd IIS:

New-Item 'IIS:\Sites\Kerberos Web Site' -bindings
@{protocol="http";bindingInformation=":80:kerb.identityplus.ch"} -
physicalPath 'c:\inetpub\kerbroot'
```

5. Configure the correct bindings and open the IIS Management Console.
6. Expand **Sites** and choose the **Kerberos Web Site**. Right-click and open bindings.
7. Add a new binding with the type: HTTPS and the hostname: kerb.identityplus.ch and choose the installed public certificate.

8. Under application pools click **add a new application pool**.

9. Name the **Kerberos Web Site** and leave the other default values.

10. Click **Advanced Settings** and change the identity to the account `svckrb`.

11. Click on the **Kerberos Web Site** and click **advanced settings**.

12. Change the application pool to the newly created one: **Kerberos Web Site**.

13. Under IIS Authentication enable **Windows Authentication** and disable **Anonymous Authentication**.

14. Go to **Windows Authentication** | **Advanced Settings** | **Clear Enable Kernel-mode**.

15. Copy the `index.htm` file from the code package to the following directory: `C:\inetpub\kerbroot`.

16. Restart the IIS.

 Claims and Kerberos Web Site represent the two types of on premise application, which we will use later in the publishing scenarios.

# Configuring the AAD/Office 365 federation

1. Log on to IDB01 with the following credentials:

   - **Username**: Domain\AdminAccount
   - **Password: Your**Password

2. Install the Azure AD PowerShell and the Microsoft Online Sign-In assistant from the code package – First: `msoidcli_64`; Second: `AdministrationConfig-en`.

3. Open the newly installed Azure AD PowerShell console: Type `Connect-MsolService` and provide your Azure AD Global Administrator credentials.

4. Next we transform our domain into a federation configuration:

```
Convert-MsolDomainToFederated –DomainName identityplus –
SupportMultipleDomain
```

5. You will find the new **Relying Party Trust** entry in ADFS.

| Relying Party Trusts | | | |
|---|---|---|---|
| Display Name | Enabled | Type | Identifier |
| Device Registration Service | Yes | WS-T... | um:ms-drs:login.identityplus.ch |
| Claims Demo Web Site | Yes | WS-T... | https://claims.identityplus.ch/ |
| Microsoft Office 365 Identity Platform | Yes | WS-T... | https://login.microsoftonline.com/ext... |

6. Next we will verify our new configuration from the Windows 10 client.
7. Open Internet Explorer and type `https://myapps.microsoft.com`.
8. Enter one of your test user credentials.

**Expected result**
You should be redirected to your ADFS infrastructure. It may take a while depending upon the changes in your Azure platform.

# Installing and configuring Azure AD Connect

Before starting the Azure AD Connect installation process we will check the local Active Directory for common misconfigurations that can disturb the identity synchronization process. We already used a correct UPN in the user creation process. Because of this we didn't check the domain before installing ADFS. For this task we will use the IdFix DirSync Error Remediation tool:

1. Log on to IDB01 with the following credentials:

   - **Username**: Domain\AdminAccount
   - **Password**: YourPassword

2. Install the IdFix DirSync Error Remediation tool from the code package **IdFix**.

3. Start the tool and click **Query**; fix the issues before you continue.

4. Next we will install the Azure AD Connect Tool from the code package **AzureADConnect**.

Review the following article to provide the correct user accounts for a productive environment `http://bit.ly/1paFUTX`.

5. Agree to the license terms and privacy notice and click **Continue**.
6. Click **Customize**.
7. Leave the optional configuration as the default.
8. Click **Install**.
9. In the **User sign-in** section choose **Do not configure** | and click **Next**.

We will manually install ADFS and the AAD Connect tool to get a better understanding of what's done with the assistants.

10. Provide your Azure AD Global Administrator credentials and click on **Next**.
11. In the **Connect your directories** section provide your local Enterprise Administrator credentials, click on **Add Directory,** and click **Next**.

12. In the **Domain and OU filtering** section we will choose the **Managed Business Objects OU** to synchronize to the Azure AD; click on **Next**.

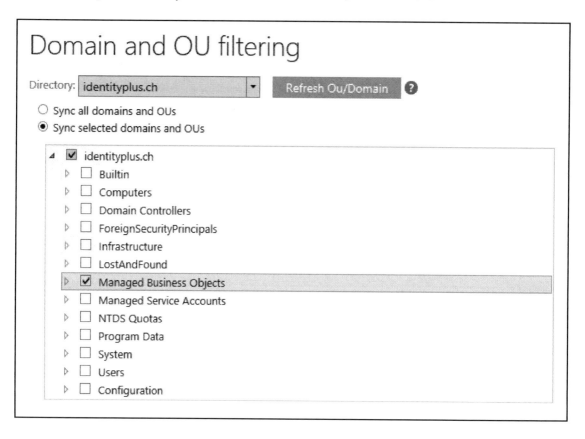

13. Make no changes to the **uniquely identifying your users** section and click on **Next**.

 We will configure this section in a complex hybrid scenario.

14. Leave the **Filter users and devices** section a the default values and click on **Next**.

15. Also leave the **Optional features** section at the default values and click on **Next**.

16. Clear the **Start the synchronization process ....** and click on **Install**.

 We will step through the complete synchronization process to get a practical understanding of the theory from the previous chapters. We also recommend always doing the Initial Load manually.

17. Go to **Configuration complete** | **Expected result**: **Azure AD Connect configuration succeeded** | and click **Exit**.

# AAD Connect stepping through the initial load

On your start screen you will find additional icons for the Azure AD Connect tool and the additional UI's.

1. Start the **Synchronization Service**.

2. Under **Connectors** you will find two connectors: **AAD** and **AD**.

3. Choose an AD connector and click **Search Connector Space** | **Search**.

**Expected result**
No records will be received, because we didn't import any object in the tool until this step.

4. Click **Run** under the **Actions** section.
5. Choose the **Full Import** run profile to bring the objects from the Active Directory into the **Connector** space of AAD Connect.

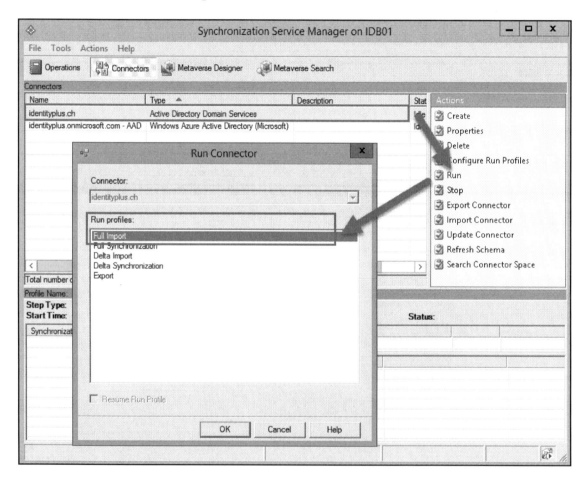

**Expected result**
You should now see a specific number of Adds in the Synchronization Statistics.

6. Click **Adds** and verify the objects were imported into the connector space with the first Full Import. You can also use the mechanism from the previous step.

7. Next we will do the same on the AAD connector.

8. Also verify the same options as we did for the AD connector.

9. Now search the connector space again from the AD connector and choose one of our demo users.

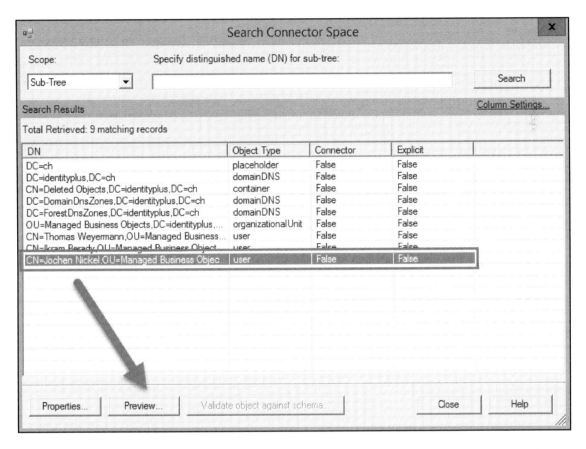

10. Click **Preview** to check the results of a synchronization preview to validate the future results in the metaverse.

11. Use **Full Synchronization** and click **Generate Preview**.

12. Now we can view the status of the object that will be **projected**. Furthermore, we will see the applied rules for the **Import Attribute Flow**.

13. Additionally, you can view the different **Export Attribute Flows**.

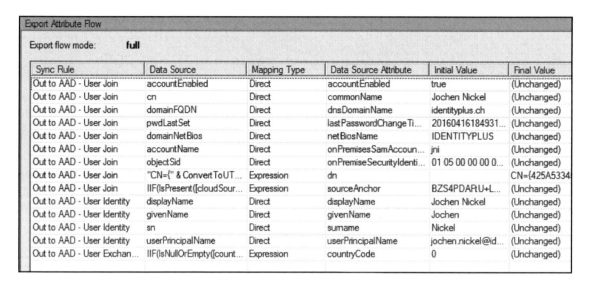

| Sync Rule | Data Source | Mapping Type | Data Source Attribute | Initial Value | Final Value |
|---|---|---|---|---|---|
| Out to AAD - User Join | accountEnabled | Direct | accountEnabled | true | (Unchanged) |
| Out to AAD - User Join | cn | Direct | commonName | Jochen Nickel | (Unchanged) |
| Out to AAD - User Join | domainFQDN | Direct | dnsDomainName | identityplus.ch | (Unchanged) |
| Out to AAD - User Join | pwdLastSet | Direct | lastPasswordChangeTi... | 20160416184931... | (Unchanged) |
| Out to AAD - User Join | domainNetBios | Direct | netBiosName | IDENTITYPLUS | (Unchanged) |
| Out to AAD - User Join | accountName | Direct | onPremisesSamAccoun... | jni | (Unchanged) |
| Out to AAD - User Join | objectSid | Direct | onPremiseSecurityIdenti... | 01 05 00 00 00 0... | (Unchanged) |
| Out to AAD - User Join | "CN={" & ConvertToUT... | Expression | dn | | CN={425A5334 |
| Out to AAD - User Join | IIF(IsPresent([cloudSour... | Expression | sourceAnchor | BZS4PDARtU+L... | (Unchanged) |
| Out to AAD - User Identity | displayName | Direct | displayName | Jochen Nickel | (Unchanged) |
| Out to AAD - User Identity | givenName | Direct | givenName | Jochen | (Unchanged) |
| Out to AAD - User Identity | sn | Direct | surname | Nickel | (Unchanged) |
| Out to AAD - User Identity | userPrincipalName | Direct | userPrincipalName | jochen.nickel@id... | (Unchanged) |
| Out to AAD - User Exchan... | IIF(IsNullOrEmpty([count... | Expression | countryCode | 0 | (Unchanged) |

Export flow mode: **full**

14. With the **Commit Preview** button, we created the first object in the AAD Connect metaverse.

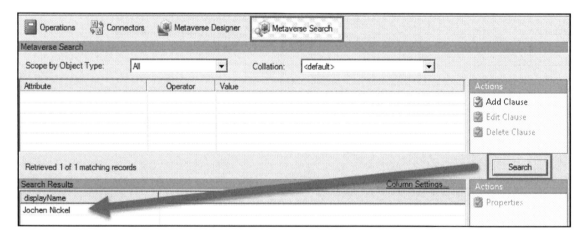

15. Next we will choose the AAD connector and run the same tasks to verify the options.

16. Run the **Export** profile on the AAD connector and we will export our first user to the Azure Active Directory. Yeah! Our first user creation.

17. Test the new user by opening IE and typing `https://myapps.microsoft.com`, then sign in with the user credentials you just created.

 17. **Expected Result**
Now you should be able to authenticate and access the Azure AD application access panel.

18. Run the **Export** profile on the AD connector to complete the run cycle.

19. Now that we have tested one single user we can run the same cycles again but with all the users – view the different stages to understand these standard run cycles.

20. In the next step we will configure the Sync Scheduler to run the process automatically. Open an evaluated PowerShell:

`Get-ADSyncScheduler`

```
PS C:\> Get-ADSyncScheduler

AllowedSyncCycleInterval               : 00:30:00
CurrentlyEffectiveSyncCycleInterval    : 00:30:00
CustomizedSyncCycleInterval            :
NextSyncCyclePolicyType                : Initial
NextSyncCycleStartTimeInUTC            : 4/18/2016 9:26:27 AM
PurgeRunHistoryInterval                : 7.00:00:00
SyncCycleEnabled                       : False
MaintenanceEnabled                     : True
StagingModeEnabled                     : False
```

21. With `Start-ADSyncSyncCycle -PolicyType Initial` you can start an initial flow.

22. Type `Set-ADSyncScheduler -SyncCycleEnabled $true` to enable the automatic sync process every 30 minutes.

**Reader note**
You will find additional information here: `http://bit.ly/1QeYgud`.

# Configuring attribute-based filtering

This configuration helps you to exclude sensible identities. You can also work with outbound rules that we will explain later in other complex scenarios:

1. Log on to IDB01 with the following credentials:

    - **Username**: Domain\AdminAccount
    - **Password**: YourPassword

2. Go to the **Start Menu** and click on **Synchronization Rules Editor**.
3. Click on **Add New Rule** and select **inbound**.
4. Configure the **Description** section.

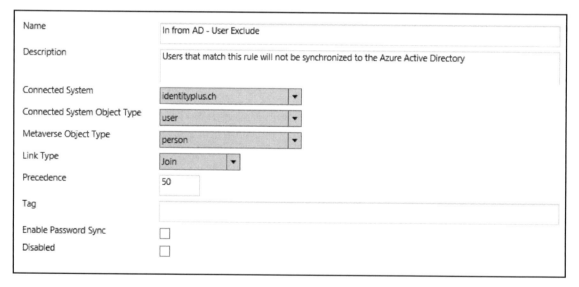

5. Select the following options:
6. In the **Transformations** section click **Add Transformation**.

7. In the **Join rules** section leave the values empty and click on **Next**.

8. Select the **department** attribute with the **Operator** EQUAL and the **VALUE Human Resources** and click on **Next**.

9. Configure the **Scoping filter** section. Click **Add Group** and **Add Clause.**

- **FlowType** = **Constant**
- **Target Attribute** = cloudFiltered
- **Source**: Type in `True`
- Click **Add** to save the rule

10. Go to **Start** – Open the **Synchronization Service Manager**.

11. What happens if you create the account in another container or OU?

12. Create a new Active Directory user in the **Managed Business Objects OU** with the **department Human Resources**.

13. Connectors – choose the AD DS connector and run a **Full Import**.

**Expected result**
You will see one **Add** in the **Synchronization Statistics** with your new created user account.

14. Run a full synchronization on the same connector.

**Expected result**
You will see one Projection in the Synchronization Statistics and you will not see an Export to the AAD connector.

So, if you try an Export on the AAD connector you will not include the newly created user account with the department attribute set to **Human Resources**.

# Enabling password writeback

Remember that you need to enable password writeback to use the self-service password reset capabilities for your federated user accounts. For this feature, password synchronization is not a required configuration:

1. Log on to IDB01 with the following credentials:

   - **Username**: Domain\AdminAccount
   - **Password**: YourPassword

2. Open an evaluated PowerShell.
3. Use `Get-ADSyncConnector` to receive the connector name.
4. View the Password writeback status on the connector: `Get-ADSyncAADPasswordResetConfiguration -Connector "Connector Name"`.
5. Enable Password writeback on the connector: `Set-ADSyncAADPasswordResetConfiguration -Connector "Connector Name" -Enable $true`.
6. Register a user for password reset as we did Chapter 4, *Building and Configuring a Suitable Azure AD*, and check the functionality.
7. Open the **Event Viewer** and verify the configuration and password result entries under **Windows Logs | Application**.

   **Expected results**:
   **Successful configuration:**
   ```
   TrackingId: 46730c64-ff7e-44bb-92fd-83d456f4750f,
   Password writeback service is in a healthy state. All
   serviceHosts for service bus endpoints are in running
   state, Details: Version: 5.0.0.686
   ```
   **Successful Password Reset:**
   ```
   TrackingId: 86fc8b58-da9e-46d1-8dd8-b810364c8e33,
   PasswordResetSuccess, Details: Context: cloudAnchor:
   User_7de3ec5c-222b-4afd-9ca5-713df8403ca7,
   SourceAnchorValue: BZS4PDAFtU+LQt7BAsnzvg==,
   UserPrincipalName: jochen.nickel@identityplus.ch,
   unblockUser: True
   ```

# Forcing a synchronization task after changes

1. Log on to ADS01 and change the **lastname** and the **UPN** of one of your users in the **Managed Business Objects OU**.
2. Log on to IDB01 with the following credentials:

   - **Username**: Domain\AdminAccount
   - **Password**: YourPassword

3. Go to the **Start** menu and click on **Synchronization Service Manager**.
4. Run a **Delta Import** on the AD connector and you will receive a **Rename** in **Synchronization Statistics**.
5. Click on **Renames** and the **Distinguished Name** of the user account you changed the last name of and UPN; you will see that the changes will apply.

| Attribute information: | | | |
|---|---|---|---|
| Changes | Attribute Name | Type | Value |
| none | cn | string | Ikram Nickel |
| none | countryCode | number | 0 |
| none | givenName | string | Ikram |
| none | objectGUID | binary | 8E D0 AB EF 2C E7 81 4D 81 76 96 97 09 59 8E 5A |
| none | objectSid | binary | 01 05 00 00 00 00 00 05 15 00 00 00 DE B8 EA C4 30 01 0 21 53 A3 DE 69 72 38 08 00... |
| none | pwdLastSet | number | 131053061723980085 |
| none | sAMAccountName | string | ini |
| none | sn | string | Nickel |
| none | userAccountControl | number | 512 |
| none | userPrincipalName | string | ikram.nickel@identityplus.ch |

6. Run a **Delta Synchronization** on the AD connector and an **Export** on the AAD connector.

7. Click **Search Connector Space** on the AAD connector and check the changes on the user object.

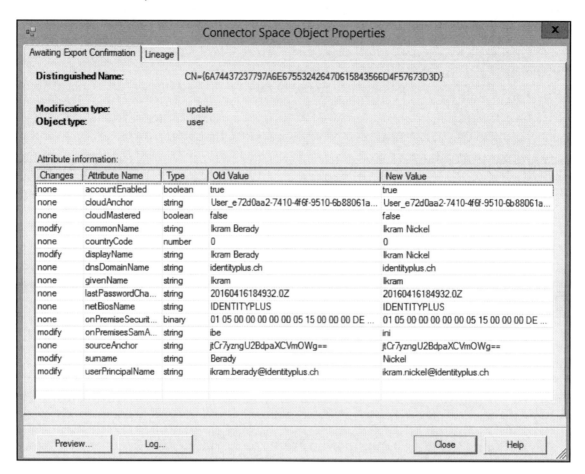

**Practical Note:**

You can also do a complete Delta cycle with:

`Start-ADSyncSyncCycle -PolicyType Delta`

This runs the following profiles:

**Delta Import**: AD connector
**Delta Import**: AAD Connector
**Delta Synchronization**: AD Connector
**Delta Synchronization**: AAD Connector
**Export**: AAD Connector
**Export**: AD Connector

# Creating dynamic groups

In this section, we will build dynamic group memberships for different purposes, such as licensing or granting application access. We will divide this section into three main parts:

- Using on premise groups for assigning licenses
- Using PowerShell to assign Office 365 licenses based on groups
- Using groups for application access assignment

You also have the option to use a custom Active Directory Attribute; see the following link to the solution: `http://bit.ly/2afrAan`.

With the following configurations you can access the capabilities of group management in a hybrid identity and access management infrastructure. Let's start!

# Using on premise groups for assigning licenses

First of all, we need to identify the different licenses that are available on our Azure tenant. Basically, we do this with the following procedure:

1. Open PowerShell.
2. Use `Connect-MsolService` to connect to your Azure AD tenant with your Global Administrator account.
3. With `Get-MsolAccountSku` you will receive the available licenses:

```
PS C:\Users\jochen.nickel> Connect-MsolService
PS C:\Users\jochen.nickel> Get-MsolAccountSku

AccountSkuId                          ActiveUnits  WarningUnits  ConsumedUnits
-----------                          -----------  ------------  -------------
identityplus:AAD_PREMIUM             100          0             4
identityplus:RMSBASIC                1            0             0
identityplus:RIGHTSMANAGEMENT_ADHOC  50000        0             0
identityplus:ENTERPRISEPACK          25           0             2
identityplus:INTUNE_A                100          0             1
```

Next we will create a group called Licensing Azure AD Premium in our local Active Directory:

1. Log on to ADS01 with the following credentials:

   - **Username**: Domain\AdminAccount
   - **Password**: YourPassword

2. Create a Global Security group called **Licensing Azure AD Premium** in the **Managed Business Objects OU** and add test users to the group.
3. Log on to IDB01 with the following credentials:

   - **Username**: Domain\AdminAccount
   - **Password**: YourPassword

4. Open PowerShell.
5. Type **Start-ADSyncSyncCycle Delta**.
6. The expected result:

# licensing azure ad premium

MEMBERS    OWNERS    PROPERTIES    CONFIGURE    SELF SERVICE ACTIVITY

| NAME | USER NAME |
| --- | --- |
| Ikram Nickel | ikram.nickel@identityplus.ch |
| Jochen Nickel | jochen.nickel@identityplus.ch |
| Thomas Weyermann | thomas.weyermann@identityplus.ch |

7. Next we need to assign the Azure AD Premium licenses to the newly created group under **Azure AD | Licenses | Azure Active Directory Premium**.
8. Choose **Assign licenses to users**.
9. Show **All Groups**.
10. Choose the **Licensing Azure AD Premium** group and click **Assign**.
11. Show **Assigned Users** and you will see that the licenses are assigned to the users of the group. For additional members of the group the users the licenses will be automatically assigned.

# Using PowerShell to assign Office 365 licenses based on group membership

Use the following steps to assign Office 365 licenses based on group membership:

1. Log on to ADS01 with the following credentials:

    - **Username**: Domain\AdminAccount
    - **Password**: YourPassword

2. Create a Global Security group called **Licensing Office 365 E3 Plan** in the **Managed Business Objects OU** and add test users to the group.
3. Log on to IDB01 with the following credentials:

    - **Username**: Domain\AdminAccount
    - **Password**: YourPassword

4. Open PowerShell.
5. Type `Start-ADSyncSyncCycle Delta`.
6. The expected Result:

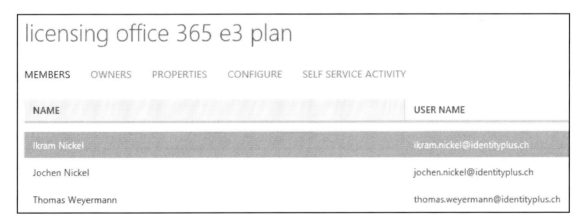

7. Use the open PowerShell and change the directory to `C:\Configuration`, where the files from the code package from this chapter are stored.
8. Type `Import-Module .\Set-LicenseToUsersInSecurityGroup.ps1`.

9. Use the following command to license the users of the group:

```
Set-LicenseToUsersInSecurityGroup -UserName <TenantAdminUserName> -Password
<TenantadminPassword> -GroupName "Licensing Office 365 E3 Plan" -
AccountSkuId identityplus:ENTERPRISEPACK
```

**Expected result**:
The users have an assigned Office 365 E3 plan and are able to access their mailbox under: `https://portal.office.com`.

# Using groups for application access assignment

With this scenario, we use on premise groups that are synchronized to Azure AD to assign specific application access based on dynamic group membership:

1. Log on to ADS01 with the following credentials:

    - **Username**: Domain\AdminAccount
    - **Password**: YourPassword

2. Create a Global Security group called **Sales Applications** in the **Managed Business Objects OU** and add test users to the group.

3. Log on to IDB01 with the following credentials:

    - **Username**: Domain\AdminAccount
    - **Password**: YourPassword

4. Open PowerShell.
5. Type **Start-ADSyncSyncCycle Delta**.
6. Log on to your Azure AD Management with the **Global Administrator**.
7. Assign the group **Sales Applications** to a CRM application that you add from the application gallery.
8. Go back to your Active Directory with the preceding credentials and add one more user to the **Sales Applications** group.
9. Start another Delta Sync Cycle.
10. Log on to `https://myapps.microsoft.com` with the newly added user.

11. **Expected result**: The user should d application.

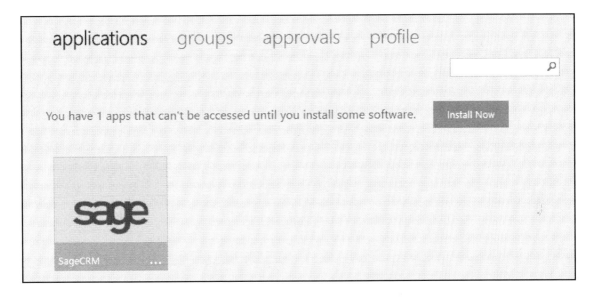

# Configuring self-service group management

With the next use case we provide the capability for self-service application access management to applications. We will use the example to enable the user to request a controlled set of social media applications in the Access Panel UI:

1. Log on to your Azure AD Management with **Global Administrator**.
2. Choose the **CONFIGURE** section and scroll down to **Users who can use self-service for security groups** = Enabled.
3. Go to `https://myapps.microsoft.com` and create a new security group called `social Media Applications` that is open to join.
4. Log on to the **Azure Management Portal (AAD)** as global administrator.
5. Under APPLICATIONS add some applications such as Facebook, LinkedIn, and Instagram and assign the group **Social Media Applications**.
6. Now log on to `https://myapps.microsoft.com` with another test user and join the **Social Media Applications** group.

7. After joining the group, refresh the browser and you should see the assigned applications.

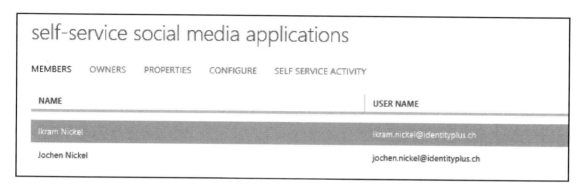

# Implementing secure remote access and SSO for on premise web applications

Now that we have worked with the basic Identity Bridge and the starter off the group capabilities, we will start to publish on premise applications with the Web Application Proxy in our environment. Right now we will focus on a Claims-based and Kerberos-based application.

# Publishing a Claims-based application

The Claims Web Application will be used as a representation of a claims-based line of business application. With this implementation you can try different claims rules and view the results in the application. Earlier in this chapter we installed and configured the application. Now we will publish the app with the Web Application Proxy URA01:

1. Log on to URA01 with the following credentials:

    - **Username**: Domain\AdminAccount
    - **Password**: YourPassword

2. Start the **Remote Access Management** console in the **Administrative tools** of the server.

3. The first step is to publish the ADFS components.

4.  Go to **Tasks** | **Publish** | **Next**.
5.  Go to **Preauthentication** | **Pass-through**.
6.  Use the following configuration and click **Next** | **Publish** | **Close**.

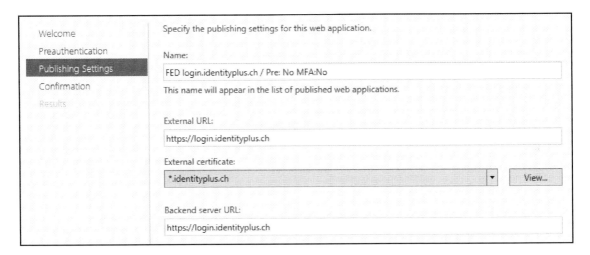

7.  Now we will publish the Claims Web Application.
8.  Click **Next** and choose the Preauthentication method: **ADFS**.
9.  Choose the ADFS relying party: **Claims Demo Web Site**.
10. Use the following then settings click **Next** | **Publish** | **Close**.

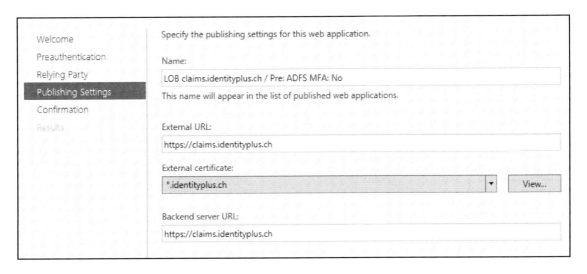

11. Test the configuration by opening your browser and typing:
    `https://claims.identityplus.ch.`

12. You should be prompted with the ADFS authentication form.

13. Log on with your administrator credentials.

14. You should see a similar site to this one:

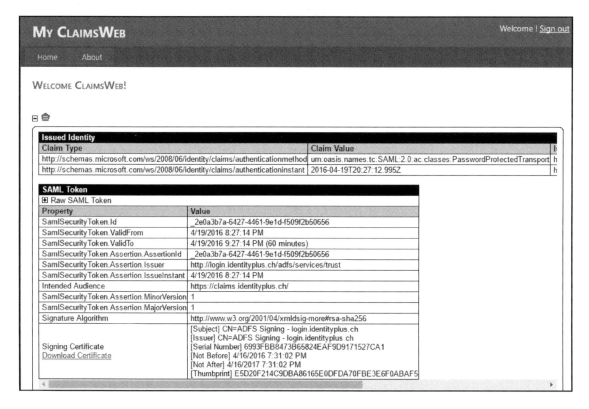

To get familiar with the Claim rules use the examples from the previous chapter and configure them in your ADFS environment, as following example:

1. Log on to IDB01 with the following credentials:

   - **Username**: Domain\AdminAccount
   - **Password**: YourPassword

2. Open the ADFS management console.

3. Go to **Trust Relationships** | **Relying Party Trusts** | **Choose Claims Demo Website**.

4. Edit **Claim Rules ....**

5. Go to **Issuance Authorization Rules** and use the following configuration:

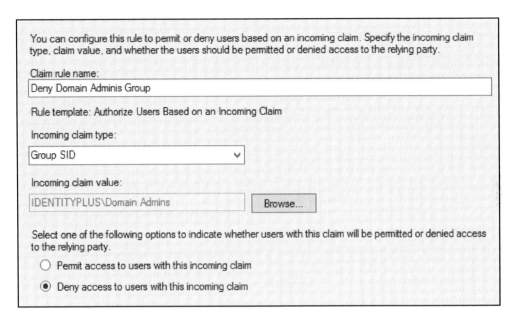

You can configure this rule to permit or deny users based on an incoming claim. Specify the incoming claim type, claim value, and whether the users should be permitted or denied access to the relying party.

Claim rule name:

Deny Domain Adminis Group

Rule template: Authorize Users Based on an Incoming Claim

Incoming claim type:

Group SID

Incoming claim value:

IDENTITYPLUS\Domain Admins    Browse...

Select one of the following options to indicate whether users with this claim will be permitted or denied access to the relying party.

○ Permit access to users with this incoming claim

◉ Deny access to users with this incoming claim

6. Test the new configuration on `https://claims.identityplus.ch` and log on with your domain admin account.

7. The expected result is that you receive the following message – try another account and you get access.

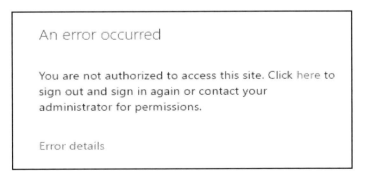

An error occurred

You are not authorized to access this site. Click here to sign out and sign in again or contact your administrator for permissions.

Error details

Try more options to limit or extend the access to this application. Also it will be a good idea to publish more claims to see the results in the Claims Demo app. Next we will publish our Kerberos application.

# Publishing a Kerberos-based application

A simple Kerberos-enabled IIS Web Site is a representation of a Kerberos enabled line of business application. We will show all the tasks required for configuring the Kerberos constrained delegation. Remember: the Web Application Proxy needs to be a domain member for such a scenario:

1. Log on to IDB01 with the following credentials:
   - **Username**: Domain\AdminAccount
   - **Password**: YourPassword
2. Start the ADFS Management Console in the Administrative tools of the server.
   - **Username**: Domain\AdminAccount
   - **Password**: YourPassword
3. Start the **Remote Access Management** console in the **Administrative tools** of the server.
4. Now we will publish the Kerberos Web Application: **Publish**.
5. Click **Next** and choose the Preauthentication method: **ADFS**.
6. Choose the ADFS relying party: **Kerberos Demo Web Site**.
7. Use the following settings – click **Next** | **Publish** | **Close**.
8. Go to **Trust Relationships** | **Relying Party Trusts** | **Add Non-Claims-Aware Relying Party Trust**.
9. Click **Start** | **Display Name: Kerberos Demo Web Site**.
10. Configure Identifiers: `https://kerb.identityplus.ch`. Click **Add** and **Next**.
11. Click **Next** and **Close**.
12. Go to **Add an Issuance Authorization Rule: Permit All Users** and click on **Apply**.

13. Log on to URA01 with the following credentials:

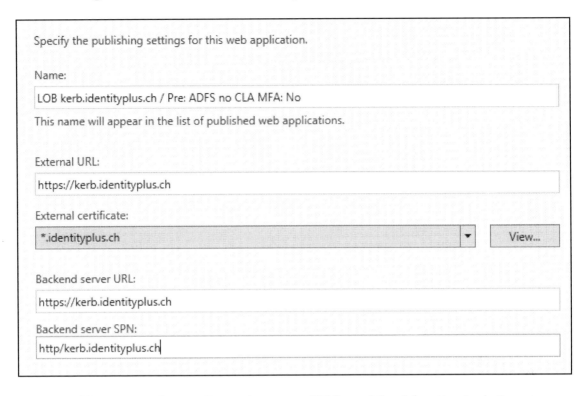

14. Next we need to configure the correct SPN's and the delegation in Active Directory.
15. Log on to ADS01 with the following credentials:
    - **Username**: Domain\AdminAccount
    - **Password**: YourPassword

16. Open the **Active Directory Users and Computers** management console.
17. Enable the **Advanced Features** under **View**.

18. Set the following SPN's on the Web Application Proxy computer account:

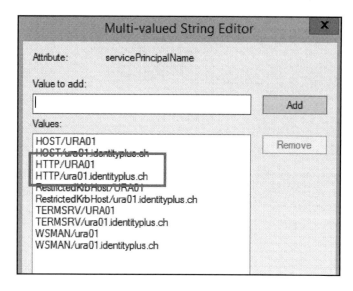

19. In our case, the hostname of the Web Application Server is URA01.
20. Next you need to set: **Trust this computer for delegation to specified services only**.
21. Choose: **Use any authentication protocol**.
22. Add the service account **svckrb** under the Kerberos Web Site is running and choose the **HTTP** service type.

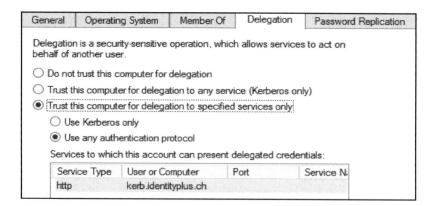

23. Now that we have configured the correct Kerberos delegation information, we are able to test the configuration.
24. Open a web browser and type: `https://kerb.identityplus.ch`.
25. Go to **ADFS forms.** Log on with a test user account.
26. The expected result looks like the following:

**You successfully signed in with Kerberos**

# Enabling and configuring Multi-Factor Authentication

After implementing the basic publishing for our on premise applications we start to integrate the Multi-Factor Authentication to protect applications with a higher security profile, which we will extend in the next chapters.

## Device Registration Service (DRS)

The first mechanism we enable is the device registration service on our ADFS infrastructure:

1. Log on to ADS01 with the following credentials:
   - **Username**: Domain\AdminAccount
   - **Password**: YourPassword
2. Open an evaluated PowerShell.
   - **Username**: Domain\AdminAccount
   - **Password**: YourPassword
3. Open an evaluated PowerShell.
4. Type `Update-WebApplicationProxyDeviceRegistration`.
5. Provide the same credentials that you used to install the components.

Use the following guidance to join a device in your local Active Directory: http://bit.ly/1IjZJQn.
Try to configure the necessary claim rules discussed in the previous chapters to get familiar with the integration of the device in the authentication and authorization process.

6. Type `Initialize-ADDeviceRegistration` and provide the ADFS service account `identityplus\svcfed$`.

7. Type `Enable-AdfsDeviceRegistration`.

8. Log on to URA01 with the following credentials:

# Enabling Azure MFA for a synchronized account

In this section, we will configure Azure MFA for a synchronized account to protect cloud services with a second factor:

1. Log on to the Azure Management Portal as Global Administrator.

2. Choose your directory and click **Configure**.

3. Go to **Multi-Factor Authentication** and click **Manage service settings**.

4. Configure the following verification options, so that you can try the different options:

verification options (learn more)

Methods available to users:
- ☑ Call to phone
- ☑ Text message to phone
- ☑ Notification through mobile app
- ☑ Verification code from mobile app

remember multi-factor authentication (learn more)

☑ Allow users to remember multi-factor authentication on devices they trust

Days before a device must re-authenticate (1-60):  1

5. Next we will configure the user we require for Azure MFA.

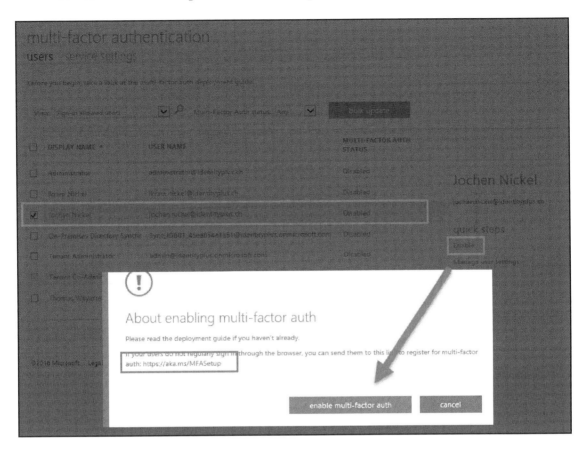

6. Register your test user under `https://aka.ms/MFASetup`.
7. Try the on premise and cloud applications. What happens? Is any MFA required?
8. You can get more information on the following links:
   `https://claims.identityplus.ch` and `https://myapps.microsoft.com`.

In the next chapter, we will extend this scenario by installing and configuring the Azure MFA Server in our local lab infrastructure. Hope you can wait!

# Summary

Working through this chapter enabled you to configure and manage your first hybrid Identity Management scenario with the basics of the central role of the Identity Bridge. In special we didn't use the assistant of the AAD Connect tool to provide you the inside of the technologies under the hood. The assistant is quite easy to understand. You are also able to address and implement the relevant security features such as claim rules, several group management ideas, and the different authentication mechanisms. This helps you to fulfil the security requirements of an organization and provide suitable solutions. In the next chapter, we will extend this basic implementation with the Azure MFA server to secure your on premise applications and services.

Furthermore, we will deploy the first information protection solution combined with more conditional access control mechanisms. And if this is not enough, we will add some new relevant features from the new Windows Server 2016. Are you ready to go?

# 10
# Implementing Access Control Mechanisms

Now that we have already installed and configured our first hybrid identity and federation environment, it's time to take the next steps to get deeper into access control mechanisms. Let's configure the Azure MFA server to protect on-premise applications for the realization of typical conditional access scenarios. Furthermore, a suitable access control solution needs a modern information protection mechanism, such as Microsoft Rights Management services. We will configure this important component in the following chapter in order to fulfill security requirements in business-relevant use cases. After looking at the currently available technologies, we will configure the latest Windows Server 2016 features so as to learn more about the new and advanced security features of Active Directory Federation Services 4.0 and Web Application Proxy. In this chapter we will cover the following topics:

- Extending the basic lab environment
- Configuring conditional access control
- Enabling and configuring information protection
- Configuring advanced security scenarios with Windows Server 2016

# Extending the basic lab environment

Until now we have worked with our basic installed lab environment. However, to configure Windows Server 2016 features, we need to extend the current structure with two additional virtual machines:

| ADS01 | Domain Controller | 2012 R2 Data Center | identitypluslabvnet-subnet2(10.0.2.0/24) |
|---|---|---|---|
| APP01 | Application Server | 2012 R2 Data Center | identitypluslabvnet-subnet2(10.0.2.0/24) |
| IDB01 | Identity Bridge ADFS and AAD Connect | 2012 R2 Data Center | identitypluslabvnet-subnet2(10.0.2.0/24) |
| IDB03 New | Identity Bridge ADFS 4.0 | 2016 TP5 | identitypluslabvnet-subnet2(10.0.2.0/24) |
| URA01 | Unified Remote Access Web Application Proxy | 2012 R2 Data Center | identitypluslabvnet-subnet2(10.0.1.0/24) |
| URA03 New | Unified Remote Access Web Application Proxy | 2016 TP5 | identitypluslabvnet-subnet2(10.0.1.0/24) |

To find out how to add additional virtual machines, follow the **Add additional virtual machines** section in `Chapter 9`, *Building Cloud from Common Identities*. After installing and joining the two machines to the domain, we need to install wildcard certificate on both machines. The configuration of ADFS and Web Application Proxy is also similar to the **Install and configure the Synchronization and Federation environment** section in `Chapter 9`, *Building Cloud from Common Identities*, with the exclusion of the AAD connect tool installation. Just for this lab, we will build two ADFS farms in one domain. Furthermore, we will configure the high availability options discussed in the following chapters:

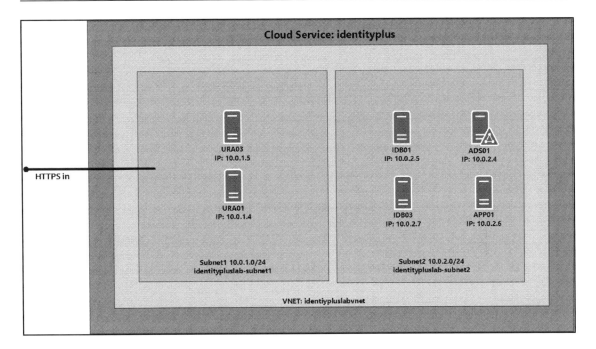

Next to these configurations we need to add the following DNS entries.

**Readers Note:**
We will turn off Windows 2012 R2-based ADFS 3.0/WAP components in the Windows Server 2016 sections. This will help you to reduce consumption and avoid misconfigurations.

# Additional internal DNS entries

The following DNS entry needs to be added to the current internal DNS configuration:

```
Add-DnsServerResourceRecord -ZoneName "identityplus.ch" -A -Name "login2" -
IPv4Address "10.0.2.7"
Add-DnsServerResourceRecord -ZoneName "identityplus.ch" -A -Name "basic" -
IPv4Address "10.0.2.6"
```

# Additional external DNS entries

The following DNS entry needs to be added to the current external DNS configuration:

| Hostname | Type | Value |
|---|---|---|
| basic.identityplus.ch New | CNAME | yourservicname.cloudapp.net for example, identitypluslabsvc.cloudapp.net |
| login2.identityplus.ch New | CNAME | yourservicname.cloudapp.net for example, identitypluslabsvc.cloudapp.net |

# Additional endpoint configuration for URA03

To allow traffic for **URA3** and our new entry point `login2.identityplus.ch,` we need to add an endpoint to the virtual machine configuration:

1. Open `https://manage.windowsazure.com` in your preferred browser and log on with your global administrator credentials.
2. Go to **virtual machines** and choose **URA03**.

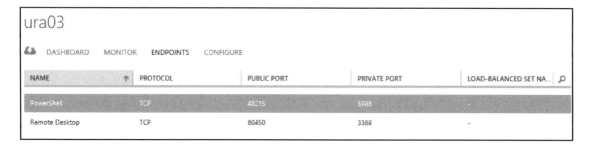

3. Open Endpoints and click **ADD** to provide the information for the new endpoint.
4. Use the option **ADD AN ENDPOINT TO AN EXISTING LOAD-BALANCED SET** and choose the existing set of your test lab.

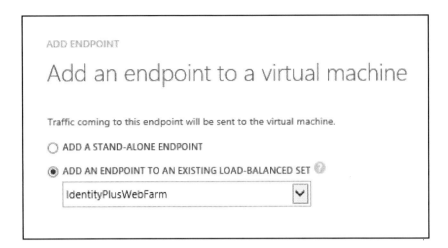

5. In the next section, add the following information and finish the configuration.

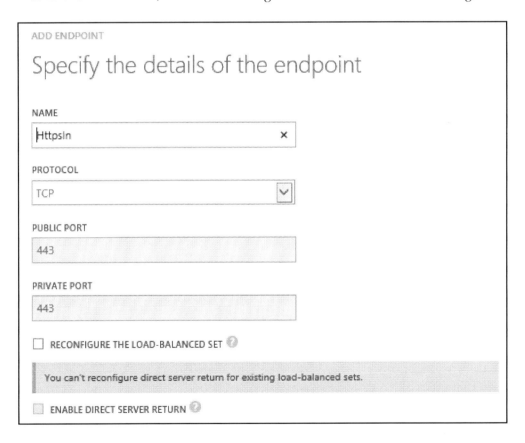

6. Reconfigure the **Load-Balanced Set**.
7. You have successfully added the new endpoint to **URA03**.

# Configuring fixed IP addresses

To configure fixed IP addresses for the new virtual machines, you can use the Azure Management Portal. Just open the configuration information for the virtual machine, as shown in the following screenshot:

Now that we have extended our test lab infrastructure, let's start to configure and use the environment.

# Configuring conditional access control

Before configuring conditional access control scenarios, we need to implement the Azure MFA server on the Identity Bridge server IDB01:

1. Open `https://manage.windowsazure.com` in your preferred browser and log on with your global administrator credentials.
2. Go to **CONFIGURE** | **multifactor authentication** | **Manage service settings**.

3. To manage advanced settings and view reports, go to the portal | **Manage advanced settings** and view reports.
4. **DOWNLOADS**: Download the **Multi-Factor Authentication Server**.
5. Click **Generate Activation Credentials**.

 The Activation Credentials (valid for **10 minutes**).

6. Click **Download**.

# Installing and configuring the Azure MFA server

After downloading the installation binaries, we need to install the Azure MFA server.

 **Practical note:**
We recommend changing the virtual machine size of IDB01 to an A2 (two cores, 3.5 GB memory).

1. Log on to the ADFS Server **IDB01** with the following credentials:

   - **Username**: Domain\AdminAccount
   - **Password**: YourPassword

2. Double-click `MultiFactorAuthenticationServerSetup.exe`.

 This software requires the **KB 2919355** update and prompts you if the update is not installed on the server.

3. Choose your preferred installation folder and click **Next** and **Finish**.

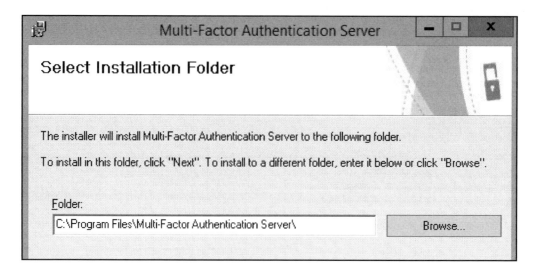

4. Click **Skip using the Authentication Configuration Wizard**.
5. Enter your credentials to activate the server.

6. Under the **Join Group** context, choose the **Existing group**.
7. We will enable and configure the replication to prepare high availability scenarios in the following chapters. Click **Yes** and **Next** until you have finished the installation process.

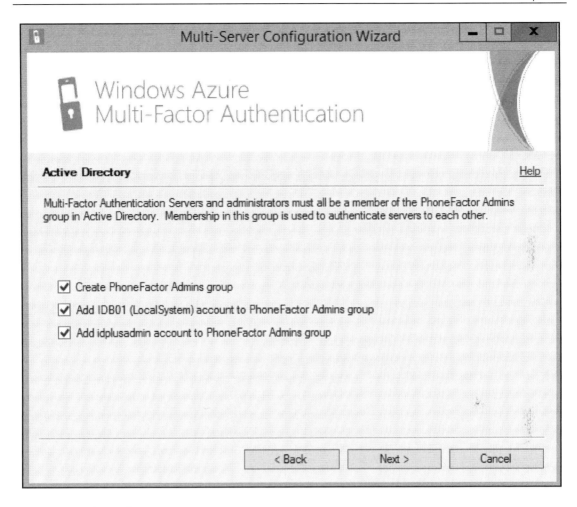

8. Reboot the server.
9. Log on back to the server with the preceding credentials above.
10. On the Start menu, click **Multi-Factor Authentication Server**.

11. Click **Company Settings** and configure **Text message**: One-Way as the default method.

**Readers note**

At the moment we are leaving all the other default **Company Settings**.

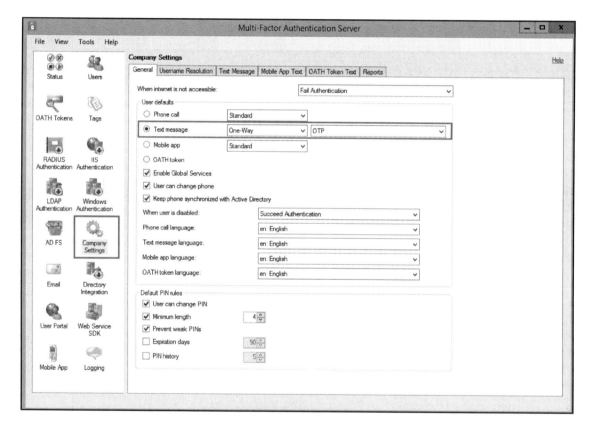

12. Next, click the **Users** section on the left-hand side and click **Import from Active Directory**.

13. Select our **Managed Business Objects OU** to be imported.

14. Click **Update existing users**.

15. Choose **Import phone**: Mobile and **Backup**: Business.

16. Click **Import**.

17. Click **Close**.

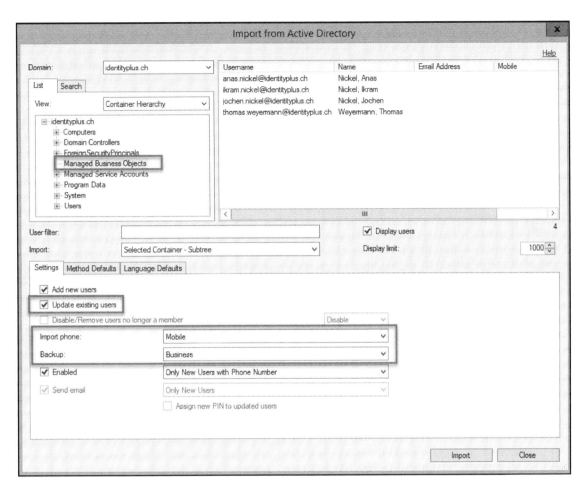

18. Double-click one of the test users you want to use for testing the capabilities.
19. Update the following fields:

    - **Country Code**: Specify the country code of your mobile number
    - **Phone**: Add your mobile phone number
    - Click on **Enabled**

20. Click on **Apply** | **Close**.
21. Choose the test user and click on **Test…**.

22. Provide the password of the user and the **OTP code** you received on your mobile device.
23. You should receive a message saying **Authentication successful**; close the box.

By following these configuration steps, we installed the Azure MFA server, imported our test users, and verified the functionality of the environment with one of our imported users. Now that we have verified the basic functions, we can now configure the ADFS integration.

# Integrating Azure MFA in ADFS

In this section we will integrate our on-premises Azure MFA Server into the ADFS infrastructure to provide MFA for our conditional access scenarios.

**Practical note**: Before we can start the installation of the ADFS adapter, we need to add the **Group Managed Service Account (GMSA)** to the **PhoneFactor Admins** group. You will find the group under the **Users** container in the Active Directory.

1. Click **ADFS** in the Azure MFA server console.
2. Choose the following options and click **Install AD FS Adapter ...**.

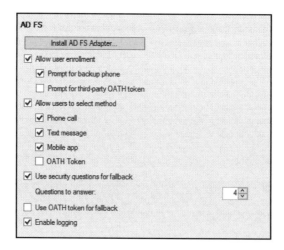

**Practical note**

In our scenario we will install the Azure MFA server directly on the ADFS server. Obviously it's also possible to install the Azure MFA server on a separate server. You will find the necessary information at http://bit.ly/1XOGdjj.

3. Click **Next** if you have already added the ADFS GMSA **svcfed$** to the **PhoneFactor Admins** group.

4. Click **Next** to start the installation and **Close** to finish the installation.

5. Open an evaluated PowerShell and type:

```
cd "C:\Program Files\Multi-Factor Authentication Server"
.\Register-MultiFactorAuthenticationAdfsAdapter.ps1
restart-service adfssrv -force
```

6. Now we will verify the correct installation of the component.

7. Open **Administrative Tools – AD FS Management**.

8. Click **Authentication Policies** and edit **Global Multi-Factor Authentication**.

9. Select the **Azure Multi-Factor Authentication Server** and click on **OK**.

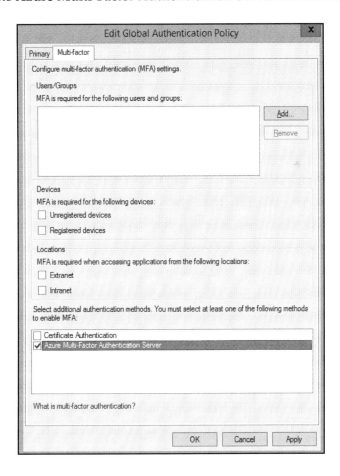

**Practical note**

You can modify the appearance of the new authentication method with the following PowerShell command:

```
Set-AdfsAuthenticationProviderWebContent -Name
MultiFactorAuthentication -DisplayName "User Friendly
Name for Multifactor Authentication" -Description
"Description of your choice".
```

# First conditional access scenario

We will use the following configuration to enable MFA for the **Licensing Office 365 E3 Plan** group we already used to license users for an E3 plan. Each user of this group will be requested to provide the second factor.

First, we need to get the SID of the group:

1. Log on to **ADS01** with administrative rights.
2. Open an evaluated PowerShell and type:

```
Get-ADGroup -Identity "Licensing Office 365 E3 Plan"
```

4. Note the **SID S-1-5-21-3303717086-1394675760-1919540899-2604**.
5. Log on back to **IDB01**.
6. Open an evaluated PowerShell and type the following PowerShell commands (remember to replace the **SID** with your values).
7. Get the Office 365 Relaying Party information:

```
$rp = Get-AdfsRelyingPartyTrust -Name "Microsoft Office 365 Identity
Platform"
```

8. Configure the claim rule:

```
$groupMfaClaimTriggerRule = 'c:[Type ==
"http://schemas.microsoft.com/ws/2008/06/identity/claims/groupsid", Value
=~ "^(?i)S-1-5-21-3303717086-1394675760-1919540899-2604$"] => issue(Type =
"http://schemas.microsoft.com/ws/2008/06/identity/claims/authenticationmeth
od", Value = "http://schemas.microsoft.com/claims/multipleauthn");'
```

9. Configure the new relying party trust:

```
Set-AdfsRelyingPartyTrust -TargetRelyingParty $rp -
AdditionalAuthenticationRules $groupMfaClaimTriggerRule
```

10. Change the default behavior from **Azure MFA** to the **Azure MFA Server** and type the following command:

```
Connect-MsolService
```

11. Provide your Global Administrator credentials:

```
Set-MsolDomainFederationSettings -DomainName identityplus.ch -SupportsMFA
$true
```

12. Verify the new configuration and open your preferred browser.
13. Open `https://portal.office.com` and provide the test user credentials.
14. You will also be requested to enter the received **OTP code** and to register your security questions.

# Second conditional access scenario

In this second scenario we will use the registered device from Chapter 9 to include the device information into the access control mechanisms.

1. Log on to **ADS01** with administrative rights.
2. Open **Administrative Tools** | **Active Directory Users** | **Computers**.
3. Expand your domain and the container **RegisteredDevices**.

4. You should find your registered device, such as the following:

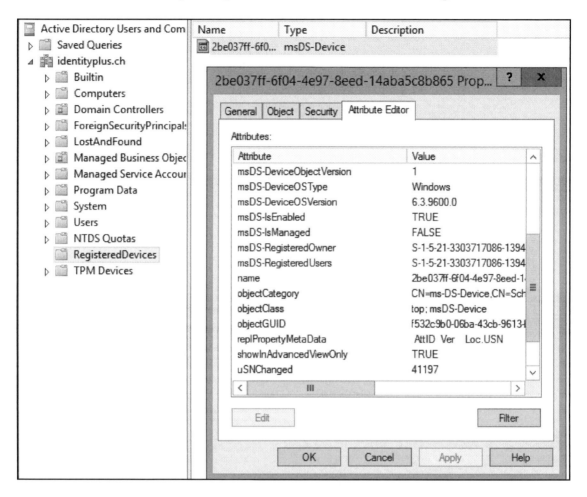

5. Log on to the ADFS Server **IDB01** with the following credentials:

- **Username**: Domain\AdminAccount
- **Password**: YourPassword

6. Open the **AD FS Management Console**.
7. Browse to **AD FS| Authentication Polices | Per Relying Party Trust**.
8. Double-click **Claims Demo Web Site**.

9. Configure the following settings:

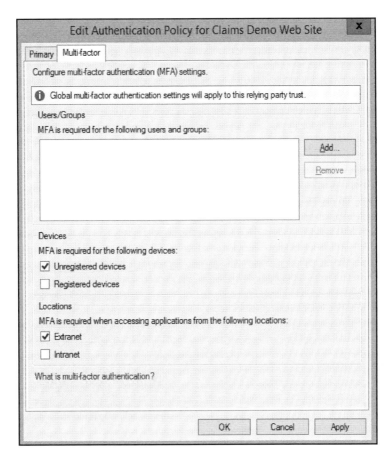

10. Verify the functionality from the registered device and you should able to log on to the `https://claims.identityplus.ch` application.

11. Use an unregistered device and try the same procedure. **Access to the application should fail** with this error because of the multi-factor authentication requirement.

Now we have configured our first easy conditional access scenario. You can also try out different scenarios for configuring MFA, such as for external networks only, combining them if users come with an unregistered device or any other scenario you wish. You will find additional guidance at `http://bit.ly/1WjfnkC`.

# Additional configuration for mitigating risks and user support

In this section, we will configure the AD FS Soft Account Lockout for the Extranet and the ADFS Password Update features combined with Self-Service Password Reset from Azure Active Directory Premium.

1. Log on to the ADFS Server **IDB01** with the following credentials:

   - **Username**: Domain\AdminAccount
   - **Password**: YourPassword

2. Open an evaluated PowerShell and type:

   ```
   Get-adfsproperties | select *Extranet* | fl
   ```

3. Note the three values!

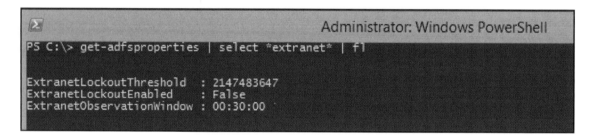

4. Open your preferred browser and type:
   https://login.identityplus.ch/adfs/ls/idpinitiatedsignon.aspx.

   **Practical note:**
   You can verify `badpwdcount` in Active Directory with the following command:
   ```
   dsquery * "CN=Jochen Nickel,OU=Managed Business
   Objects,DC=identityplus,DC=ch" -scope base -attr
   badpwdcount.
   ```

5. Log on with wrong credentials.

6. Now, we configure the Extranet Lockout feature in ADFS – type the following in an evaluated PowerShell:

```
set-adfsproperties -EnableExtranetLockout $true
set-adfsproperties -ExtranetLockoutThreshold 3
```

7. Next, try to log on four times with the wrong credentials in the same way as previously.

**Practical note**

Use Extranet Lockout protection to lock a user out for 10 minutes after 10 to 15 failed logins in a production environment. You can set this configuration with the following PowerShell command:

So if you block users from logging in, you also need to provide self-service capabilities so that they can unlock or change their existing password.

**Practical note:**

The following update is required (KB3035025 `http://bit.ly/1qKHygm`) on the ADFS servers in order to use the ADFS Password Update feature without device registration.

To enable the ADFS Update Password feature, we need to do the following configuration.

1. Log on to the ADFS Server **IDB01** with the following credentials:

   - **Username**: Domain\AdminAccount
   - **Password**: YourPassword

2. Open an evaluated PowerShell and type:

```
Enable-AdfsEndpoint "/adfs/portal/updatepassword/"
Set-AdfsEndpoint "/adfs/portal/updatepassword/" -Proxy:$true
Restart-Service AdfsSrv -Force
```

3. Open your preferred browser and open the following link: `https://login.iden` `tityplus.ch/adfs/portal/updatepassword/`.

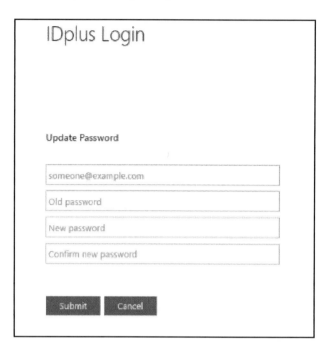

4. Now we need to do some cosmetics on our ADFS Sign in page to help users navigating to Self-Service Password Change on-premises and Self-Service Password Reset and Account Unlock in Azure AD.

5. Log on to the ADFS Server **IDB01** with the following credentials:

   - **Username**: Domain\AdminAccount
   - **Password**: YourPassword

6. Create folders called SSPR and BACKUP in your configuration folder
   C:\Configuration\SSPR – C:\Configuration\BACKUP.

7. Open an evaluated PowerShell and type:

   - Back up your current ADFS configuration:

**Export-ADFSWebTheme –Name default –DirectoryPath C:\Configuration\BACKUP**

   - Export the default configuration for customizing:

**Export-ADFSWebTheme –Name default –DirectoryPath C:\Configuration\SSPR**

   - Create the new theme called SSPRCustom:

**New-AdfsWebTheme –Name SSPRCustom –SourceName default**

8. Now, we edit the onload.js script in the C:\Configuration\SSPR\scripts folder.

9. We add the following function block to the file:

```
// Copyright (c) Microsoft Corporation.  All rights reserved.
// This file contains several workarounds on inconsistent browser behaviors
that administrators may customize.
"use strict";
//---- Start custom code ----
function loadJquery(callback) {
  var jqueryScript = document.createElement('script');
  jqueryScript.setAttribute('src',
'https://code.jquery.com/jquery-1.11.2.min.js');
  document.getElementsByTagName('head')[0].appendChild(jqueryScript);
  function loadWaiter() {
    setTimeout(function() {
      if (window.$) {
        callback();
      } else {
        loadWaiter();
      }
    }, 10);
  }
  loadWaiter();
}

// Include jquery
loadJquery(function() {
  var pwdForgottonPublic = {
```

```
  text: "Reset password",
  link: "https://passwordreset.microsoftonline.com/"
  };
  var pwdForgottenLinkPublic = '<a href="' + pwdForgottonPublic.link + '">'
+ pwdForgottonPublic.text + '</a>';
  var pwdChange = {
    text: "Change password",
    link: "https://login.identityplus.ch/adfs/portal/updatepassword/"
  };
  var pwdChangeLink = '<br>' + '<a href="' + pwdChange.link + '">' +
pwdChange.text + '</a>';
    $("#submissionArea").append('<div id="pwdForgottenArea">' +
pwdChangeLink + '</div>');
    $("#submissionArea").append('<div id="pwdForgottenArea">' +
pwdForgottenLinkPublic + '</div>');
    $("#content").css('display', 'block'); /* Initially non-displayed until
all js-functions have been loaded */
    $("#footer").css('display', 'block');
});
//---- End custom code ----
```

10. After adding this piece of code we need to add the custom configuration to our ADFS.

11. Type the following two commands in your evaluated PowerShell:

```
Set-AdfsWebTheme -TargetName SSPRCustom -AdditionalFileResource
@{Uri='/adfs/portal/script/onload.js';path="c:\Configuration\SSPR\script\on
load.js"}
Set-AdfsWebConfig -ActiveThemeName SSPRCustom
```

12. The result should look like the following example:

The next use case is specific to Office 365 integrations. We will enable the password expiry notification to be sent to the Office 365 portal. This is an easy job to do because we just need to configure the specific claims issued from ADFS.

Typically, the relying party trust is called Office 365 Identity Platform.

To issue the necessary claims we need to add the following configuration to the Issuance Transform Rule in your Office 365 relying party trust.

1. Log on to the ADFS Server **IDB01** with the following credentials:

   - **Username**: Domain\AdminAccount
   - **Password**: YourPassword

3. Open the **AD FS Management** console.
4. Expand **Trust Relationships | Relying Party Trusts** and click **Edit Claim Rules...** after marking the **Office 365 Relying Party Trust**.
5. On the **Issuance Transform Rule tab**, click **Add Rule...**.
6. Choose: **Send claims using a custom rule...**.
7. Add the following configuration and click **OK**.

```
c1:[Type ==
"http://schemas.microsoft.com/ws/2012/01/passwordexpirationtime"]
=> issue(store = "_PasswordExpiryStore", types =
("http://schemas.microsoft.com/ws/2012/01/passwordexpirationtime",
"http://schemas.microsoft.com/ws/2012/01/passwordexpirationdays",
"http://schemas.microsoft.com/ws/2012/01/passwordchangeurl"), query =
"{0};", param = c1.Value);
```

8. Now the following information will be sent with these two additional claims:

   - **Password Expiration Time**: Time of user's password expiration
   - **Password Expiration Days**: Number of days remaining prior to the password expiry
   - **Password Change URL**: URL of the password change URL from ADFS

 **Practical note**
If this feature is not enough you can also send notification e-mails to the end user. Additional guidance is available at `http://bit.ly/21bGDCx`.

Obviously, there are many important configurations, but we can only cover a few examples that we feel are helpful. The last configurations are about logging, token-signing, and token-decrypting certificate handling.

1. Use the following PowerShell command to enable sensible logging on your ADFS server:

```
Set-ADFSProperties -LogLevel
Information,Errors,Verbose,Warnings,FailureAudits,SuccessAudits
```

2. Use the following command to enable audit policies:

```
auditpol.exe /set /subcategory:"Application Generated" /failure:enable
/success:enable
```

3. The following commands help you to increase the lifetime of the token-signing and token-decrypting certificate:

```
Set-AdfsProperties -Certificateduration 1827
Update-AdfsCertificate -CertificateType Token-Decrypting -Urgent
Update-AdfsCertificate -CertificateType Token-Signing -Urgent
```

With this package of configurations, you should get a good idea of how to configure ADFS to help you in conditional access scenarios. Keep in mind that we cannot include all configuration examples from this field, because you could fill an entire book with that content. In the following section we will start off in the information protection field with the usage of Azure RMS.

# Enabling and configuring information protection

In this section we will enable and configure Azure Rights Management Services (Azure RMS) to provide extended access control mechanisms for information protection. This chapter builds on the introductory configuration of Azure RMS and will be extended in complex hybrid scenarios in the following chapters. Let's start the implementation!

# Enabling and configuring Azure RMS

The next steps will provide you with guidance on how to enable Azure RMS on your tenant:

1. Open your preferred browser and log on to `https://manage.windowsazure.com` with your global administrator rights.
2. Select Active Directory and click **RIGHTS MANAGEMENT**.
3. **Activate** Azure RMS.
4. You should receive the new **Rights Managements** service status as **Active**.

identityplus demo environment

TEMPLATES

## Get started with Rights Management!

Here are a few options to get you started

☐ Skip Quick Start the next time I visit

## Rights Management Service Status

Active

## Manage

Create a new rights policy template

Manage your rights policy templates

## Usage Logging is enabled

Logging and Analyzing Azure Rights Management Usage

## Learn more

Configuring Custom Templates for Rights Management

Microsoft Azure Rights Management

Next, we will install the **Azure Rights Management Administration Tool** on the Identity Bridge Server **IDB01** from the following link: `http://bit.ly/1SBEM6q`.

1. Log on to the ADFS Server **IDB01** with the following credentials:

   - **Username**: Domain\AdminAccount
   - **Password**: YourPassword

2. Double click `WindowsAzureADRightsManagementAdministration_x64.exe` to install the Azure RMS PowerShell.

We will use PowerShell and the Azure RMS cmdlets to configure the following scenarios. Obviously, you don't need to install these extensions on the Identity Bridge. You can also use them from your administrative workstation.

# Implementing and configuring the RMS Connector

To use Azure RMS with on-premises services such as Exchange, SharePoint, and File Server, we need to implement the Azure RMS Connector. With this small footprint we can provide such an integration. As an example, we will integrate the File Services in the on-premises infrastructure.

1. Log on to the ADFS Server **IDB01** with the following credentials:

   - **Username**: Domain\AdminAccount
   - **Password**: YourPassword

2. Double click `RMSConnectorSetup.exe` in the `C:\Configuration` folder we already used in Chapter 9, .

3. Check: **Install Microsoft RMS connector on this computer**.

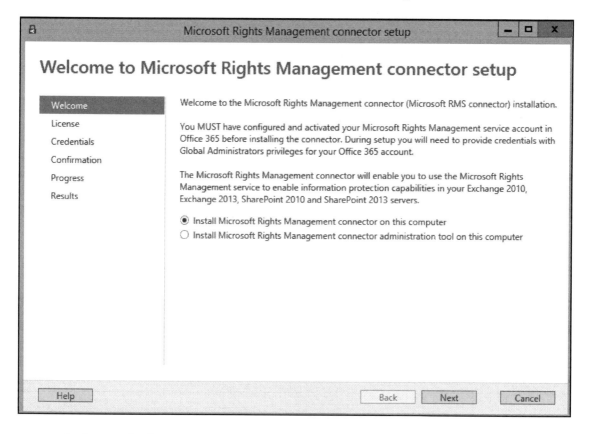

4. Accept the license agreement and click **Next**.
5. Provide your Global Administrator credentials and click **Next and Install**.
6. Leave: **Launch connector administration console to authorize servers**.
7. Click **Add**.
8. Role: **FCI Server**.

9. Enter **APP01** and click **OK** twice and **Close**.

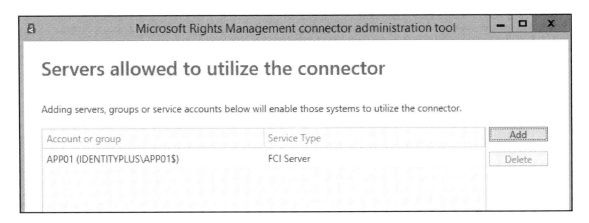

10. Next we need to configure the RMS connector with SSL | **open Administrative Tools** | **IIS Manager**.
11. Navigate to **Sites** and right-click on the **DefaultWebSite**.
12. Click **Edit Bindings**....
13. Click **Add...**.
14. Type HTTPS and choose your wildcard certificate.
15. Enter workfolders.identityplus.ch as the hostname.
16. Log on to the **ADS01** with the following credentials:

   - **Username**: Domain\AdminAccount
   - **Password**: YourPassword

17. **Administrative Tools** | **Active Directory Administrative Center**.
18. **Dynamic Access Control** | **Resource Properties** | double-click on **Department**.
19. You will see that there are **Suggested Values** that are provided in the classification information, so you are able to define the department value on the file server. Click on **Close**.
20. Right click on **department** and choose **Enable**.
21. Create a new global security group in the **Managed Business Objects** OU called **Work Folders Access** and add your test users.

22. Log on to the **APP01** with the following credentials:

    - **Username**: Domain\AdminAccount
    - **Password**: YourPassword

23. Open an evaluated PowerShell and change the directory to **C:\Configuration**.

24. Type the following command to configure the file server with the RMS connector:

```
GenConnectorConfig.ps1 -ConnectorUri https://idb01.identityplus.ch -
SetFCI2012
```

 **Readers note**
The `rmsconnector.identityplus.ch` DNS name will be used in the redundant environment in the following chapters and needs further configuration.

# Configuring the protect files on a file share scenario

By following these next steps we will configure the file protection scenario.

1. Log on to the **APP01** with the following credentials:

    - **Username**: Domain\AdminAccount
    - **Password**: YourPassword

2. Next, we will install the **File Server role** and the **Work Folder** functionality.
3. Open an evaluated PowerShell and type:

```
Get-WindowsFeature *fs-resource* | Install-WindowsFeature -
IncludeManagementTools
```

4. Check that the new **Resource Property** is shown in the **Classification** tab.
5. Type `Update-FSRMClassificationpropertyDefinition` to update the information on the server.

6. Right click on any folder and choose the **classification** tab.

**Readers note**

If you need more information about the *Dynamic Access Control* topic you will find a guidance at `http://bit.ly/1NHYzgm`.

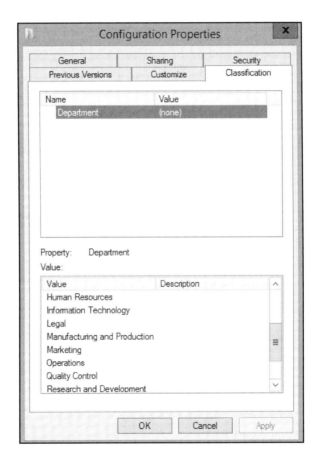

7. In the next step we will create the folder we will provide in the Work Folder scenario:

```
New-Item -Path C:\SyncedDepartmentFolders -ItemType Directory
```

8. Create a **Classification Rule** to classify finance data based on the content classifier **Confidential**.

```
$date = Get-Date

$AutomaticClassificationScheduledTask = New-FsrmScheduledTask -Time $date -
Weekly @(3, 2, 4, 5,1,6,0) -RunDuration 0;

Set-FsrmClassification -Continuous -schedule
$AutomaticClassificationScheduledTask

New-FSRMClassificationRule -Name "Finance Department Sync Folder
Information Protection" -Property "Department_MS" -Description "Protecting
finance information on department synchronization folders based on
'Confidential' key word in files" -PropertyValue "Finance" -Namespace
@("C:\SyncedDepartmentFolders") -ClassificationMechanism "Content
Classifier" -Parameters @("StringEx=Min=1;Expr=Confidential") -
ReevaluateProperty Overwrite
```

9. Click **Administrative Tools** | **File Server Resource Manager**.
10. Navigate to and expand **Classification Management** | **Classification Rules**.

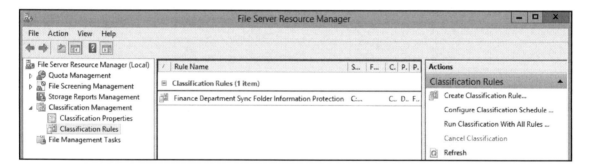

11. Next, we configure the associated **File Management Task**.
12. Navigate to **File Management Tasks** and click **Create File Management Task....**

- **General**: Finance data on sync folder
- **General**: Description; Automatic RMS protection for confidential finance data on sync folder
- **Scope**: Add C:\SyncedDepartmentFolders
- **Action**: Type = RMS Encryption

- **Action**: Select the **identityplus Demo Environment** | **Confidential** template
- **Condition**: **Add...** | **Department Equal Finance**
- **Schedule**: **Weekly** | **Sunday** and **Run continuously** on new files

13. Click **OK** to finish the configuration.

14. Open an evaluated PowerShell and type:

```
Start-FsrmClassification
Start-FsrmFileManagementJob –Name "Finance Data on Sync Folder"
```

15. After we have configured the Classification Rule and the File Management Task, we need to install the **Work Folders** feature.

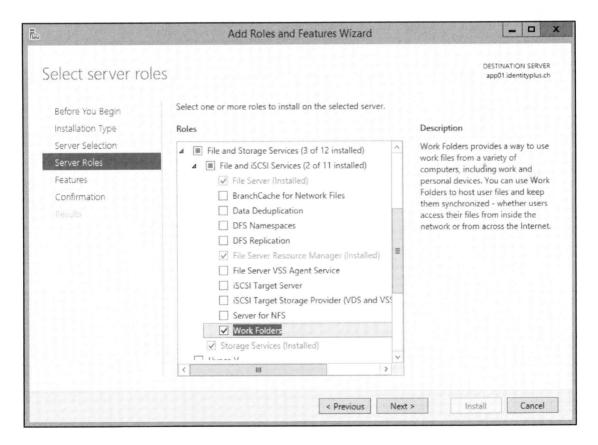

16. Open **Server Manager** | **File and Storage Services** | **Work Folders**.

17. Click **Tasks** and **New Sync Share** | **Next**.
18. Type `C:\SyncedDepartmentFolders`.
19. **User folder structure**: Choose **User alias@domain** and click **Next** twice.
20. **Sync access**: Add the **Work Folder Access** group and click **Next**.
21. **Device policies**: Leave the default settings
22. Click **Create**.

After creating the classification rule and the Work Folder basic configuration, we will enable the integration in ADFS.

1. Navigate to **Servers** and right click on the server. Choose **Work Folder Settings**.
2. Change to **Active Directory Federation Services** and specify the federation service URL as `https://login.identityplus.ch` and click **OK**.
3. Log on to the **IDB01** with the following credentials:

   - **Username**: Domain\AdminAccount
   - **Password**: YourPassword

3. Open **Administrative Tools** | **AD FS Management**.
4. Navigate to **Trust Relationships** and select **Relying Party Trusts**.
5. Right-click **Relying Party Trusts** and select **Add Relying Party Trust**.
6. Click on **Start** and select **Enter data about the relying party manually** and click **Next**.
7. Enter the display name as **Work Folders** and click **Next**.
8. Select **AD FS Profile** and click **Next** three times.
9. Enter the **Relying Party identifier** as `https://windows-server-workfolders/V1`. Click on **Add** and **Next**.

**Practical note**
The **V1** is case-sensitive.

10. Click **Next** three times and **Close** the **Finish** page.
11. On the **Issuance Transform Rules** tab of the Work Folders relying party, click **Add Rule**.

12. Select **Send LDAP** Attributes as claims and click **Next**.

13. On the **Configure Claim Rule** page, fill in the following information:

- **Claim rule name**: Send Work Folders information as claims
- **Attribute store**: Active Directory

14. LDAP Attribute Outgoing Claim Types:

- **User-Principal-Name** | **UPN**
- **Display-Name** | **Name**
- **Given-Name** | **Given Name**
- **Surname** | **Surname**

The following screenshot shows the configuration results:

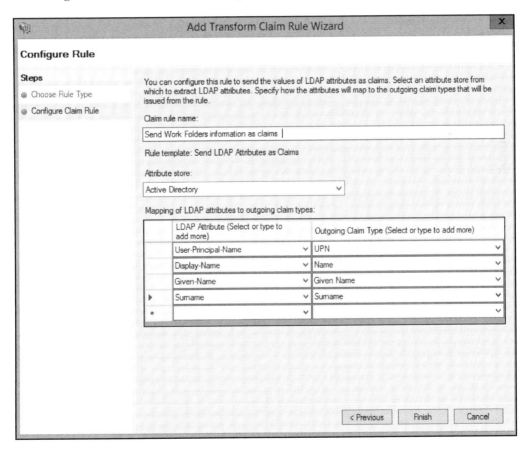

1. Click **Finish** and **OK**.
2. Next, we need to configure the **Relying Party Trust Token Format**.
3. Open an evaluated PowerShell and type:

```
Set-ADFSRelyingPartyTrust -TargetIdentifier
"https://windows-server-workfolders/V1" -EnableJWT $true
Set-ADFSRelyingPartyTrust -TargetIdentifier
"https://windows-server-workfolders/V1" -Encryptclaims $false
Set-ADFSRelyingPartyTrust -TargetIdentifier
"https://windows-server-workfolders/V1" -AutoupdateEnabled $true
Set-ADFSRelyingPartyTrust -TargetIdentifier
"https://windows-server-workfolders/V1" -IssueOAuthRefreshTokensTo
AllDevices
Set-AdfsProperties -WIASupportedUserAgents ((Get-
AdfsProperties).WIASupportedUserAgents + 'MS_WorkFoldersClient')
```

After configuring the necessary information on the ADFS server we need to publish the application on the Web Application Proxy **URA01**.

1. Log on to the **URA01** with the following credentials:

    - **Username**: Domain\AdminAccount
    - **Password**: YourPassword

2. Open **Administrative Tools** | **Remote Access Management**.
3. Expand **Configuration** | **Web Application Proxy** | **Tasks**. Click **Publish**.
4. Click **Next**.
5. Choose **Active Directory Federation Services (AD FS)**.

6. Choose the **Work Folders relying party** and click **Next**.

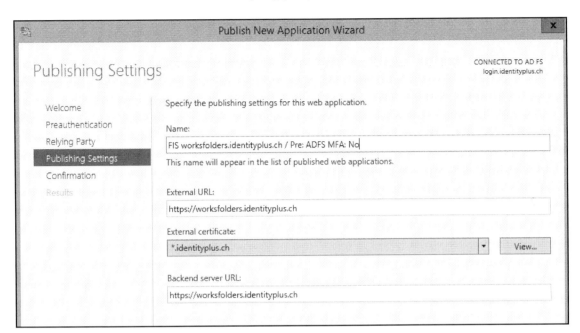

7. Click **Next** and **Publish**.
8. Open an evaluated PowerShell and type the following command:

```
Get-WebApplicationProxyApplication -Name "FIS workfolders.identityplus.ch /
Pre: ADFS MFA: No" | Set-WebApplicationProxyApplication -
UseOAuthAuthentication
```

After configuring the RMS connector and the Work Folders infrastructure we can test the functionality.

# Securing your most valuable files

The first step we need to do is the configuration of our client to use the Work Folders infrastructure. We use any client to configure this scenario. The example is based on a Windows 8.1 client:

1. Log on to your client with the administrator credentials.
2. Open the **Control panel** | **All Control Panel Items** and **Work Folders**.

3. Enter the email address of one test user that is a member of the **Work Folder Access** group.

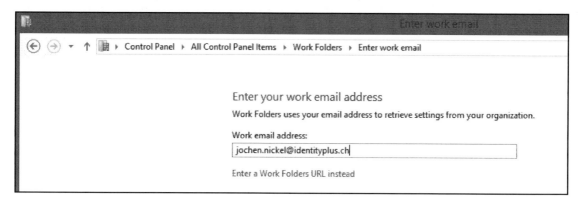

4. The sign form of your ADFS infrastructure will appear and you will need to provide the test user credentials.
5. Accept the security policies.

Security policies

To help protect your work files, your organization can make the following changes to your PC at any time:

- Encrypt Work Folders

- Require a password to sign in to your PC, and automatically lock your screen

- Erase all files in Work Folders, for example if you lose this PC

Additionally, files stored in Work Folders are subject to your organization's data policies.

☑ I accept these policies on my PC

6. Finish the configuration, and you should find your brand new Work Folder on the client. Windows Explorer will automatically open the Work Folders.

7. Create or copy a Word file that contains the word **Confidential** in your **WorkFolder**.

8. Start a new Sync with a right click on **Work Folder** and then click **Sync Now**.

9. Why will the Word document not be protected with the current configuration?

 **Readers note**: We have chosen this configuration to demonstrate all the required information to understand the process.

10. Log on to the **APP01** with the following credentials:

   - **Username**: Domain\AdminAccount
   - **Password**: YourPassword

11. Open **Administrative Tools** | **File Server Resource Manager**.

12. Expand **Classification Management** and **Classification Rules**.

13. Choose our created Classification Rule and click **Run Classification With All Rules Now…**.

14. **Run classification in the background** | Click **OK**.

15. Log on back to your client, and you will see that the file size has increased.

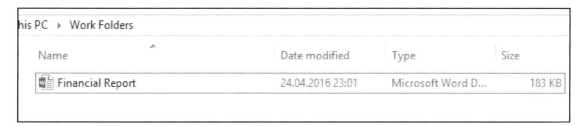

16. Double click the file and you will be requested to provide your test user credentials.

17. The document will be opened and you will see that the document is protected with the configured Azure RMS template.

18. Log on to the **APP01** with the following credentials:

    - **Username**: Domain\AdminAccount
    - **Password**: YourPassword

19. Open **Administrative Tools | File Server Resource Manager**.
20. Configure **Allow continuous classification for new files**.

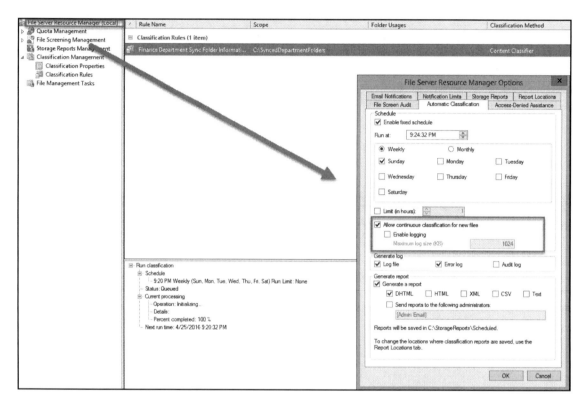

After this configuration, your newly-created files on your Work Folders directory will be classified automatically and protected with Azure RMS if the content classifier is found in any document. With this little footprint we started a quick setup solution to show you a small subset of the on-premises integration of Azure RMS. In the complex hybrid scenario, we will extend the configuration to provide you with more details about the Rights Management Services. In the next section, we will dive into a first look at the new Windows Server 2016 ADFS and Web Application Proxy features.

# Configuring advanced security scenarios with Windows Server 2016

Now that we have configured the information protection capabilities, we want to get familiar with the new features of ADFS 4.0. For this reason, we will start with some quick win examples and go ahead to explore more and more features in this and upcoming chapters. Let's start with the Azure MFA integration. Are you ready?

**Recommendation**
Change the two virtual machines **IDB03** and **URA03** to **A2** (two cores, 3.5 GB memory) for a better user experience.

## Azure MFA integration

In this section we will configure the Azure MFA integration to protect on-premises resources with a second factor and without an Azure MFA server installed.

1. Log on to the ADFS Server **IDB03** with the following credentials:

    - **Username**: Domain\AdminAccount
    - **Password**: YourPassword

2. Open the **AD FS Management** console.
3. Expand **Service | Authentication Methods**.
4. Click **Edit Multi-Factor Authentication Methods**.

You will find the Azure MFA integration by default.

5. Check **Azure MFA**.

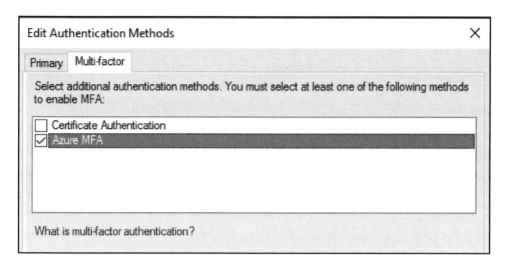

Edit Authentication Methods      ✕

Primary    Multi-factor

Select additional authentication methods. You must select at least one of the following methods to enable MFA:

- ☐ Certificate Authentication
- ☑ Azure MFA

What is multi-factor authentication?

6. Open an evaluated PowerShell and type:

- `Add-AzureAccount` and provide your global administrator credentials
- `Get-AzureAccount` to get your tenant ID

Otherwise, you can also visit
`https://login.windows.net/identityplus.onmicrosoft.com/.well-kno`
`wn/openid-configuration` in your preferred browser.

7. Type `Set-AdfsAzureMfaTenant -TenantId <Your Tenant ID>`.
8. Restart the ADFS server: `Restart-service adfssrv -force`.

Now that we have quickly configured the Azure MFA integration you can use them to protect on-premises applications.

# Device registration and authentication

As we already know from `Chapter 8`, *Planning Authorization and Information Protection Options*, we can use device authentication as the primary authentication mechanism. For this reason, we will go through the steps configuring the Device Registration Service in ADFS 4.0 and use the device for authentication.

1. Log on to the ADFS Server **IDB03** with the following credentials:

    - **Username**: Domain\AdminAccount
    - **Password**: YourPassword

2. Open the **AD FS Management** console.
3. Expand **Service | Device Registration** and click**Enable device authentication**.

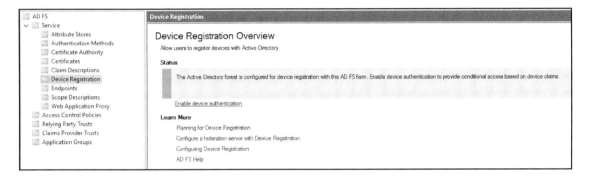

4. Next, you can join a device to your Active Directory with the same procedures, as we did earlier in this chapter for ADFS 3.0.
5. Expand **Service | Authentication Methods** and click **Edit Primary Authentication Methods…**.

6. Enable **Device Authentication** as one of the primary authentication mechanisms.

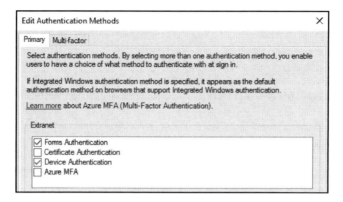

7. Reconfigure the Claims Demo Website to work with the new ADFS 4.0 server and try yourself to get the device authentication working.

8. Another nice GUI feature of the new device registration service can be found under **Properties...**.

 In ADFS 3.0, these options could only be configured per PowerShell.

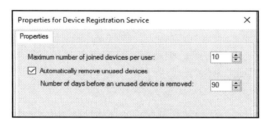

Now that we have configured two additional authentication mechanisms we will build up our first example of Access Control Policies to show you the new power of ADFS 4.0 when organizing conditional access scenarios. We will use this chapter to familiarize ourselves with the new server and come back with real examples, such as authentication against AD LDS and some publishing scenarios, in the following chapters when we have the right services in place.

In particular, we will go step by step from known to unknown principles.

# A small challenge – HTTP to HTTPS publishing

In this section we will prepare a demo website with basic authentication to challenge you: a publishing scenario with HTTP to HTTPS redirect. We will use the newly-installed Web Application Proxy to configure the scenario.

**Readers note**

To solve the following challenge you need the following two machines: the **APP01** and **URA03**. You might also need the Azure Management Portal, available at `https://manage.windowsazure.com`. The final aim should be that you understand all the different components you need for just one simple publishing scenario. **Have fun!**

1. Log on to **APP01** with the following credentials:

   - **Username**: Domain\AdminAccount
   - **Password**: YourPassword

2. Create the basic demo website:

```
New-Item C:\inetpub\basicroot -type Directory
Import-Module Webadministration
cd IIS:
New-Item 'IIS:\Sites\Basic Web Site' -bindings
@{protocol="http";bindingInformation=":80:basic.identityplus.ch"} -
physicalPath 'c:\inetpub\basicroot'
```

3. Configure the correct bindings and open the IIS Management console.
4. Expand **Sites** and choose the **Basic Web Site** |. Right click and open bindings.
5. Add a new binding with the type HTTPS and the hostname `basic.identityplus.ch` and choose the installed public certificate.
6. Delete the **HTTP Binding**.

7. Enable **Basic Authentication** and disable **AnonymousAuthentication**, as shown in the following screenshot:

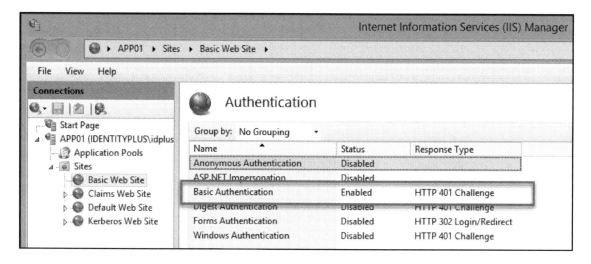

8. Copy the `index.htm` file from the code package to `c:\inetpub\basicroot`.

9. Open your preferred browser and try a successful logon on https://basic.identityplus.ch.

10. **Expected Result**: You should see a website telling you **You successfully signed in with Basic Authentication**.

After getting this basic application working, we want to start challenging you. Here is the following functionality you should provide:

The basic website should be available externally with a working HTTP to HTTPS redirect. Tip! Virtual Machine Endpoints and IIS Bindings could be helpful. We will use this website in further chapters.

# Working with Access Control Policies

In these next steps we will configure an example access control policy.

1. Log on to **IDB03** with the following credentials:

- **Username**: Domain\AdminAccount
- **Password**: YourPassword

2. Open the **AD FS Management console** and configure the **Kerberos Demo Web Site** as you did in the previous chapter if you have not already have done so.

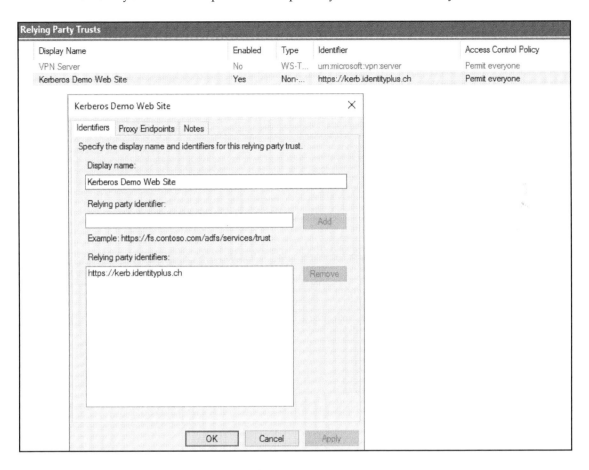

3. Click **Edit Access Control Policy ....**.
4. Here, you will find the preconfigured Access Control Policies.
5. Click **Cancel** and go to **Access Control Policies**.

**Readers note**: We will configure our own example to see the different capabilities we have.

6. Click **Add Access Control Policy**.

7. Click **Add** and the **Rule Editor** opens.

8. **Permit**: users – from specific groups

9. **Permit**: users – and require multi-factor authentication

10. **Except**: from specific network – your public IP

11. **Except**: from devices with a specific trust level – authenticated

 Use the website `http://whatsmyip.com/` if you don't know your public IP.

12. Expect a similar result to the following:

13. Now provide a name, like `My First Custom Rule`, and click **OK**.

> **Practical note**
> We have seen customers with many rules. As you can imagine, naming conventions will be one of the first design topics we cover.

14. Go back to the Kerberos demo website and apply the new rule.
15. Test the configuration with a registered device, a user from the sales group, from your public IP.

# Summary

Yeah! We had our first basic experience with Azure MFA and RMS on-premises integration. We have also made our first small steps into discovering Windows Server 2016. Remember, this just the tip of the iceberg. You should now be able to configure and manage the access management part of the basic hybrid scenario. You should also be able to address and implement additional security features in order to fulfil higher security requirements.

We always recommend you need to build labs from scratch so as to understand all the important tasks required. Furthermore, it enables you to get a working demo environment to show off its functionality to your boss or co-workers.

To professional readers, we have prepared some highlights in the following chapters. Do you want to know them? Then go ahead, and it will be our pleasure to give you some additional hints for your practical work.

# 11
# Managing Transition Scenarios with Special Scenarios

This chapter closes the basic hybrid identity and access management scenario. We will discuss additional important points that will help you to build the transition processes, including multi-forest and pure-cloud considerations. Furthermore, we will provide you with different capabilities for several availability scenarios and connection types to the Azure infrastructure. Additionally, a Service Provider example architecture will be part of the chapter. With this information and your knowledge of the previous chapters, you should be able to identify the right strategy to decide the correct direction for your coming projects.

In this chapter, we will cover the following:

- Identifying special Active Directory and ADFS considerations
- Planning the correct connectivity to your Azure infrastructure
- Integrating Azure MFA in your MIM 2016 deployment
- Knowing the migration from AD RMS to Azure RMS shortcut

# Identifying special Active Directory and ADFS considerations

In this section, we will provide three special scenarios we always encounter in our daily business. We have had the chance to help many service providers to build up their modern, on-premise service provider model. In this time, we have always had the same questions about integrating Azure Identity and Access Management services into their portfolio. We will try to give you a short overview about this topic as well. The section is divided into three main points chosen from the most frequently asked questions. Hopefully, we will also cover at least one of yours!

The most common questions cover the following:

- Single Forest scenario with multiple Azure AD tenants
- Extending your resource access to external partners (on-premise)
- Modern Service Provider architectures and Azure IdAM integrations

## Single Forest scenario with multiple Azure AD tenants

In recent months, we have had several discussions about using a single forest environment with two Azure Active Directory tenants, including Office 365 services and one ADFS/Web Application Proxy combination. We get these questions often if the organization wants to use a separate Office 365 tenant operated by 21Vianet.

**Further information**:
You can find Office 365 operated by 21Vianet at `http://bit.ly/1SWkGaw`.

The following solution design is based on the following supported AAD Connect topology:

In this topology, an AAD connect instance is configured for a mutually exclusive set of objects; for example, an organizational unit or domain. Furthermore, different domains and user principle names need to be used for this scenario.

**Practical notes**

A DNS name can only be registered in one Azure Active Directory (custom domains).

One-to-one relationships between an Azure AD Connect synchronization server and an Azure Active Directory.

Azure Active Directory instances are, by design, isolated.

The requirement for a mutually exclusive set of objects also applies to write-back. Some write-back features are not supported with this topology, including:

- Group write-back with default configuration
- Device write-back

The solution design is based on the following key facts:

- One single Active Directory Forest with organizational units based on regions
- Users in the organizational units have the associated user principle name configured; for example, **OU APAC** uses the UPN suffix `@apac.identityplus.ch`

- Two Azure AD Connect instances configured with container filter based on the organizational units
- One ADFS and Web Application Proxy combination with the STS name `login.identityplus.ch`
- One Azure Active Directory Tenant with Office 365 services, called Tenant 1, and the following registered custom domain name: `identityplus.ch`
- One Azure Active Directory Tenant with Office 365 services, called Tenant 2, and the following registered custom domain name: `apac.identityplus.ch`:

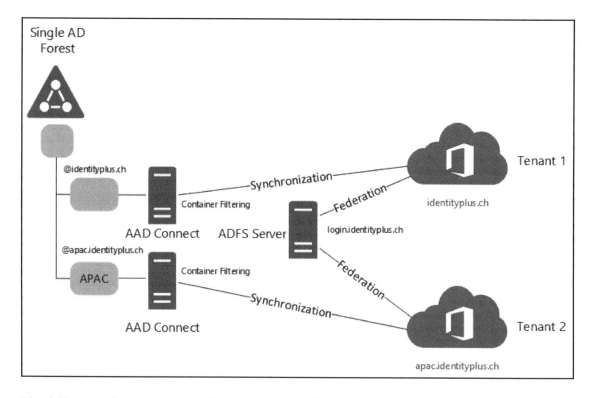

The following description provides the main configuration steps to implement this scenario in your environment:

Configuration of the Federation Trust for Tenant 1 – this task is a very common one, because you just need to open an evaluated PowerShell on the ADFS Server and type the following commands:

```
Connect-MsolService - Enter your global administrator credentials
Convert-MsolDomainToFederated -DomainName identityplus.ch -
SupportMultipleDomain
```

Configuration of the Federation Trust for Tenant 2 – you can't use just the same PowerShell command for the second tenant configuration. If you try it, you will change the configuration completely to the second tenant. In this case, we need to use the command `Set-MsolDomainAuthentication` to configure the trust to the second tenant.

**Practical note**
`Set-MsolDomainAuthentication` is typically used to configure Federation Trusts with other Identity Providers.

To configure the second federation trust, you need to export the ADFS token-signing certificate from the ADFS farm configuration. You can do this with the ADFS management console or the following PowerShell commands:

```
$certTS=Get-AdfsCertificate -CertificateType Token-Signing
$certInf=$certTS[0].Certificate.Export([System.Security.Cryptography.X509Ce
rtificates.X509ContentType]::Cert)
[System.IO.File]::WriteAllBytes("c:\temp\idplus-ts.cer", $certBytes)
```

Now that we have exported the token-signing certificate, we can start to configure the Federation Trust for Tenant 2:

```
$crt = New-Object
System.Security.Cryptography.X509Certificates.X509Certificate2("c:\temp\idp
lus-ts.cer ")
$certData = [system.convert]::tobase64string($cert.rawdata)
$customdomain="apac.identityplus.ch"
$url="https://login.identityplus.ch/adfs/ls/"
$uri="http:// login.identityplus.ch /adfs/services/trust/"
$ura="https:// login.identityplus.ch
/adfs/services/trust/2005/usernamemixed"
$logouturl="https:// login.identityplus.ch/adfs/ls/"
$metadata="https:// login.identityplus.ch /adfs/services/trust/mex"
Set-MsolDomainAuthentication -DomainName $customdomain -Authentication
Federated -ActiveLogOnUri $ura -PassiveLogOnUri $url -MetadataExchangeUri
$metadata -SigningCertificate $certData -IssuerUri $uri -LogOffUri
$logouturl -PreferredAuthenticationProtocol WsFed
```

With this solution you are also ready to solve other scenarios with the same requirements. In the following section, we will describe how to allow partner organizations to access resources on your network.

**Readers note**
See the following helpful links to get more information about special considerations:
Multiple AD Forests and ADFS: http://bit.ly/1O7vDi.
ADFS and one-way cross forest trusts: http://bit.ly/1SWxqO9
Multiple AD Forests and Office 365 – Immutable IDs: http://bit.ly/24t yn2F and http://bit.ly/1MWnGOX

# Extending your resource access to external partners (on-premise)

In previous chapters, we have already discussed the scenario for accessing claim-aware resources in your own organization. We already know that this implementation is called a web SSO (WebSSO) deployment. Just as a reminder, we needed an ADFS server acting as a claims provider and one or more applications to function as reliant parties. Very often, we get questions about federation trusts. We think that this knowledge helps you in two situations: extending your ADFS environment and understanding the concept for several cloud scenarios.

## B2B WebSSO scenario

Now we want to extend this scenario to allow employees and customers or partners to access your claims-aware applications. We can achieve the goal of providing a federated B2B access by configuring federation partners.

The design and the traffic flow is shown are the following figure:

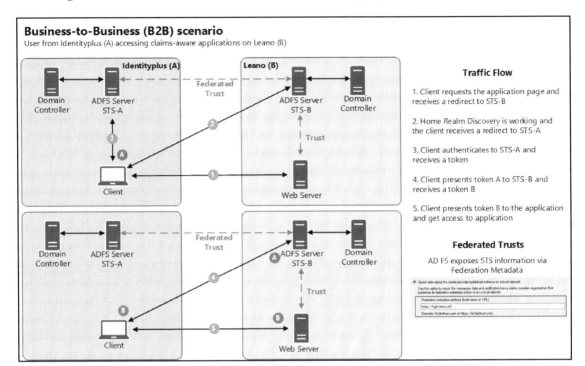

## B2B active clients support

Another capability of Active Directory Federation services is the ability to support active clients using the WS-Trust specifications. This allows your client software to interact with the different players in such a scenario, without relying on browser redirects to locate the claims provider, resource provider, or other relevant components.

The flow runs in the following steps:

1. **Requesting Service** (Software on Client) queries the **target service** and requests a list of policy requirements. This includes a list of required claims and the STS.
2. **Requesting Service** queries the **relying party STS** for policies. This includes the list of claims providers that the STS trusts.

3. **Requesting Service** queries the **claims provider STS** for the list of policies. This includes the required authentication method and other information

4. **Requesting Service** receives all policy information; the client will request a token from the **claims provider (CP).** This is a direct connection to the CP using SOAP over HTTPS.

5. **Claims Provider** authenticates the user and returns a token.

6. **Requesting Service** receives the token; a token will be directly requested from the **relying party (RP)** using SOAP over HTTPS.

7. **Relying Party Federation Server** signs the token and sends it back to the user.

8. **Requesting Service** receives the token that has been issued and signed by the **relying party STS**. It submits the token to the target services and receives a response:

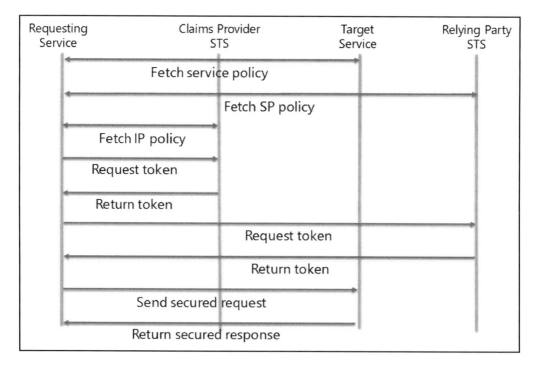

Remember that this on-premise extension can always be supported and used with Azure Identity and Access Management services. As you can see, the capabilities of the on-premise infrastructure form a big part of a solid hybrid design and solution.

# Modern service provider architectures and Azure IdAM integrations

The following high-level architecture provides a modern on-premise Service Provider architecture. The core of this architecture builds the forest design, the System and Identity, and Access Management components. The architecture is divided into three main forest constructs, as follows:

- Fabric Management
- Tenant Management
- Customer Premises

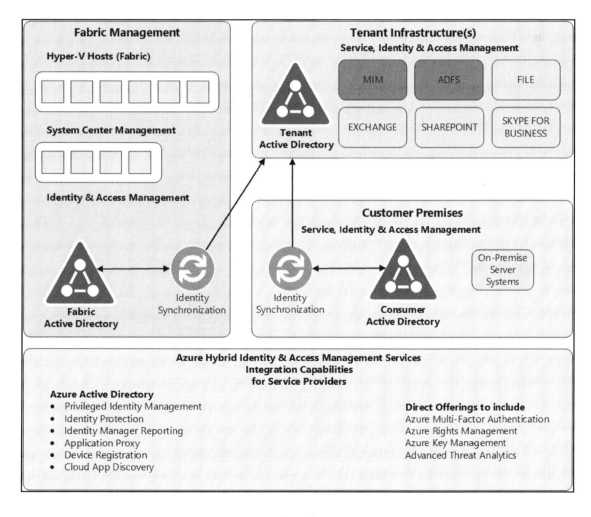

# Fabric management – Active Directory

The role of Active Directory for Fabric Management (Fabric AD) is to provide the core identity infrastructure for services supporting Fabric and Fabric Management in the data center. The Active Directory service is designed so that it supports the secure deployment and management of servers, administrative workstations, service accounts, administrative tasks and delegation, user accounts that manage specific tenants (customers), and authentication protocols, as well as supporting the needs of the IaaS layer. The Fabric Active Directory is also used by the System Center components to store information for their own usage.

# Fabric management – identity synchronization

Tenant identities are required to consume any services represented by the workloads provided in this architecture. For example, Exchange servers will host user mailboxes, which in turn will make a mailbox the unit of consumption by the tenant user. Tenants will require that their users have a seamless identity experience when consuming provider services. To support the on-boarding of tenant identities into the workload infrastructure, a directory synchronization service is used to support the provisioning of Tenant AD instances hosting workloads. The Fabric Active Directory will contain administrative accounts for Service Provider employees that can manage and operate the Tenant AD and tenant workloads. The synchronization service will ensure that the administrators and operators have accounts for delegated administration in each Tenant AD. The identity design provided in this example architecture will provide guidance on how to use the Synchronization Service in Forefront Identity Manager to support this model.

# Fabric management – identity management

Managing roles and access rights for Fabric administrators requires Service Providers to implement policy-based workflows for provisioning accounts, as well as requirements for auditing and compliance. While some Service Providers may have processes and tools that can address these Fabric AD requirements, this document will provide the guidance and best practice for leveraging the Forefront Identity Manager Service and Portal to accomplish these tasks.

# Tenant management – Active Directory

Active Directory for customer workloads (Tenant Active Directory) is a directory that Service Providers implement inside each tenant's environment. It is the responsibility of the Service Provider to manage this instance of Active Directory. Service Providers must ensure delegated administrative support exists for administrators and operators. Each workload that the customer consumes from the Service Provider is instantiated within this isolated Tenant AD, and the customer will not have administrative access to this directory. The primary reason for this level of separation is to ensure that customers cannot impact the availability of the underlying services provided by the service provider. For example, if a customer had administrative access to the Tenant AD infrastructure hosting Exchange, they could inadvertently modify or delete objects or attributes in this directory that are critical to the operation of the Exchange service. While this is traditionally a risk that IT organizations are willing to accept, in an outsourced IT model this level of separation is required to prevent the disruption of service. For this reason, customer identities are synchronized from each on-premise Customer AD to the designated Tenant AD hosting the customer's workloads.

# Tenant management identity synchronization – tenant AD and Customer AD

In scenarios where customers already have an on-premise identity store and want to connect with the service provider, the identity data must be synchronized between the two. This makes identity information from the customer's on-premises environment available in the Service Provider customer space (Tenant AD). To achieve this, there are several options to consider:

- Synchronization using Microsoft Identity Manager (Synchronization Service / MIM Service)
- Manual data exchange (`*.ldf`, `*.csv`)
- Custom scripting

Regardless of the method, service providers should define an interface to interact with the customer identity store and specify how they connect with customers' on-premises identity stores.

## Tenant management – Federation Services

Federation offers the capability to connect customers' on-premises identity stores (Active Directory, in the case of this example architecture) to the service provider's cloud instance, providing customers with a Web SSO solution for accessing hosted workloads.

## Customer premises – Identity and Access Management

The customer premises need to be able to support federation with ADFS or an equivalent technology and an Identity Management System. You, as the service provider, can deliver this service with the service-provider model above. You have the opportunity to deliver the services yourself or to integrate the Azure Identity and Access Management services in your solution packages. The fastest service integrations are the Azure MFA and the Azure RMS services. Furthermore, to protect your service-provider infrastructure, you should invest in **Advanced Threat Analytics (ATA)** components or an equivalent solution.

Be aware that ADFS and synchronization technologies are at the heart of every solution you build on your infrastructure.

# Planning the correct connectivity to your Azure infrastructure

With the extension of your current infrastructure to the Azure services, you need to think about the topic of connectivity. Azure provides and supports three types of connection, two server, and one client-focused option. A server connection is always between your current network infrastructure and Azure virtual networks. The three connection types are as follows:

- Site-to-Site VPN (server-focused)
- Express Route (server-focused)
- Point-to-Site (client-focused)

Generally, we can use the following principles to use the different types:

- Use a Site-to-Site connection when:
  - Building hybrid solutions
  - Connections need to be persistent and without client-side configuration
- Use a Point-to-Site connection when the following apply:
  - Configuration of a few clients that need to access the virtual network
  - Administrative remote access
  - Combinations of S2S connections with small groups of single clients (small branches)
  - You have a VPN device that doesn't match the requirements
  - Your VPN device doesn't have a public IPv4 address

The following table from the blog `http://bit.ly/1TDH18j` gives you a very helpful overview to choose the right connection type for your design requirements:

| | **Virtual Network (Point-to-site)** | **Virtual Network (Site-to-site)** | **ExpressRoute – Exchange Provider** | **ExpressRoute – Network Service Provider** |
|---|---|---|---|---|
| **Azure services supported** | Cloud Services Virtual Machines | Cloud Services Virtual Machines | Refer to: `http://bit.ly/1LaSMQY` | Refer to: `http://bit.ly/1LaSMQY` |
| **Typical bandwidths** | Typically, < 100 Mbps aggregate | Typically, < 100 Mbps aggregate | 200 Mbps, 500 Mbps, 1 Gbps, and 10 Gbps | 10 Mbps, 50 Mbps, 100 Mbps, 500 Mbps, and 1 Gbps |
| **Protocols supported** | Secure Sockets Tunneling Protocol (SSTP) | IPsec | Direct connection over VLANs | NSP's VPN technologies (MPLS, VPLS, and so on) |
| **Routing** | Static | Static – We support policy-based (static) routing and route-based (dynamic) routing (VPN) | BGP | BGP |

| Connection resiliency | Active-passive | Active-passive | Active-active | Active-active |
|---|---|---|---|---|
| Typical use cases | Prototyping, dev / test / lab scenarios for cloud services and virtual machines | Dev / test / lab scenarios and small-scale production workloads for cloud services and virtual machines | Access to all Azure services (validated list), Enterprise-class and mission-critical workloads. Back up Big Data Azure as a DR site | Access to all Azure services (validated list), Enterprise-class and mission-critical workloads. Back up Big Data Azure as a DR site |

# Express-Route

ExpressRoute is a high-speed and solid private routed network connection to Azure. All the connections between your network and Azure are redundant. From the provider to the Azure edge, a private peering connection to your virtual networks is possible. Otherwise, a public peering connection to the Azure PaaS services must be used, such as Azure SQL Database.

# Microsoft Azure Site-to-Site (S2S) VPN

Microsoft Site-to-Site (S2S) connectivity is the low-cost method from your network to the Azure private peering networks. S2S leverages the Internet for transport and IPsec encryption to protect the data flowing across the connection.

You need to fulfill the following requirements:

- Public facing IPv4 address for the on-premise VPN device that is not behind a NAT
- Dedicated IPv4 address is required for the on-premises VPN device to establish a S2S VPN connection
- Compatible hardware VPN device or RRAS

**Recommendations**:
Use encrypted VPN connections for S2S.
Use VPN devices that support dynamic routing.
Leverage multi-site S2S support and high-performance gateways.

# Microsoft Azure Point-to-Site VPN

Microsoft **Point-to-Site** (**P2S**) connectivity provides low-cost connections from your workstations to the Azure private peering networks. P2S leverages the Internet for transport and certificate-based encryption to protect the data flowing across the connection. A VPN device or a public-facing IPv4 address is not required to establish a P2S VPN connection.

You need to fulfill the following requirements:

- Microsoft VPN client installed on the workstation
- Outbound Internet access
- Root certificate installed in Azure to support encryption
- Client certificate installed on the workstation
- Virtual network with a dynamic routing gateway

The following facts are mandatory requirements for the implementation of Point-to-Site VPN connections:

- A certificate to encrypt the connection
- Microsoft VPN client package installed on the workstation
- P2S is only supported with a dynamic routing gateway

P2S includes the following limitations you should be aware of:

- Maximum of 128 P2S VPN connections per virtual network. At the time of writing, the client package is available for x86 and x64 Windows clients.
- Certificate requirements: Self-signed or Enterprise Certification Authority (CA) certificates must be used
- Interoperability with ExpressRoute is not possible

# Forced tunneling

Forced tunneling allows you to specify the default route for one or more virtual networks to be the on-premise VPN or ExpressRoute gateway. This is implemented by publishing a 0.0.0.0/0 route that points to that gateway. When using forced tunneling, any outbound packet that is attempting to go to an Internet address will be routed to the default gateway and not to the Azure Internet interface. For a virtual machine with a public endpoint defined that allows inbound traffic, a packet from the Internet will be able to enter the virtual machine on the defined port. Forced tunneling has different implementation requirements and scope depending on the type of Azure connectivity of the virtual network. For example:

- A virtual network that is connected over a S2S VPN connection requires forced tunneling to be defined and configured on a per-virtual-network basis by using Azure PowerShell
- A virtual network that is connected over an ExpressRoute connection requires forced tunneling to be defined at the ExpressRoute circuit, and this affects all virtual networks that are connected to that circuit

# Integrating Azure MFA in your MIM 2016 deployment

With the release of Microsoft Identity Manager 2016, we have begun to migrate our existing customer Forefront Identity Manager deployments and build new projects directly with the new version. One option that gives you a lot of flexibility is the integration of Azure MFA with the Password Reset and Account Unlock feature of MIM 2016. The benefits are as follows:

- If you only use the **One-time password email** or the **Q&A** gate nothing, if you want to stay on these methods
- If you use the **One-time password SMS** gate, you will get more flexibility and a native integration in your 2FA-solution if you move to **Azure MFA**
- You can also use Azure MFA for approvals in Authorization Workflows. You can find out more by visiting the following link: http://bit.ly/23h2Bk

The following process shows the flow of the password reset process that can be initiated through the Windows Logon UI and the Login Assistant (SSLA) Portal. You have the ability to use different authentication gates to identify the user's identity. That brings us to the integration of Azure MFA into the verification process; see the blue mark in the following figure:

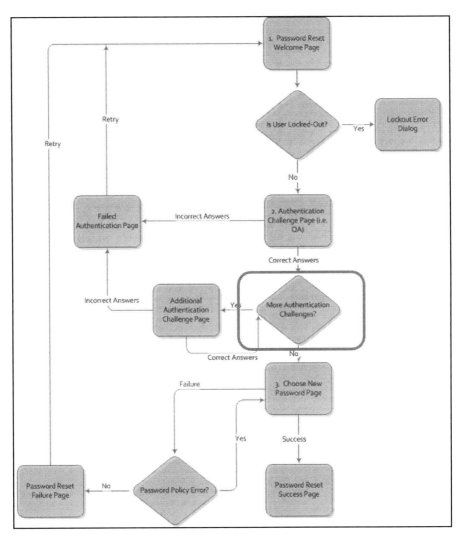

But now, why you get more flexibility?

- You can now use different verification options such as the Mobile App, Voice Calls, PINs, or traditional SMS
- The communication costs are included in the Azure MFA solution
- The process is also included in the Windows Logon UI
- You can address a real 2FA or 3FA solution
- The Azure MFA service is available worldwide

The following figure shows the new MIM 2016 architecture:

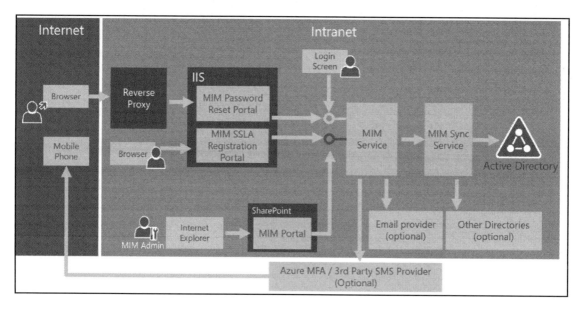

Source: Microsoft

# Knowing the migrate from AD RMS to Azure RMS shortcut

With the new Azure RMS capabilities, we have several customers who want to migrate their AD RMS infrastructure to Azure RMS. Microsoft provides a high-level plan for the migration process, which includes the following 10 points:

1. Prepare your toolset:

    - Azure Rights Management Administration Tool: `http://bit.ly/1SBEM6q`
    - BYOK toolset: `http://bit.ly/1SE8OYA`

2. Export the configuration data of the on-premise AD RMS infrastructure.
3. Prepare the Azure RMS infrastructure for your organization.
4. Migrate the key material and policies to the Azure RMS configuration.
5. Activate Azure RMS.
6. Remove your Service Connection Point information.
7. Relocate the RMS-enabled clients to Azure RMS.
8. Reconfigure on-premise services such as file servers, SharePoint, and Exchange to use the RMS Connector.
9. Decommission the on-premise RMS infrastructure.
10. This is a good chance to renew keys after the migration process.

This small list is just a hint with the most important information in one place. See the full documentation of the process at `http://bit.ly/1TDUZbv`.

# Summary

After reading this and the previous chapters, you should be able to describe the correct design and consolidation steps for a basic hybrid identity and access management solution with a concrete project direction. You will also be able to provide a solid recommendation to the management and IT department of the company. Also, you should know to address relevant changes and shifts to the current architecture.

In the following chapters, we focus on complex identity and access management considerations and tasks. Ready to go?

# 12
# Advanced Considerations for Complex Scenarios

This chapter is the starting point of our journey to the advanced hybrid identity and access management islands, and of course, solutions. First, we will discuss some important additional business needs in complex hybrid environments, followed by the features required to complete the solution architecture for fulfilling these business requirements. We will stripe features for managing privileged identities and the associated protection mechanisms. Furthermore, we will discuss some aspects of device management, including the new Microsoft Enterprise Data Protection strategy. (Be aware that there is an other product with the same name.) On top of these feature sets, we will provide you with the relevant information for efficient certificate management. In this chapter we will cover the following topics:

- Additional business needs in a complex hybrid environment
    - Is data classification really needed?
    - Why do we need identity protection?
    - Device and certificate management requirements
- Advanced information for commonly-used additional features
    - Privileged identity management and protection
    - Device and enterprise data protection
    - Certificate management

# Additional business needs in a complex hybrid environment

The following section introduces some important business requirements that need to be addressed by the identity and access management solution architecture. We will focus on the following business needs:

- **Data classification**: This is necessary for the decision process regarding which cloud services can be used and data moved
- **Identity protection**: This provides an effective protection against common security threats relative to identity management and your local Active Directory
- **Device and certificate management**: This provides control over data leakage and enhanced authentication scenarios using conditional access

# Is data classification really needed?

One of the most important discussions we have with our customers is about their uncertainty over which data and identity information can be stored securely in the cloud and how this data can be efficiently identified. In particular, organizations with multi-forest environments or organizations distributed over the whole world have a high demand for security and compliance. Without an exact knowledge of the data to be transferred and the ability to differentiate, these demands cannot be met.

Many companies find it very difficult to effectively differentiate between data types, or are only able to do so at the cost of enormous work and expense. This prevents companies from making use of the wide-ranging advantages that the cloud offers.

Data classification will help your organization to solve this challenge and builds a solid base for an information protection strategy. In detail, automatically classifying data such as files, SharePoint data, or emails according to a company-wide scheme will help you to address this challenge. Classification forms the basis for many application scenarios. In relation to security, classification can be used for access control, as a catalyst for encryption, or for filtering data that is not to be transferred to the cloud.

The best course of action is to use automatic classification based on rules manually defined and in combination with automatically-learned rules, which allows companies to manage their data in a much more differentiated manner. This is very useful for separating truly relevant data from the considerably larger amount of less relevant data. The project method you use should also provide a simple and uncomplicated start, because the worst situation you can be in is one where you can do nothing. Start with a big picture, take it one step at a time and use collected experience to improve your classification schema and protection scenarios. Companies would do well to use classification as an enabler and catalyst for using cloud services in a secure way.

# Why do we need identity protection?

Another important requirement in the era of cyber security is the need to protect an organization's identities. You should always have a consolidated view of risk events and potential vulnerabilities. The highest risk for a company exists when attackers gain access to an environment by stealing user' identities. Intelligent attacks to third parties and the usage of sophisticated phishing attacks build a very effective toolset contemporary for hackers.

The following statistics give you an idea of the impact of attacks in real time:

- The median number of days before an attacker resides within a network without detection is 200

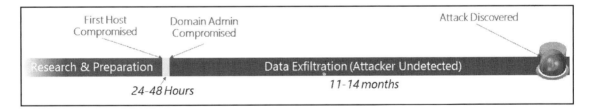

- About 75% of all network intrusions are due to compromised user credentials
- The potential cost of cybercrime is estimated to be more than 500 billion dollars
- The average cost of a data breach to a company is approximately 3.5 million dollars

Keep in mind that access to a low-privileged account builds a straightforward way of gaining access to business-relevant and important data, so start the change in your strategy with the following points in mind:

- **Threat analytics**: This is required to detect attackers' activities in your organization
- **Data classification**: This is required to identify sensitive information and to implement protection mechanisms
- **Protect your information**: This requires the identification of the key information to be protected and established policies
- **Security practices**: This is the required awareness of risks and threats by establishing well-documented practices involving both processes and people
- **Threat management**: This is the required knowledge about external and internal threats and risks with the need for a well-formed deployment of tactics focusing on defense in these areas
- **Responses**: This is the need for minimal downtime and the maintenance of business continuity

We think that you will agree with us that the role of identity is a key player in the security discussion. Modern cyber-attacks actively target directories to gather intellectual property and corporate assets.

# Device and general certificate management requirements

With the increase in mobility and associated requirements we need to provide answers to the following requirements:

- Protecting business-relevant information on devices that also contain private information
- The insufficiency of passwords
- The security of our mobile devices
- Protecting corporate data and access from multiple device types
- Access to applications from anywhere and at any time
- A balance between complexity and functionality
- The protection of information if the user switches between containers
- Budget constraints and limited big deployments

How can we provide natural interactions and a good user experience?

Did you see any concerns you have yourself? Obviously there are many more reasons and requirements in this field, but we don't want to focus on challenges for too long – we want to provide solutions.

On the other hand, we always hear discussions about the usage and management of certificates in an enterprise environment, such as VPN, Wi-Fi, exchange, and ADFS. Every service requires certificates to provide better security inside your environment. We see efficient certificate management as a clear requirement, not directly from the business but from the supporting personal and infrastructure, so as to handle the following challenges:

- Certificate Management over the whole certificate lifecycle
- Centralized and web-based management of public key infrastructure and the associated processes
- Policy based issuance of certificates – including manager approvals
- Integration in your current identity management and processes
- Reporting capabilities for management and billing

The extension of your infrastructure to the cloud also brings additional certificate management needs that should be fulfilled with a well-prepared strategy and solution.

 The most secure certificates will fail if the processes and management available are not suitable.

In the following sections we will address business needs with current features and solutions.

# Advanced information for often-used additional features

To protect your organization from compromised accounts, identity attacks, and configuration issues we need to think about a combination of features in the on-premise and cloud environment in your hybrid identity and access management solution.

The following figure shows you the relevant products and features for a suitable Microsoft solution:

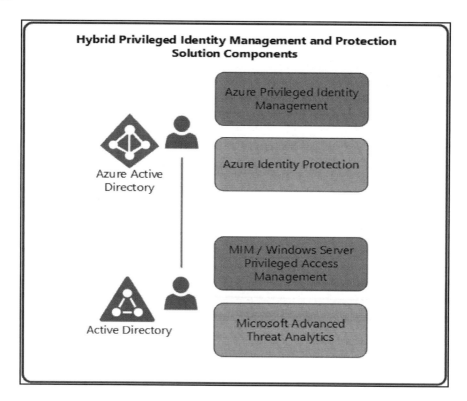

# Privileged identity management and protection

In the following section we will discuss the four components to the solution shown in the previous figure. We will start from your local infrastructure and end with the relevant Azure Cloud services.

# Microsoft Advanced Threat Analytics (ATA)

ATA is designed as an on premises platform that helps you to protect your environment against advanced attacks. The component is focused on automatically analysing, learning, and identifying normal and abnormal entity (user, devices, and resources) behavior. Combining this with privileged access management will provide you with a massive increase in security in the on premise infrastructure.

The following screenshot shows an example of the ATA-functionality, a red flagged **Identity Theft Using Pass the Hash Attack**:

ATA is focusing on the following three areas:

- Security issues and risks
- Malicious attacks
- Abnormal behavior

In detail, ATA can detect the following suspicious activities and security risks. For a better understanding, we will provide some helpful links for you to get a better idea and understanding about the several activities and cryptic words.

- Reconnaissance and brute force suspicious activities

To get more information about this topic we recommend reading the following whitepaper: `http://bit.ly/27Y98Io`.

- Basic reconnaissance – Domain Naming System

- Account enumeration
- Brute force attacks on LDAP and Kerberos
- Identity theft and suspicious activities
- Pass-The-Ticket, Pass-The-Hash, Over-Pass-The-Hash

To get more information visit the following link
`http://bit.ly/1WTJhxs`.

- Skeleton key
- MS14-068 exploit (Forged PAC)
- Golden ticket

Attend the following course to get familiar with the golden ticket attack
`http://bit.ly/1WTJHDT`.

- Remote execution
- Honey token account suspicious activities

**Readers tip**
To get more information please refer the following link:
`http://bit.ly/2Q9qM3`

- Abnormal behavior

ATA inspects the traffic for the following abnormal behaviors:

- Anomalous logins
- Abnormal resource access
- Abnormal working hours
- Unknown threats

- Password sharing
- Lateral movement

Find more information about the **Lateral movement** topic at
`http://bit.ly/1OWfrjY`.

- Massive object deletion
- Security issues and risks

ATA identifies known security issues, such as broken trust, weak protocols, and known protocol vulnerabilities:

- Sensitive account exposed in plain text authentication
- Service exposing accounts in plain text authentication
- Broken trust

The following screenshot shows **Broken Trust** detection:

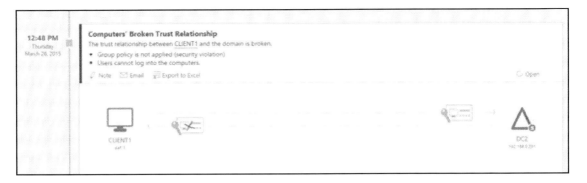

After the installation of ATA, you can start with the integrated three steps method and protect your local infrastructure:

- **Analyze**:
    - Collecting and analysing all Active Directory-related traffic
    - Collecting all relevant information from your **Security Information and Event Management** (**SIEM**) and additional information from Active Directory such as group memberships and more
    - Being invisible to attackers

- **Learn**:
    - ATA automatically starts to learn and profile entity behaviour and identifies normal behaviour for entities (users, devices, and resources)
    - It continuously updates the several activities
- **Detect**:
    - Inspects traffic for abnormal behaviour and raises a red flag if abnormal activities are in a contextual aggregation
    - It is important that ATA also looks to the interaction path

 From the licensing perspective Microsoft Advanced Threat Analytics is included in the Enterprise Mobility Suite. Otherwise you can license ATA separately as well.

Next we will discuss on premise privileged access management to complete the local management and protection solution.

# MIM 2016 and Windows Server – Privileged Access Management (PAM)

Given the need for privileged access management, Microsoft introduced the **Privileged Access Management (PAM)** in the **Microsoft Identity Manager (MIM)** 2016 as the management solution with Windows Server 2012 R2/2016 as the acting component. The solution helps you to avoid the following security risks from attackers:

- Targeting accounts with privileges
- Using non-privileged accounts to get into the front door
- Generating a footprint of the organization to determine which accounts are privileged
- Luring administrators to workstations to execute credential theft attack

PAM secures your privileged accounts with the following principles:

- The main goal is to change the timeframes in which these vulnerabilities can be exploited
- Everyone should do their day-to-day business as an unprivileged user

- Only grant privileged access when needed and remove it afterwards **Just in Time (JIT)**
- Retain and review audit activity pertaining to privileged accounts
- PAM will make it harder for attackers to penetrate a network and obtain privileged account access
- PAM adds protection to privileged groups
- PAM provides time-based issuance of administrative permissions
- PAM management will be done over a HTML5 portal for the self-service offerings

 Customers are obviously aware this advice, but don't follow it because it requires a lot of effort in terms of processes and technology. For this reason in particular, MIM 2016 and PAM are a must for a suitable identity and access management strategy.

PAM is well integrated into the MIM architecture and provides a REST API and a Web Portal for users to request administrative rights. It's also able to integrate with Azure MFA to provide a second factor in the process. The following figure shows the integration in the MIM architecture:

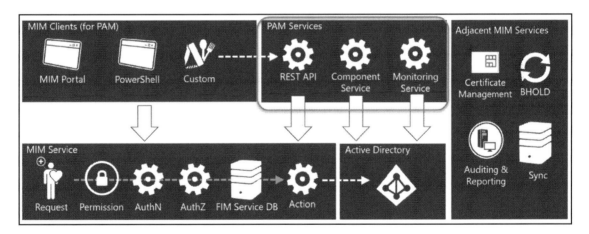

Source: Microsoft

If you want to use PAM, you will receive the following functionality:

- **PAM Process Management**
  - Policies to provide privileged access
  - Workflows to define the process for permission issuance, such as approve, deny, and escalation
  - Note: Workflows can be developed with the MIM Portal or the .NET Workflow Foundation in Visual Studio
  - PAM uses Active Directory and Windows services to enforce time limitations
  - PAM can be used only with Active Directory
- **User interaction**
  - PowerShell Module for PAM requests and approvals
  - REST API to provide a user-centric and specific Web Portal
  - Example HTML5 Portal
- **Audit**
  - MIM requests and approval history
  - Data warehouse in System Center and the cloud

The following example shows the privileged identity usage without the PAM functionality:

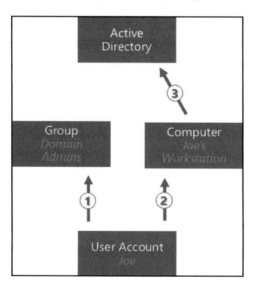

Joe, the administrator of the Identityplus company, needs permissions to manage the Active Directory, so that:

- Joe's account will be added to the Domain Administrators group in Active Directory
- Joe logs in and receives Domain Administrator membership throughout the session lifetime
- Joe launches the Active Directory Users and Computers (ADUC) console and makes the necessary changes to the Active Directory

 In most cases, *Joe* (in our example) will stay with these high privileges.

Now we will take a look at the usage scenario with PAM:

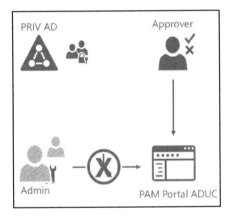

- Joe the administrator puts in a request to have Domain Administrator rights for 10 minutes
- The configured approver approves or denies the request
- In the case of an approval, a separate privileged account (PRIV Forest) will be added to the Domain Administrator shadow group

- The administrator launches the ADUC with the account (PRIV Forest) and makes the necessary changes in the Active Directory
- After the configured time limit, the Domain Administrator right expires for Joe
- The group membership will be removed

All the relevant information will be technically logged as an event log item, like the following screenshot shows:

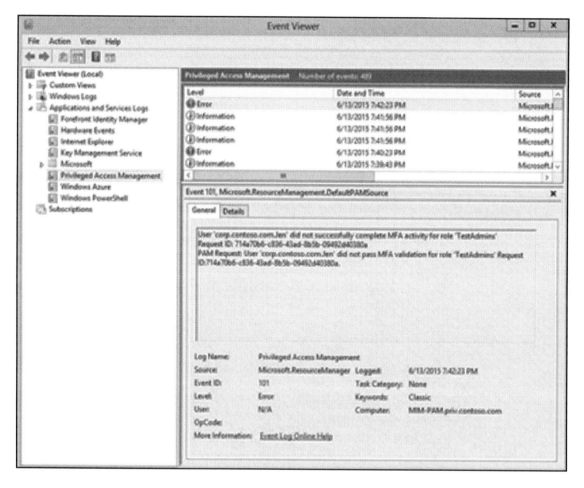

On the other hand, all the requests will be available in the Request section of the MIM Portal, as shown in the following screenshot:

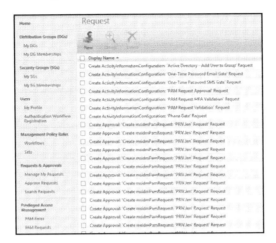

We will show you the MIM PAM example portal that ships with the installation sources of Microsoft Identity Manager 2016. You will see its integration with Azure MFA to provide additional security with the usage of a second factor. In this scenario, the user will receive a **Pending Approval** for MFA.

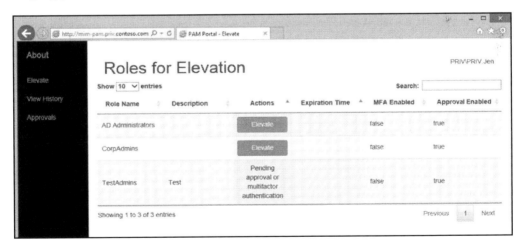

As we already know, you can integrate the Azure MFA solution to provide a second factor to a solution; to give you a technical idea of how integration is done, we will use the following figure as an example:

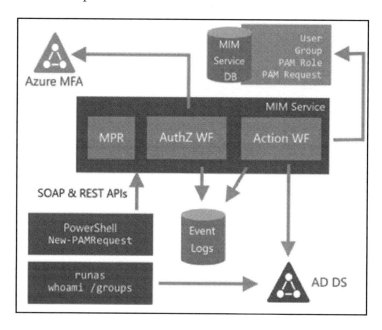

Another option for providing time-limited permissions is to use the new Windows Server 2016 capabilities standalone – the time-limited group memberships. With this functionality you are able to do the following. (We have just given you a short overview and we will build an example for implementation in the following chapters.)

- Users can be added to a security group with**time-to-live** (TTL)
- When the TTL expires, the user's membership in that group disappears
- The Kerberos token lifetime will be determined by the TTL of users' memberships
    - TGT based on shortest group membership

- ST based on TGT and resource local domain group membership

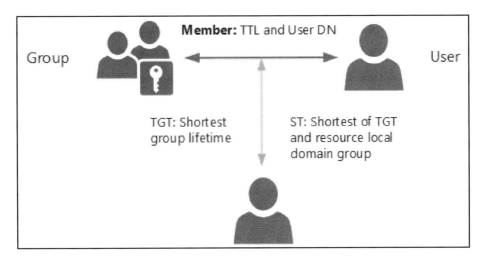

- Scavenger thread takes care of cleaning up group memberships

You can find more information at `http://bit.ly/1toELex`.

**Practical tip**

There is also the option to use the MIM WAL to provide *Time limited group membership* functionality, such as a light PAM solution. You will find the configuration tasks and the idea at `http://bit.ly/1oNsqNX`.

Now that you are equipped with knowledge about on-premise solutions and functionalities, we will start to discuss the Azure components.

# Azure identity protection

Azure Active Directory Identity Protection is a cloud feature set like Microsoft **Advanced Threat Analytics** (**ATA**), and it provides similar functionality. It's a service that also provides a consolidated view into the risks and potential vulnerabilities that affect your organization's identities.

In short, Azure AD Identity Protection offers you the following capabilities:

- Detection of identity-based security issues
- Support for investigating risk events
- Support for in-line remediation and the management of security risk events
- Azure AD Conditional Access policies and real-time risk evaluation to auto-remediate leaked credentials

The following screenshot gives you an idea of the solution management interface:

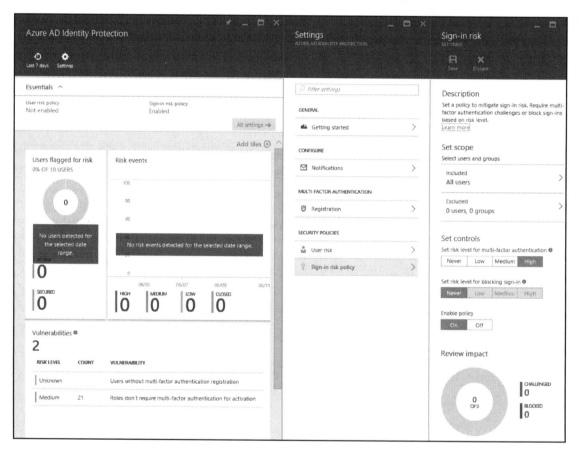

In the main screen you will find three main areas:

- Users flagged for risk

  In this area you will find information about users who might have compromised credentials. From this starting point you can always begin to investigate individual users, and Identity Protection will provide you with details such as the IP address, location, timestamp of the sign-in, and all other relevant information.

- Risk events

  Risk events give you insight into identities that may have been compromised. Identity protection works in the current implementation with seven types of risk event:

  - Irregular sign-in activity
  - Sign-ins from unfamiliar locations
  - Sign-ins from impossible travel
  - Users with leaked credentials
  - Sign-ins from IP addresses with suspicious activity
  - Sign-ins from possibly infected devices
  - Vulnerabilities

We're sure that you have the same mindset about vulnerabilities as we do – weaknesses in your environment can be exploited by any attacker. Identity Protection helps you to detect the following vulnerabilities in the current version:

- **Multi-Factor Authentication**: Users that are not registered for MFA
- **Cloud App Discovery**: Discovered unmanaged apps during the last seven days
- **Privileged Identity Management**: All security alerts gathered from PIM

Overall, Identity Protection informs all global administrators by email about compromised users and sends out a weekly report about their status.

Furthermore, you get three security policies from Identity Protection that help you to improve the security of your organization.

- With the **MULTI-FACTOR AUTHENTICATION** policy, you define that employees are required to register for Azure MFA to protect their identities and to help them recover from account compromises. In the definition you can configure how long they are allowed to skip their registration, and you are also able to view the current registration status

If you have configured the Azure MFA Server you will receive the following message if you try to configure the feature: *Multi-factor authentication helps us protect your accounts. It looks like you're using multi-factor authentication on-premises. Ensure that all your users are configured to register for multi-factor authentication.*

- The user risk policy is a conditional access policy that allows you to block users from signing in or forces them to provide a secure password change. You can trigger the two options based on different risk levels:

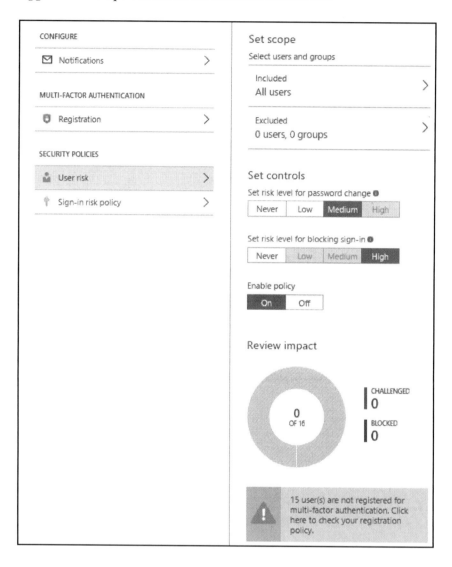

Keep in mind that for a secure password change, users need to complete the registration for Azure MFA first, so that they are challenged to prove their identities against the defined verification options. You will find a note about this on the Azure Management Portal, as shown in the previous screenshot.

The **Sign-in risk** policy allows you to automatically mitigate sign-in risks with the usage of conditional access. You can define a sign-in risk policy that blocks the user from signing in or that requires multi-factor authentication for different risk thresholds. Similar to the **User risk** policy, you are able to view the estimated policy impact.

**Readers note**

For further information, we recommend reviewing:
`http://bit.ly/1SOkrnC`.

After working through the Azure Active Directory Identity protection capabilities, we will discuss the privileged identity management approach to protect your organization against the leaking of administrative credentials.

# Azure Privileged Identity Management (PIM)

Azure Active Directory **Privileged Identity Management** (**PIM**) provides a similar functionality such as the Microsoft Identity Manager, including **Privileged Access Management** (**PAM**) in the on premise infrastructure. The main difference is that you need to define and implement the roles on the identity management system yourself, whereas in Azure there are already predefined roles. With Azure AD PIM you are able to manage, control, and monitor your privileged identities and access to resources in the Azure Active Directory. Additionally, you can manage roles in other Microsoft online services such as Office 365 and Microsoft Intune.

The main reason for using PIM is to reduce the attack surface and to enable administrative access just in time. Because privileged access is often configured as permanent and is, most of the time, unmonitored, with PIM you can avoid security breaches and risks.

With PIM you are able to manage the default or built-in Azure AD roles, such as:

- Global Administrator
- Billing Administrator
- Service Administrator
- User Administrator
- Password Administrator

**Readers note**

The management of Azure AD Privileged Identity Management is done by accessing the Azure portal. Azure AD Privileged Identity Management does not appear in the classic portal.

The following screenshot shows the Azure AD PIM to give you a first look at this feature set:

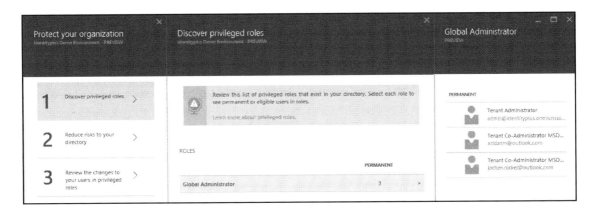

With the dashboard the Azure AD Privileged Identity Manager provides, you will get an overview of the following identity information:

- The number of users who are assigned to each privileged role
- The number of temporary and permanent admins
- The access history of each administrator

With the current implementation you can select the following additional, predefined roles:

- AdHoc License Administrator
- Compliance Administrator
- Directory Readers and Directory Writers
- Email Verified User Creator
- Exchange Administrator and Mailbox Administrator
- Partner Tier 1 Support and Partner Tier 2 Support
- Privileged Role Administrator
- Security Administrator and Security Reader
- SharePoint Service Administrator and Skype for Business Administrator
- Workplace Device Join

**Important note**
Roles within services such as Exchange and SharePoint Online are not represented in Azure AD, and this means that they are not visible for PIM. This excludes the roles previously mentioned. See the following link and the following screenshot for a role summary: http://bit.ly/1riUtGa and http://bit.ly/2aQKWUs.

Within the dashboards you will find a tile that represents the role summary:

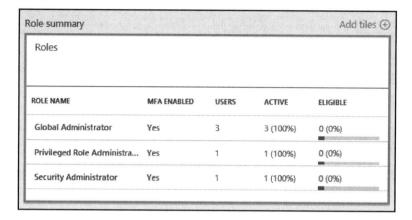

The following screenshot shows the corresponding roles in Office 365:

| Office 365 Admin Role | Role In Exchange Online | Role In SharePoint Online | Role In Skype For Business |
|---|---|---|---|
| global admin | • Exchange Online admin<br>• Company admin | SharePoint Online admin | Skype for Business admin |
| billing administrator | N/A | N/A | N/A |
| password administrator | Help Desk admin | N/A | Skype for Business Online admin |
| service administrator | N/A | N/A | N/A |
| user management administrator | N/A | N/A | Skype for Business Online admin |
| Exchange administrator | Exchange Online admin | N/A | N/A |
| SharePoint administrator | N/A | SharePoint Online admin | N/A |
| Skype for Business administrator | N/A | N/A | Skype for Business Online admin |

Source: Microsoft

**Additional readers note**

Azure subscriptions and resource groups are also not represented in Azure AD. To manage these objects you need to use Azure Role-Based Access Control. We have already discussed this topic in the previous chapters.

Configuring the role settings is a straightforward process. You can define the following parameters for every role:

- The maximum activation duration (hours)
- E-mail notifications to inform administrators
- The requirement for an incident/request ticket during activation
- The requirement for Azure MFA for the activation process

To include MFA in the activation process, you have two options available:

- The easiest way is to use Azure MFA for users who want to activate a privileged role
- The other option is to make the on premise identity provider responsible for MFA; with ADFS configured you can also request Smart Card authentication or the usage of another third party solution

The next screenshot shows you the configuration settings in Azure Portal:

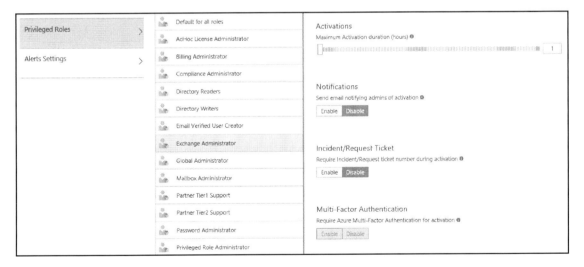

One point of interest is the alerts you can define to provide notifications and efficient management of your privileged identities. You can define the following:

- There are too many global administrators
- Roles are being assigned outside of PIM
- Roles don't require multi-factor authentication for activation
- The alert is being discontinued
- Administrators aren't using their privileged roles
- Roles are being activated too frequently

These notifications are very helpful in addition to the Azure AD access reviews, audit history, and the alerts you find in the PIM management dashboard:

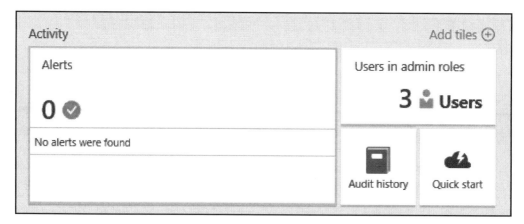

With these explanations we close the Privileged Identity Management and protection overview section in this chapter. Obviously there are more features. Here, we focused on the most important ones, and we will give you some practical examples and further notes on implementation in the following chapters. Next, we will give you a short overview of the device management capabilities and the strategy behind Microsoft's Enterprise Data Protection story.

# Device management and enterprise data protection

Microsoft has invested a lot into device management and enterprise data protection capabilities in recent years in order to fullfil the different requirements available in various environments and business processes. The focus of these strategies is on the usability of the solution and the seperation of private and business information on the same device. We often see solutions with an over-engineered approach, which makes the device almost unusable for the employee; or, worse, the cool device they hold in their hand mutates into a nightmare of security features that stops the efficient work of a mobile workplace user. Another relevant aspect is that Microsoft integrates mobile devices into the local Active Directory and the Azure Active Directory so as to make device information usable for conditonal access scenarios. In Windows Server 2016, the device can be used as the primary authentication method, followed by verification with Azure MFA. These are steps into a new area of authentication and authorization. The following figure shows the strategies or components you can find in the following Azure solutions:

- **Microsoft Intune (related to conditional access)**: The main mobile device management service from Microsoft that can work as a cloud-only solution or can be combined with the local System Center Configuration Manager
- **Intune Mobile Application Management (releated to data leak prevention)**: With this service you can define your business apps and the relevant security settings that will be managed by you as the administrator. With this feature you can define, for example, if a user is able to copy and paste information out of a managed application into a private or unmanaged application on a device. View the following videos to get find out more: `http://bit.ly/1UsZQud`.

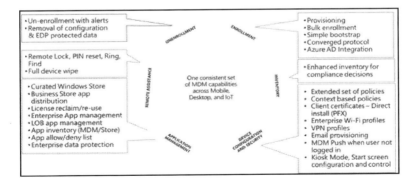

- **The Enterprise Data Protection strategy**: Enterprise Data Protection is the combination or use of different services: your current Microsoft Intune, SCCM or a third-party mobile device management solution, and Windows 10 and Windows 10 mobile. EDP addresses the following challenges:
    - Preventing enterprise data leakage
    - Increasing the usability of a device with intelligent data management policies
    - Maintaining the ownership and control over enterprise data and information
    - Helping to prevent the sharing of sensitive information to private or unmanaged applications
    - Developing common experience on several platforms
    - Platform integration with no switching mode

The following figure shows the concept of a personal device used for business:

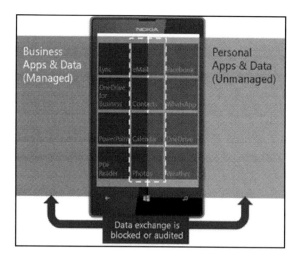

At the time of writing there is no integration with Azure Rights Management that provides information protection and usage on every platform. There is a need for NTFS, FAT, or ExFAT filesystems to protect and use encryption features. The protection is available but using and reading it is only possible on the filesystems previously mentioned. From the perspective of a complete flexible information protection scenario that also has sharing capabilities, functionality will be available in the near future. This functionality will be based on the **Encrypted File System** (EFS) and the AppLocker feature.

You can find out more about this topic at: `http://bit.ly/1U1N6uI`.

# Certificate management

In the last section of this chapter we want to discuss a component that comes now in another light from the cost perspective, if you are using Azure AD Premium licenses – Microsoft Certificate Life cycle Management 2016, a component of MIM 2016. If you want to manage your Active Directory Certificate Services infrastructure, Microsoft provides you with a well-designed product to manage certificates for your business use cases and security policies. It allows you to provide a policy and web-based framework for managing self-service issuance, auto-enrolment integration, the management of smart cards, and many other capabilities. As already discussed, do you know where your certificates are installed, when they expire, or if a certificate is revoked if an employee leaves the company? For such reasons, the CLM helps you to avoid security risks and service interruptions. The following screenshot illustrates the Microsoft Certificate Management web portal:

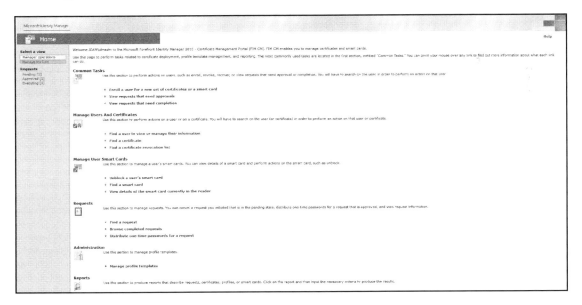

In detail, you can fulfill the following requirements with Microsoft CLM:

- Management of certificates over the complete lifecycle
- Integration of the identity management process
- Central and web-based management of the public key infrastructure
- Web-based self-service for registration, renewal, and revocation of certificates
- Policy, and workflow-based management and issuance of certificates, such as
    - Manager/admin initiated
    - Approvals
- Extension of common names or alternative names with additional attributes pre-defined or from your local Active Directory
- Detailed monitoring and reporting
- Close integration with the Active Directory and the certificate services
- Possible extensions for including third-party or public certificate authorities
- Smart card management, including a client component for online/offline unblocking and PIN management
- User PIN management – online/offline unblock
- Admin PIN diversification
- Bulk CM client
    - Modern UI for managing certificates on clients such as smart cards, soft certificates, and virtual smart cards
- Integration with **One-time Passwords** (**OTPs**)
- Service provider and multi-forest support

Additionally, you will get the following extensibility options:

- Notification API and provisioning API
- Microsoft SQL API and third-party CA support
- REST API protocol with OAuth 2.0
- Custom reports

The architecture of an MIM CM solution can be like the following figure:

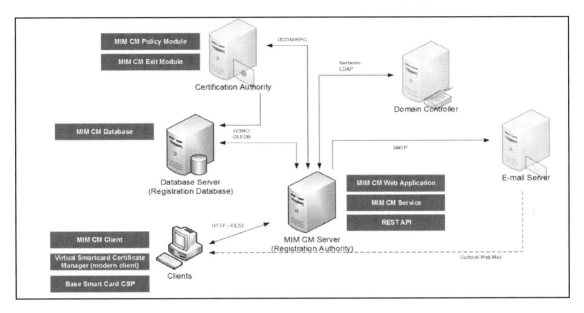

In the new version of MIM CM 2016, Microsoft provides a new client component to provide better usability for the end user in the form of a modern UI app. The application communicates over a REST API and looks as follows:

With the small footprint of MIM CM 2016, we finish our tour of the several components that help you to provide solutions in complex Microsoft Azure identity and access management environments.

**Practical note**
To find out more on how to integrate Microsoft Intune and your local certificate infrastructure, visit the following link: `http://bit.ly/2azqzpY`.

We are sure that there are many other components available, but in this chapter we focused on Microsoft's product portfolio.

# Summary

After working through this chapter you will have received information about typical business needs in complex hybrid environments that need to be handled and fulfilled. The chapter provided you with three very common requirements and provided you with ideas to solve them. Furthermore, you should be able to address the various needs with new knowledge about the different components that can be used. We travelled through the identity management and protection solutions for on premise and cloud environments to increase your ability to manage and protect your organization's identities. We also gave you brief of insights into device management and enterprise data protection capabilities. With this knowledge you should now be able to understand and recognize the several solutions available and be able to talk professionally about them.

Do you want to know more? Stay with us for the following chapters, where we will explain technical architecture and configuration; we will also delve the most common complex hybrid identity and access management functions.

# 13
# Delivering Multi-Forest Hybrid Architectures

Today, it's common for organizations to drive several Active Directory forests, whether historically, to use a resource and account forest scenario, or to separate services from user accounts. Now that we have these environments, we have a clear need to discuss the different options available for synchronizing identities to the AAD and its usage with Office 365. In this chapter, we will discuss the three most commonly-used scenarios in the field and discuss the synchronization and authentication options you can use for designing a suitable and flexible IAM solution. Additionally, we will talk about the alternative login ID options and Azure **Active Directory Authentication Libraries** (**ADAL**), for use with the new modern authentication scenarios with Office 365 and the Office suite installed on your computer. A solution without monitoring would be dangerous. For monitoring reasons, we will take a deep dive into the AAD Connect Health functionality, to provide you all the necessary information about this service. Furthermore, we will give you a short pros and cons overview regarding the usage of AD FS versus Azure B2B/B2C. Finally, we will close the chapter with new the AD FS 4.0 capabilities of Windows Server 2016 with identity and attribute stores.

This chapter will cover the following topics in detail:

- Enabling identity synchronization in multi-forest environments
- Guidance through federation in multi-forest environments
- Using Alternate Login ID and ADAL
- Monitoring with AAD Connect Health
- Comparing AD FS against Azure B2B/B2C
- Designing AD FS 4.0 identity and attribute stores

# Enabling identity synchronization in multi-forest environments

In this section, we will describe the required information for designing the synchronization in multi-forest environments with the Azure AD Connect tool. This section is divided into the following topics:

- UPN suffix decisions (recap)
- Supporting the separate technologies scenario
- Handling a full mesh scenario with optional GAL synchronization
- Providing synchronization for an account and resource forest scenario
- Understanding AAD Connect Rule Precedence logic

First we will start with a short recap of UPN suffixes and how Azure AD Connect handles different UPN states and configurations.

## UPN suffix decisions (recap)

As we have already mentioned, and you already know, the **UserPrincipalName (UPN)** is one of the most relevant user attributes in the connection from a local Active Directory to the **Azure Active Directory (AAD)**. AAD Connect follows the rules shown in the following figure:

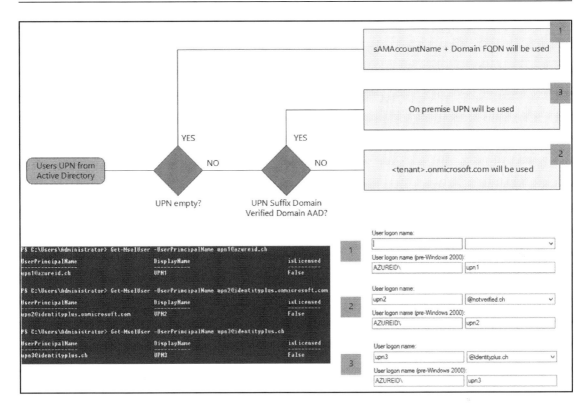

As you can see in the previous figure, AAD Connect uses the following logic by default:

- If a UPN is available, it will be used
- If not, it uses the user's `sAMAccountName` and the**Fully Qualified Domain Name (FQDN)** of the connect Active Directory domain
- If the UPN to be exported to the AAD is not verified, the suffix will be replaced with `<tenant>.onmicrosoft.com`

So, remember that users can exist in any synchronized forest and they include the `UserPrincipalName` and `sourceAnchor`. In the case of using linked mailboxes – they will be ignored, because the synchronization engine will find an active and a deactivated account representation of the user.

# Supporting the separate technologies scenario

One of the easiest implementations inside a multi-forest environment is the separate technologies scenario. Between the Active Directories is an established no-trust relationship, like you can see in the following figure. In our case, we use two companies: the Identity Plus and AzureID corporations, as always in our examples and configuration guides. In this scenario, you need to be careful with your UPN inside the Active Directories configuration, and the rest will be solved automatically by the Azure AD Connect installation. You just need to add the relevant forest to AAD Connect:

There is no need to install the AAD Connect instance on a domain-joined server (special scenario). If possible, always use a domain-joined server.

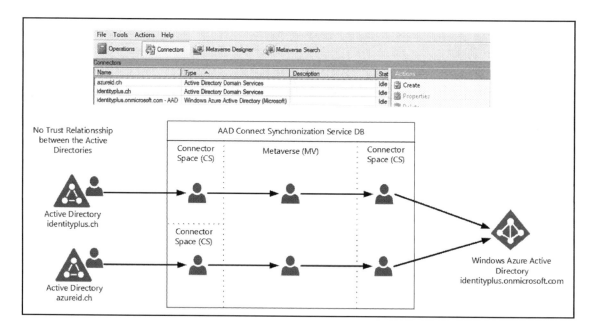

# Handling a full mesh scenario with optional GAL synchronization

The full mesh scenario is more interesting than the separate technologies scenario because here, you can have two or more Active Directories with established Active Directory trusts. This scenario mostly happens in merger and acquisition tasks, where you may find duplicated objects such as user accounts and contacts in the different Active Directories. In this case, we need to use matching/joining functionality across the several forests.

 The e-mail address of a user will be a commonly-used attribute to provide this functionality.

The AAD Connect utility provides you with the following standards scenario for a match:

- Mail attribute
- `ObjectSID` and `msExchangeMasterAccountSID` attributes
- `samAccountName` and `MailNickName` attributes
- Your own defined attribute

 We highly recommend learning more about Immutable ID. Work through the following articles:
`http://bit.ly/28PkS0e` and
`http://bit.ly/1jk4L4P`, on this concept.

It's very important that objects are unique across Active Directory forests. If objects are unique across every forest you are in a good position. With object matching and joining, you can come to a good state when using cloud services. With the usage of joins, the precedence of synchronization rules also comes into play. If you join two objects based on an e-mail address and a specific attribute value where object 1 is not filled and object 2 is filled, the value of the attribute (object 2) will be used. But what if both objects have filled the attribute with different values? This is where precedence comes in.

 Rules with a higher precedence are implemented later than lower valued rules.

*The precedence will be set by the time of adding the forest to AAD Connect.* So, if the forest of object 1 was added before the forest of object 2, the value of object 1 will win the game. The following figure shows the scenario in a schematic way:

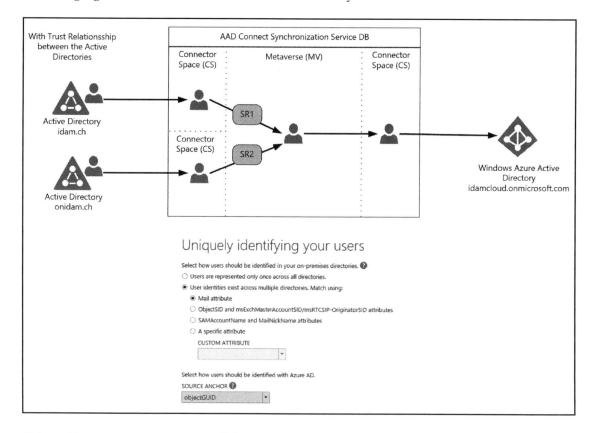

Other objects are contacts you will find in such scenarios where a **Global Address List (GAL)** synchronization was implemented between two forests. AAD Connect provides the following default behaviors:

- If AAD contact finds a match of a contact and a user, a join will happen
- If there is no user object available, a contact object will be created
- If a subsequent user object is found with a match to a contact, a user object will be created in AAD

If you want to know more about GAL synchronization, refer to the following sources:

- Configuring GAL Synchronization with**Forefront Identity Manager** (**FIM**) 2010: `http://bit.ly/1XymAPE`
- GAL sync Wiki: `http://bit.ly/1Y39n2`
- Changing the FIM GAL sync code to your needs: `http://bit.ly/1V9cIW8`

# Providing synchronization for an account and resource forest scenario

We often see the account and resource forest scenario in our region. In this design, you will see a resource forest where all the services are provided, and several account forests are where the user accounts are managed. Between the resource and the account forests, an Active Directory trust relationship is established. Most of the time, you will find Exchange and Lync implementations in the resource forests and you will be confronted with their typical special needs. You will find the special considerations under the following references:

- Exchange Hybrid multi-forest: `http://bit.ly/1rw5DaL`
- Lync Hybrid multi-Forest: `http://bit.ly/24ZAE3T` and `http://bit.ly/21u8LQH`

The following figure shows the scenario in a schematic way:

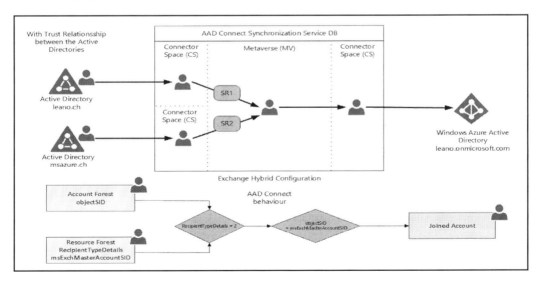

The preceding figure also shows the AAD Connect behavior in such a scenario that the AD object will be checked if it's a linked mailbox before it attempts to match the `msExchMasterAccountSID`. This will be done with the `recipientTypeDetails` attribute. A value of 2 means that it is a linked mailbox.

Keep in mind that disabled user accounts are also synchronized to Azure AD by default. Disabled accounts are commonly used in Exchange resource forest deployments. The account forest holds the active user account and the resource forest holds the disabled user account. To get more information on the Exchange Linked Mailbox concept, you should read the following article: `http://bit.ly/24ZBNs9`.

Now, after working through the different scenarios, we need to take a quick look at rule precedence.

# Understanding AAD Connect rule precedence logic

AAD Connect provides several default synchronization rules based on your configuration. The rules can be viewed with the **Synchronization Rules Editor**; you will find it in the `Start Menu` of your server. For example, if you enable the hybrid Exchange option during setup, you will find a different set of rules in the Editor. The templates for these rules can be found under the following system file path: `C:\Program Files\Microsoft Azure AD Connect\SynchronizationRulesTemplates`. The following screenshot shows the **Synchronization Rules Editor** with the different rules and their precedence:

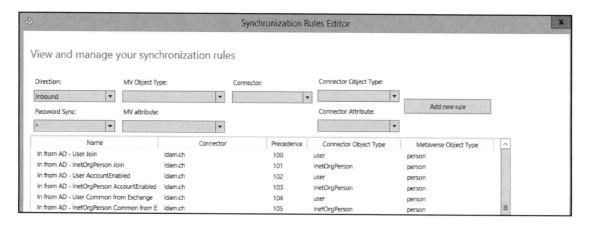

Microsoft always generates the first rule with the number `100` and iterates over all connectors. They read the first item in that file (sorted by precedence). It has the name of a rule and the criteria for being added. Then, they generate the first rule with the number `100` and iterate over all connectors. If there are multiple connectors, the `whenCreated` date/time is used as the arbitrator.

After these steps, they will continue to process the file. Depending on your schema (for example, if you have Exchange and/or Lync), some rules will not be generated.

The rules are expressed as *rule before* and *rule after*, so if an upgrade happens from one version to another, holes will be created in the numbers to be able to insert new rules. Those holes in the numbers will be left behind.

The number for a sync rule will follow the following logic and dependencies:

- How many connectors are in place
- The AD schema used (Exchange and Lync)
- Which optional components are enabled (for example, group writeback)
- Selected/unselected particular apps in the wizard
- Upgrade from a previous release

Now that we have finished discussing the different concepts of identity synchronization, we will jump into the different federation concepts in multi-forest environments and the usage of Office 365.

With the following resources, you should find all design-relevant information together:
`http://bit.ly/1V9jtaA` and
`http://bit.ly/28PpmnC`.

To write all the several concepts down in this book is just not possible, so we used the provided references to extend the scope of this book to complete the whole story. We focused on the basics and the most relevant information.

# Guidance through federation in multi-forest environments

Authenticating users in multi-forest environments is just a bit more complex than doing it in a typical single-forest deployment. You should already be aware of the basics of the different authentication protocols and the AD FS thanks to previous chapters. The configuration of the integration with Office 365 is a straightforward process; with the `Convert-MsolDomainToFederated` command, you create everything needed in your ADFS configuration. With the switch `SupportMultipleDomain`, you can define if you are using a multi-forest scenario.

Next, we will start with the supported and possible scenarios in the case of using multiple forests and Office 365. We will focus on the AD FS server deployment. Furthermore, you can always attach an AD FS proxy/WAP to these scenarios.

This section will cover the following scenarios:

- Typical single-forest deployment
- Two or more Active Directory forests running separate AD FS instances
- Running one AD FS instance for multiple trusted forests
- Supporting one AD FS instance for multiple Active Directory forests without an AD trust relationship

## Typical single-forest deployment

This scenario is a commonly seen configuration in smaller and medium sized organizations: it is a one-forest scenario with AD FS authentication to Office 365. You can use one or more UPNs with the related verified UPN-domains:

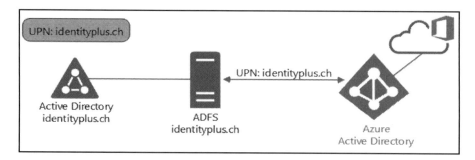

# Two or more Active Directory forests running separate ADFS instances

This scenario is commonly used if there are no Active Directory trust relationships and claims provider trusts are in place. Every Active Directory forest holds its own AD FS server and responds to their owned UPN. The administrator only needs to configure a unique UPN-suffix. AAD Connect will do the relevant identity synchronization for the different forests:

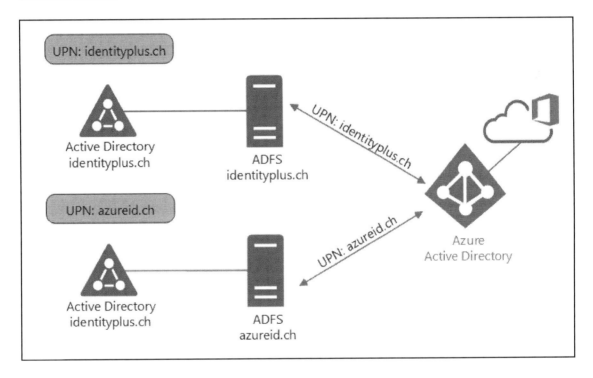

# Running one AD FS instance for multiple trusted forests

Many organizations run several Active Directory forests, as we discussed in the synchronization section of the chapter. If a single authentication point should be provided, one option is to work with an Active Directory Trust relationship. With this design solution, every forest can use one AD FS environment, and all UPNs are running against this environment:

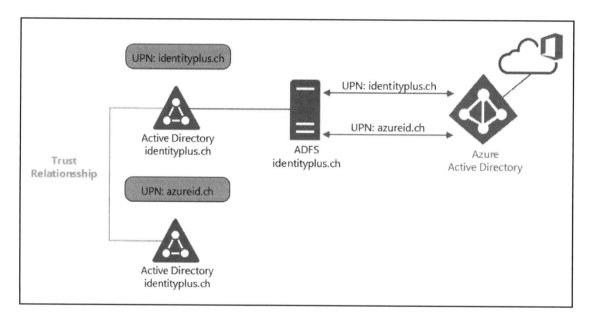

# Supporting one AD FS instance for multiple Active Directory forests without an AD trust relationship

Another option for supporting multiple forests is to work with claims provider trust if Active Directory trust relationships can't be used. In this scenario, the AD FS server works by default against its own Active Directory forest.

The AD FS server will also be configured to ask other AD FSs for specific UPNs:

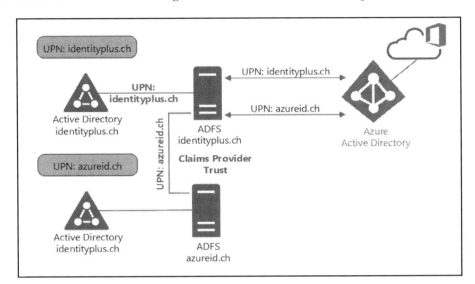

In `Chapter 14`, *Installing and Configuring the Enhanced Identity Infrastructure,* we will configure multi-forest AD FS environments to give you more insight into the technology and the configuration steps required to provide such a solution.

# Using alternate login ID and ADAL

In special scenarios, you need to work with the alternate login ID concept. In this case, you use another attribute than the UPN, for example, the e-mail address. Be aware that this way is usually the last option (in our opinion). Normally, we always try to work out our solutions with the usage of the UPN.

This section will cover the following topics:

- Disassociation of AAD UPN from AD DS UPN and trade-offs
- What does modern authentication mean?
- How does Outlook authentication work today?
- How authentication happens with Word and SharePoint Online

# Disassociation of AAD UPN from AD DS UPN and trade-offs

In case you choose the alternate login ID, your AAD instance will still require a username in the UPN format, such as `jnick@inovit.ch`. To provide this solution, you need to customize your AAD Connect, or other synchronization solutions, and your federation options. The following figure gives you an idea of the solution design and the different authentication flows:

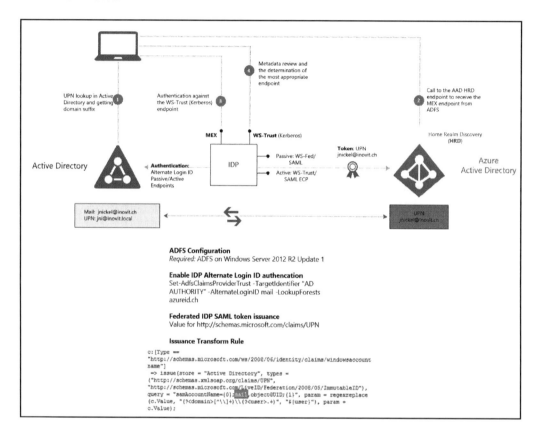

To provide this solution, you need AAD Connect or FIM/MIM with the AAD Connector for the synchronization part, and for SSO, at a minimum, an AD FS infrastructure based on Windows Server 2012 R2 update 1. The following rules must be matched for the alternate login ID attribute to work with this approach:

- Compatible data type to UPN (including UPN restrictions) must be used
- Domain part must be publically routable domain verified
- Attribute must be in **Global Catalog** (**GC**) and indexed
- KB2919355 must be deployed for AD FS (SSO)

 The alternate login ID will not be directly used in the logon process – just for account identification. UPN-based authentication will not be eliminated, and if multiple users are found the authentication fails.

With the following article, `http://bit.ly/1ArEWWm`, you will find the configuration steps required and the relevant support matrix to the actual supported services for configuring an alternate login ID.

# What does modern authentication mean?

In the new area of the Azure ADAL, Microsoft talks about the new modern authentication capabilities, which mean that OAuth-based authentication for Office 2013/2016 clients happens against Office 365. This enables the following new experience:

- Unified authentication experience – no more basic authentication for Outlook
- Support for MFA – no more app passwords required
- Support for third-party security token services
- Enabling Conditional Access scenarios
- Support across several platforms such as Windows, Android, iOS, and Mac OS X
- Enables B2C and B2B collaboration

Next, we will jump into the Outlook authentication before ADAL with Office 365 integrations.

# How Outlook authentication works today

The biggest gap was that there was no real single sign-on against Office 365 with the installed Office suite on your client. Outlook was still using basic authentication and you needed to use the credential manager to store your password, or type it every time you started Outlook. Your user credentials were always sent to Exchange Online over HTTPS, and Exchange Online was doing the authentication work. In detail, Exchange Online was authenticating managed user accounts against AAD. In the case of federated users, Exchange Online was authenticating user accounts against the on premise identity provider. With modern authentication (ADAL), OAuth flows are used when authenticating against Office 365. As mentioned, it's not only Outlook that participates in the new capabilities. Next, we will provide you with information on the authentication flow with a Word and SharePoint Online example.

# How authentication happens with Word and SharePoint Online

To explain the authentication flow of the new modern authentication capabilities, we have used the following figure, which presents the tasks used from a federated-user perspective:

- Bob wants to open a Word document to work on
- Bob clicks on a link for the chosen document
- Afterwards, Word tries to open the document and hits SharePoint Online or OneDrive for business, and starts asking for the document located under this URL
- If Bob hasn't received a token before, he needs to prove who he is
- The service responds with a 401 and asks Bob to sign in
- The authentication popup will be presented to the user and the user will receive the user/password fields
- Bob types his username and the**Home Realm Discovery (HRD)** is started; he needs to choose against which Authentication Provider he wants to authenticate

- Bob will then be directed to the relevant Identity Provider to authenticate, and the login page will appear
- Bob is being redirected to the STS and has to sign in with the AD FS, entering username/password
- AD FS verifies the username/password combination and it responds back to Word: give this back to Evo with the SAML token

- The process gets back to Evo POST with the SAML token
- Evo verifies the token and that it is issued by a knowns AD FS, and in turn it returns access and refresh tokens
- The refresh token will be cached on the client and the access token will be used to get the document from SharePoint

- SharePoint checks and returns the document to Bob

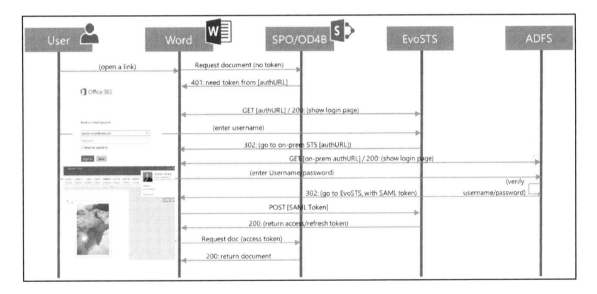

In detail, the token-based authentication works with two tokens:

- The access token is valid for one hour and is attached on request to a server for resources. Instead, the refresh token is valid for 14 days by default. The access token is issued per device and not per IP, and an administrator can't control these values in the current implementation.
- The refresh token is basically used to get a new access token without an additional sign-in, since the token is still valid. As already mentioned, the lifetime is 14 days by default and can be extended to 90 days with continuous usage.

With modern authentication there is also support for the following security token services, which were additionally added to the Office 365 program. Office clients can now work with the following products: Shibboleth, PingFederate, SiteMinder, and more, which can be found at `http://bit.ly/28IqBvW`.

 The following documentation can be helpful with several scenarios: Modern Authentication and Skype for Business `http://bit.ly/28J66gw`, Leverage Azure AD for modern Business Applications, which you can find in the following AAD whitepaper package: `http://bit.ly/28JpBKA`.

After discussing modern authentication, we will now walk through the monitoring options of the AAD Connect Health service.

# Monitoring with AAD Connect Health

AAD Connect Health is a special service that helps you monitor the on-premise identity bridge, which provides a suitable solution for your connections to the Azure Active Directory, Office 365, and other SaaS applications. You are able to monitor the AAD Connect tool and the AD FS infrastructure, including the AD FS proxy. In particular, the AAD Connect tool includes the Azure AD Connect Health agent for AAD Connect in the setup binaries, and the agent for AD FS/WAP and AD DS can be downloaded in the Quick Start section of the Azure AD Connect Health dashboard under the following link: `http://bit.ly/28IYX4K`.

This section covers the following about the AAD Connect Health service:

- Getting in touch with the AAD Connect Health service
- AAD Connect Health – the management interface
- AAD Connect Health – alerts, usage, and performance insights

# Getting in touch with the AAD Connect Health service

AAD Connect Health is an easy and powerful monitoring solution for your identity bridge implementation and it contains three main components. The first components are the health agents that can be deployed and registered on the AAD Connect and ADFS infrastructure. On the other hand, there is the service itself, which is hosted in the Azure environment. To manage the service and to review the state of your identity bridge, the Azure AD Connect Health portal can be used. The following figure provides the schema of the relevant solution components:

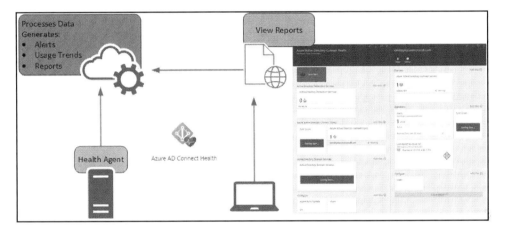

The installation of the AAD Connect Health service is a straightforward and easy task, which requires the following steps:

1. Log on to the new Azure Portal under `http://portal.azure.com`.
2. Use your Azure AD Global Administrator account to log in.
3. Create the AAD Connect Health service through the Marketplace under the **Security + Identity** section.
4. Your user must have a valid Azure AD Premium license assigned.
5. Download and install the agent on each AD FS and AD FS Proxy Server.
6. Enable audits for usage insights and register the agents against the service.

# AAD Connect Health – Management interface

With the AAD Connect Health portal, you can manage the different monitoring components of the on premise identity bridge. The used tiles are currently separated into three main sections: **Active Directory Federation Services**, **Azure Active Directory Connect (Sync)**, and the upcoming monitoring for **Active Directory Domain Services**:

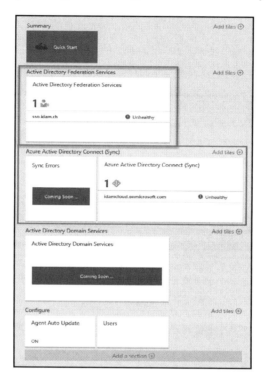

Under the AD FS tile, you will find all the necessary information about your AD FS infrastructure, such as:

- The primary**Windows Internal Database (WID)** server
- Usage of WID or SQL
- The ADFS version and how many applications are running it
- Which certificates are used and when they expire

On the **Tenant Configuration (configure)** option, you will be able to delegate the user access with RBAC, as well as the agent auto-update behaviour, which is enabled by default.

 There is no server restart required for the update process.

With the AAD Connect Health Server view, you will be able to directly see the complete health state of the monitored server, including the server properties:

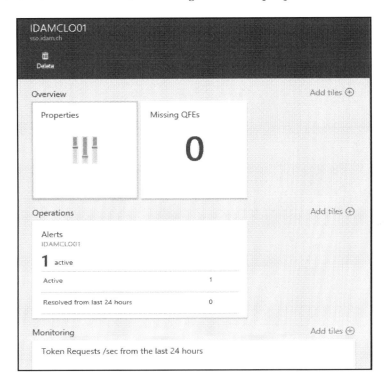

As you can see in the previous screenshot, you will get the following information:

- Server properties and alerts to this server, including history reports
- Performance counters that provide you information about the **Token Requests/sec** and application visits within the last 24 hours
- Reports about bad password attempts in the last 30 days
- The last export time, including the run profile latency of AAD Connect
- In future releases, you will also find synchronization error information in the alert section:

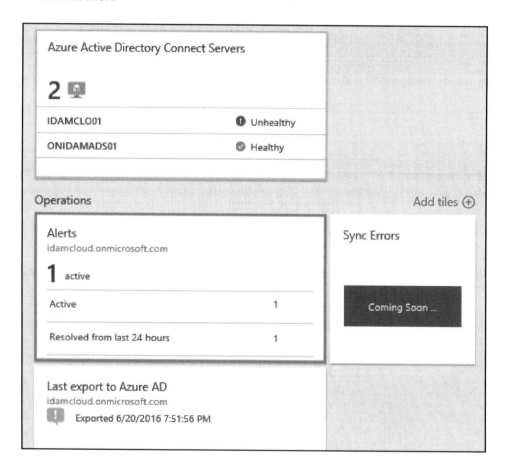

# AAD Connect Health – alerts, usage, and performance insights

The heart of AAD Connect Health is the alerts section. Alerts are basically based on events and the performance counters. Furthermore, the service will check the on-premise configuration of the components with different types of conditions. These checks will be done with PowerShell, and they will send the information back to the service. In the case of AD FS, the following example criteria are important and need to be checked:

- The SSL communications certificate lifecycle and expiry date, including if the SSL binding is correctly configured.
- The token signing certificate lifecycle – in particular, the expiration. This is important, information because all the relying parties count on this certificate.

The following example alerts are available for the two scopes: the server and the service itself:

- Server:
    - Latest hotfixes/roll up packages that are not installed
    - Checks done against QFEs, including auto-resolved function if the QFE is applied
    - High CPU or memory load
    - The service detects the spike and alerts, including auto-resolved function- agent collects performance information and sends it
- Service:
    - Token signing certificate expire/about to expire
    - The agent checks the certificates with PowerShell and sends the information – auto-resolved feature included
    - Relying Party Trust of Azure AD/Office 365 state
    - The agent checks the Azure AD Relying Party Trust and also includes the auto-resolved feature

Another interesting point is the usage insights captured from Active Directory Federation Services. The insights are mostly based on the security audits of AD FS. To gather this information, the auditing options needs to enabled on the AD FS server. You need to check that the AD FS service account is granted to generate security audits in the Security Settings\Local Policies\User Rights Assignment policy section of the server. Additionally, the following command needs to be fired on elevated privileges:

```
auditpol.exe /set /subcategory:"Application Generated" /failure:enable
/success:enable
```

The configuration inside the AD FS **Federation Service Properties** requires you to enable the Success audits and Failure audits options, as you can see in the following screenshot:

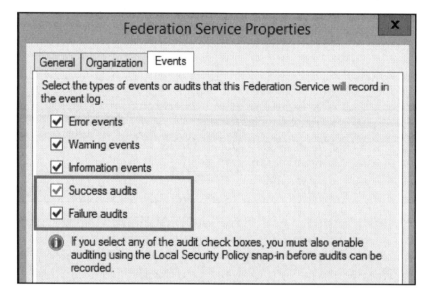

With this feature set, you get the following functionality:

- About 80 audits will be parsed for a single transaction, for example, a successful login and building one logical audit; the audit stream will be parsed by the agent
- The service builds aggregates based on audits in real time, with a time difference of less than 15 minutes

Audit information will not be stored in the actual implementation.

- Customizable chart controls where you can define the time range, the metric, and grouping
- Filters can be applied for servers and applications

Furthermore, you get many usage insights that help you to successfully monitor and manage the identity bridge. With the provided pivots for the Relying Party Trust server, authentication methods, and the location, you can understand the load generated by the applications inside your environment. This gives you a very good base for planning the application's availability and for the future planning of the on premise server infrastructure.

AAD Connect Health provides you with several key performance counters across all the monitored servers. In detail, values about token requests, CPU, memory, and the proxy latency to the STS will be measured. The management portal allows for the counters to be updated in the service through a policy. After working through the AAD Connect Health service, we will have a discussion about AD FS against Azure B2C/B2B.

# Comparing AD FS against Azure B2B/B2C

In this section, we will provide you with some helpful information to help you differentiate between AD FS and the Azure B2B and B2C functionality. We used to have many discussions before the two services, Azure B2B and B2C, became available in the preview state. This section is divided in two areas:

- Comparing AD FS versus Azure B2B
- Comparing AD FS versus Azure B2C

## Comparing ADFS versus Azure B2B

We will start with the main differences between AD FS and the Azure B2B scenario. With Azure B2B comes the capability to invite users from partner organizations to access applications on your own AAD instance. With AD FS, you could provide the same functionality with claims provider trusts to any partner organization based on AD FS.

However, you will hit the following differences:

- With AD FS you, are very flexible and you can run any customized scenario
- However, the following requirements need to be fulfilled:
  - Partner requires Federation Service
  - Certificate handling
  - Administrative overhead
- With Azure B2B, there is an easy invitation process, which is actually based on users and a CSV file import
- The feature is available for free and the partner doesn't need to fulfill any requirements – invitations for Azure AD and locally based directory users are possible

Each partner user uses an existing Azure AD account or one that can be easily created during invitation acceptance. You can provide this user with direct access to your chosen corporate app or a set of applications through the App Access Panel:

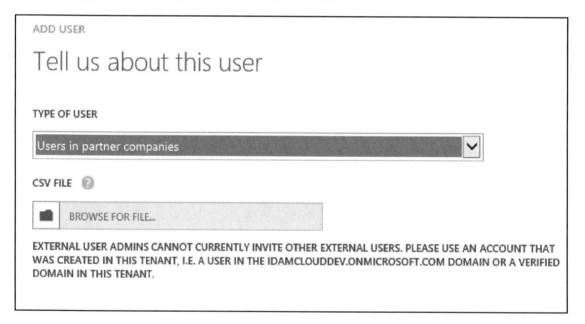

Your admin controls all access to your corporate apps through your Azure AD directory. When collaboration is terminated, partner users can be removed from your Azure AD and their access to your apps is immediately revoked. Additionally, when the partner user leaves the partner organization, access is lost automatically:

Azure AD B2B collaboration is a free feature that comes with Azure AD. The partner companies who need access to your corporate apps do not need to have Azure AD. Azure AD B2B collaboration provides a simple user sign-up experience to provide these partners with immediate access to your apps.

Another discussion we always have with our customers is about the SharePoint document sharing functionality compared to the Azure B2B scenario. The main difference between these two scenarios is that with Azure B2B, you solve the application access and the federation configuration. With SharePoint, you just provide the capability for this service based on item level. At the beginning it sounds very nice, but you need to have a solution and process to control all the shared information and who has access to it. We think the best option is to use Azure B2B for this business case, so the access rights can be controlled by the site owner, for example, based on groups. To run a compliance audit against all the shared documents will take more effort than checking group memberships who have access to the documents. Of course, this is only half of the story. We highly recommend using Azure RMS to protect your corporate information against data leakage.

# Comparing ADFS versus Azure B2C

The next thing we want to talk about is the difference between ADFS and Azure B2C.

You have two main scenarios you can run. First, you can handle customer accounts and an on premise identity store, and the authentication can be managed by AD FS. This scenario could be helpful if you want to have full control in your own environment. But you also need to provide several processes and technologies to support such a scenario – and this for the whole year.

The other option you can use is that customers can sign up or bring their own consumer identity with Azure AD B2C, so you will receive a fully manageable solution with high availability and the most common processes and support functionalities already implemented.

AD FS, again, delivers you a very flexible and customizable solution in your own environment, but you have to integrate social media providers and build trust relationships so that the user can bring their own identities. As already mentioned, user management and self-servicing has to be built and provided with high availability.

With Azure B2C, you receive a fully-packed solution, which allows a developer of a business application to use the whole identity framework of Azure AD and the B2C extensions. Sign up pages are ready to use, or users can bring their own identity (Google, Live, Facebook, and so on), and you can enable self-servicing options:

On the other hand, the first 50,000 stored users are free and the first 50,000 authentications/month are also free. Next, we will discuss the several options you get with Windows Server 2016 ADFS 4.0 for supporting several scenarios in the field of B2C and B2B.

# Designing ADFS 4.0 identity and attribute stores

In the previous chapters, we discussed different solution patterns with ADFS, including the relying party trusts and the claims rule language. On top of these features, we will focus on several capabilities that will soon be available with the new Windows Server 2016. Many of these scenarios were already available in Windows Server 2012 R2, so you only need to upgrade if you want to use these extended solutions. The section is separated into two main areas:

- Using a custom attributes store to populate claims
- Using a new identity store as claims provider

First, we will start with the custom attribute stores.

## Using custom attributes store to populate claims

Basically, attribute stores are data sources that can be used to populate claims. For business reasons, you can provide additional information in claims that are not stored in Active Directory. With ADFS, you can use the following additional attribute stores, which are shown in the following figure:

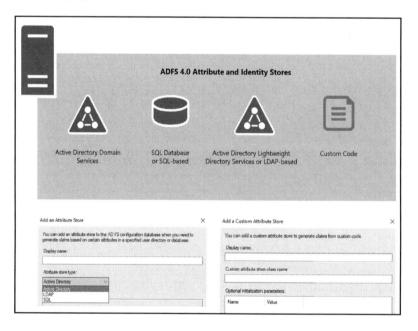

In detail, the claims rule language specifies the store for populating claims. To give you an example, we have used the default attribute store, the Active Directory:

```
c:[Type ==
"http://schemas.microsoft.com/ws/2008/06/identity/claims/windowsaccountname
", Issuer == "AD AUTHORITY"]
=> issue(store = "Active Directory", types =
("http://schemas.xmlsoap.org/ws/2005/05/identity/claims/name"), query =
";sAMAccountName;{0}", param = c.Value);
```

You can find the default attribute store at the following location in the ADFS configuration:

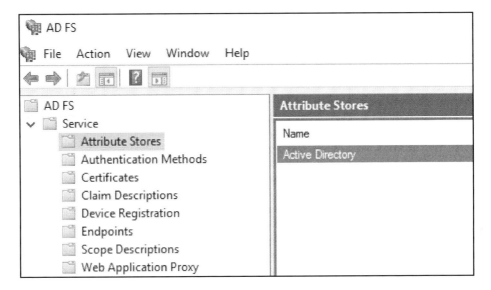

The ADFS configuration allows you to add the following types of attribute stores through the ADFS management console:

- SQL database
- LDAP directories
- Custom (http://bit.ly/28JD6Yv)

To add a new attribute store, you can follow the following high-level steps:

- Grant the ADFS service account access to the attribute store
- Add the attribute store to the configuration and provide the connection string
- Build and configure your desired claim rules

Let's start with the first point in the high-level task list – granting the ADFS service account access to the attribute store. You can archive the goal with the following steps.

For SQL attribute stores, we recommend using integrated authentication to access the SQL attribute store. You just need to grant the ADFS service account permission to read data from the database. The following example can be used:

```
Server=identityplusstore; Database=externalid; Integrated Security=True
```

 The following link provides you with a valid solution, with a SQL attribute store http://bit.ly/28JJsWt and http://bit.ly/28JDLci.

For AD LDS instances, you need to grant the ADFS service account the generic read permission using the dsacls.exe tool, as follows:

```
dsacls.exe \\identityplustore:389\ou=identities,dc=identityplus,dc=ch /I:T
/G "identityplus\svcfed$":GR
```

The following connection string can be used to connect to an LDAP-based attribute store:

```
LDAP://identityplusstore.identityplus.ch:389/ou=identities,dc=identityplus,
dc=ch
```

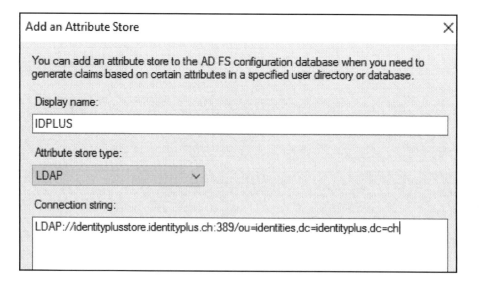

Next, we will discuss the different claims rules for SQL and LDAP attribute stores that can be used to provide such a solution. First, we start with the SQL claims rule, where we can use SQL select statements to query information. We have used the example to query the department. The attribute store will be queried and the output is a claim of the type `http://schemas.xmlsoap.org/ws/2005/05/identity/claims/Department`

```
c:[Type ==
"http://schemas.xmlsoap.org/ws/2005/05/identity/claims/emailaddress"] =>
issue(store = "IdentityPlusStore", types =
("http://schemas.xmlsoap.org/ws/2005/05/identity/claims/Department"), query
= "SELECT Department FROM attributes WHERE email = {0}", param = c.Value);
```

With the following claim rule, we provide the usage of an LDAP-based attribute store. In this case, the same syntax will be used as for the Active Directory:

```
c:[Type ==
"http://schemas.xmlsoap.org/ws/2005/05/identity/claims/emailaddress"]
=> issue(store = "ADLDS", types =
("http://schemas.xmlsoap.org/ws/2005/05/identity/claims/Department"), query
= "mail={0};Department", param = c.Value);
```

 The preceding claims rule provides the same functionality as the previous one – just using a LDAP attribute store.

Now that we have discussed the main options available with custom attribute stores, we will jump into the configuration for authentication against additional LDAP directories.

# Using a new identity store as claims provider

With ADFS 1.0 and 1.1 we already had the option of using LDAP directories as identity stores. In later releases, Microsoft decided to remove this capability. Some of us were very disappointed this option was removed. But, be happy – it's back, with Windows Server 2016 and ADFS 4.0.

The following figure shows a specific way of using this functionality; for example, if you want to store your external identities in LDAP instead of your Active Directory:

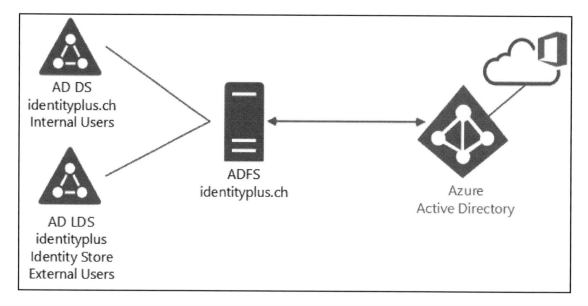

With this solution design in mind, we will discuss an on premise external user identity store, which you could also provide with a dedicated Active Directory forest and AAD.

Microsoft allows you to add any LDAP v3 directory for this use case, including an untrusted Active Directory forest. There is one speciality that you can't configure this scenario over AD FS management GUI – PowerShell is your best friend to do. The scenario has the following limitations in the case of authentication, because only forms-based authentication is supported for authenticating users from LDAP directories. Certificate-based and Integrated Windows authentication methods are not supported for authenticating users in LDAP directories.

If you don't have an existing LDAP directory, you just need to create one. You could use the following procedure to generate an example store for our next lab configuration, which we will cover in next chapters:

1. Install an example ADLDS instance.
2. Run the ADLDS setup wizard on a member server.
3. Define a unique instance.
4. Call the **Instance Name**: `IdentityPlusStore`.
5. Use the Description: Additional Attribute Store for AD FS.
6. Use the LDAP port: `389`.
7. Use the SSL port: `636`.
8. You will get asked, so yes, create an application partition:

`OU=identityplusstore,DC=identityplus,DC=ch`

9. Use the Default data files (default).
10. Use the Network service account (default).
11. Choose the option: **Currently logged on user** (default).
12. Select the `MS-User.ldf` file.
13. Configure the Organizational Structure and some test users.
14. Connect using to your instance with ADSIedit:
15. Use NC:

`OU=externalid,DC=identityplus,DC=ch`

16. Server: `<servername>:389`.
17. Create your test OU: `Identities` (commonName).
18. Create user: `exUser01` (commonName).
19. Add: `john.hill@identityplus.ch`.
20. Add DisplayName: `Ex User 01`.
21. Add Title: Sales Manager.
22. Create another user: `idplusUser1` (commonName).
23. Add mail: `idplususer1@azureid.ch`.
24. Add DisplayName: `AzureID User 1`.
25. Add Title: Customer.

Now that we have a sample ADLDS instance, we can go through the high-level tasks of the configuration. No worries – we will configure this scenario in the next lab and will authenticate it against Office 365.

1. The next step we need to do is to define the LDAP directory connection:

```
$credential = Get-Credential
$idplusdir = New-AdfsLdapServerConnection
-HostName adatum.com
-Port 636
-SslMode Ssl
-AuthenticationMethod basic
-Credential $credential
```

2. The next step will be the connection and issuance of claims from the LDAP store (example):

```
$Name = New-AdfsLdapAttributeToClaimMapping
-LdapAttribute sAMAccountName
-ClaimType "http://schemas.xmlsoap.org/ws/2005/05/identity/claims/name"
$Mail = New-AdfsLdapAttributeToClaimMapping
-LdapAttribute mail
-ClaimType
"http://schemas.xmlsoap.org/ws/2005/05/identity/claims/emailaddress
```

3. The last step is to define the new LDAP directory as an attribute store:

```
Add-AdfsLocalClaimsProviderTrust
-Name "identityplus"
-Identifier "urn:identityplus"
-Type Ldap
-LdapServerConnection $idplusdir
-UserObjectClass user
-UserContainer "DC=identityplus,DC=ch"
-LdapAuthenticationMethod basic
-AnchorClaimLdapAttribute userPrincipalName
-AnchorClaimType
"http://schemas.xmlsoap.org/ws/2005/05/identity/claims/upn" –
LdapAttributeToClaimMapping @($Name, $Mail)
-AcceptanceTransformRules "c:[] => issue(claim=c);"
-Enabled $true -OrganizationalAccountSuffix "identityplus.ch"
```

After working through this section, you should be aware of the different options you get with additional attribute and identity stores. In the following chapters, we will use this new knowledge and deploy such a solution.

# Summary

Working through this chapter you should have gathered the knowledge to be able to design a multi-forest identity synchronization and federation environment, including the AAD Connect Health service for monitoring. Additionally, you should have discovered the most relevant concepts about the new AAD Authentication Library (ADAL) and be able to describe a practical example, such as the usage of Word and SharePoint Online. Finally, you should be able, and feel comfortable, to design a complex hybrid IAM platform with multiple forests. You should also be able to compare ADFS and Azure B2B/B2C functionality for your own design needs. Last but not least, we provided ideas on using additional identity and attribute stores with new Windows Server 2016 ADFS 4.0 capabilities, which will help you to support external user scenarios with a rich subset of providing claims and authentication.

In the following chapter, we will install and configure the enhanced identity infrastructure. In particular, we will focus on multi-forest synchronization and federation, and configure an example of a conditional access scenario, including multi-factor authentication.

# 14
# Installing and Configuring the Enhanced Identity Infrastructure

In this chapter, we will configure and manage a multi-forest synchronization and Single-Sign-On High Availability identity and access management environment based on AAD Connect and ADFS to provide the necessary infrastructure for several use cases in a hybrid identity and access management solution. We also work with the capabilities across company borders and publish the most common on premise services, such as Exchange, SharePoint, and Remote Desktop Services. We will have a special look at the integration and use of the Azure AD provided functionalities.

We will cover the following topics:

- Installing and configuring the multi-forest synchronization environment
- Installing and configuring the multi-forest and high availability Federation environment
- Configuring application access with ADFS, WAP, and AAD AP
- Configuring a multi-factor authentication scenario for Conditional Access

# Important note for readers

We will have a mix between detailed and high-level configuration steps to get as many scenarios as possible into the chapter. You, as an experienced reader, should be able to configure all the scenarios with your existing knowledge and the information provided in the previous chapters, where we explained all the concepts. We will also jump between different capabilities. Furthermore, we will not provide detailed steps for configuring the services themselves – we will provide you with the necessary references from valid expert blogs on the Internet. Basically, you should use the described `azureid.ch` and `identityplus.ch` forests as internal corporate forests – where you can work with several scenarios and easy network configurations. The shown forest `idam.ch` should be used for network boundary or partner scenarios.

# Creating the extended lab environment

At the beginning of the chapter, we need to extend our example lab infrastructure to follow the steps in this guidance. You can use this lab configuration or your own. If you use your own lab configuration, then it's up to you to make the necessary adjustments. For introduction purposes, we will use Azure IaaS to provide the lab environment, but you can also choose an on premise infrastructure based on your virtualization solution. In this chapter, we will use further virtual machines to demonstrate the generic installation and configuration steps.

 We will extend our existing lab environment with a new Active Directory forest to configure the multi-forest environment solutions. In the first part, we will use the existing cloud service, so that we can use the same subnets for the solution without any routing, to provide an easy working environment with less troubleshooting, to start the effective configurations.

The following figure shows the expected lab architecture, where you can also use a cross-forest Active Directory trust relationship and the test client will be your administrative workstation from the previous labs:

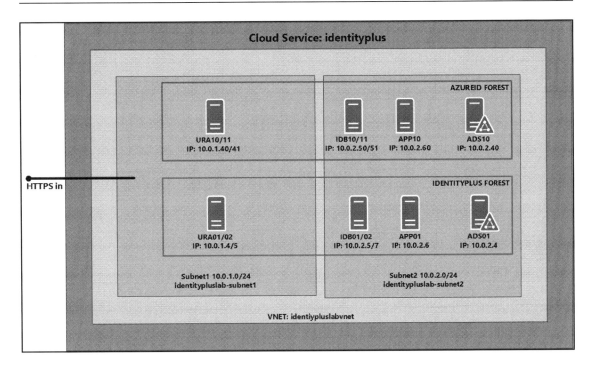

**Important note**
We will leave the configuration open so that you can use the two forests with and without a cross-forest Active Directory forest.

# Virtual machines

The lab contains the following virtual machines installed on a virtual network with two subnets based on a cloud service in Azure IaaS. The following table describes the virtual machines. We will install the additional machines manually, or you can modify the example script to provision them as you like. Important for us is that you know how to extend the lab environment so you are able to choose the method to provide additional machines yourself – by script or manually:

`identityplus.ch`, `azureid.ch`, and `idam.ch` represent the demo suffixes – replace them with your public domain name.

| Name | Role | OS | Subnet |
|------|------|-----|--------|
| ADS01 ADS02 | Domain Controller | 2012 R2 Data Center 2016 TP5 | identitypluslabvnet-subnet2(10.0.2.0/24) |
| APP01 APP10 | Application Server | 2012 R2 Data Center | identitypluslabvnet-subnet2(10.0.2.0/24) |
| IDB01/02 IDB10/11 | Identity Bridge ADFS and AAD Connect | 2012 R2 Data Center 2016 TP5 | identitypluslabvnet-subnet2(10.0.2.0/24) |
| URA01/02 URA10/11 (opt. HA) | Unified Remote Access Web Application Proxy | 2012 R2 Data Center 2016 TP5 | identitypluslabvnet-subnet2(10.0.1.0/24) |

 We highly recommend that you work with the virtual machines just in time, especially if you are using an Azure trial to have the machines available for a longer period – cost limitation! The high-availability options are just necessary in one Active Directory forest, so it's up to you how many machines you deploy.

To provision the extra forest for the partner organization, we recommend that you repeat all the steps from `Chapter 9`, *Building Cloud from Common Identities*, to get extra resources and an isolated lab infrastructure. Furthermore, we recommend subscribing to an extra trial for the several cloud services we used in `Chapter 9`, *Building Cloud from Common Identities*.

The following table and figure shows the expected lab architecture, where you can build the partner organization:

| Name | Role | OS | Subnet |
|------|------|-----|--------|
| ADS01 | Domain Controller | 2012 R2 Data Center or 2016 TP5 or RTM | identitypluslabvnet-subnet2(10.0.2.0/24) |
| APP01 | Application Server | 2012 R2 Data Center or 2016 TP5 or RTM | identitypluslabvnet-subnet2(10.0.2.0/24) |

| IDB01 | Identity Bridge ADFS and AAD Connect | 2012 R2 Data Center or 2016 TP5 or RTM | identitypluslabvnet-subnet2(10.0.2.0/24) |
|-------|--------------------------------------|---------------------------------------|------------------------------------------|
| URA01 | Unified Remote Access Web Application Proxy | 2012 R2 Data Center or 2016 TP5 or RTM | identitypluslabvnet-subnet2(10.0.1.0/24) |

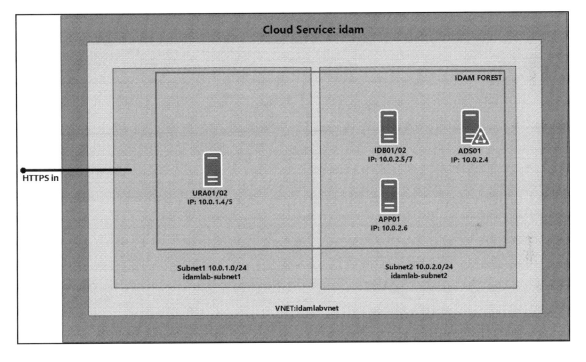

You can use the script from `Chapter 9`, *Building Cloud from Common Identities*, to automatically provision the scenario. Obviously, you need to provide the basic ADFS infrastructure manually in the upcoming environment. Furthermore, the configuration steps for the different scenarios from `Chapter 9`, *Building Cloud from Common Identities*, need to be done manually.

# Public domains and Azure AD Default Directory

You should have the following registered domains with the colored associations:

| Parameter | Value |
|---|---|
| Public domains | YourRegisteredDomain, for example, `<identityplus.ch>`<br>YourRegisteredDomain, for example, `<azureid.ch>`<br>YourRegisteredDomain, for example, `<idam.ch>` |
| Azure AD Default Directory | YourDefaultDirectory, for example,<br>`<identityplus.onmicrosoft.com>`<br>YourDefaultDirectory, for example, `<idam.onmicrosoft.com>` |

# The public SSL certificate

You should also have three public certificates for the three registered domains, like in `Chapter 9`, *Building Cloud from Common Identities*. For the lab environment, you can use an SSL certificate from Comodo or other public certificate authorities.

StartSSL is a very smart and cost-effective provider.

# Internal and external DNS entries

To use the lab configurations, you should apply the necessary DNS entries. We provided a sample set you already used in `Chapter 9`, *Building Cloud from Common Identities*. To be successful in the following labs, you always need to add the service-relevant DNS entries, always internal and external.

Use the scripts we provided in the previous chapters to get a rapid deployment.

# Additional lab environment information

We know that it will be a little bit harder working with the preceding description, but with the prerequisites, we could fill chapters and we would miss the really necessary information to configure the scenarios. We think that with the information provided and the scripts, you should be able to provide a smart environment to test the configurations. Furthermore, we will do some configurations in this and the following chapter with SharePoint, Exchange, and other services. It's up to you to install the basic services. We recommend that you have a look for the Microsoft Test Lab Guide series or installation guides for additional guidance.

 Try to keep your environment as simple as possible. From our experience, it's always helpful how the service you touch basically works – in special with the focus on identity and access management.

 You will find the test lab guides under the following link: `http://bit.ly/28Nu1RJ`.

Try to organize yourself with the free Microsoft Remote Desktop Manager, which you can find at `http://bit.ly/1wvL6ht`, or an equivalent tool.

Now that we have discussed the extension of our lab environment, we can start to work on the configuration topics. Are you ready?

# Installing and configuring the multi-forest synchronization environment

In the first configuration step, we will configure Azure AD Connect to work with two Active Directory forests. We will synchronize the two forests with one Azure Active Directory. Afterwards, we will configure AAD Connect in a high-availability scenario, with a second instance as staging server. We close the synchronization section with the configuration of the AAD Connect Health components to monitor the solution.

# Configuring AAD Connect to add the additional forest

In this first stage, we will configure AAD Connect to handle two Active Directory forests. To connect to the different forests, you need to configure the required name resolution before we can connect to the other forest. You can archive this through conditional forwarders or secondary DNS zones between the `identityplus.ch` and the `azureid.ch` forests. Furthermore, you can do this configuration with two different states: one, with a cross forest Active Directory trust to work, for example, in an account and resource forest scenario, or, two, in a separate technologies environment. We will do option two to demonstrate the steps. Our goal is to extend the actual configuration you already configured in `Chapter 9`, *Building Cloud from Common Identities*, for `identityplus.ch`.

 **Prerequisites**: Create a synchronization user account in the additional forest under which the management agent runs. Reference: `http://bit.ly/1paFUTX`.
Verify the additional forest in your Azure AD environment.

You will need to perform the following steps:

1. Log on to **IDB01**, the forest you have already configured with AAD connect:
   - **Username**: Domain\AdminAccount
   - **Password**: YourPassword

2. Open the **Azure AD Connect** configuration assistant.

3. Choose **Customize synchronization options** and click **Next**:

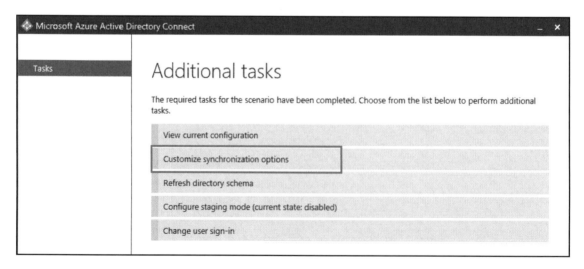

5. Under **Connect to Azure AD**, provide the global administrator credentials of your tenant and click **Next**.

6. Next, provide the forest name of the additional forest and the credentials to be used for the new management agent and click **Add Directory**:

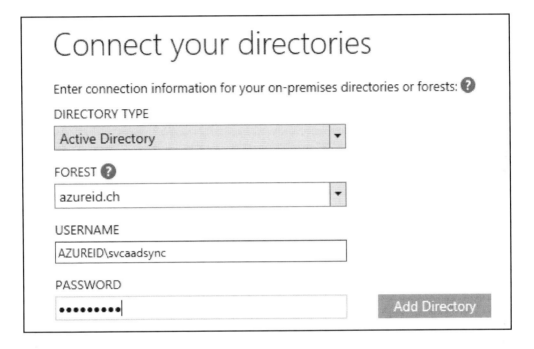

7. Click **Next** and configure the organizational units that you want to synchronize with the Azure Active Directory for both directories, then click **Next**:

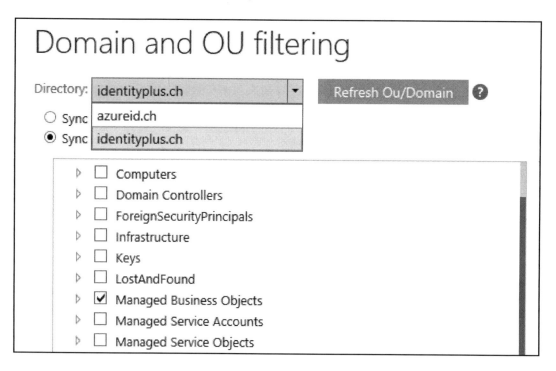

8. Under **Optional features**, configure your preferred options.

**Note**: Use Exchange Hybrid if you have or plan to use an Exchange hybrid environment – we will use this option so that we can verify the Exchange, relevant attributes that get synchronized, in particular for using the Alternate ID login functionality – with the e-mail address. Choose any other option to try more scenarios. Refer to `http://bit.ly/1U26so2` for further reference.

9. Click **Next**.

10. Clear the **Start the synchronization process** option to step through the different stages as we have done in `Chapter 9`, *Building Cloud from Common Identities*, if you like.

In productive environments, we always use the manual mode to control every stage of the process.

11. Otherwise, leave it checked and click **Install,** and after the configuration completes, click **Exit**.

12. Open the **Synchronization Service** console to verify the configuration.

13. You should find now three management agents:

| Connectors | | | |
|---|---|---|---|
| Name | Type | Description | State |
| identityplus.onmicrosoft... | Windows Azure Active Directory (Micr... | | Idle |
| identityplus.ch | Active Directory Domain Services | | Idle |
| azureid.ch | Active Directory Domain Services | | Idle |

14. We always recommend checking the connector operations for any errors:

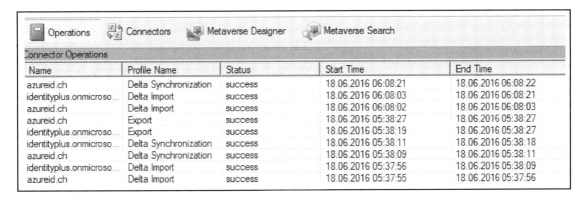

| Operations | Connectors | Metaverse Designer | Metaverse Search | |
|---|---|---|---|---|

| Connector Operations | | | | |
|---|---|---|---|---|
| Name | Profile Name | Status | Start Time | End Time |
| azureid.ch | Delta Synchronization | success | 18.06.2016 06:08:21 | 18.06.2016 06:08:22 |
| identityplus.onmicroso... | Delta Import | success | 18.06.2016 06:08:03 | 18.06.2016 06:08:21 |
| azureid.ch | Delta Import | success | 18.06.2016 06:08:02 | 18.06.2016 06:08:03 |
| azureid.ch | Export | success | 18.06.2016 05:38:27 | 18.06.2016 05:38:27 |
| identityplus.onmicroso... | Export | success | 18.06.2016 05:38:19 | 18.06.2016 05:38:27 |
| identityplus.onmicroso... | Delta Synchronization | success | 18.06.2016 05:38:11 | 18.06.2016 05:38:18 |
| azureid.ch | Delta Synchronization | success | 18.06.2016 05:38:09 | 18.06.2016 05:38:11 |
| identityplus.onmicroso... | Delta Import | success | 18.06.2016 05:37:56 | 18.06.2016 05:38:09 |
| azureid.ch | Delta Import | success | 18.06.2016 05:37:55 | 18.06.2016 05:37:56 |

Finally, we added the new forest to our synchronization configuration. Now we are ready to use the several cloud services with the new identities from the new forest. Later in the chapter, we will configure the Alternate Login ID on the ADFS side. To use the scenario, you need to customize the synchronization again and change from UPN to e-mail address.

If you have already used a trusted forest, you are already able to use single sign-on with your ADFS infrastructure. You just need to fire the following PowerShell command on your ADFS infrastructure:

```
Update-MSOLFederatedDomain
-DomainName <domain>
-SupportMultipleDomain $true
```

Otherwise, you should synchronize passwords until we have configured the relevant ADFS subsets.

The following screenshot shows a separated-technologies configuration:

| DOMAIN NAME | TYPE | STATUS | SINGLE SIGN-ON |
|---|---|---|---|
| identityplus.ch | Custom | ✔ Verified | Configured |
| azureid.ch | Custom | ✔ Verified | Not Planned |
| identityplus.onmicrosoft.com | Basic | ✔ Active | Not Available |

The following screenshot shows a configuration with Active Directory cross-forest trust:

| onidam.ch | Custom | ✔ Verified | Configured | No |
|---|---|---|---|---|
| idam.ch | Custom | ✔ Verified | Configured | No |

# Configuring AAD Connect high availability

Now that we have extended to a multi-forest configuration, we want to provide a high-availability scenario for AAD Connect with the installation and configuration of an additional AAD Connect instance in staging mode.

**Prerequisites**: Download AAD Connect from: `http://bit.ly/1JPD3qY` and place it as the second Identity Bridge Server in the `identityplus` forest.

Take a note, including the passwords, of the two service accounts for the **Management Agent (MA)** configuration, for example, `identityplus\svcaadsync` and `azureid\svcaadsync`.

Perform the following steps:

1. Log on to **IDB02**, the forest you have already configured with AAD Connect:
   - **Username**: Domain\AdminAccount
   - **Password**: YourPassword

2. Install AAD Connect with `AzureADConnect.msi`.

3. Agree the license terms on the welcome screen and click on **Continue**.

4. Click **Customize** and **Install**.

5. Under **User sign-in**, choose **Do not configure** and click **Next**.

6. Provide the credentials for the Azure AD Connect – your global administrator.

7. Click **Next**.

8. Add the two Active Directory forests, providing the noted `MA accounts`, and click **Next**:

CONFIGURED DIRECTORIES

azureid.ch (Active Directory) ✓

identityplus.ch (Active Directory) ✓

9. You should get the following on the **Azure AD sign-in configuration** like in the following figure.

10. Click **Next**.

11. Choose the same **Domain and OU filtering** options as in your first instance of AAD Connect and click **Next** three times:

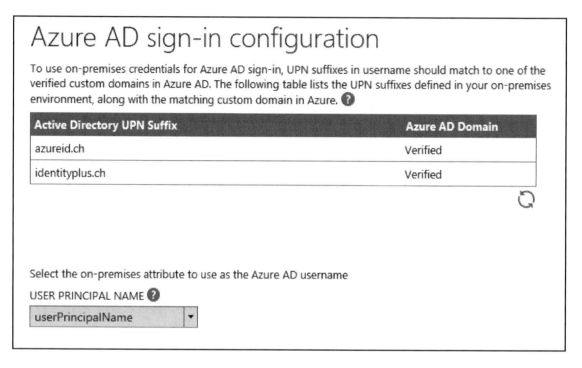

12. Choose the same **Optional features** as on the primary AAD Connect instance.
13. Under **Ready to configure:**
    - Clear the **Start the synchronization process** option
    - Check the **Enable staging mode** option
    - Click **Install**

14. You should receive the following expected result:

Azure AD Connect configuration succeeded.

> **Synchronization is currently disabled. Before a synchronization can occur, you must enable the Azure Active Directory Sync Scheduler.** Learn more

> **To sync your Windows 10 domain joined computers to Azure AD as registered devices, please run AdSyncPrep:Initialize-ADSyncDomainJoinedComputerSync for identityplus.ch.** Learn more

 The synchronization on the primary instance needs to be stopped or unavailable until you enable the synchronization on the secondary AAD Connect instance.

Check the staging mode configuration with PowerShell `Get-ADSyncScheduler`

```
PS C:\Users\Administrator.AZUREID> Get-ADSyncScheduler

AllowedSyncCycleInterval              : 00:30:00
CurrentlyEffectiveSyncCycleInterval   : 00:30:00
CustomizedSyncCycleInterval           :
NextSyncCyclePolicyType               : Initial
NextSyncCycleStartTimeInUTC           : 22.06.2016 22:11:50
PurgeRunHistoryInterval               : 7.00:00:00
SyncCycleEnabled                      : False
MaintenanceEnabled                    : True
StagingModeEnabled                    : True
```

 The secondary instance helps you to reduce **Full Import** times in larger environments. There is no active/active configuration – you need to do the tasks manually.

Now that we have configured the secondary AAD Connect instance for high availability, we can start to configure AAD Connect Health in the Azure Management Portal.

# Viewing AAD Connect Health for synchronization components

In this section, we will view the AAD Connect Health components to provide monitoring of your Identity Bridge synchronization.

Perform the following steps:

1. Log on to portal.azure.com with your global administrator credentials.
2. The **Azure AD Connect Health** tile should appear on your dashboard:

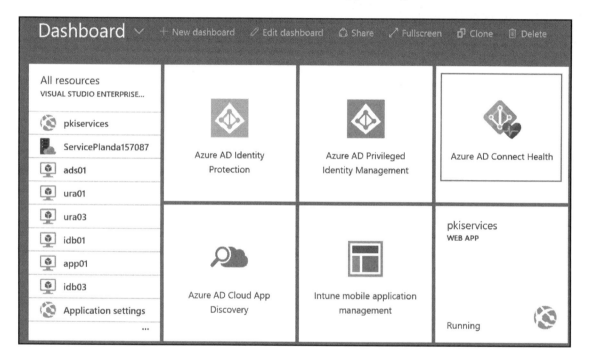

3. Click the **Azure AD Connect Health** tile:

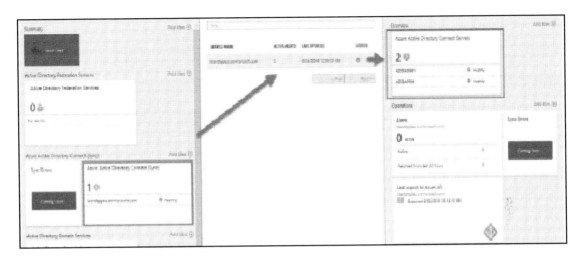

4. Navigate through the **Azure Active Directory Connect Servers** – the expected result on the secondary instance must be **Last export to AD – (No data found)**:

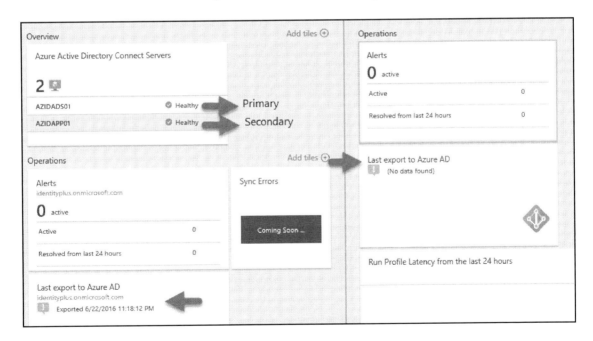

Now that we have an idea about the monitoring interface of Azure AD Connect Health, we have completed our basic synchronization installation and configuration. In the next steps, we will configure the Federation high-availability and multi-forest options.

# Installing and configuring the multi-forest and high availability Federation environments

In the following section, you will get the information to configure a high available Federation environment.

## Building high availability – ADFS and Web Application Proxy in identityplus.ch

In the following steps, we provide the high-level configuration to configure the additional ADFS server in the farm:

1. Log on to the server **IDB02** with the following credentials:
   - **Username**: Domain\AdminAccount
   - **Password**: YourPassword
2. Open the **Server Manager**.
3. Manage **Add roles and features**.
4. Click **Next** | **Next** | **Next** and select **Active Directory Federation Services**:

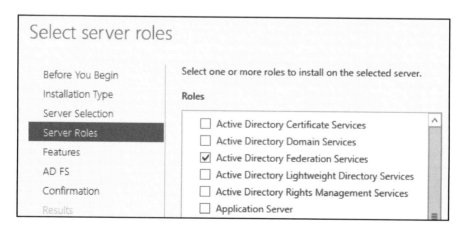

5. Click **Next** | **Next** | **Next**.

6. Click **Install**.

7. Wait for the installation to complete and then click **Close**.

8. Ensure that you are still logged on to **IDB02** with the Enterprise Administrator account.

9. Go to **Server Manager** and click on **Configure the federation service**.

10. Follow the setup instructions and add the server to the existing farm.

11. Configure an additional A entry to the DNS configuration for the FQDN of the federation service name in the internal and external DNS zones.

 Obviously, you can use a load balancer in productive environments.

After installing the additional ADFS server, we will install the second Web Application Proxy server URA02. We also provide the high-level steps because you already know the installation and configuration procedure from *Chapter 9*, *Building Clouds from Common Identities*:

1. Log on to the server **URA02** with the following credentials:
   - **Username**: Domain\AdminAccount
   - **Password**: YourPassword

2. Go to **Server Manager** |**Manage**| and click **Add roles and features**.

3. Click **Next** | **Next** | **Next** and select **Remote Access**.

4. Click **Next** | **Next** | **Next** and select **Web Application Proxy**:

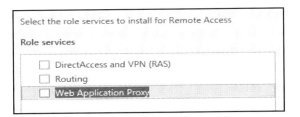

5. Click **Add Features**.

6. Click **Next** | **Install**.

7. After the installation completes, click **Close**.

8. Ensure that you are still logged in to **URA02** with the following credentials:
    - **Username**: Domain\AdminAccount
    - **Password**: YourPassword
9. Go to **Server Manager** and click open the **Web Application Proxy Wizard**.
10. Click **Next** and type `login.identityplus.ch` in the Federation service name.
11. Use the following credentials:
    - **Username**: Domain\AdminAccount
    - **Password**: YourPassword
12. Click **Next**.
13. Select the `login.identityplus.ch` certificate and click **Next**.
14. Click **Configure** and ensure that the Web Application Proxy was configured successfully, and click **Close**.

Now that we have configured the high available federation information, we will provide you with the steps to configure ADFS to support multiple forests.

 This configuration will be done for the scenario with an established cross-forest Active Directory trust relationship.

# Configuring ADFS to support multiple forests

In this section, we will show how to update the ADFS federation information to support additional forests with a cross forest trust relationship. The scenario with separated topologies will be provided in the next section.

Perform the following steps:

1. Log on to the server **IDB01** (primary ADFS) with the following credentials:
    - **Username**: Domain\AdminAccount
    - **Password**: YourPassword
2. Open an evaluated PowerShell session.
3. Type `connect-msolservice` and provide your global administrator credentials.

4. Type:

```
4. Update-MSOLFederatedDomain
   -DomainName <yourdomain>
   -SupportMultiDomain
```

# Configuring ADFS to support a partner organization

In this section, we will configure a federated trust between two federation servers, which is also typically used for separate Active Directory forests.

You can use the `azureid.ch` and `identityplus.ch` forests if you didn't create an Active Directory trust relationship. Otherwise, you can work with the `identityplus.ch` and the partner forest `idam.ch`, as described earlier in the chapter.

## Prerequisites

ADFS environments configured in both the forests you want to use for the configuration.

Remember that the forest names are just to identify the different forests – you must use your configured forest names.

Perform the following steps:

1. Log on to **IDB01** (`identityplus.ch`):
     - **Username**: Domain\AdminAccount
     - **Password**: YourPassword
2. Open the **AD FS Management** console.
3. Right-click **Claims Provider Trusts** and choose **Add Claims Provider Trust**.

`idam.ch` AD FS will take the role of an Identity Provider and thus needs to be added as a Claims Provider.

4. Click **Start** on the **Add Claims Provider Trust Wizard** welcome screen.
5. Type `login.idam.ch` in the **Federation metadata address** field and click **Next**.

The actual URL that is being used by AD FS to retrieve the federation metadata of IDAM is `https://login.idam.ch/federationmetadata/27-6/federationmetadata.xml`.

6. Type `IDAM` in the **Display Name** field and click **Next**.
7. View the tabs and see what information is available for IDAM:

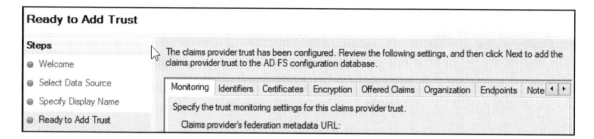

8. Click **Next**.
9. Clear the **Open the Edit Claim Rules** option and click **Close**.
10. You should see the following expected result:

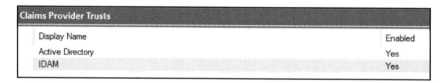

11. Log on to **IDB01** (`idam.ch`):
    - **Username**: Domain\AdminAccount
    - **Password**: YourPassword
12. Open the AD FS Management console.
13. Expand **Trust Relationships**.
14. Right-click **Relying Party Trusts** and choose **Add Relying Party Trust**.

We have to configure the opposite now and create a Relying Party Trust for `identityplus.ch`.

15. Click **Start** on the **Add Relying Party Trust Wizard** welcome screen.
16. Type `login.identityplus.ch` in the **Federation metadata address** field and click **Next**:

The actual URL that is being used by AD FS to retrieve the federation metadata of IDENTITYPLUS is `https://login.identityplus.ch/federationmetadata/27-6/federationmetadata.xml`.

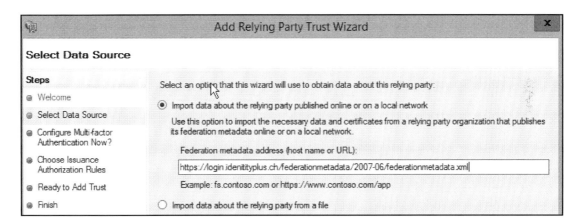

17. Type **IDENTITYPLUS** in the **DisplayName** field and click **Next** three times.
18. View the tabs and see what information is available for **IDENTITYPLUS**:

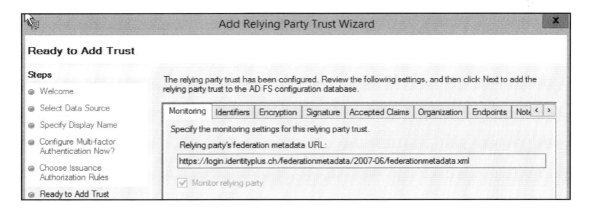

19. Click **Next**.
20. Clear the **Open the Edit Claim Rules** option and click **Close**.
21. Open your web browser, type
    `https://login.identityplus.ch/adfs/ls/idpinitiatedsignon.aspx`, and click
    **Sign-in**.
22. You should get the following expected result:

23. Click **IDAM** and you should be redirected to the IDAM ADFS server.
24. Log in with `administrator@idam.ch` and you should get the following result:

Now that we have configured the basic partner organization support, we configure an additional attribute store.

# Configuring Home Realm Discovery (HRD)

In this section, we will configure the HRD functionality. With this configuration, you can associate a claims provider to a Relying Party trust.

Perform the following steps:

1. Log on to IDB01 (identityplus.ch):
   - **Username**: Domain\AdminAccount
   - **Password**: YourPassword
2. Open an evaluated PowerShell and type the following command:

```
Set-AdfsRelyingPartyTrust -TargetName <RelayingPartyTrust e.g. Claims Web>
-ClaimsProviderName "Active Directory"
```

3. Test the configuration with your administrative workstation.
4. Use the application link of the relying party with Internet Explorer.
5. You should land directly on the logon page of the claims provider you configured in the previous steps.

For troubleshooting sessions, you should install Fiddler on your administrative workstation. You will find the binaries at:
http://bit.ly/28S4GDK
The Fiddler inspector for federation from the following reference:
http://bit.ly/28RBJog.

# Configuring ADLDS and ADFS – additional attribute store

In this section, we will configure ADFS to use an additional attribute store based on AD LDS. The store can be used for external user management or additional attribute information in this example. To configure this scenario, we need to use a Windows Server 2016-based ADFS configuration. Windows 2012 R2 cannot provide this configuration.

Perform the following steps:

1.  Log on to IDB01 (Windows Server 2016):
    *   **Username**: Domain\AdminAccount
    *   **Password**: YourPassword
2.  Use the Server Manager to add the AD LDS role.
3.  After installing the role, start the AD LDS configuration wizard:

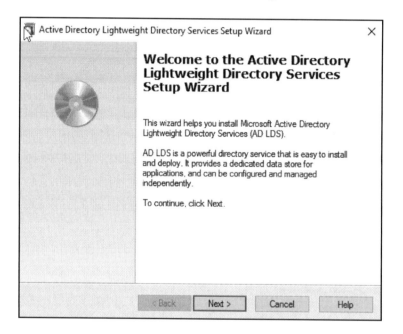

4. Choose the following options:

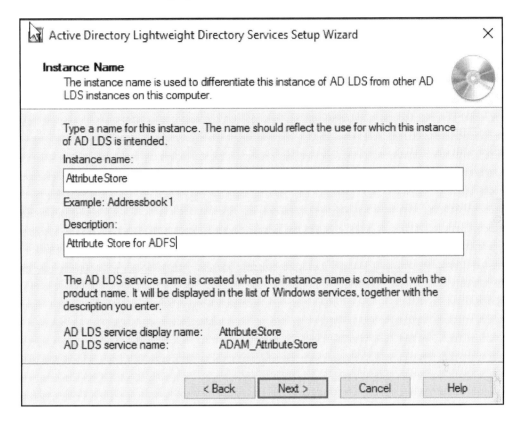

5. Configure **LDAP port**: 33334, and for **SSL**: 33335.

**Tip**: You can also use 50389 and 50636, or other free ports.

6. Configure the following application partition:

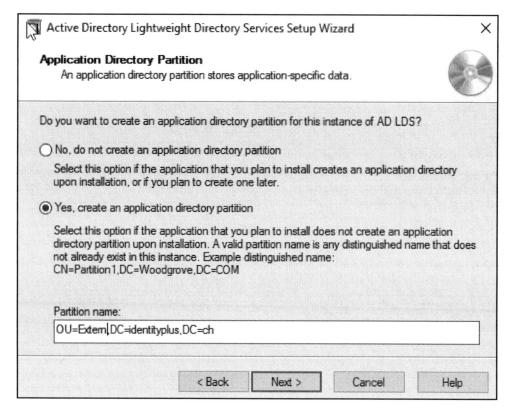

7. Use the next three default values.

8. Select the `MS-User.LDF` file to import:

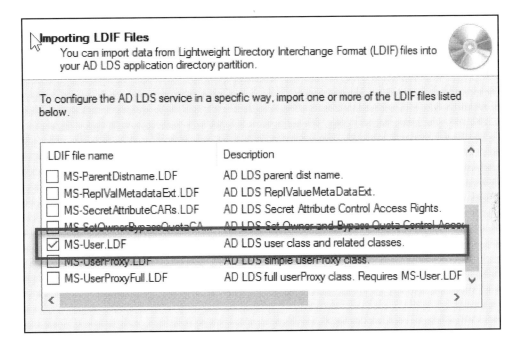

9. Click **Next** twice and **Finish**.

10. Now we have installed our new AD LDS instance to hold the external users.

11. Next, we connect to the new instance and create some test users.

12. Start the `adsiedit.msc` management console.

13. Use the following connection parameters:

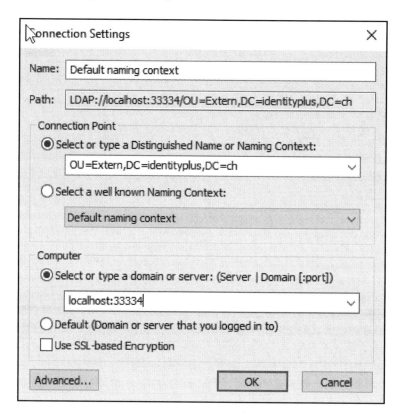

14. You should see the following configuration:

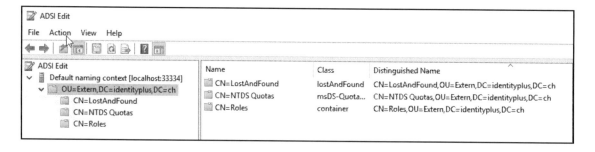

15. Create a new organizational unit called **Users**.

16. Create a user called: **ExtUser1**:
    - Add **mail: anas@identityplus.ch**
    - Add **displayName: External User 1**
    - Add **title: Sales Manager**

17. Create a user called: **CusUser1**.
    - Add **mail: ikram@idam.ch**
    - Add **displayName: Customer User 1**
    - Add **title: Customer**

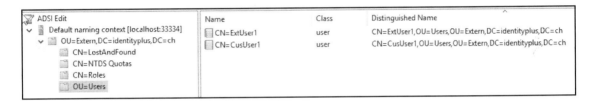

As the next step after installing and configuring the AD LDS instance, we need to grant the ADFS service account access to the AD LDS instance:

1. Log on to **IDB01 (Windows Server 2016)** with the AD LDS instance:
   - **Username**: Domain\AdminAccount
   - **Password**: YourPassword

2. Open an evaluated Command Prompt type:

```
dsacls.exe \\localhost:33334\ou=Extern,dc=identityplus,dc=ch /I:T /G
"identityplus\svcfed$":GR
```

3. You should receive the following output on your command line:

```
C:\Users\Administrator>dsacls.exe \\localhost:33334\ou=Extern,dc=identityplus,dc=ch /I:T /G "identityplus\svcfed$":GR
Owner: CN=Administrators,CN=Roles,OU=Extern,DC=identityplus,DC=ch
Group: CN=Administrators,CN=Roles,OU=Extern,DC=identityplus,DC=ch

Access list:
Allow IDENTITYPLUS\svcfed$                      SPECIAL ACCESS
                                                READ PERMISSONS
                                                LIST CONTENTS
                                                READ PROPERTY
                                                LIST OBJECT
Allow CN=Instances,CN=Roles,CN=Configuration,CN={110C4973-85C1-431A-A224-02195D1BA93D}
                                                SPECIAL ACCESS
                                                READ PERMISSONS
                                                LIST CONTENTS
                                                READ PROPERTY
                                                LIST OBJECT
Allow CN=Readers,CN=Roles,OU=Extern,DC=identityplus,DC=ch
                                                SPECIAL ACCESS
                                                READ PERMISSONS
                                                LIST CONTENTS
                                                READ PROPERTY
                                                LIST OBJECT
Allow CN=Administrators,CN=Roles,OU=Extern,DC=identityplus,DC=ch
                                                FULL CONTROL
Allow CN=Instances,CN=Roles,CN=Configuration,CN={110C4973-85C1-431A-A224-02195D1BA93D}
                                                Replicating Directory Changes
Allow CN=Instances,CN=Roles,CN=Configuration,CN={110C4973-85C1-431A-A224-02195D1BA93D}
                                                Replication Synchronization
Allow CN=Instances,CN=Roles,CN=Configuration,CN={110C4973-85C1-431A-A224-02195D1BA93D}
                                                Manage Replication Topology
Allow CN=Instances,CN=Roles,CN=Configuration,CN={110C4973-85C1-431A-A224-02195D1BA93D}
                                                Replicating Directory Changes All

Permissions inherited to subobjects are:
Inherited to all subobjects
Allow IDENTITYPLUS\svcfed$                      SPECIAL ACCESS
                                                READ PERMISSONS
                                                LIST CONTENTS
                                                READ PROPERTY
                                                LIST OBJECT
Allow CN=Readers,CN=Roles,OU=Extern,DC=identityplus,DC=ch
                                                SPECIAL ACCESS
                                                READ PERMISSONS
                                                LIST CONTENTS
                                                READ PROPERTY
                                                LIST OBJECT
Allow CN=Administrators,CN=Roles,OU=Extern,DC=identityplus,DC=ch
                                                FULL CONTROL

The command completed successfully
```

Next, we need to add the ADLDS instance as an ADFS attribute store:

1. Log on to **IDB01 (Windows Server 2016)** with the AD LDS instance:
   - **Username**: Domain\AdminAccount
   - **Password**: YourPassword

2. Open the **ADFS Management** console.
3. Open **AD FS** | **Service** | **Attribute Stores**.
4. Right-click **Attribute Stores**, and then click **Add an attribute store**.
5. Add an attribute store with the following parameters:
   - **Display name**: ADLDSEXT
   - **Attribute store type**: LDAP
   - **Connection string**:
     `LDAP://localhost:33334/ou=Extern,dc=identityplus,dc=ch`

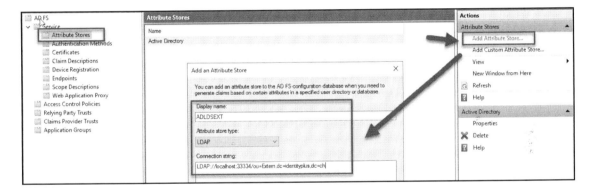

Now that we have configured the ADLDS attribute store in ADFS, we start using the store for issuing claims from a custom attribute store. We want to issue the job title as a claim. To retrieve the job title from ADLDS, we will use a lookup of the email address to identify the user. The e-mail address is a property of the user in the `identityplus` Active Directory.

Perform the following steps:

1. The following attributes are set for `anas@identityplus.ch`:

   - **mail**: `anas@identityplus.ch`
   - **title**: will be retrieved from ADLDS:

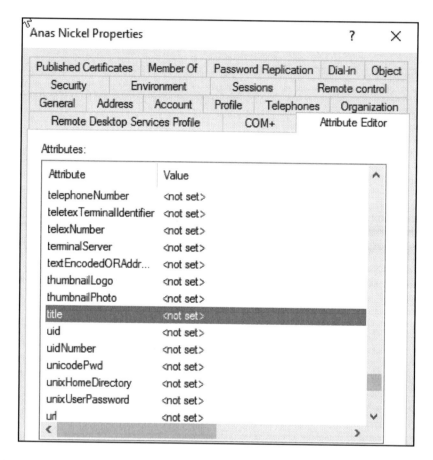

2. To query the AD LDS attribute store, we need to configure claim rules for an existing Relying party trust of your choice, for example, Claims Web.

3. Edit an RP and choose **Edit Claim Issuance Policy** and configure the following example claim rules.

# Sending information from an AD claim rule

We need to configure the following claim rule:

```
c:[Type ==
"http://schemas.microsoft.com/ws/2008/06/identity/claims/windowsaccountname
", Issuer == "AD AUTHORITY"]
=> issue(store = "Active Directory", types =
("http://schemas.xmlsoap.org/ws/2005/05/identity/claims/name",
"http://schemas.xmlsoap.org/ws/2005/05/identity/claims/emailaddress"),
query = ";sAMAccountName,mail;{0}", param = c.Value);
```

# Sending claims using a custom rule

With the following steps, we will configure the custom rule:

1. In the claim rule name field, type **Lookup Title based** on **Email Address**.
2. In the **Custom rule** field, type the following rule:

```
c:[Type ==
"http://schemas.xmlsoap.org/ws/2005/05/identity/claims/emailaddress"] =>
issue(store = "ADLDS", types = ("http://identityplus.ch/title"), query =
"mail={0};title", param = c.Value);
```

3. Click **Add Rule**.
4. Select **Pass Through Or Filter an Incoming Claim**.
5. Click **Next**.
6. In the **claim rule name** field, type `Pass Through Email Address`.
7. Select **E-Mail Address** in **incoming claim type**.
8. Click **OK** twice.

Now that we have configured the issuance of claims from the attribute store, we want to authenticate and issue claims from the ADLDS instance.

**Prerequisites**

To configure the scenario, you need to use the wildcard certificate we requested in the previous chapters. The certificate is needed for the SSL connection to the AD LDS instance.

Perform the following steps:

1. Log on to **IDB01 (Windows Server 2016)** with the AD LDS instance:
   - **Username**: Domain\AdminAccount
   - **Password**: YourPassword

2. Use the following procedures to configure the scenario:
   - http://bit.ly/28TEavL
   - http://bit.ly/28RpdaS

After running through this guidance, you should be able to authenticate against the ADLDS identity store. We used the two valid articles because they provide all the necessary information so that you can successfully implement the solution.

# Delegating the administration of ADFS

With the new delegation option of the AD FS 4.0 service, you can grant access to administer the AD FS service without using local administrator rights.

Next, we delegate the administration of the AD FS Service:

1. Log on to **IDB01 (Windows Server 2016)** with the AD LDS instance:
   - **Username**: Domain\AdminAccount
   - **Password**: YourPassword

2. Open the **ADFS Management** console.
3. Edit the **Federation Service Properties**.

4. Add a group with the **ADFS Administrator members ACL-IDF-Administrators** our example and check **Allow Local Administratorgroup for service administration**:

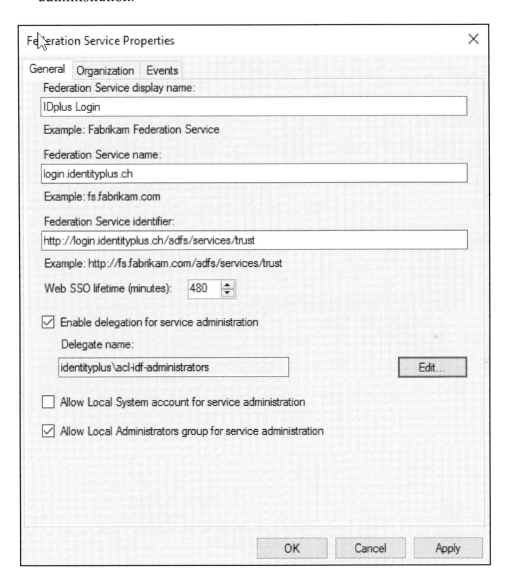

5. Click **OK**.
6. Close the **ADFS Management** console.
7. Type `lusrmgr.msc` and press Enter.
8. Expand the groups.
9. Double-click **Event Log Readers**.
10. Click **Add**.
11. Type `ACL-IDF-Administrators` and click **check names**.
12. Click **OK**.
13. Click **OK**.
14. Double-click **Remote Desktop Users**.
15. Click **Add**.
16. Type `ACL-IDF-Administrators` and click **check names**.
17. Click **OK**.
18. Click **OK**.
19. Log off and log in to validate the delegation with a member of the group **ACL-IDF-Administrators**.
20. Open `eventvwr.msc`.
21. Select application, security, and system event log.
22. Check **Application and Services\AD FS\Admin event log**.
23. Type `services.msc` and press Enter – try to restart the service!

Now you should be able to work with the delegated administrators. In the next section, we will configure the monitoring for the federation components.

# Configuring AAD Connect Health for Federation components

In this section, we will configure AAD Connect Health to monitor the federation components:

1. Log on to portal.azure.com with the global administrator for `identityplus`.
2. Choose **AAD Connect Health**.

3. Click **Quick Start** and **Get tools**:

4. Download the ADFS agent and distribute it to **IDB01** and **URA01**.
5. Log on to **IDB01 (Windows Server 2016)** with the AD LDS instance:
   - **Username**: Domain\AdminAccount
   - **Password**: YourPassword
6. Install **AdHealthAdfsAgentSetup.exe** and configure AAD Connect Health.
7. Provide your global administrator credentials in the logon form.
8. Configure the following audit settings, `http://bit.ly/28TaXhT`, because you receive a warning on the command-line output – if you have already configured auditing on your ADFS server, no warnings should appear.
9. Open the **ADFS Management** console.
10. Edit **Federation Services Properties** and move to **events**.
11. Enable all the audit options:

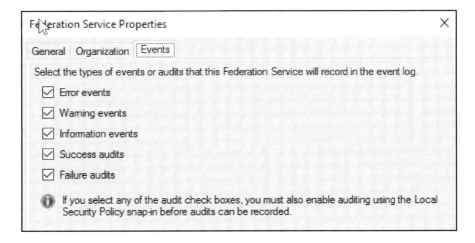

12. Type `auditpol.exe /set /subcategory:"Application Generated" /failure:enable /success:enable` on the command line.
13. Repeat the installation on URA01.
14. Now you can view the two servers in the AAD Connect Health portal:

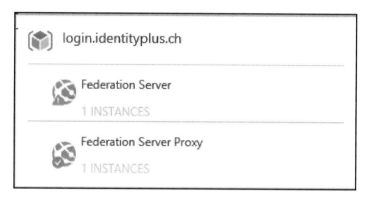

 It may take some time to update the status of the federation service if you didn't enable the audit options at registration time.

Now we have configured the monitoring solution for our complete Identity Bridge, and we will follow up with the support for Windows Integrated Authentication.

# Configuring AD FS to support Windows Integrated Authentication on certain browsers

In this section, we will configure ADFS to support several browsers to use Windows Integrated Authentication. Furthermore, the one we want that they use the form based authentication. The relevant property on ADFS is called the `WIASupportedUserAgents` property. With this property, you can control which browsers, determined by their user agent string, will perform windows integrated authentication. If you do not list a browser, form-based authentication will be used.

Perform the following steps:

1. Log on to **IDB01 (Windows Server 2016)** with the AD LDS instance:
   - **Username**: Domain\AdminAccount
   - **Password**: YourPassword

2. Start an evaluated PowerShell.

3. Type `Get-AdfsProperties | select -ExpandProperty WIASupportedUserAgents`

4. You should see something similar to the following User Agents:
   - MSAuthHost/1.0/In-Domain
   - MSIE 6.0
   - MSIE 7.0
   - MSIE 8.0
   - MSIE 9.0
   - MSIE 10.0
   - Trident/7.0
   - MSIPC
   - Windows Rights Management Client
   - MS_WorkFoldersClient

5. Now we will configure the Microsoft Edge browser to use (**WIA**Windows Intergrated Authentication (WIA):

```
[System.Collections.ArrayList]$UserAgents = Get-AdfsProperties | select -ExpandProperty WIASupportedUserAgents
$UserAgents.Add("Edge/12.10240")
Set-ADFSProperties -WIASupportedUserAgents $UserAgents
```

6. Test the configuration with your administrative workstation and the Edge browser.

7. With this option, you can add several user agents and also the usage of own generated user agents that you can deploy of group policies inside your Active Directory environment:

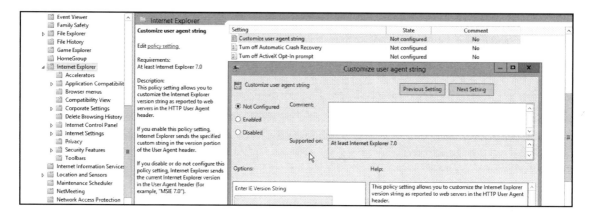

Now that we have configured the support for WIA, we will follow up with the configuration of Alternate Login ID.

# Configuring alternate login ID

The most recommended option to log on to ADFS is to use the `userPrincipalName` that matches the e-mail address. Some organizations cannot change the UPNs in Active Directory to match the e-mail addresses, for instance, if an application is dependent on the UPNs. For this reason, you can configure the alternate login ID with the following procedure:

1. Log on to **IDB01** in `identityplus.ch`:
   - **Username**: Domain\AdminAccount
   - **Password**: YourPassword

2. Start an evaluated PowerShell.

3. Type the following command:

```
Set-AdfsClaimsProviderTrust -TargetIdentifier "AD AUTHORITY" -
AlternateLoginID mail -LookupForests identityplus.ch
```

Test the configuration with the Claims Web application and you should be able to use the email address to log in.

# Configuring application access with ADFS, WAP, and AAD AP

In this section, we will provide the high-level steps to use ADFS, WAP, and **Azure AD Application Proxy** (**AAD AP**) to publish your hybrid service infrastructure. We will show the use case and refer to valid expert blog entries so that you get an idea of the solution and the necessary configuration steps.

 Remember the steps and explanations from the previous chapters, about publishing Kerberos-based applications. We don't provide the steps again in this chapter.

We used the `idam.ch` forest and configured the following ADFS relying parties for our scenario cases:

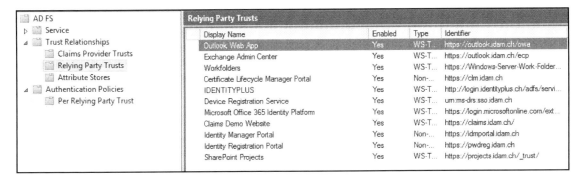

In the following section, we will start to use Azure AD Application Proxy to publish applications.

# Using Azure AD Application Proxy to publish applications

In this scenario, we will configure the Azure AD Proxy to publish the Claims Web demo site, to provide you with the principles for this configuration type:

1. Log on to `manage.windowsazure.com` and navigate to your Azure Active Directory.
2. Choose **Applications**.

3. Click **Add**:

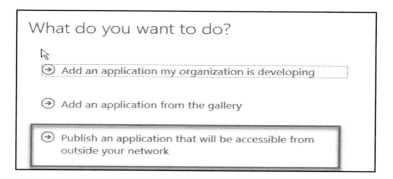

4. Define the name and provide the following information:
   - **Name**: Claims Demo Website
   - **Internal URL**: https://claims.idam.ch/
   - **Pre-Authentication Method**: Azure Active Directory

5. Finish the configuration and open the newly configured application.

6. Click **Configure** to review your configuration:

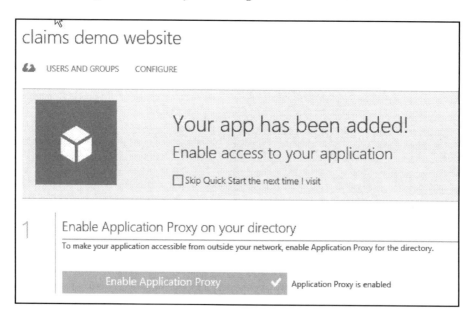

7. Next, click **Download a connector** to install your WAP URA01:

8. Install the connector on URA01:

9. Next, you can assign users or better groups to access the new application – put your test user in this group:

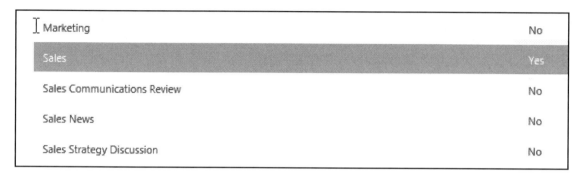

Now you can test the access to your new published application through `https://myapps.microsoft.com`.

You should be able to access the application.

With these principles, you can publish further applications. You can use the following links for further configurations:

- Skype for Business: `http://bit.ly/28SntyL`
- Remote Desktop Services: `http://bit.ly/28Si2Bt`

Next, we will show the scenarios for Exchange and SharePoint on-premises.

# Publish Exchange and SharePoint on premise

With the following scenario, you will see the idea of publishing Exchange and SharePoint on-premises that you can include MFA in the process.

With the following references, you will be able to configure the following use case:

- `http://bit.ly/28UZwYR`
- `http://bit.ly/292qf4g`
- `http://bit.ly/28QLLrD`

| Relying Party Trusts | | | |
|---|---|---|---|
| Display Name | Enabled | Type | Identifier |
| Outlook Web App | Yes | WS-Trust / SAML / WS-Federation | https://outlook.idam.ch/owa |
| Exchange Admin Center | Yes | WS-Trust / SAML / WS-Federation | https://outlook.idam.ch/ecp |

Perform the following steps:

1. The user will open `https://outlook.idam.ch/owa` to access Outlook Web Access:

> G https://outlook.idam.ch/owa

2. With the provided configuration, the user will be redirected to the login form of ADFS:

3. Provide your credentials, and next you will be prompted for MFA, because the application is activated for MFA:

4. You need to click**Continue** and prove your identity with the Azure Authenticator app on your registered device.
5. The user will be able to access Outlook Web Access protected with the on premise Azure MFA server we configured in the previous chapters.

We can use the same idea for publishing SharePoint access:

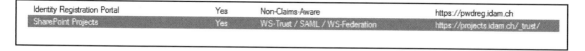

| Identity Registration Portal | Yes | Non-Claims-Aware | https://pwdreg.idam.ch |
| SharePoint Projects | Yes | WS-Trust / SAML / WS-Federation | https://projects.idam.ch/_trust/ |

Obviously, you are not only configuring ADFS, you need also to publish the services over your Web Application Proxy, as you can see in the following screenshot:

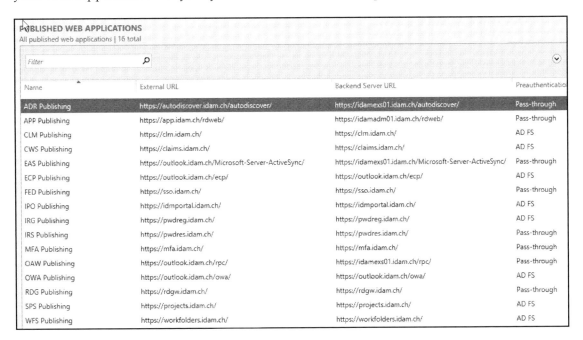

| Name | External URL | Backend Server URL | Preauthenticatio |
|------|-------------|-------------------|------------------|
| ADR Publishing | https://autodiscover.idam.ch/autodiscover/ | https://idamexs01.idam.ch/autodiscover/ | Pass-through |
| APP Publishing | https://app.idam.ch/rdweb/ | https://idamadm01.idam.ch/rdweb/ | Pass-through |
| CLM Publishing | https://clm.idam.ch/ | https://clm.idam.ch/ | AD FS |
| CWS Publishing | https://claims.idam.ch/ | https://claims.idam.ch/ | AD FS |
| EAS Publishing | https://outlook.idam.ch/Microsoft-Server-ActiveSync/ | https://idamexs01.idam.ch/Microsoft-Server-ActiveSync/ | Pass-through |
| ECP Publishing | https://outlook.idam.ch/ecp/ | https://outlook.idam.ch/ecp/ | AD FS |
| FED Publishing | https://sso.idam.ch/ | https://sso.idam.ch/ | Pass-through |
| IPO Publishing | https://idmportal.idam.ch/ | https://idmportal.idam.ch/ | AD FS |
| IRG Publishing | https://pwdreg.idam.ch/ | https://pwdreg.idam.ch/ | AD FS |
| IRS Publishing | https://pwdres.idam.ch/ | https://pwdres.idam.ch/ | Pass-through |
| MFA Publishing | https://mfa.idam.ch/ | https://mfa.idam.ch/ | Pass-through |
| OAW Publishing | https://outlook.idam.ch/rpc/ | https://idamexs01.idam.ch/rpc/ | Pass-through |
| OWA Publishing | https://outlook.idam.ch/owa/ | https://outlook.idam.ch/owa/ | AD FS |
| RDG Publishing | https://rdgw.idam.ch/ | https://rdgw.idam.ch/ | Pass-through |
| SPS Publishing | https://projects.idam.ch/ | https://projects.idam.ch/ | AD FS |
| WFS Publishing | https://workfolders.idam.ch/ | https://workfolders.idam.ch/ | AD FS |

The following reference provides the steps to configure SharePoint with the Azure ACS: `http://bit.ly/28Wu9fT`.

Now that we have seen the idea of publishing on premise applications with the Web Application Proxy, we will move on to the Lync or Skype for Business procedures.

# Publishing Lync/S4B on premise

For this scenario, we only provide the necessary configuration references, because we see no real scenario where you would install Lync or Skype for Business in our lab environment under Azure IaaS. You can use the following configuration references to provide this service over your Web Application Proxy:

- `http://bit.ly/28RTeVu`
- `http://bit.ly/28SntyL`

Next, we will provide you with the information necessary to publish your Remote Desktop Services to provide a solid publishing scenario in a hybrid identity and access management solution.

# Publishing Remote Desktop Services on premise

In this section, we will provide you with the idea to secure your Remote Desktop Services with publishing through the Web Application Proxy, and the proof of your identity with the local Azure MFA server. For this option, you can only use the call or app options to provide your second factor.

The use case will be that an administrative user wants to access a server from outside the network over the Remote Desktop gateway. The user opens a Remote Desktop session with the following Remote Desktop Gateway configured:

The user needs to be verified with the Azure Authenticator app on your mobile device during the connection process:

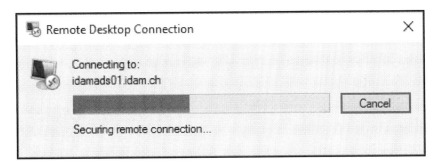

With this option, you can protect direct connections over Remote Desktop sessions and the **Remote Desktop Web Access** page. To configure this scenario, you need to configure the following main components:

- The RDG publishing on the Web Application Proxy:

| OWA Publishing | https://outlook.idam.ch/owa/ | https://outlook.idam.ch/owa/ | AD FS |
| RDG Publishing | https://rdgw.idam.ch/ | https://rdgw.idam.ch/ | Pass-through |
| SPS Publishing | https://projects.idam.ch/ | https://projects.idam.ch/ | AD FS |

- The Azure MFA server:

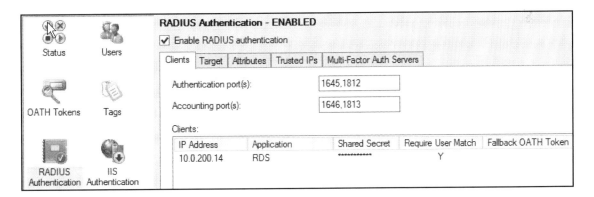

- The Network Policy Service:

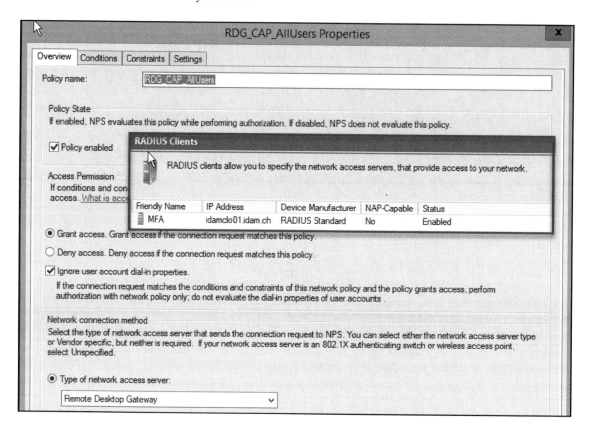

With the following references, you will be able to configure these scenarios and the publishing of **Remote Desktop Server (RDS)** over the AAD AP:

- http://bit.ly/28Suvn6
- http://bit.ly/1ws1uX2
- http://bit.ly/28V4tRq

Next, we will show you the idea of publishing your local Identity Manager to provide a self-service solution for modifying your own profile and password reset.

# Publishing Microsoft Identity Manager

In this scenario, we will give you all the tips necessary to securely publish your local identity management solution for Self-Service. The example we will start with the password reset functionality started with a login to your local ADFS environment. Let's say a user tries to login to a Relying party and needs to reset his password. We provided the configuration for ADFS in the previous chapters:

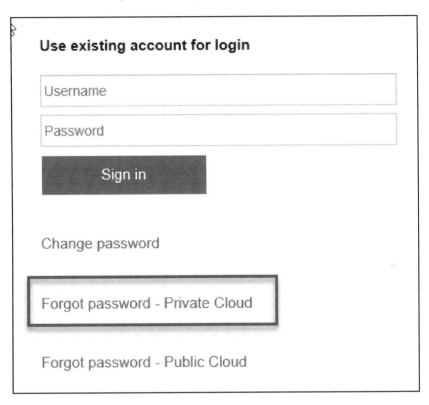

The user clicks on the link and gets redirected to the published Password Reset Portal of the local Identity Manager, and can reset his password. After resetting his password, he will automatically be sent back to the ADFS to log in:

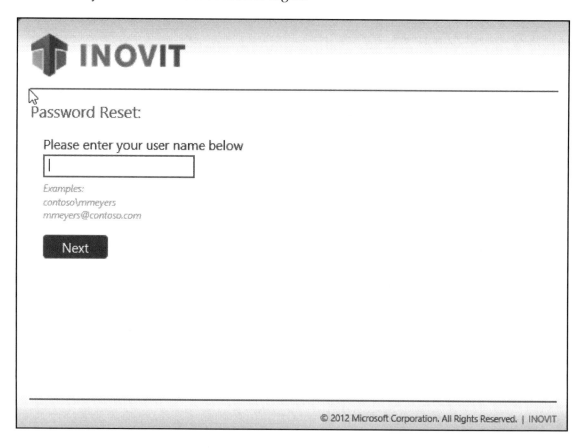

You will need the following main configurations to provide the solution:

1. You need to configure Kerberos Constrained Delegation with the Web Application Proxy to access the Password Reset Registration portal that will be secured with a login to ADFS.

2. You need to create the ADFS configuration (Relying parties):

| | | | |
|---|---|---|---|
| Identity Manager Portal | Yes | Non-Claims-Aware | https://idmportal.idam.ch |
| Identity Registration Portal | Yes | Non-Claims-Aware | https://pwdreg.idam.ch |
| SharePoint Projects | Yes | WS-Trust / SAML / WS-Federation | https://projects.idam.ch/_trust/ |

3. The publishing rules on your Web Application Proxy are as follows:

- **Password Reset Portal**: Pass-through
- **Password Reset Registration Portal**: ADFS Pre-Authentication

| | | | |
|---|---|---|---|
| IRG Publishing | https://pwdreg.idam.ch/ | https://pwdreg.idam.ch/ | AD FS |
| IRS Publishing | https://pwdres.idam.ch/ | https://pwdres.idam.ch/ | Pass-through |

You will find all the detailed steps to configure this scenario at: `http://bit.ly/295qudI`.

With this configuration, we provided the realized password solution we discussed in the solution architecture for password resets in the previous chapters. Now we will configure certificate-based authentication for conditional access scenarios.

# Configuring Multi-Factor authentication scenarios for Conditional Access

In this section, we will provide the necessary steps to configure certificate-based authentication that you can use in conditional access scenarios.

To complete the configuration, you need a deployed PKI in your environment, with externally published CRL information. You can use the following test lab guide if you want to deploy a two-tier PKI in your environment: `http://bit.ly/292h5Vh`.

For the external publishing of the CRL, you can use a website on Azure, such as that in the following example. You just need to change the CRL paths to the newly created website and copy the files. You are able to use FTP to upload the files:

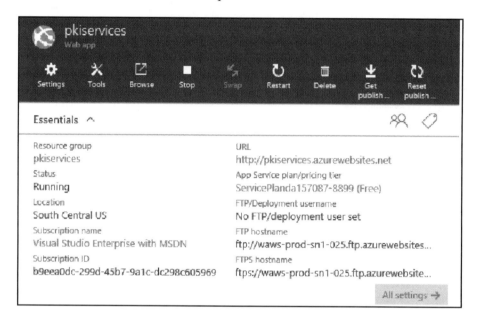

 We used the `idam.ch` forest to deploy all the different services, including the PKI.

Next, you need to provide a certificate template for the user authentication.

You just need to duplicate the User template and use only the client authentication usage:

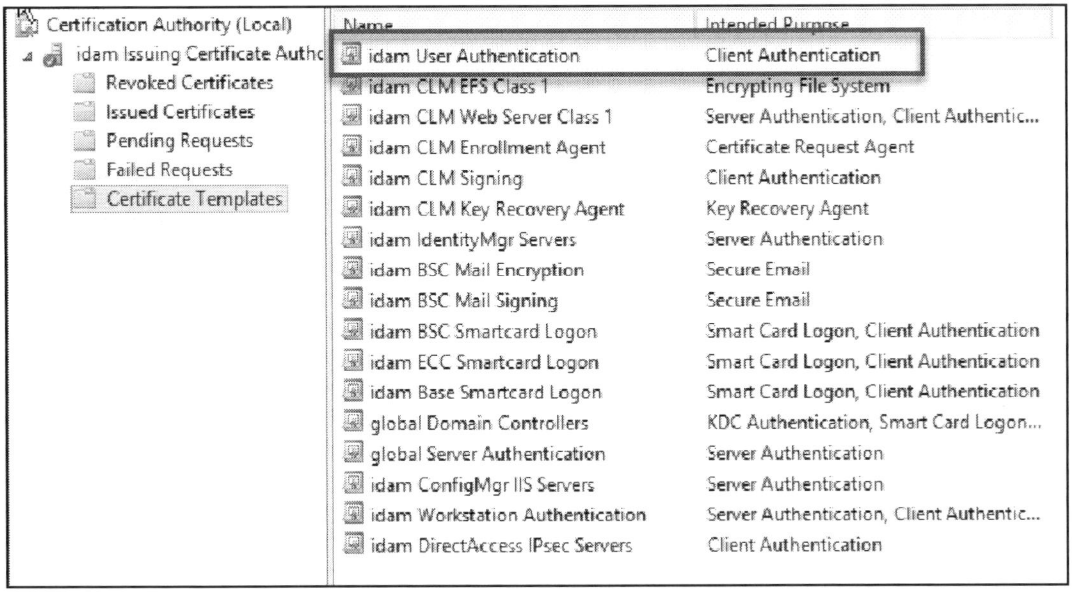

Register a new certificate for your administrative user so that you can test the functionality in the following configuration procedure.

# Configuring certificate-based authentication

In this section, we will configure AD FS so that users need to specify both a valid username/password and certificate. You can use any Relying party. In our configuration, we use the claims web application.

Perform the following steps:

1. Log on to **IDB01** in `idam.ch`:
   - **Username**: Domain\AdminAccount
   - **Password**: YourPassword
2. Open the **ADFS Management** console.
3. Go to **Relying Party Trusts**, right-click **Claims Web Site** and choose **Edit Access Control Policy**.

4. Permit everyone and require MFA, and click **OK**.
5. Go to **Service | Authentication Methods**.
6. Click **Edit Multi-Factor Authentication Methods** in the **Actions** pane.
7. Click **Certificate Authentication**:

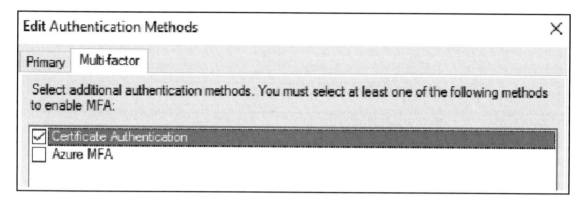

8. Open Internet Explorer on the administrative workstation where you have requested the certificate.
9. Open the Claims website and you should be prompted for the certificate.
10. Provide your credentials and you should be able to log in.
11. Remove the MFA requirement after you have tried the solution.

 Refer to http://bit.ly/28Sf8c2 and http://bit.ly/28SdE5t for configuring this scenario.

Now we have provided the basic implementation for using certificates in the authentication process for on premise published applications.

# Summary

After working through this chapter, you should be able to configure and handle an identity and access management solution with multiple forests. You should also be able to provide this functionality across company borders for secure application and information access. We used the approach to provide you the idea for several scenarios, which we always get asked about in our customer discussions, to provide a suitable hybrid structure. It's impossible to bring all the configuration steps into the book, because the page count would explode, so we used qualified references to help you configure such scenarios. Otherwise, we have configured many on premise services. We see it in the field to really provide a hybrid strategy and a lot of services are still on premise; because of this reason, we choose to integrate these configurations.

In the following chapter, we will focus on more extended scenarios and on access management features.

# 15
# Installing and Configuring Information Protection Features

In this chapter, we will configure information protection features with Azure RMS to secure access to sensitive data to provide an extended access management solution. We will start with the extension of the basic infrastructure that we already deployed in previous chapters. The focus of the starting configuration tasks will be on Exchange on-premise, Exchange Online, and SharePoint. Afterwards, we will configure and publish custom rights policy templates, enable RMS logging, and provide you with a first view on the new Azure Information Protection capabilities.

We will cover the following topics:

- Preparing your admin workstation to manage Azure RMS
- Configuring onboarding controls
- Delegating administrative permissions
- Enabling Azure RMS super users
- Configuring Exchange to use Rights Management capabilities
- Configuring Exchange Online to use Rights Management capabilities
- Configuring SharePoint to use Rights Management capabilities
- Creating and publishing custom Rights Policy templates
- Verifying Azure RMS logging
- Preview of Azure Information Protection
- SAP Integration as a special integration
- Configuring a BYOK scenario

# Preparing your admin workstation to manage Azure RMS

To manage our Azure RMS information protection solution, we need to prepare the administrative Windows 10 workstation with the necessary tools. You need to download and install the following setup files:

- Microsoft Online Services Sign-In Assistant (`http://bit.ly/28Y8P9F`)
- Azure Rights Management Administration Tool (`http://bit.ly/28TYaN`)

After installing the administrative toolset, we test the correct installation and the connectivity to the activated Azure RMS service from the previous chapter:

1. Open an evaluated PowerShell and type the following command: `Connect-AadrmService` and provide your global administrator credentials.
2. Check the current state of the service with `Get-Aadrm`.
3. The expected result should be **enabled**.

In the next section, we will start with the configuration of the on boarding mechanisms you can use with Azure RMS.

# Configuring onboarding controls

It's a recommended way to do a planned rollout of the RMS functionality in an organization. For this reason, Microsoft has implemented the on boarding controls feature.

You can check the default configuration with the following command: `Get-AadrmOnboardingControlPolicy` on an elevated PowerShell after you have established a connection to the Azure RMS service with the `Connect-AadrmService` command.

You should see a result like the following if you didn't touch it before:

```
Administrator: Windows PowerShell
PS C:\Windows\system32> Get-AadrmOnboardingControlPolicy

UseRmsUserLicense SecurityGroupObjectId Scope
----------------- --------------------- -----
            False                         All
```

To enable the onboarding controls, you can use the following command:

```
Set-AadrmOnboardingControlPolicy
```

 **Practical note**
You can run this command before or after you activate Azure RMS. But you must have at least version 2.1.0.0 of the Azure RMS Windows PowerShell module installed.

To check the version of your installed PowerShell module, you can run `(Get-Module aadrm -ListAvailable).Version`:

```
Administrator: Windows PowerShell
PS C:\Windows\system32> (Get-Module aadrm -ListAvailable).Version

Major  Minor  Build  Revision
-----  -----  -----  --------
2      4      0      0
```

Let's start with the example that you only want to allow a specific group to be able to protect content for a proof of concept. In our example, we want to use the Human Resources group:

1. First we need to determine the object ID of the group we want to use. Open an elevated PowerShell and type the following commands:

   - `Connect-MsolService` to connect to your Azure AD – provide your Azure AD global administrator credentials

- `Get-MsolGroup` to find the related group, as shown in the following screenshot:

```
PS C:\Windows\system32> Connect-Msolservice
PS C:\Windows\system32> Get-MsolGroup

ObjectId                                 DisplayName                        GroupType             Description
--------                                 -----------                        ---------             -----------
664826e2-0264-42ec-ae82-6afab63f8a7a     SSPRSecurityGroupUsers             Security              SSPRSecurityGroupUsers
0ef95a30-9277-490e-b07c-487e2f4e75a8     All Users                          Security
239d9a09-9d9e-434e-83a4-3a554df3ffae     Self-Service App Access for Cl...  Security              This system-generated group c...
f7f1249a-9e5f-4717-828e-2347d7403988     Self-Service App Access for Gr...  Security              This system-generated group c...
4e4419cd-8437-4ca5-a622-47e261dec1b1     Marketing                          DistributionList
363802eb-d4a3-4319-a7f0-b0ac173fc9b6     Sales                              DistributionList
61a99c41-a75e-470c-a991-41d66fe8f0e5     Sales Strategy Discussion          DistributionList
c1c87fe2-5beb-4a5f-bbd3-5abc5e5b0c79     Sales Communications Review        DistributionList
0de8fa9f-5764-48cd-bd11-de3f3ece2e32     Sales News                         DistributionList
20c78dcf-f0b5-43f7-b88f-ead0b1f39566     Identityplus SharePoint            Security              identityplus B2B SharePoint
ef36c6e3-e1cb-4ddc-aa9b-f8e600ab2718     Licensing Office 365               Security
d17702a7-94f1-4dc6-b6a6-cd9dd037ee73     Licensing Azure Active Directo...  Security
7daeedc7-31dc-4ff6-89b8-dc1924023798     Licensing Dynamics                 Security
e027af51-8cfa-47a7-baba-5df3c5e1e972     Licensing Enterprise Mobility      Security
9b78b258-f885-4dfe-a400-ce3ae68f13da     Licensing Intune                   Security
8fcbf032-be05-44c9-8e95-d798c20e283f     AAD DC Administrators              Security              AAD DS Administrators
493ca20e-a34d-44c2-8fb9-a414aaf7bcfd     Finance                            Security
b8941bc9-c973-4ac6-93cc-5937e0096e50     Test                               Security
aea6c17a-fcdf-407e-98b1-df8322a0651e     RMSSuperUsers                      DistributionList     RMS Super Users Group
d6819dd7-2cec-4dae-9272-ebbc53033690     Human Resources                    MailEnabledSecurity
```

> In our example, we use the group with the display name `Human Resources` that needs to be mail enabled and the object ID `d6819dd7-2cec-4dae-9272-ebbc53033690`.

2. Next, we enable the onboarding policy for this group with the following command:

```
Set-AadrmOnboardingControlPolicy - SecurityGroupObjectId
d6819dd7-2cec-4dae-9272-ebbc53033690
```

```
PS C:\Windows\system32> Set-AadrmOnboardingControlPolicy -Securitygroupobjectid d6819dd7-2cec-4dae-9272-ebbc53033690

cmdlet Set-AadrmOnboardingControlPolicy at command pipeline position 1
Supply values for the following parameters:
UseRmsUserLicense: y
WARNING: The tenant user on-boarding control policy will be updated by this operation.

Confirm
Are you sure you want to perform this action?
Performing the operation "Set-AadrmOnboardingControlPolicy" on target "current organization".
[Y] Yes  [A] Yes to All  [N] No  [L] No to All  [S] Suspend  [?] Help (default is "Y"): y
The tenant user on-boarding control policy for the Rights Management service has been successfully set.
PS C:\Windows\system32>
```

**Practical note**

For this configuration option, you must specify a group; you cannot specify individual users.

3.  With the next option, we want to ensure that only users who are correctly licensed to use Azure RMS can protect content.
4.  Type `Set-AadrmOnboardingControlPolicy -UseRmsUserLicense $true`
5.  Verify your configuration.
6.  Type `Get-AadrmOnboardingControlPolicy`

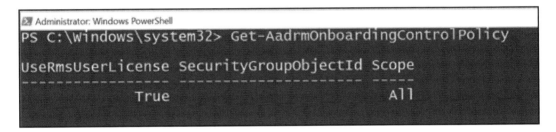

Using onboarding controls always allows all users in your organization to consume protected content that has been protected by your subset of users. But they are unable to apply information protection themselves. They will not see the default templates that are automatically published after you activated Azure RMS for your organization:

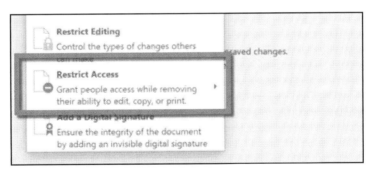

# Delegating administrative permissions

In this section, we will discuss and configure the delegation of administrative permissions, especially the question: are there global administrator permissions needed or can I delegate the tasks to other administrators?

By default, global administrators can obviously do all the administrative tasks for Azure RMS. But in fact, we don't want to use or assign global administrator rights to some individuals every time. With the command `Add-AadrmRoleBasedAdministrator`, you can assign this administrative role to a user account or a group.

Two roles are available:

- **Global administrator**: This will run all administrative tasks on Azure RMS without granting global administrator rights to other cloud services.
- **Connector administrator**: This will just run the RMS connector. First, we check the default configuration using the following steps:

1. Open an elevated PowerShell and type the following command:

   ```
   Get-AadrmRoleBasedAdministrator
   ```

2. Normally, if you didn't touch the feature before, you should have no entry.
3. Next, we add a user to the role.
4. Type `Add-AadrmRoleBasedAdministrator -EmailAddress <mail>` (in our example, `jochen.nickel@idam.ch`):

```
Administrator: Windows PowerShell
PS C:\Windows\system32> Add-AadrmRoleBasedAdministrator  -EmailAddress jochen.nickel@idam.ch
jochen.nickel@idam.ch was added to the list of administrators for the Rights Management service.
PS C:\Windows\system32> Get-AadrmRoleBasedAdministrator

ObjectId                               DisplayName     EmailAddress                                            Role
--------                               -----------     ------------                                            ----
5e4583c3-9571-4651-a59b-25b0d5e24a47 Jochen Nickel smtp:jochen.nickel5265@idamcloud.onmicrosoft.com GlobalAdministrator
```

5. Verify your configuration with the following command:

   ```
   Get-AadrmRoleBasedAdministrator
   ```

6. Test your configuration by connecting to the Azure RMS service and configuring some functions.

**Practical note**

By default, no administrator for Azure RMS, even the global administrator for your Azure tenant, can automatically remove protection from documents or e-mails that were protected by Azure RMS. This functionality is only available for users who are assigned as super users for Azure RMS.

Also, remember that super users can only be assigned from the tenant global administrator and the global administrator for Azure RMS, including their own account. Furthermore, these actions are recorded in the Azure RMS administrator log.

Now that we have successfully delegated administrative rights for Azure RMS, we will configure the Azure Super Users feature.

# Enabling Azure RMS super users

The super user feature is your fallback scenario to ensure that you can inspect and unprotect RMS secured information. The super user always has full owner rights.

Remember the following best practices:

1. Check that the super user feature is enabled with the following command:

```
Get-AadrmSuperUserFeature
```

The results will be disabled or enabled.

2. Limit and monitor the administrators who are assigned global administrator rights or in special assigned with the Add-AadrmRoleBasedAdministrator command.

3. You can check the actual configured administrators with the following command:

```
Get-AadrmRoleBasedAdministrator
```

```
Administrator: Windows PowerShell

PS C:\WINDOWS\system32> Get-AadrmRoleBasedAdministrator | fl


ObjectId      : 5e4583c3-9571-4651-a59b-25b0d5e24a47
DisplayName   : Jochen Nickel
EmailAddress  : smtp:jochen.nickel5265@idamcloud.onmicrosoft.com
Role          : GlobalAdministrator
```

4. If you want to check which users and accounts are assigned to the super users, you can use the command `Get-Aadrm-SuperUser`:

```
Administrator: Windows PowerShell                                            —

PS C:\WINDOWS\system32> Get-AadrmSuperUser
Aadrm_S-1-5-21-3123384963-3601710319-2843089171-1118@b934de73-2597-4922-9a7b-c97c5d6d4c7a.rms.eu.aadrm.com
PS C:\WINDOWS\system32>
```

5. To get the log information for all administrative tasks, you can use the `Get-AadrmAdminLog -Path "C:\ActualLog.log"` command and you will receive the whole details, as shown in the following example:

```
2016-05-27T12:39:16    admin@idamcloud.onmicrosoft.com GetTemplateById -templateId d9f53841-9861-4646-8fcf-1559ae049a56        Passed  Begin TemplatePrope
TemplateID = d9f53841-9861-4646-8fcf-1559ae049a56
Names:
1033 -> idam Demo Environment - Human Resources Confidential
Descriptions:
1033 -> idam Demo Environment - Human Resources Confidential
Status = Published
RightsDefinitions:
HumanResources@idam.ch -> VIEW, EXTRACT, REPLY, REPLYALL, PRINT, OBJMODEL
ContentExpirationDate = 1/1/0001 12:00:00 AM
ContentValidityDuration = 0
ContentExpirationOption = Never
LicenseValidityDuration = 7
ReadOnly = False
LastModifiedTimeStamp = 6/23/2015 2:39:00 PM
ScopedIdentities:
EnableInLegacyApps = False
End TemplateProperties
```

6. We recommend that the super user feature is used on a need basis. So if you don't need it, disable it with the following command:

`Disable-AadrmSuperUserFeature`

If you need to protect and unprotect files, you can use the RMS Protection Toolkit under `http://bit.ly/1RM3UGE`.

 **Practical note**
**If** you need the RMS 2.1 SDK, you can download it from the following link: `http://bit.ly/298QzMn`.

With this toolkit, you receive the following two cmdlets:

- Protect-RMSFile
- Unprotect-RMSFile

To use the commands, you need to determine the **TemplateID** or **License**; in our example, we used the command, `Get-AadrmTemplate`, to get the templates listed, including the **TemplateID**. Afterwards, you can use the `Protect-RMSFile` command to protect files manually by PowerShell:

And you will get a result like the following one with the policy applied:

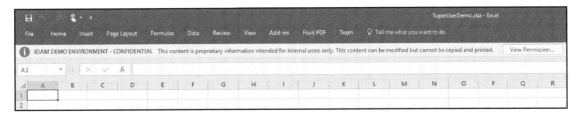

Obviously, you can unprotect the file with the command, `Unprotect-RMSFile`:

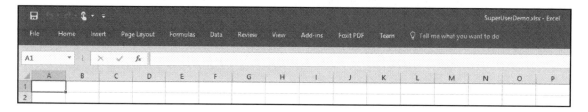

And you will get an unprotected file:

Now that we have configured and tested the tools and options for the Super Users, we will configure Exchange Online to use the Rights Management capabilities.

# Configuring Exchange Online to use Rights Management capabilities

In the following section, we will configure Exchange Online to work with the Azure RMS capabilities. You need to perform the following steps:

1. Log on to your administrative workstation.
2. Open an evaluated PowerShell.
3. Type the following command:

   ```
   $Cred = Get-Credential
   ```

4. Enter your global administrator credentials.

5. Type the following commands:

```
$Session = New-PSSession -ConfigurationName Microsoft.Exchange -
ConnectionUri https://ps.outlook.com/powershell/ -Credential $Cred -
Authentication Basic -AllowRedirection
Import-PSSession $Session
```

```
Enable-OrganizationCustomization
```

Configuration note: Exchange needs a copy of your tenant keys in order to be able to work with protected content.

6. Type the following command with the correct tenant region:

```
Set-IRMConfiguration -RMSOnlineKeySharingLocation
"https://sp-rms.eu.aadrm.com/TenantManagement/ServicePartner.svc"
```

**Region note**: Tenant regions – North America **na**; **eu** for Europe; **ap** for Asia-Pacific; or **sa** for South America.

7. Type the following commands:

```
Import-RMSTrustedPublishingDomain -RMSOnline -name "RMS Online"
Set-IRMConfiguration -InternalLicensingEnabled $true
```

This enables the IRM support in Exchange Online.

8. Use `Get-IRMConfiguration` to receive the current configuration:

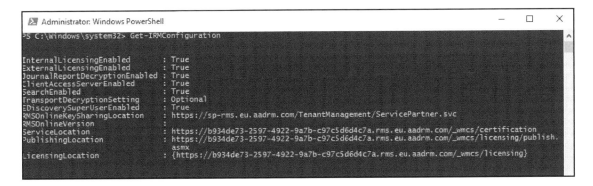

9. Verify that the values for the following parameters are set to **true**:
   - **InternalLicensingEnabled**
   - **ExternalLicensingEnabled**
   - **JournalReportDecryptionEnabled**
   - **ClientAccessServerEnabled**
   - **SearchEnabled**

Now we are able to use Azure RMS features in Exchange Online:

1. The first test we will do is to see the Outlook Web App experience a user gets if they try to create a protected message:
2. Sign in with a test user, in our case ,anas.nickel@idam.ch, to the Access Panel http://myapps.microsoft.com:

3. Click on the **Office 365 Exchange Online** tile.
4. Click **New Mail** to create a new mail message.
5. Send a protected mail with a test user, in our case, jochen.nickel@idam.ch.

6. Click the ellipsis (…) button, click **Set permissions**, and select the template corporate confidential template:

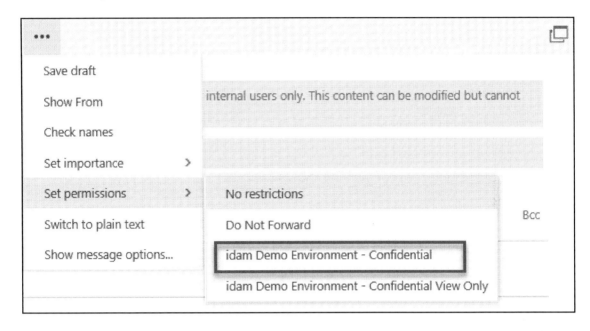

7. Sign out and log on with the other user to view the newly received protected mail.

The second test will be to automatically apply protection to sensitive information. For this reason, we can use Transport Protection Rules to apply RMS protection to e-mails in transit based on triggers configured by the administrator.

We will use a sensible project name, Project Identity and Access Management Private Preview, which contains the phase **Azure Information Protection**. Next, we need to create the transport protection rule that automatically protects messages that contain the phase**Azure Information Protection**:

1. Use your browser to log in on `https://login.microsoftonline.com` with your global administrator credentials.
2. Click on the **Admin** tile to open the **Office 365 admin center**.
3. Select **Exchange** in the left navigation bar.

4. Under the mail flow section, click on **rules** and choose **+**:

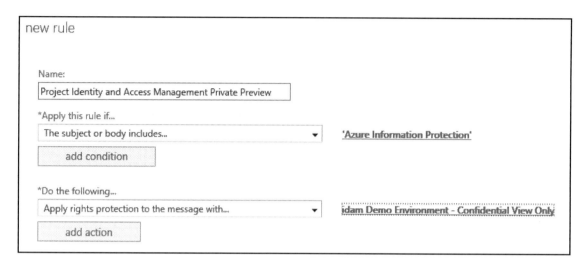

5. Review the additional options available and click **Save**.

6. Send a mail with the following content from one test user to the other:

```
Subject: Project Identity and Access Management Private Preview important
notes
Body:
Hi <Employee>
I have some important notes for the project.
We will add the new feature Azure Information Protection were you can
classify, label and protect sensitive information.
Best regards
<Employee>
```

7. Notice that the message is unprotected and click **Send**.

8. Log in with the recipient user and you should find the automatically protected e-mail protected with the Company Confidential View Only template protected.

With this section, we have configured Exchange Online to use Azure RMS with a manually and automatically protected scenario. Next, we will configure Exchange and SharePoint on premise to use Azure RMS.

 We will use the same procedure that we have done to authorize the servers in the RMS connector as we have done for the file server integration. So you need to have the relevant Exchange and SharePoint servers authorized before you follow the next sections.

So you should have an RMS connector configuration.

Open the **Microsoft RMS connector administration tool** and provide your global administrator credentials or the RMS connector credentials depending on your delegation configuration:

You should have a list of authorized servers like the following:

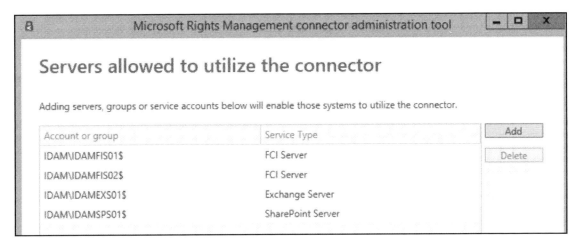

Now that all servers are authorized, we can start with the next sections to configure the servers to use the RMS connector.

# Configuring Exchange to use Rights Management capabilities

With the following steps, we will configure Exchange Server 2010 and 2013 to use the Rights Management capabilities; the following Exchange roles are especially relevant for this configuration:

Hub transport server for:

- Transport Protection
- Journal Decryption
- Prelicensing
- Transport Decryption

Client access server for:

- Outlook Web Access IRM capabilities
- IRM capabilities in Search

**Practical Note**
On this server, the Rights Management Client needs to be installed and configured like a normal client.

Basically, there are two options to configure this scenario. The first option is to use the RMS connector administration tool and the other one is to do the steps manually. We will use the manual mode, so that you understand the steps under the hood:

1. The first step we need is to retrieve the Azure RMS URL for the tenant.
2. Open an elevated PowerShell and type `Connect-Aadrm-Service`.
3. Provide your global administrator credentials.

4. Type the following command: `Get-AadrmConfiguration`, as shown in the following screenshot:

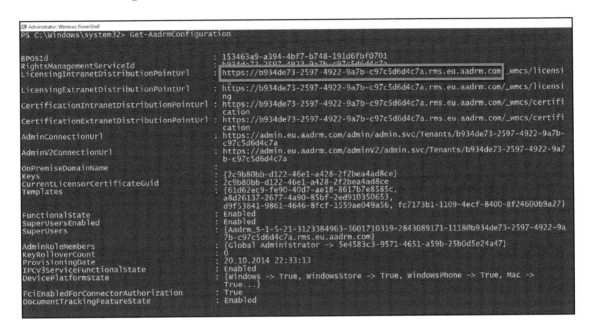

5. You will receive the Microsoft RMS URL that you need to copy to your Exchange server for configuring the correct registry entries. In our demo environment, we receive:

   `https://b934de73-2597-4922-9a7b-c97c5d6d4c7a.rms.eu.aadrm.com`

6. With the next step, we need to configure the registry entries on the Exchange server to point to our installed RMS connector.

7. Log on to your local Exchange server with the appropriate administrative credentials.

8. Start the **Registry Editor** and navigate to the following registry key:

   `HKEY_LOCAL_MACHINE\SOFTWARE\Microsoft\MSDRM\ServiceLocation\Activiation`

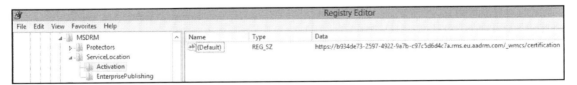

**Practical Note**: If any keys within the path do not exist, create them.

9. Create a new **Reg_SZ** in the **Activation** node and leave the default value.
10. Double-click the new **Reg_SZ** and enter the Azure RMS tenant URL; click **OK**.
11. Navigate to the next registry key:

```
HKEY_LOCAL_MACHINE\SOFTWARE\Microsoft\MSDRM\ServiceLocation\EnterprisePubli
shing
```

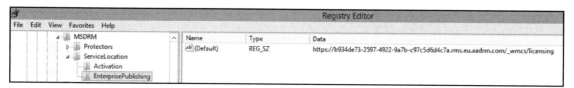

12. Create a new **Reg_SZ** in the **EnterprisePublishing** node and leave the default value.
13. Double-click the new **Reg_SZ** and enter the Azure RMS tenant; click **OK**.
14. Next, navigate to the following registry key:

```
HKEY_LOCAL_MACHINE\SOFTWARE\Microsoft\ExchangeServer\v15 or
v14\IRM\CertificationServerRedirection
```

15. Create a new **Reg_SZ** in the **CertificationServerRedirection** node with a value of the Azure RMS tenant URL.
16. Double-click the new **Reg_SZ** and enter the RMS connector URL in the **Data** field – in our example, `https://idamclo01.idam.ch` – and click **OK**.
17. Next, navigate to the following registry key:

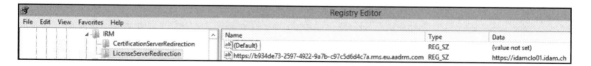

18. Create a new **Reg_SZ** in the **LicenseServerRedirection** node with a value of the Azure RMS tenant URL.

19. Double-click the new **Reg_SZ** and enter the RMS connector URL in the **Data** field – in our example, `https://idamclo01.idam.ch` – and click **OK**.

**Practical note**

You need to repeat the steps on every Exchange server that runs the relevant roles.

Now that we have configured the correct registry entries, we can configure the Outlook Web Access IRM and IRM Search support:

1. Open the Exchange Management Shell.

2. First, we enable the Outlook Web Access IRM capabilities and type the following command: `Get-OWAMailboxPolicy`

3. We need to look for the **IRMEnabled** parameter:

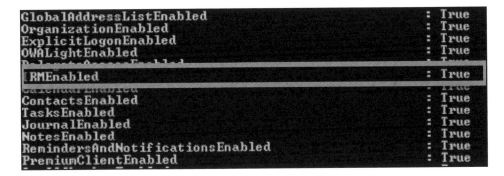

4. If the parameter is not set to `True`, we need to run the following command:

```
Set-OWAMailboxPolicy –Identity Default –IRMEnabled $true
```

5. Next, we will verify if indexing for search of protected content in Outlook Web Access is enabled.

6. Type `Get-IRMConfiguration` and see the **SearchEnabled** parameter:

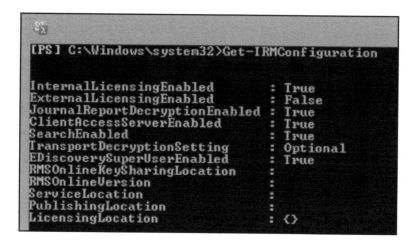

```
[PS] C:\Windows\system32>Get-IRMConfiguration

InternalLicensingEnabled         : True
ExternalLicensingEnabled         : False
JournalReportDecryptionEnabled   : True
ClientAccessServerEnabled        : True
SearchEnabled                    : True
TransportDecryptionSetting       : Optional
EDiscoverySuperUserEnabled       : True
RMSOnlineKeySharingLocation      :
RMSOnlineVersion                 :
ServiceLocation                  :
PublishingLocation               :
LicensingLocation                : {}
```

7. If the parameter is not set to `True`, we need to run the following command:

   `Set-IRMConfiguration -SearchEnabled $true`

8. So that all the functionality works as expected, the `InternalLicensingEnabled` parameter also needs to be enabled.

9. Type `Get-IRMConfiguration` and see the `InternalLicensingEnabled` parameter.

10. If the parameter is not set to `True`, we need to run the following command:

    `Set-IRMConfiguration -InternalLicensingEnabled $true`

11. Now that we have configured Exchange to work with the RMS connector, we can start to create Transport Protection Rules to test our configuration.

12. You can repeat the configuration we have done in Exchange Online by opening **Exchange Admin Center** | **Mail flow** | **Rules**:

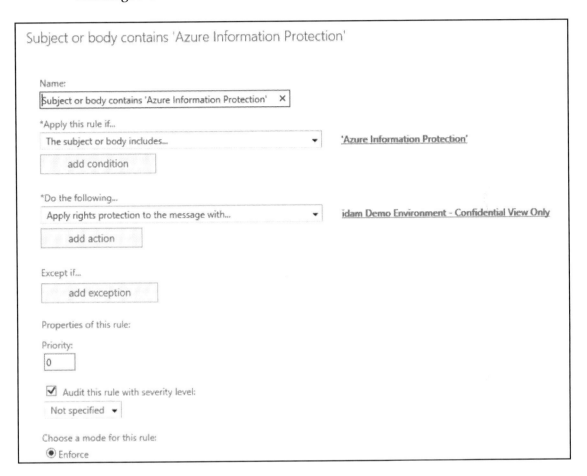

**Practical Note**: You can repeat the steps from the Exchange Online configuration, including the test mail, to verify the functionality.

13. To enable Transport Decryption, you need to type the following command in the Exchange Management Shell:

    ```
    Set-IRMConfiguration –TransportDecryptionSetting Mandatory
    ```

14. To enable Journal Decryption, you need to type the following command in the Exchange Management Shell:

    ```
    Set-IRMConfiguration –JournalReportDecryptionEnabled $true
    ```

15. In the next step, we integrate the **Exchange Data Loss Prevention** feature with RMS.

16. Open the **Exchange Admin Center** and click **compliance management**.

17. Click on the **data loss prevention** tab:

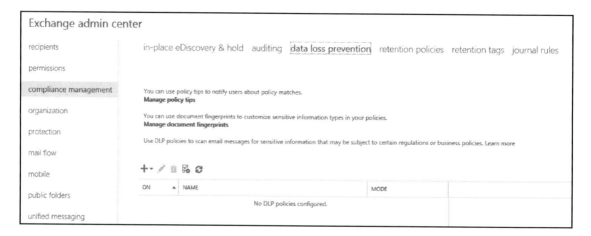

18. Click the plus icon and select from template.

19. We use an example to identify**German Financial Data**:

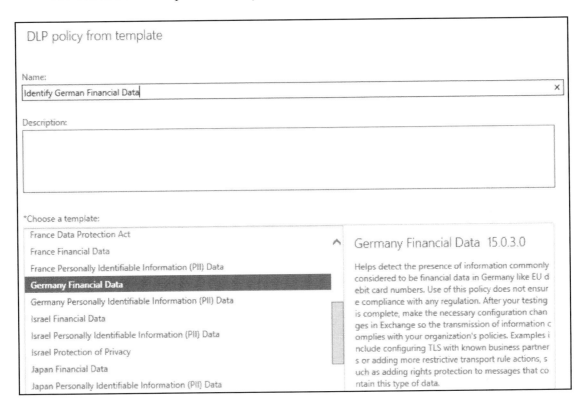

20. Next, click **Save**.

21. Edit the policy again to enforce it:

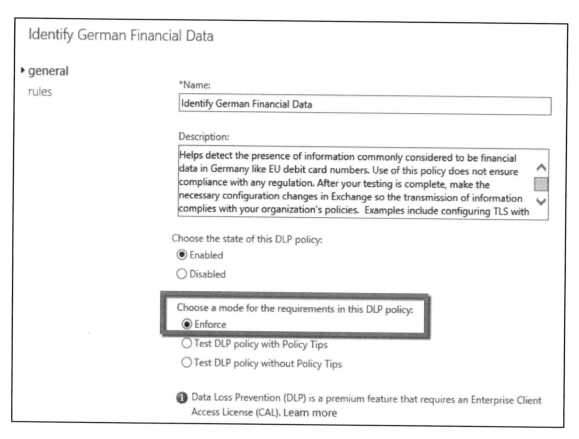

22. Next, we need to identify what the policy does for us – click **rules**:

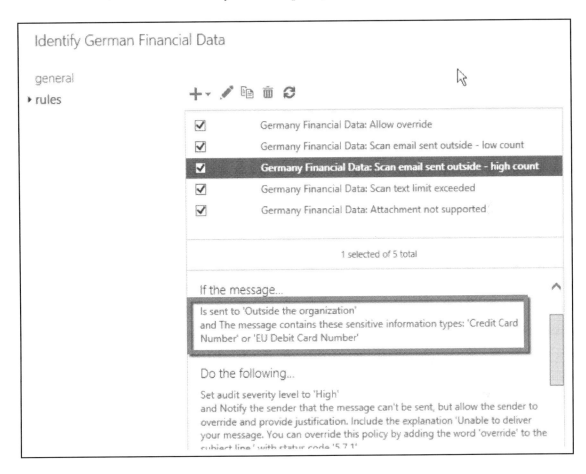

23. Verify what the policy is looking for – in our example, it looks for **Credit Card Number** in messages that are sent **Outside the organization**.
24. Next, we need to integrate RMS to our newly created policy.
25. Click the **mail flow** tab.
26. Double-click one of the rules that were created from the DLP policy.
27. Under the **Do the following** section, click the drop-down list, point to **Modify the message security**, and select **Apply rights protection**.

28. Select the appropriate rights policy template – in our example, **idam Demo Environment –Confidential** – and click **OK**:

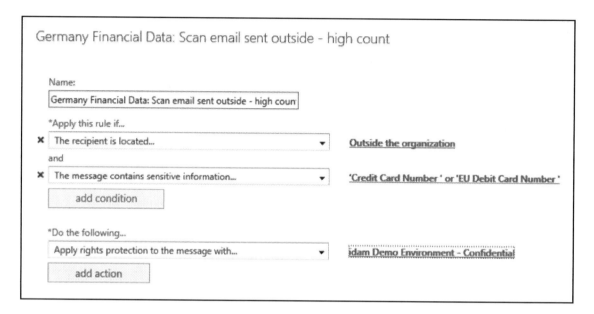

29. Click **Save**.
30. Now you can try this functionality with a mail that contains a credit card number.

**Practical Note**
You can use the following credit card number generator for testing:
`http://bit.ly/1qYwaGT`.

31. Verify that the message sent outside the organization is protected with the chosen Azure RMS template.

Now that we have successfully configured and tested the integration of Azure RMS in our on premise Exchange environment, we can jump to the next service – *SharePoint*.

# Configuring SharePoint to use Rights Management capabilities

In this section, we will configure SharePoint 2010/2013 and SharePoint Online to use the Rights Management capabilities. As a prerequisite on SharePoint 2013 servers, the latest RMS client version 2.1 needs to be installed. For SharePoint 2010, the MSDRM client that includes support for RMS Cryptographic Mode 2 needs to be installed:

> **Practical note**
>
> SharePoint 2010 needs the following additional prerequisites:
> Windows 2012/R2 (`http://bit.ly/29ror7U`)
> Windows 2008 R2 (`http://bit.ly/29IrwwA`)
> Windows 2008 (`http://bit.ly/291rrR6`)

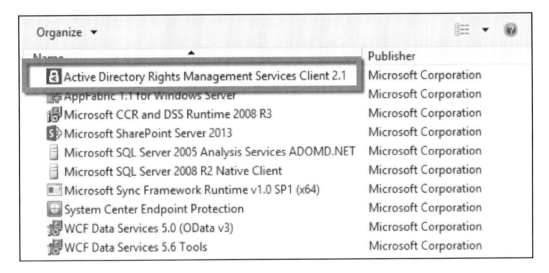

In our scenario, we will use SharePoint 2013 and the already installed RMS Connector. Perform the following steps:

1. First, we need to retrieve the Azure RMS URL for your tenant.
2. Open an elevated PowerShell and type `Connect-Aadrm-Service`
3. Provide your global administrator credentials.
4. Type the following command: `Get-AadrmConfiguration`

5. You will receive the Microsoft RMS URL that you need to copy to your SharePoint server for configuring the correct registry entries. In our demo environment, we receive
`https://b934de73-2597-4922-9a7b-c97c5d6d4c7a.rms.eu.aadrm.com`

6. With the next step, we need to configure the registry entries on the SharePoint server to point to our installed RMS connector.

7. Log on to your SharePoint server with local administrative permissions or your SharePoint farm account with local administrative rights.

8. Start the registry editor by typing `regedit` in the search field.

9. Navigate to the `HKEY_LOCAL_MACHINE\SOFTWARE\Microsoft\MSIPC\ServiceLocation\LicensingRedirection` registry key.

10. Create a new **Reg_SZ** in the **LicensingRedirection** node and enter the RMS URL.

11. Double-click the new **Reg_SZ** and enter the URL of the RMS Connector – in our demo, `https://idamclo01.idam.ch` – and click **OK**:

12. Navigate to the `HKEY_LOCAL_MACHINE\SOFTWARE\Microsoft\MSIPC\ServiceLocation\EnterpriseCertification` registry key.

13. Create a new **Reg_SZ** in the **EnterpriseCertification** node and leave the default value.

14. Double-click the new **Reg_SZ** and enter the RMS connector URL; click **OK**:

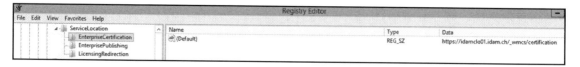

15. Navigate to the `HKEY_LOCAL_MACHINE\SOFTWARE\Microsoft\MSIPC\ServiceLocation\EnterprisePublishing` registry key.

16. Create a new **Reg_SZ** in the **EnterprisePublishing** node and leave the default value.

17. Double-click the new **Reg_SZ** and enter the RMS connector URL; click **OK**:

**Practical note**

Repeat these steps for each SharePoint server that will use Azure RMS.

18. Next, we will enable SharePoint to use Azure RMS.

19. Log on to the SharePoint server with Full Control over the document library.

20. Open the SharePoint 2013/2010 Central Administration.

21. Navigate to **Security**.

22. Click **Configure information rights management**:

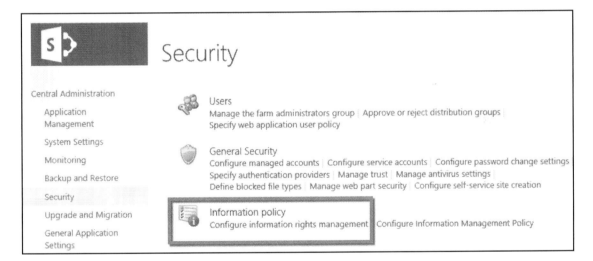

23. Configure your RMS Connector URL as the RMS server:

## Information Rights Management

Information Rights Management

IRM helps protect sensitive files from being misused or distributed without permission once they have been downloaded from this server.

Specify the location of Windows Rights Management Services (RMS):

○ Do not use IRM on this server

○ Use the default RMS server specified in Active Directory

⦿ Use this RMS server:

`https://idamclo01.idam.ch`     ✕

☐ Check this box in multi-tenant configurations to allow tenants to configure tenant level IRM settings.

24. Next, we can go RMS protect a document library.

25. Navigate to a **SharePoint** document library using your credentials with **Full Control** over the document library.

26. Click the **Page** tab and click **Library Settings**.

27. Click **Information Rights Management**, located under the **Permissions and Management** column.

28. Select the **Restrict permission to documents in this library on download** option.

29. Enter a name and description for the permission policy.

30. Click **OK**.

31. Try out your configuration with some test files.

In addition to the SharePoint on premise configuration, we will configure SharePoint Online to get all configurations done.

We will use the following steps to configure SharePoint Online for RMS capabilities:

1. Log on to Office 365 at `https:// portal.office.com` with global administrator credentials.

2. Click **Admin** and **SharePoint**.

3. Navigate to **Settings**:

**Information Rights Management (IRM)**

Set IRM capabilities to SharePoint for your organization (requires Office 365 IRM service)

⦿ Use the IRM service specified in your configuration

○ Do not use IRM for this tenant

Refresh IRM Settings

We successfully refreshed your settings.

4. Choose **Use the IRM service specified in your configuration** and **Refresh IRM Settings**.

5. Click **OK**.

Now that we have configured the RMS integration, we will RMS protect a document library:

1. Navigate to a **SharePoint** document library using your credentials with **Full Control** over the document library.
2. Click the **Page** tab and click **Library Settings**.
3. Click **Information Rights Management**, located under the **Permissions and Management** column.
4. Select the **Restrict permission to documents in this library on download** option.
5. Enter a name and description for the permission policy.
6. Click **OK**.
7. Try your new feature with some test files.

Now that we have configured and tested the SharePoint Online RMS integration, we will start to create and publish custom Rights Policy templates in the next section.

# Creating and publishing custom Rights Policy templates

To support additional use cases, we will configure custom rights policy templates in addition to the two default templates.

We want to reach the following configuration, where we configure one policy template for human resources and one for an external sharing scenario:

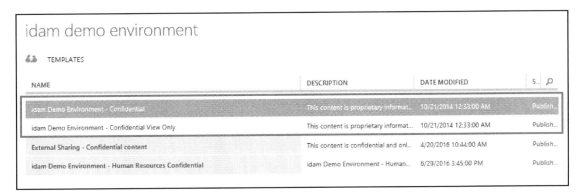

# Creating a custom rights policy template

In the first step, we will configure the human resources policy template with the following steps:

1. Log in to the **Azure Management Portal** with global administrator credentials.
2. Navigate to **Active Directory** and choose **RIGHTS MANAGEMENT**.
3. Choose your active instance:

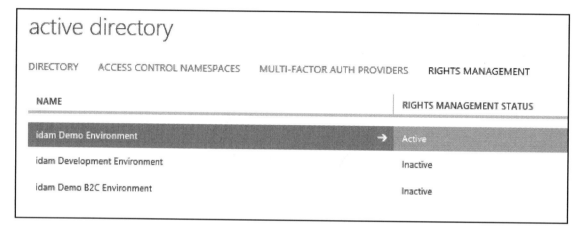

4. Click **Create a new rights policy template** to start the **Rights Policy Template** wizard:

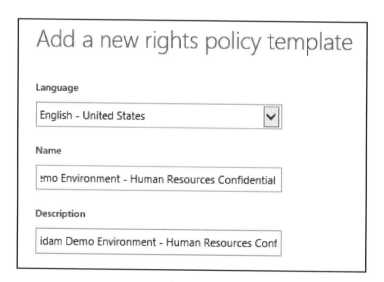

5. Click your newly created template to configure the options.
6. Under **Configure rights for users and groups**, click **Get started**.
7. Configure the Human Resources group:

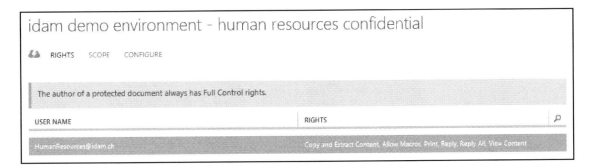

8. Configure the following custom rights:

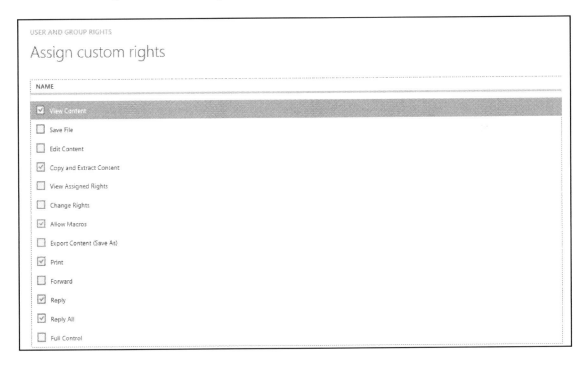

9. If you like, you can also do the following:

- Add the template name and description in additional languages:

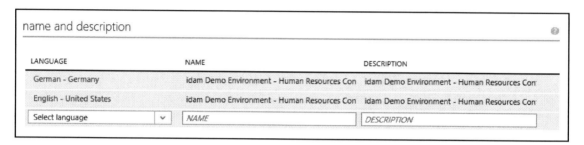

- Configure the content expiration by date or number of days:

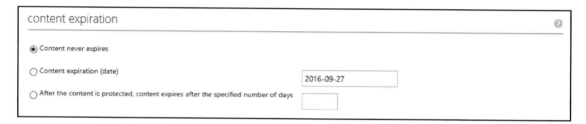

- Configure offline access:

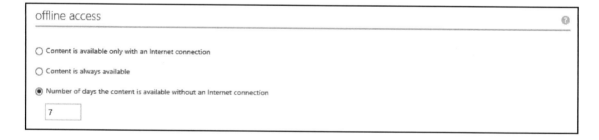

10. Additionally, we will configure the scope of the template so that only users from HR will see the template in the RMS-enabled applications:

11. Next, publish the custom rights policy template:

12. Now we will test the configuration. Open Word with a user that is a member of the Human Resources group and you should see the newly generated template:

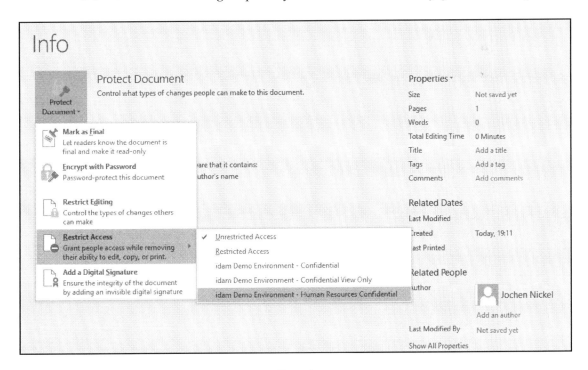

In the second scenario, we will provide a solution to include external users in our policy template. We will build up a small example that shows this principle and how to use it. The example contains a template for the marketing department of IDAM that sends protected content to the engineering department of the IdentityPlus company. Obviously, you will use your own company and organization names. The result we want to achieve looks like the following:

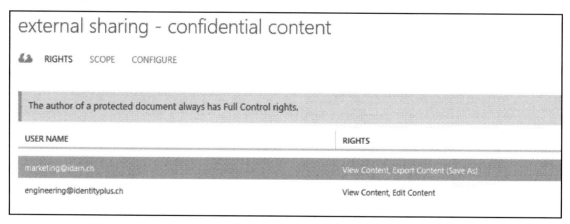

external sharing - confidential content

RIGHTS    SCOPE    CONFIGURE

The author of a protected document always has Full Control rights.

| USER NAME | RIGHTS |
| --- | --- |
| marketing@idam.ch | View Content, Export Content (Save As) |
| engineering@identityplus.ch | View Content, Edit Content |

 As a further reference, you can use `http://bit.ly/29rUyEl`.

Remember that you can have a maximum of 500 custom templates in Azure AD. The configuration for this custom template can be done with the following PowerShell commands:

- `Add-AadrmTemplate` – this adds a new template
- `Set-AadrmTemplateProperty` – this modifies an existing template

The main configuration we do to provide this example is to add the external e-mail addresses we want to use in the rights definition object.

Let's go through this example step by step to get familiar with the different options you can configure to solve such requirements:

1. First, we connect to the Azure RMS service with `Connect-AadrmService` and provide your global administrator credentials.

2. For a better understanding, we provide the result from the PowerShell perspective:

```
PS C:\windows\system32> Get-AadrmTemplateProperty -Templateid fc7173b1-1109-4ecf-8400-8f24600b9a27 -RightsDefinitions | fl

Key   : RightsDefinitions
Value : {marketing@idam.ch -> VIEW, EXPORT, engineering@identityplus.ch -> VIEW, DOCEDIT}
```

3. Next, we will prepare a short script to define the specific rights:

```
$templateid = " 1ca2cd41-ba33-4681-85a9-a6b3d929a5cc"
[array]$r = New-AadrmRightsDefinition -EmailAddress marketing@idam.ch -
Rights "VIEW", "EXPORT"

$r += New-AadrmRightsDefinition -EmailAddress engineering@identityplus.ch -
Rights "VIEW,DOCEDIT"

$CurrentRightsDefinitions = [array]((get-aadrmtemplate -templateid
$templateid).RightsDefinitions)

$ResultingRightsDefinitions = $CurrentRightsDefinitions + $r
Set-AadrmTemplateProperty -TemplateId $templateid -RightsDefinition
$ResultingRightsDefinitions
```

4. Now we will add the template with the `Add-AadrmTemplate` command, as following:

```
$names = @{}
$names[1033] = "External Sharing - Confidential content"
$descriptions = @{}
$descriptions[1033] = " This content is confidential and only
shared with specific partner organizations"
$r1 = New-AadrmRightsDefinition -EmailAddress marketing@idam.ch
-Rights "VIEW","EXPORT"
Add-AadrmTemplate -Names $names -Descriptions $Descriptions
-LicenseValidityDuration 5 -RightsDefinitions $r1
-ScopedIdentities marketing@idam.ch -Status Published
```

5. Note the created template ID, put it in the prepared script, and run it to change our rights definitions.

 For practical reasons, you can combine the tasks and choose a better-designed naming convention than we have done in the example. It should only show how to solve the requirement and get you familiar with the needed PowerShell commands.

Check your result and you should have created your first rights policy template with external recipients. Now that we have worked with custom templates, we will now configure the RMS logging capabilities.

# Verifying Azure RMS logging

In this section, we will verify the by default enabled Azure RMS logging. Perform the following steps:

1. To verify the functionality, we will create one entry with these two commands:

   - `Protect-RMSFile`
   - `Unprotect-RMSFile`

```
PS C:\Users\jochen.nickel\Desktop> Protect-RMSFile -TemplateID 61d62ec9-fe90-40d7-ae18-8617b7e8585c -File .\SuperUserDem
o.xlsx

InputFile                                               EncryptedFile
---------                                               -------------
C:\Users\jochen.nickel\Desktop\SuperUserDemo.xlsx C:\Users\jochen.nickel\Desktop\SuperUserDemo.xlsx

PS C:\Users\jochen.nickel\Desktop> Unprotect-RMSFile -File .\SuperUserDemo.xlsx

InputFile                                               DecryptedFile
---------                                               -------------
C:\Users\jochen.nickel\Desktop\SuperUserDemo.xlsx C:\Users\jochen.nickel\Desktop\SuperUserDemo.xlsx
```

2. Now you can use `Get-AadrmUsageLog -Path "C:\ActualUsage.log"` to download the usage logs to your local hard disk.

Now that we have tested the Azure RMS logging feature, we will have a preview look at the new Azure Information Protection features.

# Preview of Azure Information Protection

In this section, we want to provide you with a short intro about the new upcoming capabilities of Azure Information Protection. The solution is based on the integrated solution of Secure Islands, an acquisition from last year. Microsoft builds up a solution that follows the following protection process:

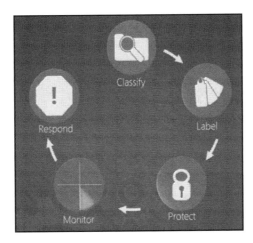

Source: Microsoft

With this approach, Microsoft closes an existing gap in their solution. Now they are able to provide a complete process and make it usable for cloud services and on premise infrastructures.

We will receive the following key features from this solution:

- Automatic, user-driven, and recommended classifications
- Classification overrides and justifications
- Flexible policy and rules engine
- Protection using encryption, authentication, and use rights
- Document tracking and revocation

Now that we know the new key features, let's jump a bit in the new technology.

First of all, you can manage the new service over the new Azure Portal under https://portal.azure.com and not the classic Azure Portal, which makes sense because it's the strategic way of Microsoft to use this portal.

The first screen provides you with an overview of the labels that can be used:

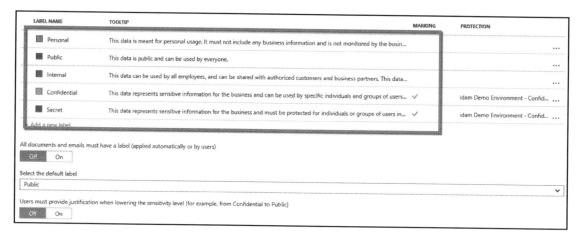

Under this **Label** option, you can use the predefined labels or create your own. Furthermore, you can configure the default label and behavior. Inside the different labels, you can configure the conditions they should apply. We will use the **Confidential** label as an example:

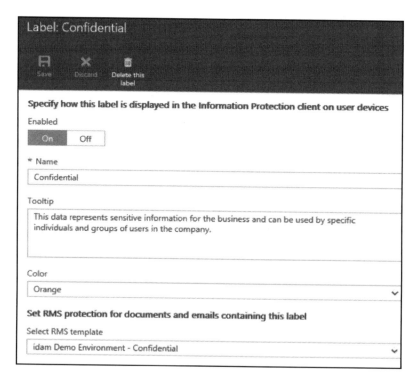

In this configuration step, you can define the characteristics of this label and, for example, the Azure RMS template that should be applied if this label will be attached. Furthermore, you can define the watermarking options that should be applied:

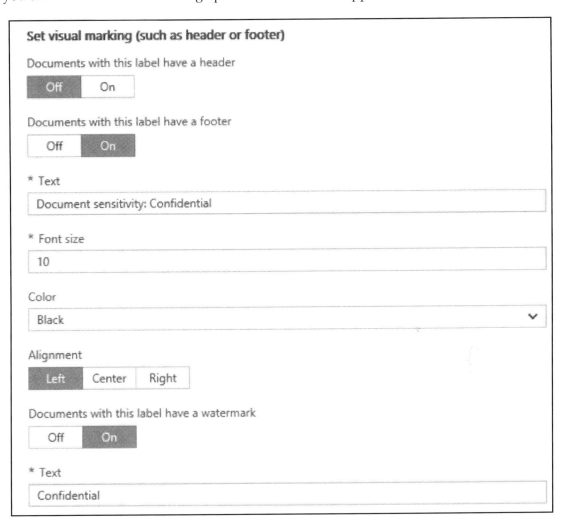

Additionally, you provide the conditions to apply this label. In our example, we choose an IBAN number, which is a predefined condition. Obviously, you can define your own custom conditions as well:

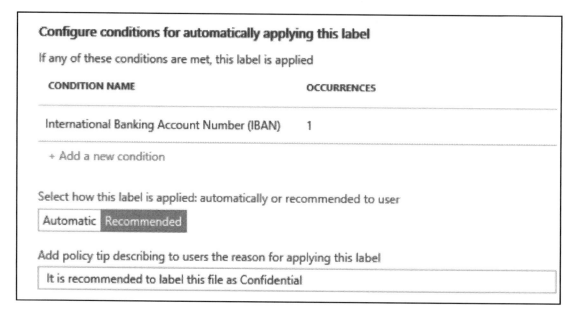

We also configured this label as **Recommended**, which means that the user will get information that this label is the recommended one to use and it will not be automatically applied. Now that we have seen the service configuration, we want to see the results from the user's perspective. We used the recommended label, and the result looks like the following:

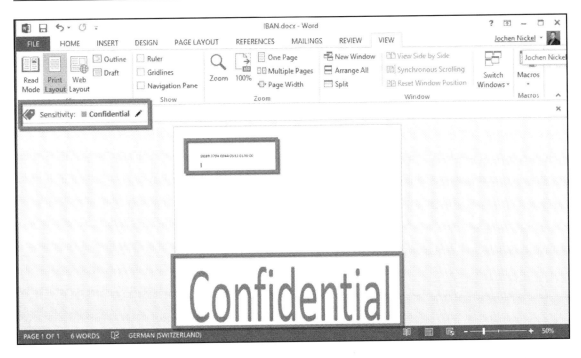

Additionally, the correct RMS template is applied, if we look at the **Info** part of Word:

With this first example, we provided a small intro about the Azure Information Protection features and configuration steps. Azure Information Protection is currently in the preview progress, but it already provides very powerful functionality.

If you want to see more demonstrations, we highly recommend viewing the following video: `http://bit.ly/2912DJI` from Dan Plastina.

# SAP integration as a special scenario

This scenario is just a demonstration that RMS can happen in or around nearly every system. Halocore, a product of Secude, brings a native integration of RMS in SAP. We will provide examples for different data that gets out of SAP and will be protected based on classification with Azure RMS. We will provide the following examples:

- Financial information
- Personal information

For example, if you export defined content or information from specific transactions or tables, the content will be classified and you can choose the protection level. Halocore provides the best matching RMS policies to protect the information, as in the following example:

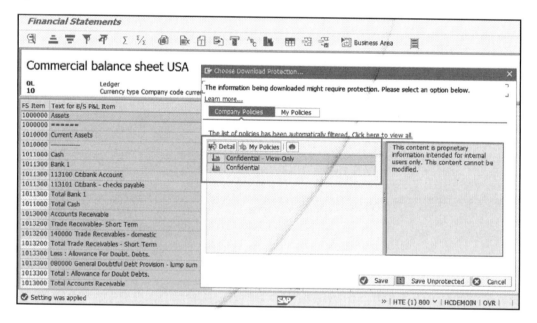

As a result, for example, you will get a protected Excel sheet:

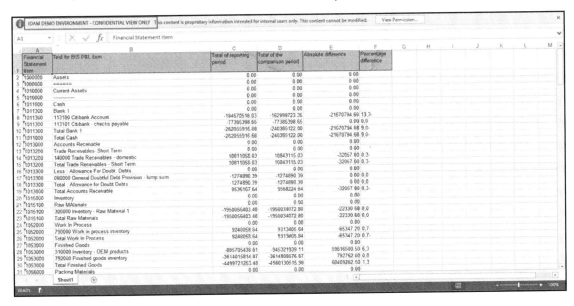

The other way you can choose is that Halocore determines the best match and classifies and protects the information transparent to the user. The following configuration shows the different options – an activated **Policy Selection UI** and an **Own Use Decision** option:

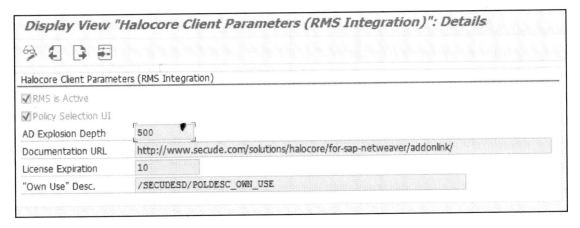

If you change this option, you can provide a completely transparent process to the user. Another example is to classify and protect the information based on personal information or on a specific field of work, such as Human Resources. In this example, we will protect information that is identified as PII from the **Flexible Employee Data**:

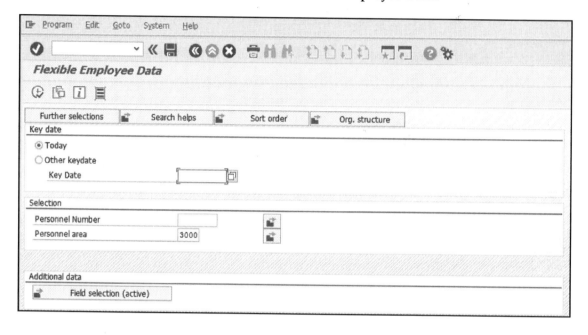

You can see that there is information such as birthday and other details in this example, so we will protect this typical HR information with a specific rights policy template:

**Flexible Employee Data**

# Flexible Employee Data

**Key date: 01.03.2016**

| Last Name | First Name | Personnel Number | Date of Birth | Entry Date | Nationality | Number of Children | Total basic pay | Crcy | Wage Type |
|---|---|---|---|---|---|---|---|---|---|
| Zubke | Carsten | 00010870 | 25.01.1970 | 01.01.2002 | American | 0 | 1.250,00 | USD | |
| Fredericks | Frank | 00010960 | 12.10.1960 | 01.06.1999 | American | 0 | 2.250,00 | USD | |
| Henning | Anne | 00010961 | 11.02.1960 | 01.06.1999 | American | 0 | 1.750,00 | USD | |
| Jensen | Steve | 00010962 | 10.03.1960 | 01.06.1999 | American | 0 | 1.750,00 | USD | |
| Kyne | Kevin | 00010963 | 13.03.1960 | 01.06.1999 | American | 0 | 1.750,00 | USD | |
| Blackton | Barbara | 00010964 | 10.05.1960 | 01.06.1999 | American | 0 | 1.750,00 | USD | |
| Francis | Nancy | 00010965 | 15.05.1960 | 01.06.1999 | American | 0 | 1.500,00 | USD | |
| Anderson | Andrew | 00010966 | 11.01.1960 | 01.06.1999 | American | 0 | 1.500,00 | USD | |
| Olbright | Ellen | 00010967 | 10.07.1960 | 01.06.1999 | American | 0 | 1.500,00 | USD | |
| Parker | Alan | 00010968 | 22.02.1960 | 01.06.1999 | American | 0 | 1.250,00 | USD | |
| Tendy | Jessica | 00010969 | 19.09.1960 | 01.06.1999 | American | 0 | 1.750,00 | USD | |
| Peter | Russel | 00080012 | 01.03.1969 | 01.01.2006 | American | 0 | 2.000,00 | USD | |
| Porter | Susan | 00080014 | 01.03.1969 | 01.01.2006 | American | 0 | 3.000,00 | USD | |
| Jones | Bobby | 00080090 | 08.09.1960 | 11.10.2004 | | 0 | 1.750,00 | USD | |
| Jones | Robert | 00080091 | 09.11.1964 | 11.10.2004 | | 0 | 2.500,00 | USD | |
| Stark | Allison | 00080200 | 14.09.1974 | 25.03.2002 | | 0 | 2.500,00 | USD | |
| Jones | Gary | 00080201 | 14.02.1964 | 16.08.2003 | | 0 | 2.000,00 | USD | |
| Reynolds | Andrea | 00080202 | 14.02.1974 | 04.06.2002 | | 0 | 1.250,00 | USD | |

» | HTE (1)

You will receive the following results that the correct classification and RMS template will be applied – the **HUMAN RESOURCES CONFIDENTIAL** template is applied:

| Last Name | First Name | Personnel Number | Date of Birth | Entry Date | Nationality | Number of Children | Total basic pay | Currency |
|---|---|---|---|---|---|---|---|---|
| Zubke | Carsten | 10870 | 1/25/1970 | 1/1/2002 | American | 0 | 1250.00 | USD |
| Fredericks | Frank | 10960 | 10/12/1960 | 6/1/1999 | American | 0 | 2250.00 | USD |
| Henning | Anne | 10961 | 2/11/1960 | 6/1/1999 | American | 0 | 1750.00 | USD |
| Jensen | Steve | 10962 | 3/10/1960 | 6/1/1999 | American | 0 | 1750.00 | USD |
| Kyne | Kevin | 10963 | 3/13/1960 | 6/1/1999 | American | 0 | 1750.00 | USD |
| Blackton | Barbara | 10964 | 5/10/1960 | 6/1/1999 | American | 0 | 1750.00 | USD |
| Francis | Nancy | 10965 | 5/15/1960 | 6/1/1999 | American | 0 | 1500.00 | USD |
| Anderson | Andrew | 10966 | 1/11/1960 | 6/1/1999 | American | 0 | 1500.00 | USD |
| Olbright | Ellen | 10967 | 7/10/1960 | 6/1/1999 | American | 0 | 1500.00 | USD |
| Parker | Alan | 10968 | 2/22/1960 | 6/1/1999 | American | 0 | 1250.00 | USD |
| Tendy | Jessica | 10969 | 9/19/1960 | 6/1/1999 | American | 0 | 1750.00 | USD |
| Peter | Russel | 80012 | 3/1/1969 | 1/1/2006 | American | 0 | 2000.00 | USD |
| Porter | Susan | 80014 | 3/1/1969 | 1/1/2006 | American | 0 | 3000.00 | USD |
| Jones | Bobby | 80090 | 9/8/1960 | 10/11/2004 | | 0 | 1750.00 | USD |
| Jones | Robert | 80091 | 11/9/1964 | 10/11/2004 | | 0 | 2500.00 | USD |
| Stark | Allison | 80200 | 9/14/1974 | 3/25/2002 | | 0 | 2500.00 | USD |
| Jones | Gary | 80201 | 2/14/1964 | 8/16/2003 | | 0 | 2000.00 | USD |
| Reynolds | Andrea | 80202 | 2/14/1974 | 6/4/2002 | | 0 | 1250.00 | USD |
| Rae | Angela | 80203 | 3/25/1980 | 11/28/2004 | | 0 | 2250.00 | USD |
| Jones | Stephanie | 80204 | 5/23/1970 | 2/12/2005 | | 0 | 2250.00 | USD |

With the Halocore solution, you are also able to simulate the different policies to identify the best match criteria before they get productive. The following screenshot shows such a simulation and shows the deep integration:

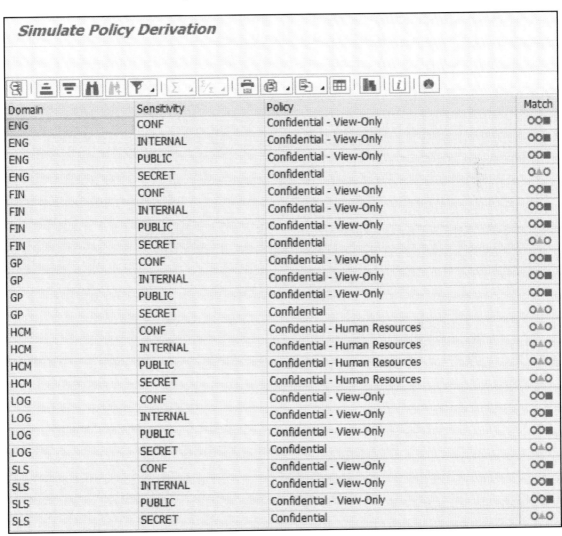

*Simulate Policy Derivation*

| Domain | Sensitivity | Policy | Match |
|--------|-------------|--------|-------|
| ENG | CONF | Confidential - View-Only | OO■ |
| ENG | INTERNAL | Confidential - View-Only | OO■ |
| ENG | PUBLIC | Confidential - View-Only | OO■ |
| ENG | SECRET | Confidential | O▲O |
| FIN | CONF | Confidential - View-Only | OO■ |
| FIN | INTERNAL | Confidential - View-Only | OO■ |
| FIN | PUBLIC | Confidential - View-Only | OO■ |
| FIN | SECRET | Confidential | O▲O |
| GP | CONF | Confidential - View-Only | OO■ |
| GP | INTERNAL | Confidential - View-Only | OO■ |
| GP | PUBLIC | Confidential - View-Only | OO■ |
| GP | SECRET | Confidential | O▲O |
| HCM | CONF | Confidential - Human Resources | O▲O |
| HCM | INTERNAL | Confidential - Human Resources | O▲O |
| HCM | PUBLIC | Confidential - Human Resources | O▲O |
| HCM | SECRET | Confidential - Human Resources | O▲O |
| LOG | CONF | Confidential - View-Only | OO■ |
| LOG | INTERNAL | Confidential - View-Only | OO■ |
| LOG | PUBLIC | Confidential - View-Only | OO■ |
| LOG | SECRET | Confidential | O▲O |
| SLS | CONF | Confidential - View-Only | OO■ |
| SLS | INTERNAL | Confidential - View-Only | OO■ |
| SLS | PUBLIC | Confidential - View-Only | OO■ |
| SLS | SECRET | Confidential | O▲O |

With this short introduction into SAP, you have seen that the RMS integration to different systems is really not like in the past. RMS brings more and more advantages to a company with a broad support of different solutions to protect sensitive information in an organization. Next, we will discuss the configuration of a **Bring Your Own Key (BYOK)** scenario.

# Configuring a BYOK scenario

For the configuration of the BYOK scenario for Azure RMS, we will use the following reference, where you will find a detailed configuration guide. With this reference, you will be able to configure this scenario:

- **Whitepaper**: BYOK with Azure Rights Management (`http://bit.ly/28YVjF1`)

# Summary

Now that you have worked through this chapter, you will be able to configure a flexible information protection solution with on premises and online services. You will be able to provide security for several use cases in the main services of your environment. Furthermore, you received the needed information to configure Azure RMS logging, and a preview of the new Azure Information Protection functionality.

In the next chapters, we will provide further information that you need to know for complex and multi-forest environments to build suitable identity and access management solutions.

# 16
# Choosing the Right Technology, Methods, and Future Trends

In the final destination of our journey, we will discuss additional information that will help you to manage several cloud scenarios and support new initiatives to bring you back to your daily business. We will jump into some upcoming features and innovations of Microsoft. Finally, we will provide you with some extra information about the upcoming features of **Microsoft Identity Manager** (**MIM**) 2016 and Windows Server 2016 to be prepared in the on-premises environment for suitable hybrid cloud usage:

- **MIM 2016** improvements include:
  - Synchronization Engine merger
  - REST API support
  - **Privileged Access Management** (**PAM**) improvements
  - MIM and Exchange online integration
  - MIM compatibility updates
- Advanced Conditional Access Helper
  - Conditional Access Client scenarios – Mail access
  - Conditional Access Client scenarios – SharePoint access

Let's dive into the different functions available. First, we will start with MIM. Obviously, there are more functions that we could describe in the Windows Server 2016. If you need more Windows Server 2016 knowledge, we recommend the book *Mastering Windows Server 2016*, by *Jordan Krause, Packt Publisihing*. You can find more information on this at `http://bit.ly/2614kA8`.

# MIM 2016 future improvements

We have already discussed the role and importance of MIM 2016 in the On-Premise IAM landscape. As you already know, there are two synchronization engines in place at the moment – the **Azure Active Directory** (**AAD**) Connect and the MIM 2016 synchronization engine.

# Synchronization engine merger

One of the main strategies of Microsoft is to combine these two engines into one for better usability and the fulfillment of all requirements with one engine. Microsoft actually recommends using AAD Connect for synchronization with Azure AD and MIM 2016 to synchronize with all the On-premise directories and repositories. The first steps of consolidation are already done for building the identity bridge, as you can see with all the rich functionality of Azure AD Connect. The consolidation process is still in progress.

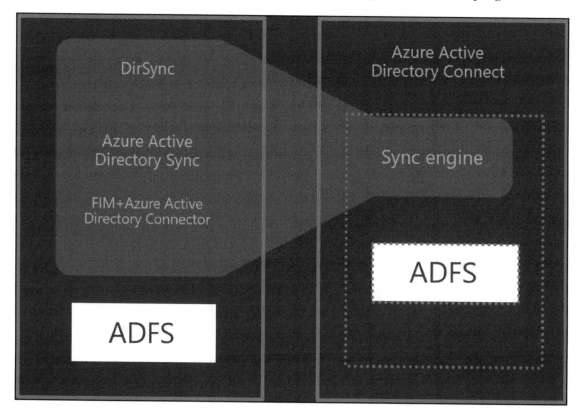

# REST API support

Another planned strategy is to provide a complete REST API for the MIM Service. You will find a partial implementation with the MIM PAM portal that is based on a REST API already in place. In the meantime, you will have already had the chance to work with the Lithnet FIM/MIM Service REST API implementation, which provides you with a wrapper for the FIM/MIM Service SOAP/WCF endpoint. This gives you a perfect opportunity for CRUD operations via a series of standard HTTP calls. The API uses JSON-formatted data for a broad range of compatibility.

 You can find the project on github.com under the following shortcut: `http://bit.ly/1PsgEjp`.

To give you an idea, we will provide you with a short example done in our development environments. In this example, we want to better retrieve a resource from the MIM Service, and this implementation provides us with the following request capabilities:

| Method | URL |
|--------|-----|
| **GET** | /v1/resources/{id} |
| **GET** | /v1/resources/{objectType}/{anchorAttributeName}/{anchorAttributeValue} |

You can use the following URL parameters for your request:

| Parameter name | Description |
|----------------|-------------|
| {id} | The object ID of the resource |
| {objectType} | The type of object to query |
| {anchorAttributeName} | The name of the attribute that can be used to find this resource by its unique anchor value |
| {anchorAttributeValue} | The value of the anchor attribute that uniquely identifies this resource |

 You can find the complete reference at `http://bit.ly/237WpPE`.

The example output of the request with `GET /v1/resources/{id}` with an `HTTP/1.1 200 OK` response looks like the following:

```json
{
"ObjectType": "Person",
"ObjectID": "62f62491-c255-442a-aee4-481a46313725",
"ObjectSID": "ADUADAFACCUVABBACYKkaG46nJrWb04iFacCBB==",
"CreatedTime": "2015-06-02T09:13:57.037",
"Creator": "fa68cafa-4fa1-38c1-7690-ace7745d3497",
"DomainConfiguration": "1aff46f4-5511-452d-bcbd-7c7f35a0de11",
"Manager": "34d32151-a223-233c-bba4-441c36204326",
"AccountName": "jnickel",
"DisplayName": "Jochen Nickel",
"Domain": "AZIDMIM01",
"Email": "Jochen.nickel@azureid.ch",
"FirstName": "Jochen",
"JobTitle": "Architect",
"LastName": "Nickel",
"MVObjectID": "{A86B659F-062F-E611-80DD-00155D00C83D}",
"jobTitles": [
"Manager",
"Chairman"
],
}
```

These capabilities are helpful. You can also create mobile applications for MIM with *Microsoft PowerApps* and *Microsoft Flow*. Peter Stapf, an MVP (Identity and Access), provides a straightforward example on his blog, where he shows the creation of such an app.

We don't need to reinvent the wheel, so we will use the following screenshot from his blog to give you an idea of these powerful tools:

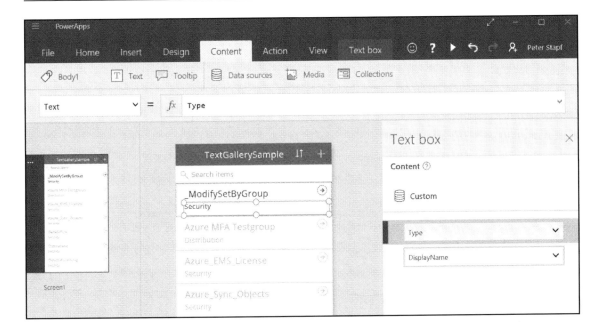

Source: `http://bit.ly/1roipbg`

You can find the full blog post at
`http://bit.ly/1roipbg`.

To give you a fast ramp up with such powerful tools, we have provided the following links:

- Lithnet FIM/MIM Synchronization Service PowerShell Module,
  `http://bit.ly/1UxTWYy`
- Certificate Management Monitoring CMMonitor for MIM/FIM,
  `http://bit.ly/24OYAac`
- Lithnet FIM/MIM Service .NET Client Library, `http://bit.ly/1VXPM1c`

# PAM improvements

Another area where Microsoft is working very hard is on the improvement of PAM for administration across forests. There are two principal concepts:

- The focus on user access management and not on the credentials
- The extraction and isolation of administrative user accounts from existing AD forests

In the following diagram you can see the current idea and architecture of MIM/PAM:

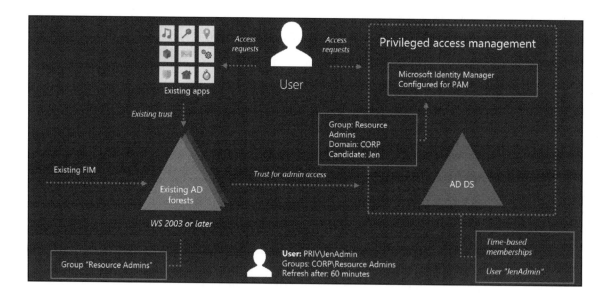

Source: Microsoft

The main improvement for the future in this area is the usage of the Windows Server 2016 Active Directory functionality. So, for example, a user's Kerberos ticket will be time-limited to the remaining time of their role activation. In other news, the MIM Portal will be supported for additional browser access; until now, only Internet Explorer was the supported browser.

**Practical Note**

To install Windows Server 2016 at functional level you can use the following command:

```
Install-ADDSForest -DomainMode 7 -ForestMode 7 -
DomainName azureid.ch -DomainNetbiosName azureid -Force -
NoDnsOnNetwork
```

**Privileged Forest**

```
Install-ADDSForest -DomainMode 7 -ForestMode 7 -
DomainName priv.azureid.ch
-DomainNetbiosName priv -Force -CreateDNSDelegation -
DNSDelegationCredential $ca
```

The following commands can be used to configure the PAM feature in Windows Server 2016:

```
$of = get-ADOptionalFeature -filter "name -eq 'PAM feature'"
Enable-ADOptionalFeature $of -scope ForestOrConfigurationSet -target
"priv.azureid.ch"
```

Another helpful command we want to introduce to you is security-focused to harden the security of a PAM deployment. During the installation of a PAM deployment you create an authentication policy. By default, this policy is enabled and you can activate and check it with the following commands:

```
Set-PAMAuthenticationRestriction -Domain "Priv" -Credentials (Get-
Credentials) -EnforcePolicy $true
Get-PAMAuthenticationRestriction
```

# MIM and Exchange Online integration

Until now we always worked with local exchange servers to send approvals and notifications. With this new functionality you can send and receive e-mail messages using Office 365 Exchange Online.

You will be able to configure this new functionality through the traditional setup or configuration routine:

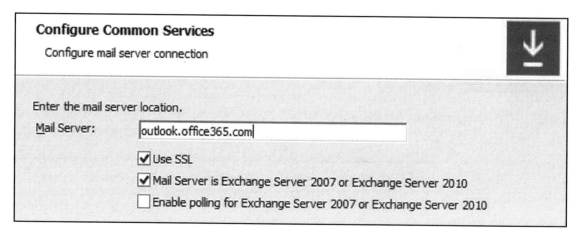

## MIM compatibility updates

We always get many questions about new version support. Here you can find a small list of the compatibility updates that arrive with the GA of the new update of MIM 2016:

- MIM Sync and MIM Service using SQL Server 2016 on Windows Server 2012 R2 to hold its database
- MIM Sync and MIM Service communicating with Exchange Server 2016 on Windows Server 2012 R2
- MIM Portal installed with SharePoint Server 2016 on Windows Server 2012 R2
- MIM add-ins and extensions installed with Outlook 2016 on Windows 10

- Multiple browser support to address the following issues:
    - Browsers that did not support the JavaScript windowing functions were unable to view or edit resources in the MIM Portal
    - Browsers on mobile devices were unable to view the MIM Portal

You can find the actual supported configuration of MIM 2016 at `http://bit.ly/1VXWnc5`.

# Advanced Conditional Access Helper

We wrote a lot of practical tips in previous chapters, but we missed some helper tables that can provide you with packed information regarding which scenarios work with each other.

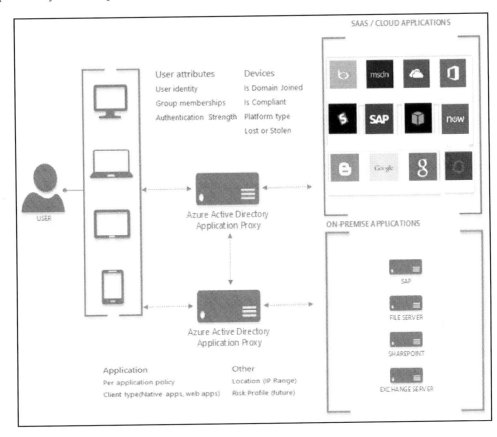

The four main focus area conditional access in the case of knowing it's the right user are:

- Providing and requiring stronger authentication with Azure MFA in the cloud and On-premise
- Proof of the user's location to increase trust, for example, with the definition of trusted networks
- A combination of the authentication method and the location to provide security with usability

- Access Control based on the risk

There is always a combination of the knowledge of the user and the managing and protecting of data on devices. The following diagram shows the main management tools of this area in a solution architecture:

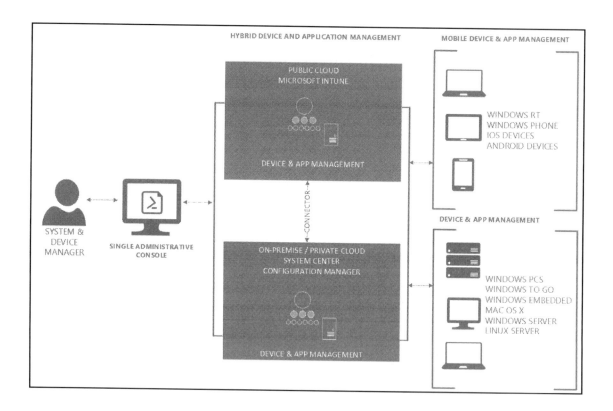

The following main principals are relevant in a Conditional Access context:

- The compliance status against Microsoft Intune and SCCM policies
- Reflected status about the knowledge of the device AD joined or Azure AD joined

- Managed applications compliant with policies
- Usage location of the device, such as VPN, DirectAccess, or a trusted network

To be sure, we need to conduct a short overview of the several configuration points for conditional access. There are three main technologies in the game:

- Exchange Online Conditional Access

  The usage of this method is only relevant for Active Sync access against Exchange Online

- Intune and Azure AD Conditional Access

  This option is relevant for ADAL- enabled Office clients with access to Exchange and SharePoint Online. Web browsers are not covered with this method and there is a need for Intune or/and Office 365 Mobile Device Management and Azure Device Registration as well.

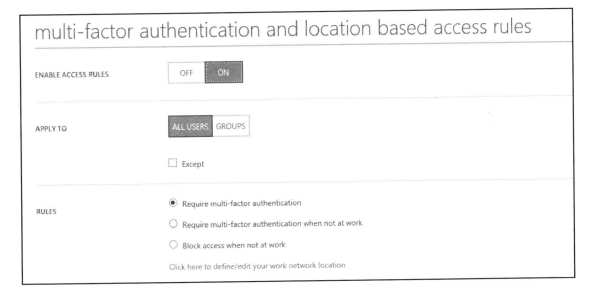

You can find more information about ADAL at `http://bit.ly/1S4xdBL`.

- AD FS Conditional Access

  This option uses the three main functions of AD FS to provide Conditional Access

- ADFS authentication rules – typically On-premise MFA is required; provides flexible authentication rules:
  - Windows 2016 Device Authentication as a primary method
  - Windows 2016 Microsoft Passport Authentication

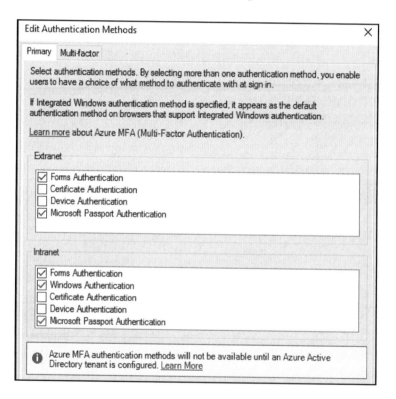

- AD FS authorization rules – required for flexible security policies; practically, many claims rules are needed

Windows Server 2016 provides access control policies

| Access Control Policies | | | |
| --- | --- | --- | --- |
| Name | Built-in | Parameters | Usage |
| Permit everyone | Yes | No | Not in use |
| Permit everyone and require MFA | Yes | No | Not in use |
| Permit everyone and require MFA, allow automatic device registration | Yes | No | Not in use |
| Permit everyone and require MFA from unauthenticated devices | Yes | No | Not in use |
| Permit everyone for intranet access | Yes | No | Not in use |
| Permit specific group | Yes | Yes | Not in use |
| Permit everyone and require MFA for specific group | Yes | Yes | Not in use |
| Permit everyone and require MFA from extranet access | Yes | No | Not in use |

- AD FS transformation rules – with this, rule claims are sent to Azure AD after the AuthN and AuthZ
- Now that we have gone over the basic information we need to take a look into several client scenarios; we will focus on e-mail and SharePoint access because they represent the most relevant cases

# Conditional Access Client scenarios – mail access

The following client scenarios describe the available conditional access capabilities for the mail access.

# Client scenario Outlook 2010 on domain joined computer

This scenario provides the following options:

- Exchange Online Conditional Access – *working functionality*
- Intune and Azure AD Conditional Access – *no option*
- ADFS AuthN (MFA Trigger) – *no option*
- ADFS AuthZ – *working with groups and the User Agent string*

# Client scenario Outlook 2013 on domain joined computer

This scenario provides the following options:

- Exchange Online Conditional Access – *working functionality*
- Intune and Azure AD Conditional Access – *no option (non-ADAL)*
- ADFS AuthN (MFA Trigger) – *working with groups and the User Agent string*
- ADFS AuthZ – *working with groups, User Agent string and DRS managed*

# Client scenario Outlook 2013/16 on domain joined computer with Windows 7/8.1

This scenario provides the following options:

- Exchange Online Conditional Access – *not working*
- Intune and Azure AD Conditional Access – *working, also with Intune ADAL*
- ADFS AuthN (MFA Trigger) – *working with groups, User Agent string and DRS managed*
- ADFS AuthZ – *working with groups, User Agent string and DRS managed*

# Client scenario Outlook 2013/16 on domain joined computer with Windows 10

This scenario provides the following options:

- Exchange Online Conditional Access – *not working*
- Intune and Azure AD Conditional Access – *working scenario*
- ADFS AuthN (MFA Trigger) – *working with groups, User Agent string and DRS managed*
- ADFS AuthZ – *working with groups, User Agent string and DRS managed*

# Client scenario iOS and Android ActiveSync Mail Clients

This scenario provides the following options:

- Exchange Online Conditional Access – *working functionality*
- Intune and Azure AD Conditional Access – *working for Active Sync*
- Mobile Application Management – *not working*
- ADFS AuthN (MFA Trigger) – *no options*
- ADFS AuthZ – *working with groups, User Agent string*

# Client scenario Outlook for iOS and Android

This scenario provides the following options:

- Exchange Online Conditional Access – *not working*
- Intune and Azure AD Conditional Access – *working (ADAL)*
- Mobile Application Management – *working with or without MDM*
- ADFS AuthN (MFA Trigger) – *working with groups, User Agent string*
- ADFS AuthZ – *working with groups, User Agent string*

# Client scenario OWA for iOS and Android

This scenario provides the following options:

- Exchange Online Conditional Access – *not working*
- Intune and Azure AD Conditional Access – *working (ADAL)*
- Mobile Application Management – *no option*
- ADFS AuthN (MFA Trigger) – *working with groups, User Agent string*
- ADFS AuthZ – *working with groups, User Agent string*

# Client scenario Outlook WP8.1

This scenario provides the following options:

- Exchange Online Conditional Access – *working functionality*
- Intune and Azure AD Conditional Access – *working with Active Sync*
- Mobile Application Management – *no option*
- ADFS AuthN (MFA Trigger) – *working with groups, User Agent string*
- ADFS AuthZ – *working with groups, User Agent string*

# Client scenario Outlook 2016 Mac OS X

This scenario provides the following options:

- Exchange Online Conditional Access – *not working*
- Intune and Azure AD Conditional Access – *working with ADAL*
- Mobile Application Management – *no option*
- ADFS AuthN (MFA Trigger) – *Azure MFA and User Agent string*
- ADFS AuthZ – *working with groups, User Agent string*

# Conditional Access Client scenarios – SharePoint access

The following client scenarios describe the available conditional access capabilities for SharePoint access.

## Client scenario Browser from domain joined PC Windows 7/8.1

This scenario provides the following options:

- Intune and Azure AD Conditional Access – *future planning*
- Mobile Application Management – *no option*
- ADFS AuthN (MFA Trigger) – *Azure MFA, User Agent string*, DRS (isManaged)
- ADFS AuthZ – *User Agent string – DRS* (isManaged), *group*

## Client scenario Browser from domain joined PC Windows 10

This scenario provides the following options:

- Intune and Azure AD Conditional Access – *future planning*
- Mobile Application Management – *no option*
- ADFS AuthN (MFA Trigger) – *Azure MFA, User Agent string,* DRS (`isRegisteredUser`)
- ADFS AuthZ – *User Agent string,* DRS (`isRegisteredUser`), group

## Client scenario Browser from Mac OS

This scenario provides the following options:

- Intune and Azure AD Conditional Access – *no option*
- Mobile Application Management – *no option*
- ADFS AuthN (MFA Trigger) – *Azure MFA and User Agent string*
- ADFS AuthZ – *User Agent string and group*

## Client scenario OD4B Client from domain joined PC Windows 7/8.1

This scenario provides the following options:

- Intune and Azure AD Conditional Access – *working functionality*
- Mobile Application Management – *no option*
- ADFS AuthN (MFA Trigger) – *Azure MFA, User Agent string,* DRS (`isManaged`)
- ADFS AuthZ – *Azure MFA, User Agent string,* DRS (`isManaged`), *group*

## Client scenario OD4B Client from domain joined PC Windows 10

This scenario provides the following options:

- Intune and Azure AD Conditional Access – *working functionality*
- Mobile Application Management – *no option*
- ADFS AuthN (MFA Trigger) – *Azure MFA and User Agent string,* DRS (`isRegisteredUser`)
- ADFS AuthZ – *Azure MFA and User Agent string,* DRS (`isRegisteredUser`), *group*

## Client scenario non-ADAL OD4B client

This scenario provides the following options:

- Intune and Azure AD Conditional Access – *not working (non-ADAL)*
- Mobile Application Management – *no option*
- ADFS AuthN (MFA Trigger) – *no option*
- ADFS AuthZ – *UserAgent string, group*

## Client scenario OD4B Client from mobile devices

This scenario provides the following options:

- Intune and Azure AD Conditional Access – *working functionality*
- Mobile Application Management – *working for iOS and Android*
- ADFS AuthN (MFA Trigger) – *Azure MFA, UserAgent string*
- ADFS AuthZ – *UserAgent string*

Working through this section should help you to design the Conditional Access scenarios for Exchange and SharePoint access with different client scenarios.

# Summary

After working through this final chapter you should now be able to create modern IAM architectures with future improvements and have knowledge of the upcoming features of MIM and Windows Server 2016. In this chapter, we focused on the different client scenarios, because in every project we answer the same questions about the different capabilities – perhaps you are in the same situation. During the different chapters, we always described the different Windows Server 2016 capabilities for designing and implementing the new features of this server product. With this knowledge you should be well prepared and able to take the right decisions. We want to thank you for choosing this book and hope that you take some relevant and important knowledge out of these chapters. We wish you happiness and success when working with your hybrid IAM solutions with Microsoft Azure. We will follow up on these topics on www.inovit.ch and blog.idam.ch.

# Index

# N

# O

# P